Praise for *Cries of the Savanna*

Winner of the:

2022 Readers Favorite Gold Medal in Animal Category
2022 Professional Outdoor Media Association Pinnacle Award
2022 Kindle Book Review Non-fiction Semi-finalist
2022 The Wildlife Society Conservation Education Award

"...Tidwell took me back to my first hunting trip to Africa. Her innocence and sense of discovery is powerful, making for an easy entertaining read..."
—Dan Cabela, The Cabela Family Foundation

"...Written in an engaging and first person style...Africa has always generated fantasies, but Tidwell shows us where the realities lie."
-- Glen Martin, Author of *Game Changer: Animal Rights and the Fate of Africa's Wildlife*"

"Mesmerizing, captivating, raw. Sue Tidwell's debut book is a must-read to understand Africa's conservation model.…"
— Gabriella Hoffman, Award-winning Journalist, *District of Conservation Podcast*

"…I urge those who are opposed to the sustainable utilization of wildlife to read this thoroughly researched well-written book with an open, unbiased mind. Do this, and you may be surprised when your opinion changes!"
--Dr. Kevin Robertson, veterinarian, author and dedicated conservationist.

"… an honest note to the hearts of non-hunters in hopes of understanding and reconciliation."
--**Brittany Boddington,**
Founder of She Hunts Skills Camp

"…She will make you laugh out loud, scare you more than once and probably coax a tear or two along the way. Whatever your feelings might be about big game hunting and wildlife conservation, there's a great deal for you in these pages!"
--**Dwight Van Brunt**, author of *Born a Hunter*

"…Reading the story … brought me back to my first trip to Africa many years ago, with all the awe, wonder, and curiosity of all things about the continent it inspired in me..."
--**John McAdams,** *Big Game Hunting Blog/Podcast*

"... Like Sue, I am not a hunter, but I respect my fellow Africans and value African wildlife. If you do, too, then join Sue for an educational adventure."
--**Gail Thomson, Co-director,**
Felines Communication and Conservation

"...If you can only read one book on Africa, make it this one!"
--**Tommy Serafinski,** *Tommy's Outdoors Podcast*

"...All hunters should read this book, and they'll be moved to share it with non-hunters and anti-hunters...*Cries of the Savanna* is sure to enthrall and provide a bridge of understanding between the hunting and non-hunting communities."
--**Claire Fortenberry,** *Hunting Life Magazine*

"… I found *Cries of the Savanna* to be an authentic transformation of one women's naive perspective of the necessities of life in the Serengeti..."
—**TA Opre, Director/Cinematographer** *Killing the Shepherd*

"...an unflinching, and eye-opening, account of the
realities of life on a continent many imagine but
few ever rarely spend the time to get to know."
**--Dr. Adam Hart, Professor of Science Communication,
Biologist, Broadcaster, Author**

"...Honest, clear and raw... a must-read for hunters and
non-hunters alike."
— Huntersinc.com

"...At least we have some good people somewhere to speak
for us so that the world will understand."
– Lilian Peter Mremi, Game Warden, Tanzania

"...I believe the book has and will in time bring change
to the perception of the hunting world…"
**—Kyle Burelli, Wildlife and Tourism Manager,
FHT Project Wildlife, South Africa**

"...It is a captivating writing debut by Sue....well worth the read, especially for any
first-time hunting safari observer. While the camps, setting, and people may
change, the actual day-to-day experience is universal and one that everybody
should experience, even if only through this book."
**--Mike Angelides, SAFARI ROYAL TANZANIA and
African Professional Hunters Association (APHA) President**

"...If you have ever dreamed of going to Africa to hunt, Sue presents an eyes wide
open perspective to what it will be like."
— Dr. Robbie Kroger, Biologist, Blood Origins

"To know Africa is to love her, and also to fear for her. Sue Tidwell captures the
magic of safari and the wonder of Africa's wildlife and people…with a keen sense
of understanding the problems of that troubled land. With a new and unique
perspective, *Cries of the Savanna* is a valuable addition to the rich body of Africana.
– Craig Boddington, Author, Journalist, Hunter

"...Even most hunters who embark on an African Safari don't realize the tremendous benefits that safari hunting imparts to the local people and animals, which is why I highly recommend this book to hunters and non-hunters alike. Both will benefit from accompanying Tidwell on her journey to understanding Africa and its wildlife. Not only is *Cries of the Savanna* an engaging adventure story, it is a well-researched and well-written book that opens the door to a full appreciation of the present and future conservation realities of a complex and captivating continent."
—**Diana Rupp, Editor-in-Chief,** *Sports Afield*

"...*Cries of the Savanna* depicts Tidwell's unforgettable, surprise-packed trip to Africa's wilderness and the harsh truths she discovered about nature... Even as an African, I learned a great deal about Africa from *Cries of the Savanna*... Apart from being quite informative, this is an incredibly fun, addictive read. The choice of words and sense of humor brought a smile to my face...It's as entertaining as a thrilling adventure movie yet brimming with enough information to be a documentary film. If Sue Tidwell takes another trip and writes about it, I'm reading that book as well."
--**Foluso Falaye, Reader's Favorite**

CRIES of the
Savanna

SUE TIDWELL

Circle T Publishing, Idaho

Cries of the Savanna
An Adventure. An Awakening. A Journey to understanding African wildlife
conservation.

Circle T Publishing Company
Cottonwood, Idaho
info@circletpublising.com

Paperback ISBN 978-1-7379039-0-1
Hardback ISBN 978-1-7379039-2-5
Ebook ISBN 978-1-7379039-1-8
Library of Congress Control Number (LCCN) 2021918291

Printed in the United States of America

Editing by Jocelyn G. Engel
Cover design and interior graphics by Gerdi E. Fullard

First Paperback Edition

"The use of traveling is to regulate imagination with reality, and instead of thinking of how things may be, see them as they are."

— Samuel Johnson

DEDICATION

For Africa, whose magical wild places stirred my soul.
For Tanzania, whose conservation efforts opened my eyes.
For *Masimba* Camp, whose people captured my heart.
For the beasts, whose cries filled me with wonder.
For my husband, whose dreams changed my life.

CONTENTS

Foreword

Huntersinc.com LLC has had the great privilege of supporting author Sue Tidwell on her journey to create and publish her debut book, *Cries of the Savanna*.

Sue, a non-hunter herself, accompanied her hunting-husband Rick on an epic 21-day leopard and buffalo safari in Tanzania. During the course of that safari, Sue's eyes were opened to the complex and multi-faceted issues of conservation through hunting. Largely through what developed as a close friendship with a young female game scout named Lilian, Sue experienced an emotional awakening to the vital impact that regulated sport hunting has on Africa's wildlife and the intricacies of local populations' often tenuous relationship with game species.

Told amidst the backdrop of riveting hunting adventures, Sue tackles the very real and relevant complexities of African conservation and the often brutal assaults on the hunting industry by the anti-hunting opposition. Sue's scope of understanding and research on the topics at hand are extraordinary and her support of well-regulated hunting is endorsed by both hunting professionals and non-hunting scientists alike. Sue's aim—to offer an enlightened apologetic in favor of hunting—to those otherwise opposed to it, hits not only the mark, but the bullseye.

Honest, clear and raw, *Cries of the Savanna* is a must-read for hunters and non-hunters alike.

Yours in hunting,

The Huntersinc.com Team

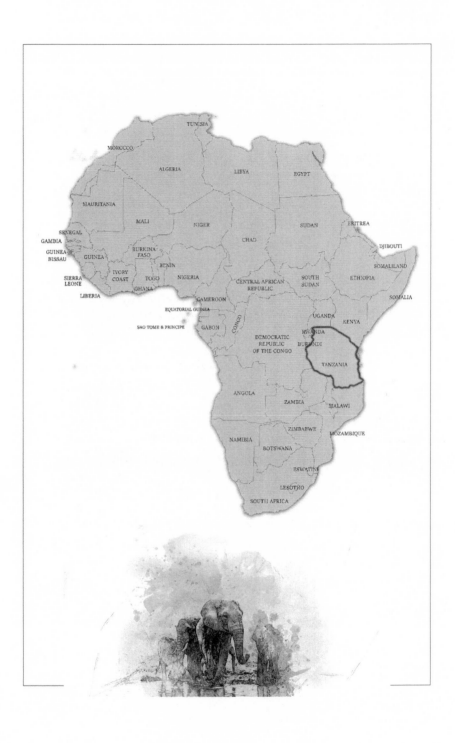

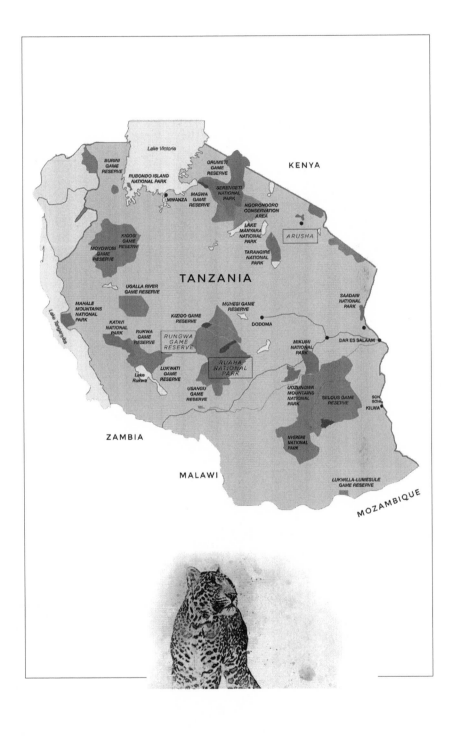

Lake Victoria

BURINI
GAME
RESERVE

RUBONDO ISLAND
NATIONAL PARK

MWANZA

MASWA
GAME
RESERVE

ORUMETI
GAME
RESERVE

SERENGETI
NATIONAL
PARK

NGORONGORO
CONSERVATION
AREA

LAKE
MANYARA
NATIONAL
PARK

TARANGIRE
NATIONAL
PARK

KENYA

ARUSHA

KIGOSI
GAME
RESERVE

MOYOWOSI
GAME
RESERVE

UGALLA RIVER
GAME RESERVE

TANZANIA

MUHESI GAME
RESERVE

SAADANI
NATIONAL
PARK

MAHALE
MOUNTAINS
NATIONAL
PARK

KIZIGO GAME
RESERVE

DODOMA

KATAVI
NATIONAL
PARK

RUKWA
GAME
RESERVE

RUNGWA
GAME
RESERVE

RUAHA
NATIONAL
PARK

MIKUMI
NATIONAL
PARK

DAR ES SALAAM

Lake
Rukwa

LUKWATI
GAME
RESERVE

USANGU
GAME
RESERVE

UDZUNGWA
MOUNTAINS
NATIONAL
PARK

SELOUS GAME
RESERVE

SON
SON
KILWA

Lake Tanganyika

ZAMBIA

NYERERE
NATIONAL
PARK

MALAWI

LUKWILLA-LUMESULE
GAME RESERVE

MOZAMBIQUE

1
THE AFRICAN SYMPHONY

Umphh. Umphh. My eyes blinked open in alarm and confusion as the unfamiliar sound pierced the night air, instantly forming a knot in my gut. It was no human sound. At least, not one that I had ever heard. No, it was a low-pitched guttural cry--something raw, distinctive, and primal. *Umphh.* Again, the primal call cut through the darkness, sending another wave of chills up and down my spine.

As I lay paralyzed in fear, the fog of my slumber gradually lifted, allowing pieces of reality to slip into place. Rick and I weren't snuggled side by side on our king-size bed. No. He was sleeping in a narrow bunk, similar to mine, six feet away and the new sleeping arrangement wasn't behind the secure walls of our rural Idaho home. We were behind the canvas panels of a wall tent, but unlike most of our outdoor excursions, we weren't in Idaho's backcountry wilderness. The distinctive *umphh* belonged to none of the wild critters we were familiar with. Instead, we were in a remote expanse of the Tanzanian bush: an exotic land where the people, terrain, and animals were far different than anything we had ever experienced; a place where lions, hyenas, leopards, and elephants roamed freely throughout the landscape.

With that awareness, I puzzled over the bestial grunt. The *umphh* sounded nothing like the king of beast's ferocious roars from MGM movie introductions. Still, there was little doubt that the foreboding sound belonged to anything other than a real, live, honest-to-goodness African lion. *Simba*, a simple but potent Swahili word. The dread I felt told me that it could be nothing else. We were, after all, in the heart of lion country, a fact that gave *Masimba* Camp its name.

Three days of international travel and sensory overload had turned us into little more than zombies when we crawled into our beds earlier that first night. Accordingly, we expected to fall asleep as soon as we hit the sheets. That didn't happen. The second the generator spit to silence and the staff vanished into their quarters, the din of camp life was replaced by an unfamiliar barrage of primal voices. *Whoop whoooooop whoop* followed by eerie chortles, *heeheehees*, and cackles. Then another *whhhoopp whooop*.

"Hyenas," Rick whispered from the darkness across the tent.

Fisi, I thought to myself. The animal's Swahili name had been used at dinner in the retelling of a gruesome story, a tale that might have been better left unsaid, especially with a fearful reluctant greenhorn like me gobbling up every word.

Lying wide-eyed, I listened to *Fisi's* insane chorus—an ensemble of squeals, roars, growls, and a maniac-like hysteria—as it seeped through the canvas barrier from every direction.

Next, a deep bellowing oozed through the tent's walls. With this new vocal came Rick's best guess. "Has to be a hippo."

The next few hours continued like that, with Rick doing his best to decipher each new dialogue. A conglomeration of chittering, chattering, cooing, cawing, shrieking, growling, grunting, and crying. A symphony, so to speak, of bestial serenades. Still, during those first few hours, *Simba's* cries had been missing from the ghostly composition. We listened and waited, but none had come.

When exhaustion overpowered the unsettling vocals, we drifted off--at least, until that first hair-raising *umphh* shattered our sleep. The deafening silence on the opposite end of the tent told me that Rick was also wide awake. After sleeping with someone for 15 years, the sound of their breathing is as telling as any words; he, too, was listening to the lion. How could he *not* be? The canvas walls with eight mesh windows offered little in the way of soundproofing. Even more alarming, the fabric provided laughable protection against deadly predators. Suddenly, our tent which had felt cozy and secure in the light of day felt vulnerable and exposed.

Rick's and my tent at Masimba Camp along the dried-up Mzombe river.

Tense energy filled the air as we listened to the lion's guttural calls. After a few moments, Rick whispered, "Our first lion."

With my gut twisted in a knot, a meek "Aha" was all I could muster. Neither of us moved a muscle. We stayed frozen in our separate bunks with our ears focused on the unfamiliar sounds.

Eventually Rick's hushed revelation, "Honey, we aren't in Kansas anymore" was the straw that broke the camel's back.

"No kidding!" I quietly hissed as I slid out of my cot and climbed into his. Cramped. Uncomfortable. Overflowing. It mattered not.

While traveling to Africa had been a dream of mine since childhood, I never imagined sleeping in a primitive encampment where my slumber was cut short by wild creatures conducting their nightly shenanigans. Tromping through terrain riddled with deadly snakes was certainly not on my bucket list, and I *definitely* didn't fancy the idea of being a sidekick on a hunting safari.

Although I am a non-hunter, the tradition wasn't new to me; out of a family of eight, five were hunters--my dad and all four brothers. In rural Pennsylvania where we grew up, deer hunting was almost a religion. As you might imagine, our lives revolved largely around hunting seasons with wild game making up a huge part of our diet. Truth be told, I loved that *the boys* hunted. Not only did they put meat on the table, but their gearing up in fluorescent orange meant they'd be spending long days in the woods, giving me a testosterone-free house for hours on end. A fact that made my teenage self want to jump up and do a jig.

Still, the idea of killing doe-eyed critters myself was out of the question. I could barely make it through a Hallmark commercial without one of the boys sprinting to the kitchen, amid a bunch of giggles, to fetch a bucket for my tears. Still, hunting by association was such a part of my life that I had an innate understanding of its general merits, especially for subsistence and population control.

Therefore, it had not been a deal breaker when I met Rick and learned that he was also a dedicated hunter. As the strong silent type, he was the yin to my yang in many ways. His serious, quiet nature balanced out my more social, lighthearted disposition. Aside from that, he was a kind, intelligent, competent, hard-working country boy who grew up on a small ranch. As the cherry on top, he nursed a passion for the outdoors. That part of our personalities was totally in sync.

Like me, he also dreamt of Africa. His vision, however, was the polar opposite of mine. As a hunter, Rick wanted nothing more than to see wildlife in its natural state in some far-flung section of the bush, away from civilization and all of its trappings. He wanted to spend his days creeping through the savanna in pursuit of wild game and his nights sleeping in a primitive shelter where beastly serenades could be heard through the walls. He had zero desire to sleep in a fancy lodge, take an afternoon dip in a swimming pool, or cram on top of a safari vehicle with a slew of photo-tourists. That also meant no electricity, no solid walls, and no nearby medical facilities--in a place where danger lurked everywhere. He wanted to experience the *real* Africa, not the watered-down, sugarcoated version.

Understandably, as a non-hunter, I *did* want the watered-down sugar-coated version. My concept of Africa included morning excursions through the national park systems teeming with wildlife. Wildlife who, by the way, paid little heed to the oodles of vehicles streaming by, accompanied by a cascade of *oohs* and *ahhs*. Sweltering afternoons would be spent lounging in a sparkling blue pool. Evenings would include dinner with like-minded safari-goers gasping in wonder at extraordinary photos of the day. Nights would be spent cozied up in a safe air-conditioned lodge. Sleeping would be a peaceful proposition on a cushy mattress nestled under a ceiling fan's gentle breeze. It was a wonderful dream.

Instead of all that, I found myself in a cluster of grass huts hundreds of miles away from such luxuries. You know the saying *"Happy wife, happy life."* Well, that works both ways. Marriage is about compromise. Although Rick's version of the dream was insanely different from mine, it still allowed me to experience Africa.

Still, accompanying him wasn't without reservations. Aside from the danger factor, lions and snakes for example, it was hard to surrender to the idea of Rick hunting some of the world's most beloved species. Extraordinary animals that had filled me with awe and admiration for five decades.

While many kids were enthralled with Mickey Mouse and the Flintstones, I was held spellbound every Saturday morning with the cartoon adventures of Kimba, a brave white lion cub. Even though "Kimba the White Lion" only aired a few years in the mid-'60s, it kick-started my obsession with Africa. Next, I fed my fixation by watching as many "Tarzan" movie reruns as I could muster, especially on cold winter weekends.

It wasn't an easy undertaking. In those early days, our family had only one television. Therefore, the shows we watched typically followed the unspoken guidelines of majority rules, especially if Dad was part of that majority. Just as Tarzan was about to rescue Jane from a pit of hissing vipers, my dad and the boys would waltz into the room and--click--*"...the Pittsburgh Steelers kicked a field goal."* To this day, I am still traumatized by such interruptions. So many ghastly deeds in the wilds of Africa were left hanging in the air. Sometimes, literally.

Tarzan, of course, didn't fight the evils of the world on his lonesome. Aside from Jane, Boy, and Cheetah, he had the whole animal kingdom at his disposal. The fact that the exciting adventures with fur-covered stars were fictitious did little to take away from their charm. Therefore, like so many others, I fell in love with Africa's iconic residents. A devotion that followed me into adulthood.

Who isn't captivated by six-ton monstrosities with sail-like ears and accordion noses; towering creatures of mottled gold whose soaring necks allow them to browse the treetops; mane-covered beasts who are killing machines, as well as doting parents; or horse-like grazers whose black and white stripes dazzle the landscape with striking grace? From my biased view, the Maker's creativity seemed absolutely uninhibited and ingenious when designing Africa's hodgepodge of wildlife.

The idea of hunting such exotic specimens seemed different from hunting deer, turkey, and elk, all of which enjoy healthy populations and provide food for the table. What kind of hypocrite would I be to judge hunters poorly as I slurped up the family favorite, spaghetti sauce made with ground deer meat? It is also understandable that some animal populations must be controlled when faced with limited space. Mutilated deer carcasses littering Pennsylvania's roads make that point grotesquely clear. So, even though I hated the idea of hunting myself, essentially, I *got it*. Even so, when it came to hunting in Africa, I was deeply torn, especially regarding certain prized species.

Just like in the States, hunting would provide food, population control, and money for conservation. Yada yada yada. My head told me one thing, but my heart asked questions.

Weren't many of Africa's species endangered? If so, why could they sometimes be legally hunted? Human-wildlife conflict is a huge and growing problem in rural Africa but how does well-managed hunting help that problem? Why is population control even needed in lands that seem endless? What purpose does harvesting a leopard or lion serve? What about poaching? With illegal killing and wildlife trafficking already an issue, isn't legalized hunting just adding another nail in the coffin? Doesn't Africa have a reputation for corruption? Is such misconduct a widespread issue or confined to only a few nations and, most importantly, how does it affect wildlife conservation? Why is there such conflicting information regarding the actual threats to wildlife? Above all else, isn't general tourism--a non-lethal approach to helping local communities and conserving wildlife--a better alternative?

All these doubts, as well as the outright fear of sleeping amid wild critters, almost caused me to stay safely tucked away in our Idaho home. Ultimately, my zest for adventure and desperation to experience Africa trumped my misgivings. I put on my big girl pants, packed a bag, and headed for the Tanzanian bush.

Umphhh. The lion's grunt jolted me from my reverie. Still wedged against Rick on his tiny bunk, I returned my attention to *Simba's* primal serenade, *Fisi's* insane choruses, and the rest of Africa's beastly symphony. A realization surged through me. Finally, after years of anticipation, my African dream was coming true. It was nothing like I had envisioned, but nestled in a tent, hours from civilization, there was absolutely no turning back. Nor did I find myself wanting to. Even though apprehension filled my entire being, it became crystal clear that Rick's version of the dream was far more than anything I could have imagined for myself.

No doubt, there would be difficult and unsettling moments. Rick would very likely be harvesting some of the creatures that I had treasured since my first "Kimba the White Lion" cartoon. It was also clear that our adventures would be partnered with aspects of danger. I couldn't help wondering how my romanticized view of Africa, after dreaming about it for so many years, would stand against reality.

Even with uncertainty gnawing at me, my feelings of apprehension and exhaustion floundered as other emotions trickled to the surface. Fascination. Excitement. Awe. Astonishment. Curiosity. And thankfulness. Lying wide-eyed--covered in goosebumps listening to the chortles, bellows, growls, squeaks, whistles, cooing, cawing, *whoooops*, and *umphhs* of the African Symphony--I realized that I had never felt so terror-stricken and yet, at the same time, so alive and exhilarated by the promise of the days to come.

2
MASIMBA CAMP

I t had taken two layovers and 23 hours of flying before touching down at the tiny international airport outside the city of Arusha, Tanzania. Fortunately, Rod and Sue, our friends and travel companions, had several African trips under their belts. Our good fortune was their misfortune; during the months of planning, we had bombarded them with questions. Yet, the answers did little to prepare us for the real thing. From the moment we stepped off the jet onto the oven-baked tarmac, the world was no longer as we knew it.

The first 30 minutes en route to our hotel took us through a barren countryside interspersed with shanties, some homes and other ramshackle storefronts. Brightly dressed cattle farmers and their children herded small bunches of cattle down the road using nothing but long canes. No horses, ATVs, or pickups--none of what Rick's family uses when moving cattle.

Shortly thereafter, we came upon Arusha, the third largest city in Tanzania, home to over 400,000 people. The countryside and sporadic dwellings were replaced by noisy crowded streets of makeshift shacks, all squished together with people selling their wares. Many outdoor furniture stores displayed their stock, including couches and beds, right on the dusty ground. Most of the roads were little more than packed dirt. Pavement seemed to be scarce, at least where we traveled.

The crude streets were jumbled with beautifully adorned women wearing traditional *kangas,* a large piece of colorful patterned fabric draped around their bodies. Most of the women carried five-gallon buckets or bulky feed sacks balanced expertly on their heads. Some, miraculously, carried both a bucket *and* a large sack. Still others carried these loads with infants draped across their bodies. My head pivoted from one woman to another, spellbound by the grace and seemingly effortless manner in which they accomplished such feats.

Women weren't the only ones doing the inconceivable. Men were pushing carts or riding bicycles while carrying loads of overflowing wood, sacks, corn, and other supplies. These supply-laden human-powered modes of transportation, along with tons of motorcycles, far outnumbered cars and trucks. Even within the hustle-bustle of the city, small herds of cattle could be seen plodding their way through the chaotic hodgepodge of traffic and weighted-down pedestrians. Arusha was a city bursting at the seams.

The dizzying world was a huge contrast from our hometown, a farm and ranching community of roughly 800 people located in Idaho's panhandle. Rick's family owns a modest ranch originally homesteaded by his grandparents. Along with a few hundred tillable acres, they raise about 80 head of cattle, a few milk cows, horses, chickens, and a host of other farm-life misfits. The plump Black Angus-Hereford cattle grazing in the Idaho pastures were a huge contrast to the scraggly multi-colored bovine of Tanzania. Still, the rawboned cattle were far more familiar looking than anything else we'd seen.

As enthralling as the city was, the previous two days spent in a cramped space, jet lag, and the lack of sleep had taken their toll on us. Understandably, we resembled the walking dead more than excited tourists starting a grand adventure. As a tease, the hotel offered a crystal blue swimming pool surrounded by palm trees and exotic flowering shrubs. The alluring refuge was everything I had wished for in *my* dream of Africa, but we weren't interested in any of it. An air-conditioned room with a comfy bed was the only thing that mattered.

Bright and early the next morning, without even dipping my big toe in the pool, we were off again. An hour later, we pulled into a small airport with bush planes dotting the tarmac. After piles of supplies and our packs were loaded into a turbo-prop Cessna Caravan, our little group hopped aboard for the last leg of our journey. Hilary Daffi, a Tanzanian professional hunter and the owner of the safari outfitting business, joined us as well. Only minutes into our flight, the cluttered roadways with women performing balancing acts on their heads disappeared. The mass of humanity was replaced by the Miombo woodlands, a vast region of tropical grasslands, savannas, and scrublands that cover much of central and southern Africa.

Gaping out the window, I watched as 400 miles of desolate landscape passed beneath me. Chartering the bush plane had been a difficult decision and troubling expense. Without it, the 2-hour flight would have been replaced by a punishing 16-hour drive. At that point, an overnight stay in a village would have been necessary, essentially adding two days to our journey at each end. Facing the reality of our remote destination suddenly made the charter seem essential rather than a luxury.

Finally, the runway--or rather a cleared strip of land in the Rungwa West Game Reserve--appeared below us. Minutes later, we were on the ground taxiing to meet our waiting hosts.

As we stepped from the airplane, we were slammed with a wall of heat even worse than the day before. While adjusting to the sudden temperature change, *Masimba* Camp's staff scurried to transfer the gear and supplies into two Land Cruisers for the final leg of our journey.

"It's a short drive. Only 45 minutes" they assured us. "Maybe we'll even see animals."

That perked us up a bit. After quick introductions, Rod, Sue, Rick, and I crammed into the open-air bench seat positioned high above the enclosed cab of the Land Cruiser, giving us a great vantage point for the wildlife we were sure to see.

Nothing, and I mean *nothing,* could have prepared us for what awaited us.

Almost the moment we left the airstrip, we were attacked by a battalion of ravenous miniature vampires with wings. Keep in mind, I'm not talking about the righteous vampires from the "Twilight" movies that were popular a few years back. I'm talking about Africa's infamous Tsetse flies, bloodsuckers that hurt worse than any bee sting I've ever experienced. Also, just like vampires, they refuse to die. Swatting them against your thigh or arm deters them for just a bit. Then they come back with a vengeance.

In our months of preparation, we had been warned of the Tsetse flies' presence in the Tanzanian bush and had, therefore, packed accordingly. We had mosquito nets, long-sleeved shirts, leather gloves, bug sprays, bug-repellent bracelets, and even insect-repelling body oils—all stashed on the *other* Land Cruiser. Definitely, a rookie move.

Wearing T-shirts and lacking our Tsetse-fly arsenal, we made easy pickings for the gorging insects. Our long hiking pants also did little to help. Even through the fabric, they drew blood. Tsetse flies have a special awl arrangement on their bills enabling them to bore through three layers of canvas, or so we'd read in Robert Ruark's "Horn of the Hunter." Surely, he exaggerated, we naively presumed. Unfortunately, the insects lived up to their loathsome reputation. Even Rod and Sue had never dealt with them on their previous safaris and therefore were just as surprised by the insatiable assault.

Wedged in like sardines in a can while bouncing down a bumpy Tsetse-fly-infested road, we performed a slapstick comedy routine resembling "The Three Stooges." Our arms flailed about wildly, swatting and whacking at the bloodsuckers while our legs took their own evasive actions, stomping and kicking erratically. It was *not* each man for themselves. As friends, we took liberties to swat each other *wherever* necessary to keep the nasty buggers from landing long enough to draw blood. Suddenly, the unexpected onslaught coupled with extreme exhaustion caused us to burst into hysterical laughter.

Who would have guessed that our first truly memorable experience in the African bush had absolutely nothing to do with one of Africa's iconic species? No majestic lion, lumbering elephant, or browsing giraffe. No. Our first notable memory was of a tiny little fly.

Surprisingly, for the wallop they punch, they are a rather innocent-looking insect, tinier and more delicate-looking than the American housefly. Even the name Tsetse fly has a cutesy-sounding ring to it. Their name and appearance are a total deception. There is nothing innocent, dainty, or adorable about them. *Ndorobo,* their Swahili translation, at least strikes a more menacing tone --one that more aptly describes the sinister instruments of pain.

Finally, after 45 minutes, which honestly felt like hours, we rounded a bend to see a welcoming cluster of thatched huts, fences and shade shelters, a few with tents resting underneath. The whole conglomeration of structures was nestled under a shade-producing canopy of woodland trees.

Just like that, the *ndorobo* were gone. Simply vanished. In their place, we were delighted to find smiling Tanzanians rushing to greet us warmly. Feeling like celebrities, we were soon introduced to all 20 members of Hilary's staff.

Yes. You heard that right. Twenty people, not counting Hilary, were to take care of four Americans. I had always prided myself on being a rather low-maintenance female; but as I gazed at the faces of those who were to assist in our stay, it became perfectly clear that I was kidding myself.

As men scrambled to take our belongings and unload supplies, Joel, the primary host and camp manager, ushered us to the dining hall. The *mesi* was a large, open-air pavilion with branches forming its framework. The roof's supports were covered with thatched grasses. The partial walls, only three-foot high to allow for plenty of air movement, were made of grasses as well. Nestled under a thatched roof and a canopy of shade trees, the open structure allowed for a gentle breeze to create a refreshing oasis, comparatively speaking, of course. Unshielded, the midday sun's rays were absolutely brutal. Even better than the shade was the miraculous lack of Tsetse flies.

After some fabulous hartebeest meat sauce over spaghetti and friendly banter, we were finally shown to what would be our quarters for the next 23 days. As I noted earlier, much of my apprehension about our trip, aside from the harvesting of particular species, revolved around our sleeping arrangements.

Masimba Camp's dining hut or mesi

For months I had envisioned waking up to see a deadly spider crawling up my arm or, even worse, a venomous snake hanging from the rafters above my bed. The only thing that outweighed my concern for slithering or creeping crawling guests was the thought of trips to the outhouse in the middle of the night. A midnight rendezvous to the latrine in Idaho's backcountry offered little more than a nerve-wracking trek through the blackness, along with a cold butt. In Africa, a midnight excursion could lead to a six-foot hole in the ground.

Peter Hathaway Capstick's book, "Death in the Long Grass," made this point loud and clear: "The only thing more abundant in Africa than life is death. It takes a thousand forms...It walks, crawls, creeps, flies, swims, and runs in untold disguises."[1] Capstick's harrowing book revolves around big game hunting adventures in the African bush. As the name aptly implies, the pages are filled with gruesome stories of death as a result of Africa's wild species. The chapter titles are very basic: Elephant, Leopard, Cape buffalo, Hippo, Crocodile, Rhino, Snakes, and, of course, Lion. Yet the stories in each chapter are far from ordinary. With vivid vocabulary, he recounts grisly scenes and ghastly deaths bringing you face to face with some of the most ferocious killers in the world.

While the book will have you sitting on the edge of your seat chewing your fingernails from start to finish, it is not the ideal book to read *before* a trip to Africa. Please take my word for it.

Some people claim that Capstick tends to exaggerate. That may or may not be true. Either way, his style of writing takes you on a journey that places you right there with him, stalking through the blinding long grasses or sitting around the crackling fire when untold horrors erupt. Once his graphic words enter your head, embellished or not, they stick to you like tar.

I'd read the book several years before our trip to Africa so, thankfully, the gory details of each horrific death had slightly faded. Still, the dread of each scene remained embedded in my psyche.

With ghastly stories of man-eating lions, venomous black mamba snakes, and cunning hyenas implanted in my mind, I almost kissed the ground in blissful relief when I saw that our sleeping quarters were not just a grass hut like I had pictured. Underneath the thatched structure was a large tent. A fully enclosed tent--impenetrable by at least the creeping, crawling, slithering variety of varmints. The canvas floor was attached to the tent's walls and the front and back door flaps were secured by zippers. Neither spiders nor serpents could enter unless we were stupid enough to leave the zippers open. Believe me, that would not happen. Forgetting to wear our

Tsetse-fly arsenal is one thing; leaving the tent open for truly nasty buggers is quite another.

The tent setup was far different from what I was familiar with when camping in Idaho's backcountry where staying warm and dry was the main concern--especially if Rick wanted his always-too-cold wife to join him. Therefore, to keep me happy, a small wood-burning stove was typically set up in one corner of the tent, which incidentally had no attached floor. A large piece of canvas was simply laid on the ground to keep our gear and feet off of the earthen floor.

While the system worked great to keep me toasty and free from wallow-ing in the dirt, it did little to prevent the intrusion of tiny critters; mice, spiders, and snakes could, and did, easily slink into our cozy little nest. That reality kept me slightly on edge, especially because the knowledge of such visits was often conveniently withheld. We never did tell my brother, who hates snakes, about the small serpent we found under *his* sleeping mat.

A snake in Tanzania is vastly different from a snake in Idaho. I can just hear my hardened, ranch-savvy mother-in-law Betty calmly stating, "Don't worry; a bite probably won't kill ya," when I ran into her house frantically yelling that a prairie rattler had just chased me through the pasture.

In all fairness to the coiled rattlesnake vigorously shaking its tail at me, it only broke its stance and pursued me *after* I approached it for the *third* time. The annoyed rattler was blocking the gate; so, thoughtfully, I walked away for a few minutes, allowing it to clear out. Unfortunately, patience has never been my virtue. Instead of minutes between intrusions, it was probably more like seconds. On my third approach, the snake had had enough of my foolery. Rather than turning tail, it uncoiled and came right at me—quite speedily, I might add. Needless to say, I did a frantic 180 and ran flailing through the pasture screaming like a lunatic. My wild sprint didn't stop until the snake took a right turn and I took a left.

As unhappy as I was with Betty's casual indifference to my rattlesnake encounter, she was right. A rattlesnake "*probably* won't kill ya."

Rattlesnakes also have another great advantage over Africa's litany of lethal snakes; their distinctive rattle sound is as attention-grabbing as any high-tech alarm system. Their warning has saved Rick and me on multiple occasions.

Black mambas, cobras, and puff adders, the three African snakes that I feared the most, were silent and deadly. They didn't have a handy-dandy rattle to warn you away. Their venom is also far deadlier than most anything we have in the States.

The black mamba's bite, for instance, is so lethal that even with an antivenom in hand, which is highly unlikely in the bush, you are likely to be pushing up daisies before you even get done saying your goodbyes. I read one story of a crocodile hunter found dead of a black mamba bite with the antivenom kit clenched in his hand, presumably dying before he could administer it.

Their name is actually derived from the jet-black color of their mouth. Even a picture of the inky abyss makes you feel like you are staring into the pit of hell. Yes, like an idiot I googled 'Black Mamba Pictures' *before* leaving for Africa. At the time it seemed like a good idea to know what the legendary snake looked like.

Again, stupid move. Immense size. White fangs. Black forked tongue. The utter black cavity of its mouth. Their sinister look just reinforced what I'd already learned; its lethal venom results in an agonizing death often within twenty minutes. Understandably, the black mamba filled my innards with dread.

The silent instrument of death, as with most snakes, also ate mice as a regular part of their diet. A rather troubling thought since settlements tend to draw mice. The woven grasses of native huts create perfect nooks and crannies for opportunistic rodents and snakes to hide in.

You might wonder what any of this has to do with me. Well, knowing the thoughts that were swimming around in my head, and why, might help you understand my fear. A zipped-up, totally enclosed, tent meant that no snakes would offer a deadly wake-up call.

In addition to offering peace of mind, the tent was immaculate. Aside from the two single bunks which were a definite upgrade from our sleeping arrangements in an Idaho wall tent, there were a few wooden shelves for clothing and a small end table beside each bed. Solar panels outside even provided us with an overhead light. A thatched roof was built above the tent to offer shade. The tent's screened windows, with their flaps rolled up, also allowed a slight breeze to filter through.

While this cozy nest offered protection against snakes and such, it offered little protection against the larger four-legged creatures of the night. Mainly *Simba*. If a lion truly wanted inside, his power and arsenal of weapons would make mincemeat of the tent's canvas walls. Many people argue that only sick or injured lions kill people. Yet, there are oodles of grisly tales of perfectly healthy lions acquiring a taste for humans. Unarmed, our species are easy pickings. Once a lion or its pride recognizes that it is a recipe for disaster.

Probably the most notorious case is the tale of "The Man-Eaters of Tsavo" which was made into a book of the same name and later as a movie, "The Ghost and the Darkness." The two man-eaters halted construction of the Uganda Railroad at the turn of the twentieth century. According to the book, the lions "...treated the project as one extended buffet table." A vibrant account of a human's remains, or what was left of them, brought home in a coffee can comes to mind.

Lions, overall, may be afraid of man, but I, for one, didn't want to bump into the one that felt differently. You get the point. I'd read enough to know that ending up as kitty chow, no matter what the state of the lion, was not a pleasant way to go.

Just as my thoughts had turned back to the carnivores of Africa, Joel unzipped the back flap of the tent, or *hema*, to finish the tour of our quarters. There before us was a bathroom! Yes, in the bush of Tanzania, we had functioning facilities of sorts. A totally unexpected and welcome surprise. Less than 10 feet from the relative safety of our tent was a flushing toilet, a small sink with running water, and a makeshift shower on a small hand-poured slab of cement. The rest of the washroom had a dirt floor. All of these conveniences were nestled between grass walls that practically butted up to the tent.

Since the toilet area adjoined our tent, another of my biggest fears was crossed off the list; I would not have to slink to an outhouse in the middle of the night. That meant less likelihood of me becoming a rump roast dinner.

Rick's Idaho backcountry elk camps didn't include bathrooms, especially not adjacent to the tent. For obvious reasons, the so-called toilets were always placed quite a distance away. In places where we could ride ATVs and carry more equipment, a bottomless five-gallon bucket was often placed over a hole dug in the ground. Then a camping toilet seat was placed on top of the bucket. Ta-da! A toilet. It was a little wobbly at times, but compared to other methods, it was quite nice. Still, taking care of business entailed a jaunt into the woods, several hundred yards from the tent.

A flushing toilet in the African bush!

For more remote camps, accessible only on foot or horseback, it wasn't feasible to carry a five-gallon bucket and toilet seat--especially on the way out. Nasty business for sure. Consequently, another method was often used. A hole was dug between two well-placed trees. Then branches were tied between the trees creating a sort of chair over the pit. You then hung your butt over the bottom branch while placing your back against the top branch, doing the deed while balancing in this awkward position. Not an easy task by any measure. In the dead of night, it is even less fun.

On one pitch-black evening, deep in the backcountry, I found myself sitting above a yuck-filled hole in that preposterous position with wolves howling in the distance. Even on the best of days, willing *things* to happen is not easy while your butt is teetering over a branch with your pants crumpled around your ankles. Believe me, the mournful howling of wolves intensifies the experience. Skittish and on high alert, I used my headlamp's narrow beam of light to scour the blackness for any signs of glowing eyes. Catching movement, I jerked my head up to see a supersized packrat walking on a tree branch 10 feet above my head! Looking into the eyes of an 18-inch rodent with a bushy tail and beady eyes was as terrifying as any wolf. Well, almost.

Instinctively, I let out a bloodcurdling scream sending Rick and the rest of camp into a flurry of activity. Before the cavalry arrived to have my humiliating position burned into their memory, I gained my composure enough to assure them it was okay. It wasn't a wolf.

Anyway, because of my past experiences with howling predators and oversized rodents, I was dreading any midnight trips across *Masimba* Camp. While the Idaho experience definitely rattled me a bit, there was no real danger. Africa, however, is an altogether different ballgame. Bumping into a skulking lion, leopard, or hyena while traipsing across camp in the dark of the night might cause more than a loss of dignity.

Masimba Camp's bathroom, as wonderful as it was, still wasn't without risks. The tour of the latrine area came with Joel's unique goodhearted assurances mixed with foreboding: "Bath hut very safe. Very safe *but* you look first. Keep your eyes open. Snakes sometimes like to hide. Snakes are very bad. OOOhhhh very bad."

The makeshift shower in the bathroom hut behind the tent.

Believe me, my eyes were wide open any time I left my zippered sanctuary.

We were also issued strong warnings to *never* leave our tent or bath hut at night. No way. No how. Not for any reason. That was the primary reason the bathroom was basically connected to the tent, so we *didn't* have to step outside. Then, almost comically, we received another contradictory message from Joel: "Oh, don't worry. *Masimba* Camp is very safe. Very safe. Animals will stay away."

It was inferred that wildlife looked at the canvas walls as impenetrable. Therefore, as long as we didn't exit our protective cocoon after dark, there was *supposedly* nothing to worry about. How the lions, leopards, hyenas, and elephants communicate their thoughts to our hosts was never mentioned. Still, the optimistic part of me chose to believe them.

Many rural Africans are not fortunate enough to have a bathroom essentially attached to their quarters as we did; when nature calls, they saunter off into the bushes. Sometimes for the last time. I, for one, had no intention of pushing my luck. The urgency in Joel's and Hilary's voices when it came to these instructions spoke to me loud and clear.

Once all of this was sufficiently drilled into our heads, we were off for the next part of our mini-tour. Our *hema* was located about ten yards from the *mostly* dried-up riverbed of the Mzombe River. Rod and Sue's tent was also along the riverbed but on the other side of the dining hut. During the rainy season, the river would swell with rising waters and become a haven for crocodiles. Yet by the time of our arrival in October, the flowing river had been reduced to pockets of water scattered along a ribbon of dirt. One of those 15-foot oversized puddles was only about 40 feet from our tent and provided much-needed water to a whole variety of thirsty beasts.

It also offered a watery sanctuary to our nearest neighbor, a resident crocodile that we soon dubbed Freddy. How could we not slap a name on a critter who was a permanent fixture of our so-called yard? Luckily, Freddy was only four feet long. Crocodiles typically latch onto their victims with their razor-sharp teeth, dragging them underwater to drown them before feasting. Freddy's small size made me pretty confident that he wouldn't be dragging my 125-pound hunk of flesh into that nasty pool. *Getting eaten by a crocodile* was therefore crossed off my list of things to worry about.

Finally, it was time to check out the hippo pond which I had been looking forward to for months. Knowing that I had reservations about joining Rick on the hunt, Hilary had enticed me with the promise of a pod of hippopotamuses only 300 yards from camp. After seeing the dried-up-river bed and the few scattered puddles, I was highly skeptical of any nearby populations of *Kibokos*. Accordingly, when Joel finally mentioned hippos, I snapped to attention.

Following Joel, we passed our hut, a skinning shed, and a small clearing before scrambling up an embankment of rock boulders. True to his word, below us in a 100-foot length of putrid river, or what was left of it, was a group of about 15 hippos and their calves. Most of the *Kibokos* only had their heads poking above the stagnant liquid filth and frothing excrement. Apparently, exiting their watery refuge when nature calls isn't high on a hippo's priority list.

Seeing our rotund neighbors lounging in the pool of nastiness and hearing their deep throaty bellows caused a grin to spread across my face: real live hippopotamuses in the wilds of Africa. How spectacular was this?

The hippo pool that was located 300 yards from our tent.

3
Follow-the-Leader

W ith darkness still engulfing the tent, the cries of the savanna melted away, replaced by muffled voices, footsteps, and stirrings from the kitchen area. Glancing at my watch, I blinked in disbelief. At only 4:30 a.m., the camp was already coming to life. Beside me, Rick also stirred. Sleep had evaded us much of the night, a combination of *Simba's* otherworldly dialogue, *Fisi's* deranged giggles, and the sad reality that a single bunk no longer did the trick for two rather-seasoned adults.

Moments later, a gentle whisper seeped through the canvas walls. "Rick. Sue. *Chakula.*"

Food. A simple but clear indication that another day in Tanzania was about to begin. Just as promised, Michael, our tent attendant and human alarm clock, woke us for breakfast. By then it was 5 a.m., still the middle of the night in my book. After our long journey and barely sleeping a wink, I just wanted to roll over, turn my brain off and fall into a deep slumber for at least a week. Rick's reaction was the opposite of mine. He practically leaped out of bed, almost throwing me on the floor in the process.

Knowing there was no escaping my fate, I sluggishly slipped into my safari attire as Rick offered cheery encouragement to quicken my progress. Who was this man? My normally laid-back reserved husband was practically beaming.

Within minutes we looked like we'd walked right off the pages of a safari hunting magazine. Camouflage, the pattern used in the States for such outings, was prohibited in Tanzania and was reserved instead for the Tanzanian army. Having spent eight years as a gunship pilot in the United States Army, Rick had no desire to step into that role again. Thus, a mini shopping spree had outfitted us in a sea of beige, browns, and greens.

Next, we filled our backpacks with everything but the kitchen sink: a journal, gloves, extra shirt, wet wipes, Kleenexes, cameras, ibuprofen,

Band-Aids, Moleskin for blisters, energy bars, Chapstick, sun block, bandanas, and an arsenal of Tsetse-fly paraphernalia. Unlike the trip from the airport, we were geared up and ready for battle. Last, but not least, I tossed in the brightly colored Maasai blankets that Hilary had gifted us at dinner the night before. What possessed me to grab those blankets in a land that got hot enough to scald a lizard is beyond me. Apparently, I'm a little psychic.

We had barely stepped from the tent when Michael sprinted toward us like a leopard chasing a gazelle. Instead of wanting to eat us for lunch, however, he wanted our packs. For two people used to pitching hay bales and remodeling a different fixer-upper each year, having someone carry our gear seemed unnecessary. Our resistance had about the same effect as punching him in the gut. Struck by his reaction, we handed over packs, allowing Michael to return to his cheery self.

Breakfast found Rod and Sue looking like they'd also stepped out of a safari magazine. Rod's face, however, made us do a double take. *Had Sue used Rod as a punching bag during the night?* we wondered. Rod is quite the character and a practical joker, so it's understandable why Sue might want to knock him around a bit. As a spirited, strong-minded, capable woman, she is nobody to mess with. Still, she is also kind and warmhearted, so we knew she wasn't the cause of Rod's swollen face. Those blood-sucking Tsetse-flies had left Rod a calling card; their bites had caused an allergic reaction, convincing us to double check our Tsetse-fly arsenal.

While scarfing up a delicious mystery-meat breakfast, the staff loaded the vehicle with water, coolers, lunches, tarps, packs, rifles, and other necessary odds and ends. All these preparations were made without us so much as lifting a finger. This was quite a jolt to our systems when typically, these chores all fell to us. Nevertheless, helping was out of the question.

At 6 a.m. sharp we were ushered to the ready-to-go safari vehicles. Unlike the trip from the airport, we weren't crammed in like sardines. Rod and Sue were assigned their own Land Cruiser with five staff members and we were assigned another with our own crew.

All foreign hunters in Africa must be accompanied by a Professional Hunter, or "PH", for many reasons. Most notably, to make sure clients go home via an airplane seat and not in a pine box. Even a skilled, well-seasoned hunter is like a babe in the woods when it comes to hunting in Africa, especially the first time. Aside from keeping clients safe, the PH must make sure the hunt is done legally while also making it as successful as possible. These talented individuals wear a lot of different hats; they are tour guides, interpreters, hosts, storytellers and educators just to name a few.

Our PH was a soft-spoken, reserved, and modest man who exuded confidence and skill with few words. Raphael had worked with Hilary for almost 23 years, starting as a tent attendant and then moving up the ranks to become a head tracker. Ultimately, after years of training, he earned his PH license.

Raphael Erro, the Professional Hunter (PH)

Raphael always sat on the right side of the bench seat. Rick was always positioned on the opposite side, and I was nestled in between. Like the day before, the seating platform was elevated in the open air above the enclosed cab to offer the best vantage point.

Directly behind our seat was a roll-bar-encircled cargo hold with a spare tire mounted on each side. The nine feet of storage held most of the supplies, as well as our trackers.

Mgogo, the head tracker, had many years of experience in the Rungwa West Game Reserve. He lived in the nearest village, a four-hour drive away, and worked for the previous outfitter before Hilary took over the hunting concession. Mgogo, therefore, knew the area like the back of his hand. As such a valuable asset, he always stood behind Raphael which enabled easy communication between the two. Abdalah, young and less experienced, was the assistant tracker and always positioned himself behind Rick.

That left two people sitting in the cab of the pickup. The Tanzanian game scout, or what we might call a wildlife ranger, always sat in the passenger seat. As government employees, their duty was to oversee each hunting safari, document everything, and ensure that all regulations were followed.

I'm not sure what I was expecting from an African law enforcement officer, but it certainly wasn't Lilian, a beautiful young woman in a green uniform slinging a Russian AK47 over her shoulder. While her beauty and rifle made a big statement, it was her intelligence that made her so incredible. Not only was she a wealth of information, but she also spoke three languages: her tribal tongue, Swahili, and English. Her ability to speak easily with us was a godsend that opened the doors for friendship and learning.

The final member of our safari crew was Mike, our very capable and trusted driver. Anyone unfamiliar with the African bush might assume his job to be the easiest. They would be dead wrong. Mike wasn't driving smooth paved roads sitting in an air-conditioned vehicle. He was trapped in the stifling heat of a non-air-conditioned cab in temperatures that would fry an egg on the dashboard. Maneuvering over bumpy, pitted terrain required him to keep a death grip on the steering wheel. Lilian, too, suffered with Mike. As a passenger, she was trapped in the same rattling inferno.

The fact that our driver's name was Mike and our tent attendant's name was Michael seemed uncanny to me. What are the chances of having not one, but two, Mikes in a foreign country on the other side of the globe? A place where the majority of names--Mgogo, Kaumba, Salum, Maugo, Ima, and Musa--reflect their tribal origins. I don't believe in coincidences; having two men with that particular name central to our team could not have been a fluke. My brother's name was Mike. After a brief but courageous battle with lung cancer, he died at the age of 50.

This is how we roll! Mike and Lilian in the cab. Me in the middle on top. Raphael on my right. Rick on my left. Mgogo behind Raphael. Zefania behind Rick. (Abdalah replaced him the third morning)

As the oldest of our family's little tribe--me, four brothers, and finally a sister--I was a self-appointed mini-mom from the moment each sibling poked their head into the world. Our childhood included endless games of Hide-n-Seek, searching for salamanders in nearby creeks, hanging out at Grandma's river camp, and exploring the woods behind our house.

As we became teenagers, our interests changed. My mom, sister, and I were drawn to endless hours at the river camp while my dad and the boys pursued hunting and fishing. Even with different interests, our lives were intertwined.

When Mike died, everything changed. Our world was turned upside down and thrown into an agony that my family had yet to experience. Torment. Heartbreak. Loss. It didn't matter that Mike was a capable adult; first and foremost, he was my little brother. Losing him felt like I lost a piece of my heart. A part of my history. A part of who I am. The pain was tangible. Like my heart had been ripped from my chest and twisted into a knot.

Mike's loss not only shattered my heart, it changed me. What once seemed important suddenly seemed trivial, giving me a whole new perspective on life. Rick and I recognized our mortality for what it was; each of us is here on earth for a finite amount of time, maybe 20 minutes, maybe 20 years. Every single day is a gift *not* to be taken for granted. It must be lived with joy, love, purpose, and wonder, just like Mike had always done.

Rick and I had put off our desire to travel to Africa for years. It was never the right time. Jobs. Money. Family obligations. There were lots of excuses. Losing my brother made us realize that you can't just wait for the *right* time, you have to *create* the right time. It meant making sacrifices; we sold our pack mules, ATV, camper, and other items to make our dreams come true.

Eighteen months later, we found ourselves on a Tanzanian safari with two Mikes in a staff of 21 Africans. Call me crazy, but I had no doubt that my brother Mike was riding shotgun. After all, you never *truly* lose a person you love; they remain forever a part of your memories, heart, and soul. Even so, the tangible reminders of him during our excursions brought me peace, joy, and knowing. His death sparked the action leading us to *Masimba* Camp and, finally, the safari was ready to begin.

The anticipation in the air was palpable. With our gear loaded and everyone situated, we puttered away from the bustle of camp. As calm washed over the vehicle, we took notice of everyone's garb. Most of our crew were wearing multiple layers. Heavier coats. Knit scarves. Caps. Gloves. At only 6 a.m. the sun was still just a promise. It may have been a tad chilly by some standards, but it certainly didn't seem cold enough to warrant so much clothing. We were definitely baffled.

Before we could explore it further, two humongous, blurred shapes materialized in the murkiness of the pre-dawn light only 20 yards in front of us. Elephants! Two mystical, seemingly floating, colossal forms. Then a second later they were gone, a mirage that disappeared into the early morning haze as quickly as it had appeared. Seeing, or *kind of* seeing, elephants only 500 yards from camp caught us totally off guard.

"The resident elephants," Raphael calmly informed us.

Apparently, the two hulking giants were regular visitors of the temporary cluster of grass huts and tents making up *Masimba* Camp.

Quickly, we learned that the roads, or *so-called* roads, could hardly be classified as such. They were bumpy, pitted, and filled with craters. Elephant craters. During the rainy season, the water-logged soil becomes as malleable as a fresh can of Play-doh, creating cookie-cutter-like imprints from six-ton pachyderms and other brawny beasts. When the dry season hits, the soppy mess dries into a network of oven-baked craters, making our gravel driveway in Idaho feel like a freeway.

We bounced, bobbed, and lurched like a can of paint in Home Depot's mixing machine. When there were fewer crusted-over cavities we were able to reach the dizzying speed of 15 mph. It became abundantly clear: no one goes anywhere fast in the bush.

With bodies pitching to and fro, the morning haze faded, replaced by the orangish-pink hues of sunrise, highlighted by stunning silhouettes of umbrella acacia trees. Skirting the dried-up riverbed, the terrain held a ribbon of more densely forested terrain compared to the sparser route we'd traveled from the airport.

Soon the ghost-like elephants faded from our thoughts as a host of other animals took center stage. Each sighting brought on a whole new round of excitement as Raphael pointed in one direction or the other softly stating, "waterbuck, warthog, vervet monkey, dik-dik."

After a few miles, he tapped on the window, signaling Mike to turn from the riverbed onto another track of slightly rolling terrain scattered with trees, open savannas, and mounds of rocks jutting randomly from the soil. Some of the boulders were the size of pickup trucks, others the size of houses, and still others as vast as an apartment building. When placed against the ground's relative flatness, the arbitrary displays somehow looked out of place, leaving me wondering what geological events had created such erratic displays.

A couple of miles later, Mgogo lurched forward, tapping Raphael on the shoulder, immediately spurring Raphael to rap on the cab window telling Mike to stop. The two men jumped off, ran a dozen yards, and peered at the ground amidst a parley of Swahili. Rick and I watched eagerly, trying to decipher the gist of the conversation.

A minute later Raphael came back and whispered, "Fresh *Nyati* tracks heading towards the riverbed. Alone. A *dagga* boy."

Dagga boy? I wondered. Raphael explained that young stronger Cape buffalo bulls drive the old males from the safety of the herd, often in brutal displays of dominance. These old buffalos tend to enjoy wallowing in the mud, or *dagga*--a fact that often leaves them encased in a muddy suit of armor. Hence the name, *dagga* boy.

Unfortunately for the companionless bovine, buffalo steak is one of *Simba's* favorite meals. A single bull with up to a ton of brute strength will put up a savage defense against a lion. When outnumbered by a pride, however, the lone buffalo's chances dwindle. *Dagga* boys therefore often band together in a bachelor group to help even out the odds.

While it seems harsh, Lilian explained that forcing old bulls from the herd is nature's way of ensuring that the genes of the biggest and strongest buffalo are passed to the next generation, furthering the health of the species overall. The often-resulting premature death of the *dagga* boy leaves more grasses and territory for the younger generation, completing the cycle of life by becoming food for the lion, leopard, hyena, jackals, vultures and a host of other scavengers.

Even with Mother Nature doing her part, habitats--even ones as vast as Africa--can become stressed from overgrazing. It is no secret that many of Africa's four-legged inhabitants are big. Really big. These supersized creatures require colossal amounts of food and huge chunks of real estate. Wildlife management is crucial everywhere, but in Africa, a continent of developing nations where local people and their livestock are competing for the same resources, it is even more important.

That I understood. It also helped that the *Nyati* is ultimately a member of the bovine family, fierce deadly versions, but still relatives of the cattle grazing in our pastures at home. Right or wrong, it was easier for me to wrap my head around harvesting an animal similar to domestic livestock whose meat filled our freezers at home. It also helped that they lacked the endearing qualities that we equate with so many African species.

Raphael estimated the *dagga* boy track to be less than an hour old. The hunt was on. Single file, we headed into the bush like a serpentine column of withering old men: backs hunched, shoulders rounded, and heads slumped. A position that made us look smaller and less human-like. We crept along, mirroring the crouched person in front of us while stepping almost exactly in each carefully placed footstep, avoiding kicking rocks and breaking twigs that would give us away. Mike was the only crew member that stayed behind. His job, as the driver, was to remain with the vehicle in the event of curious elephants or other destructive visitors.

There was also a precise order to the snake-like formation. When tracking dangerous game, Mgogo was always in the front, intent on reading each piece of displaced dirt, snapped twig, crushed blade of grass, or partial hoof print while Raphael followed close behind with his rifle ready. The *dagga* boy could be concealed behind any mound of dirt, thicket, or stand of grass, bursting out at any time. Cradling his rifle as well, Rick followed behind Raphael. I followed in Rick's footsteps with Abdalah behind me. Lilian and her automatic weapon always brought up the rear.

Since a firearm in the hands of an untrained person is more deadly than any buffalo, everyone was safer without me carrying a rifle. The trackers, too, never carried a weapon. This could have been for a host of reasons. Possibly, it hindered their movements and ability to do their jobs. Maybe they weren't trained or didn't have access to a gun. Possibly, too many rifles in the field were just as dangerous as too few. Whatever the reason, the firepower rested squarely on the shoulders of Raphael, Rick, and Lilian.

Stealthily, we weaved through brush, open areas, and stands of towering grass often reaching 10 feet tall. Sneaking through the thick walls of vegetation kept me on pins and needles. Since my fear of *Nyati* had yet to manifest, my unease centered on the multitude of deadly snakes that could be lurking in the dense, sometimes trampled and matted, network of dried foliage.

Tanzania is home to four kinds of spitting cobra alone. All of which are plenty deadly. Everyone is familiar with these serpents with their unique expandable hoods flaring out in warning. In fact, I'd go as far as to say spitting cobras, with their throats inflated and hissing in their full intimidating glory, are even more sinister looking than the black mamba.

Second on my most-feared list was the puff adder. It is a short serpent, three to four feet long, with a stout chevron-patterned body that blends perfectly with the environment. While this snake's venom isn't as deadly as the black mamba's, it is responsible for up to 90 percent of all snakebites in Africa, killing more people than any other snake.

There are several reasons the puff adder holds this honor: they are widespread across most of Africa; they are often found near settlements since rodents, their favorite food, are found there in abundance; and they are sluggish, nocturnal snakes who ambush their prey by sitting motionless for hours. Its lazy attitude is countered by utter swiftness when it strikes. Unfortunately, for all too many rural Africans, the slothful snake doesn't flee when unsuspecting, often barefoot, villagers travel the same well-worn trails that the snake's prey uses. If stepped on or threatened, the puff adder strikes quickly in retaliation.

As I crept through the savanna, stepping in the footsteps of those in front of me, I convinced myself that being fourth in line meant I would *not* be the first to encounter one of the short, fat, lazy reptiles. Surely, Raphael or Mgogo would spot it first. Also, it was nocturnal, and we were hunting in broad daylight. Certainly, Mr. Puff Adder was hiding from the blazing sun, holed up in some cool dark place.

The black mamba was a different story. As I mentioned, the lethal, slithering giant was the object of my nightmares. Their extreme length allows them to rear several feet off the ground, peering above the grasses like a telescope on a submarine. Because of this ability, they often strike victims in the head, face, and neck, another factor making them so deadly. Knowing my fear, Raphael assured me that black mambas are shy; their acute senses would feel our approach and they would be long gone before we got anywhere near them. This deadly snake supposedly only becomes a threat if it is cornered or threatened. Both of which I had no intention of doing.

Rick likes to refer to me as a *bull in a china shop*. While that trait may not have been great for slinking noiselessly through the savanna, it may have worked in my favor when it came to alerting any snakes en route. Still, I took no chances. With each footstep, I alternated between scouring the ground and scanning for steely-black eyes peering above the grasses.

This hushed and meticulous game of "Follow-the-Leader" continued as we weaved through game trails, sparsely vegetated clearings, burnt-out sections of scrubland, and tall-grass thickets; I breathed a sigh of relief each time we exited one of the jungle-like enclaves. No one spoke. The only sound was fabric rubbing against the grasses or the slight scuff of a boot against the ground. Quiet obedience kept us stepping one foot in front of the other as we blindly followed Mgogo and Raphael through the bush in the wake of the *dagga* boy.

Though skulking through terrain with an abundance of death-dealing creatures was unnerving, to say the least, I soon found myself transitioning from fearfulness to fascination as I watched Mgogo and Raphael's every move trying to determine what narrative they were reading in the dirt. It was utterly riveting.

After almost two hours of this intense version of a childhood game, they unexpectedly straightened from their withered-old-men impression and began speaking openly. Confused, we looked at Raphael.

"The *dagga* boy crossed into the national park," he explained.

It was only then that we realized we were standing in a dried-up riverbed. In fact, it was the Mzombe river, the same dehydrated waterway that bordered our camp. It turns out that the river was the border between Ruaha National Park and the Rungwa West Game Reserve. The *dagga* boy had chosen his route well. The second his hooves touched that sand, he was off limits. Hunting in the park was prohibited. Just like that, the hunt was over. Ended by that magical invisible line. Score one for the *Nyati*, zero for us. As most hunters would say, *that is why they call it hunting and not killing.*

At the time, we were clueless that our little nest at *Masimba* Camp was butted up against the national park's boundary, another great reason that foreign hunters aren't set loose in Africa on their own. The PH *does* know such crucial information. We had been so intent on the tracking that we barely noticed transitioning from the savanna into the strip of sand and rocks.

Initially, we were slightly dumbfounded by the turn of events and, of course, a little disappointed; but, as the excitement dissipated, another realization washed over us. My gosh. We had just followed in the tracks of a Cape buffalo in Tanzania, Africa. How blessed were we to have such an amazing visceral experience? The fact that we had spotted neither hide nor hair of the old boy in our two-hour quest was irrelevant. The pursuit itself *was* the reward. Watching Mgogo and Raphael expertly read the buffalo's almost imperceptible spoor, or tracks, was the absolute cherry on top--a true privilege.

With the hunt over, we wormed our way back to the Land Cruiser and continued. Heading away from the waterway, we entered open savannas with a spattering of decrepit-looking trees. With the change in terrain came an increasing number and variety of antelopes, keeping me in a constant state of delight. You never knew what would make an appearance around the next bend: herds of grazing zebras, impalas, and hartebeests; warthog families dashing for their burrows; oribis and dik-diks darting about; or giraffes browsing the treetops in the distance before erupting to flee, their long legs giving the illusion that they were running in slow-motion.

Raphael didn't miss a beat. Noticing my fascination for the tall browsers, he signaled Mike to stop each time we spotted *twiga* so we could enjoy their presence as long as possible. Soon, he did the same with the warthogs. Those hideous-looking creatures cracked me up every time.

Since we were in a game reserve and not a national park, the wild residents rarely stuck around to pose for pictures. Not being used to an endless train of tourist vehicles parading by, they hoofed it whenever our vehicle approached. While animals habituated to humans would have been great for photos, it would also have made them sitting ducks for a rifle.

Ethical hunting requires that the "rules of fair chase" are followed. That entails a whole list of rules and lifestyle choices to live by: obey all laws and regulations; respect the land and customs of the locals; only shoot when a quick precise kill is possible; and pursue game in a respectable manner. That means no motorized chases, confinement to small enclosures, or trapped, drugged, or helpless prey. These are just a few of the guidelines followed by principled hunters. There are plenty more, varying a bit for each hunter and each form of hunting.

Each time anyone spotted a species that Rick was hunting, Raphael would either have Mike stop immediately or signal him to drive further along depending on the situation and the distance between us. Mgogo could spot the ear of a kudu poking out of the brush at 300 yards. No joke. Often Rick and I were left peering in bewilderment at a cluster of trees or brush in the distance while Raphael and Mgogo scrutinized whatever hind leg, tail section, or piece of horn protruded from concealment. A hushed burst of Swahili decided the next plan of action. If a harvestable male was spotted, we would quietly exit the vehicle and form our serpentine-style formation to begin a stalk.

Stalking is different from tracking. The desired quarry is already in sight. The trick then becomes getting within 20-50 yards for dangerous game or within 200 yards for others. It doesn't matter how much experience or accuracy a hunter exhibits, long-distance shooting in Africa is highly frowned upon. Africa's game is unbelievably tough with a strong sense of self-preservation. It is critical to get as close as possible to allow for a precise shot, preferably killing instantly and painlessly.

If the target is wounded, it is followed up as quickly as possible to mitigate any suffering. No ethical hunter wishes to prolong a living creature's death.

Still, no one is perfect. Even the most diligent, well-trained hunters do make mistakes from time to time. A few years back, Rick injured an elk that we were never able to find, even after hours and hours of searching. The bull fled *up* the mountain--no easy feat in Idaho's steep rugged terrain. A critically injured bull would typically take the easier route, fleeing downward. Also, there was very little blood trail. For these reasons, Rick felt sure the bullet passed through the muscle cleanly, causing minimal damage.

Even so, without finding the elk, there was no way to be sure. He had one tag and as far as he was concerned, he had used it--even though by Idaho law he *legally* could have continued to hunt.

Typically, whether hunting or not, Rick loves being in the woods. Despite that, he was so disgusted with himself that the next morning we tore down camp, packed the mules, and headed home. That hunt is burnt into his memory. A memory that fills him with loathing, regret and sorrow.

Most ethical hunters who've made similar blunders carry that burden forever. Having said that, it is the weight of that mistake that causes them to take the steps necessary to lessen the chance of it ever happening again.

In Africa, another factor comes into play. Money. For example, when you buy a license in Tanzania, it has a list of specified animals on it that are available for harvest, with each species assigned a monetary value, or trophy fee. Each country's government determines these figures based on population statistics, scientific conservation data, and other factors. If you wound any game, it is considered harvested whether you retrieve it or not. That also means you pay the trophy fee and your tag is filled. Fundamentally this is a great system. After all, with deadly carnivores lurking about, a wounded creature typically doesn't survive long. Also, for the few hunters who don't factor in the ethical equation of a difficult shot, hopefully, the sizable price tag of a misplaced bullet will.

Most people save for years for the experience. Dishing out thousands of dollars for an inaccurate shot while simultaneously ending the hunt for that particular species is disheartening. In Africa, every bullet counts.

In sparse terrain offering little cover, getting close to wild game is no easy feat. While we assumed the same hunkered-down position as we did when tracking, stalking was quite different. Instead of moving slowly and methodically, we scrambled quickly from cover to cover in a linear grouping with Raphael always in the lead. Rick, Mgogo, me, Abdalah and Lilian followed, always in that order. Our line moved as one unit moving perpendicular to the target to create one single blob instead of a fanned-out pack of two-legged predators. The smaller we could appear, the better.

On Raphael's cue, all five of us darted to hide behind an acacia tree. Next, he'd aim for a 6-inch scrub tree. In unison, we dashed behind him. Zigging from one tree, zagging to another. Finally, the whole huddled mass would end up behind one itsy-bitsy "Charlie Brown" tree. It was a bizarre combination of "Follow-the-Leader" and "Hide-n-Seek" while imitating the hunchback of Notre Dame.

No matter how ridiculously skilled we became at the kooky version of childhood games, more often than not, the targets won. Aside from tracking the *dagga* boy, we stalked a group of roans, two groups of zebras, and a group of impalas--all before early afternoon. Yet, all we succeeded in getting was tired, hot and hungry.

Dashing about under Africa's unrelenting sun, then bobbing along mercilessly on elephant-potholed roads wiped me out. By the time we pulled under a large shade tree to stop for lunch, I was toast. Literally.

During these hours we also discovered the reason for all the layers of clothing that had stumped us earlier. Tsetse flies. Of course. Not all the time. But enough. The crew's extra layers of clothing were not to combat the morning chill as we had assumed, they were a shield against the *angry little devils*, as Lilian referred to them. The Maasai blankets that I had instinctively tossed into our packs also came in quite handy. Draped across our shoulders or legs, they added another layer of protection. Those lifesavers, along with the rest of our arsenal of *Ndorobo* weapons, were a definite improvement over the ride from the airport.

Lilian and Mike suffered the most. With no air-conditioning and their windows down to keep from having a heat stroke, the cab acted like a wasp trap; the flies got in but couldn't get out. In their entrapment they attacked, inflicting untold pain on the confined humans. Mike, with both hands wrestling the steering wheel, couldn't even swat them off. Lilian, with her hands free and dressed for an Antarctic expedition, fared slightly better.

We couldn't figure out rhyme or reason for the flies' appearance. One minute, we'd be fighting the stifling heat with sweat dripping down our backs and the next we'd be battling a battalion of those little devils. Then, mysteriously, they'd be gone.

The minute we pulled under the spreading crown of a massive, green-leafed tree, it became abundantly clear why lunch had been delayed until that very moment: dense luxurious shade and no Tsetse-flies. The *Lucky Bean Tree*, as Raphael referred to it, was a mini refuge of sorts, a haven tucked away in Tanzania's harsh countryside.

Resembling wet noodles, Rick and I melted into the two folding chairs that Raphael produced from the cargo hold. Since the Tsetse flies were gone, we even risked taking off our hats and rolling up our sleeves and pant legs to expose as much flesh as possible, hoping to feel a little relief from the debilitating heat. Quite frankly, we were miserable. We barely slept a wink thanks to *Simba's* chilling serenade; endured hours of abuse jostling about in the Land Cruiser; trekked miles through the bush; and suffered multiple bouts with the *Ndorobo*. All under a sun hot enough to cook a goose.

Our first few hours on safari had been thrilling but also grueling. Sitting under that shade tree, soggy, whipped, and heavy-eyed, it seemed impossible to survive another 21 days.

Me at lunch, already wiped out!

While we licked our wounds, Raphael brought us an Americanized lunch: some type of game meat burrito, chips, a piece of fruit, and even a candy bar that somehow survived in the cooler without turning into a puddle. Slumped in our chairs, the crew left us to wallow in our misery alone.

It took a few minutes before we realized the crew hadn't been given chairs or even a bagged lunch. Nor were they relaxing. They were busy with some activity behind a tree about 10 yards away. As dog-tired as I was, I couldn't stand it; curiosity trumped exhaustion. I wolfed down my quickly melting chocolate and slogged over to see what all the fuss was about.

Mike and Mgogo had built a small fire against a large rock and were cooking mielie-meal, or *ugali,* a type of coarse cornmeal porridge cooked in water until it reached a stiff dough-like consistency. After removing it, they cooked some vegetables in broth using the same pan. When the stew was finished, a portion of the mixture was pulled off the mound, rolled into an oblong chunk, and used kind of like a spoon to scoop up the cooked vegetables.

Mgogo cooking mielie-meal, or ugali.

According to Lilian, *ugali* is the staple food of Africa and is eaten in one form or another at almost every single meal, especially in the villages. The porridge-type mixture reminded me of extremely thick grits minus the butter, salt, cheese, and milk. It can also be eaten with milk, beans, and, when protein is available, stewed meats. Lilian was nice enough to instruct Rick and me on the rolling and scooping technique for us to try some. Alone, the concoction was very bland but when dipped in the vegetable relish, it was quite yummy.

After eating, Raphael taught us about the Lucky Bean Tree. Aside from its umbrella-like canopy, the highly beneficial tree offered a little something for everybody. Bees and birds love the nectar from the spring flowers. Vervet monkeys eat the flower buds. Kudu, klipspringer, and baboons graze on the leaves. Elephants and rhinos eat the bark. Bush pigs like the roots. Insect-eating birds feed on the insects sheltered in its canopy. Snakes curl in their branches, waiting for their next meal. The thick foliage provides sanctuary and nesting areas for all kinds of small critters. People use the wood to make canoes, roof shingles, and other building materials. Also, hanging from the tree are copious amounts of cylindrical pods containing clusters of large, black, bean-like seeds. After the flowering is over, the pods dry and burst open, scattering the kernels all over the ground to be enjoyed by a whole host of herbivores, especially kudu. As you might suspect from such a valuable specimen, parts of the tree also have medicinal qualities.

With all these attributes, it is no wonder that many indigenous people believe that the Lucky Bean Tree has magical properties. Raphael gathered some of the seeds, presenting them to us for good luck. Not opposed to a little magic, we carried our *Lucky Beans* everywhere as tokens of luck.

Much too soon, lunch and our little stint in heaven were over. Many of Tanzania's four-legged inhabitants were smarter than we were; they did their best to stay out of the midafternoon sun's scorching rays. Not us. We continued to jerk, dip and bob over the rough roads scanning for anything of interest. While many animals were bedded down in the shade, we still spotted impala, hartebeest, oribi, duiker, steinbok, and dik-dik. We even played another game of Hide-n-Seek with a herd of zebras, or *punda milias*. Apparently, the magic of our *Lucky Beans* hadn't kicked in yet. The striped equines outmaneuvered us again.

By late afternoon, I looked and felt like a worn-out rag doll. I spent the last two hours of our first day on safari sound asleep. Sitting up. One minute I was draped against Rick's shoulder and the next pitch of the vehicle would send me flopping onto Raphael's. If he minded, he never let on. Friendships are cemented pretty quickly when you've spent from sunrise to sunset bouncing off of each other, especially with a man as quiet, competent, and kindhearted as Raphael.

My jiggling slumber ended with the sounds of *Masimba* Camp greeting us as we pulled in under the thatched parking pavilion just as darkness set in. It was a bit after 7 p.m., completing a 13-hour excursion that felt like 13 days.

The camp came alive. The staff scurried like ants out of an anthill, dropping whatever task they were doing, and again, greeted us like we were celebrities. Rod and Sue and their crew had pulled in shortly before us.

We learned that Sue had, astonishingly, harvested a zebra soon after daylight while we had chased them all day with no success. While I was happy for her success, my emotional attachment to zebras made it hard to accept the idea of harvesting the species, causing more than a few heated discussions between Rick and me. With mixed emotions I listened to Sue's account of the stalk, mentally preparing myself to view the lifeless animal, but it was all for naught. The *punda milia* was long gone; hours earlier, it had been transformed into slabs of meat and its hide placed in a bed of salt to preserve it for later use.

If you count success by the harvesting of game, then you could say their safari was more successful than ours. Yet, in a million years, you couldn't convince me that our day had been any less wonderful. Grueling? Yes. Priceless? Absolutely!

We dragged our spent bodies into our neat-as-a-pin tent. Not one speck of sand or dust marred the immaculate canvas floor. Each of our wooden beds had been turned down like the beds of a cruise ship. The only thing missing was the folded towel monkeys. Instead, there was a stack of ironed and perfectly folded clothes, our outfits from the previous day. Even my underwear was pressed and folded into a tiny square! I was mortified and guilt-ridden. Ironing is barely a part of my realm. For crying out loud, that's why they make wrinkle-free fabrics. My hiking pants had never seen a crease in their life. As far as skivvies go, crumpled up and stashed in a drawer worked just fine.

We had little choice. Aside from our travel clothes, we had specifically been instructed to bring only three outfits: two safari outfits and one set of camp clothes. I did cheat a bit, but I certainly didn't waste that cheat on gobs of underwear. After seeing my pressed undies displayed like a beacon atop my freshly laundered clothes, I wished I'd reconsidered that decision.

Although our first day on safari left me depleted and feeling like I'd gone a few rounds in a washing machine, I was lucid enough to grasp the enormous effort it had taken to present our tent, amid a dust-entrenched wilderness, as the finest room in a five-star resort.

After recovering from the shock of our pristine sleeping quarters, we luxuriated in the bath hut's makeshift shower. Yes, I was still in awe that no PTA bath (Pits, Tits and Ass) would be necessary. We were uptown living high on the hog for sure.

In Idaho's backcountry, we rarely rigged up a shower. Filling a solar shower bag, finding a suitable place to hang it, and standing in the cold air letting lukewarm water drizzle over your body was too cold and too much effort for this chickadee. Instead, I heated water on the wood stove, also warming the tent, and washed my vitals with a washcloth. Hence the nickname PTA. So, if you ever find yourself talking to a rural Idahoan and they mention a PTA, you can be sure they aren't talking about a Parent Teacher Association meeting.

Having a real shower with warm water to wash away the day's grime felt like heaven itself. Another thing very much appreciated and *not* taken for granted.

With the shower's intoxicating effect, and the stink gone, we went to the dining hut to see the glorious sight of ice cubes piled high in our glasses. Never could I have imagined that simple chunks of frozen water could look so magnificent. A few hours in Africa will cause you to gain a new respect for that simple luxury.

I didn't want to look a gift horse in the mouth, but I couldn't help wondering how this amazing feat was possible--amid the wilderness and off the grid. Recognizing our delight, Joel proudly introduced us to a tiny ice machine nestled in the corner of the *mesi*. Each day, to cater to clients, a generator was turned on long enough to fill the belly of the little dream machine with those glorious ice cubes, making just enough for a few chilled drinks each evening at dinner.

And the meal was scrumptious. Thanks to the previous clients, eland steak was the main course. It was the leek soup, however, that really had me in seventh heaven. Normally, I'm not a soup lover but the concoctions that Moses prepared each evening were my favorite part of every meal.

Even more fabulous than the food was the camaraderie. Joel, our host, was full of energy and anecdotes that kept us in stitches. Hilary was just plain full of it. I say that with deep affection. He was always instigating, teasing, or recounting captivating tales from when he, himself, was a PH. Rod was also a jokester who kept the banter going and even Rick, my normally reserved husband, was lively in the conversation. Sue, not the prankster like her husband, still had plenty of stories to add to the pot. Raphael and Paul were much quieter and more matter-of-fact than the rest of us, adding stories of pissed-off buffalos, charging hippos, elephant poachers, and horrific hyena accounts. We also got to relive our own adventures in its telling while sharing in Rod and Sue's escapades as well.

Some stories prompted laughter. Others filled us in awe. More than a few blurred our eyes with emotion. And many scared the living crap out of us. The tales, along with the melding of cultures and personalities, created an enchanting evening every single night.

As if all of this wasn't enough, Michael and Joel waited on us like Rod, Sue, Rick, and I were the Kings and Queens of Sheba. Heck, just trying to pour our own glass of water caused a wild sprint across the room grabbing the pitcher from our hands. As a past waitress and already perceiving the staff as friends, it was hard to control my instincts to jump up and clear the dishes.

After dinner, Rod, Sue, Rick and I moved to a small fire built in the center of the patio area overlooking the dry riverbed. After all, no camp is complete without a campfire, or cowboy TV, as it is known in Idaho. With full bellies, we gazed at the flames. No matter where you are in the world, campfires are the same everywhere. A place to gather. Mesmerizing. Comforting. Warm.

Then plop. A second later, another plop. And another. *Could it really be raining during the dry season?* We wondered. We surveyed the sky in confusion. Soon we noticed supersized bats with long pointy ears darting for insects in the branches above our heads. Another plop. This time in Rod's drink. Plop. Now Rick's shoulder. Another Plop. My arm. We studied the whitish pasty drops with puzzled expressions for a few moments before realization dawned on us. It wasn't raindrops. It was bat poop. In our defense of such sluggish awareness, our lights weren't burning too bright at that point. The exhausting day had taken its toll.

That was it. Being pelted by the feces of flying mamals was our limit. We cleaned off the white goo, said our goodnights, and ambled off to our respective tents. As I fell into bed, the African symphony had already

begun its ghostly composition. We could hear the hyena's howls and ghastly giggles; the hippo's throaty bellow; and other squeals, squeaks, chirps,
whistles, and cries that are impossible to put into words. *Simba* was still
quiet, at least at that moment.

In many ways, the day had been punishing: many long arduous hours of
hunting but no harvesting. We had tracked a *dagga* boy, stalked multiple
zebra, eaten lunch under the canopy of a Lucky Bean tree, and were exposed to countless new experiences, wildlife, and lands. Heck, we'd even
been showered with feces from giant-sized bats. I couldn't remember ever
having a day as exhausting, sweltering, grueling and sometimes frustrating.
Yet, unbelievably, I couldn't wait to do it all over again. One thing was for
certain, our first day on safari had been crazy. Bat-shit crazy. Literally.

4
Horns Curling to the Heavens

"*Tandala*," Mgogo stated as he leaned forward pointing towards a thicket of trees in the distance.

Following his fingers, Rick and I peered towards the *supposed* flicker of an ear hidden in scrub trees 300 yards away. Zip. Zilch. Nada. We saw absolutely nothing. Yet, on day two, we already had total faith in our crew's seemingly superhuman senses. They could hear an ant peeing on cotton or spy a toothpick in a bale of hay. At least that's how Rick's Grandma would have put it. If Mgogo said a kudu was hiding in the brush, you could bet your bottom dollar a kudu was hiding in the brush.

Kudu bulls have very long, distinctive, corkscrew-like horns making them, quite possibly, the most well-known antelope in all of Africa. With the average male weighing about 550 pounds, they are slightly smaller than a bull elk. Like elk, the females have no horns. Thus, it doesn't take much between the ears to determine the beautiful silhouette of a kudu bull. What *is* challenging is knowing its approximate age and, therefore, if it is harvestable or not.

As with most African quarry, having horns on their head doesn't automatically make them fair game. The goal being to harvest animals towards the end of their life span and no longer spreading their genes puts a whole new spin on things.

In America, it works a little differently. Each species, of course, has its requirements, but, typically, regulations are more relaxed. For instance, in most cases, it is perfectly legal for a hunter to harvest a 3 x 3 mule deer buck or a spike elk--animals still in the prime of life. In general, this would be highly frowned upon or illegal in most African countries, unless culling (the need to control overpopulation en masse) or some other factor is in play.

Kudu

Rick and I may know what a mature elk looks like, but a mature kudu, or any African species for that matter, is a different kettle of fish. That, my friend, is why a PH is so critically important. They *do* know how to read the minute details that are a dead giveaway of an animal's maturity. Rick and I most certainly did not.

Making these comparisons between African antelopes and our deer species--whose protein is a regular part of our Idaho diet--is probably what allowed me to accept the idea of harvesting these types of animals while questioning the ethics of hunting others, specifically the exotic and endearing ones that I adored since childhood.

Unlike America's ungulates who have adapted to feed on grasses or browsing material, kudus don't have that luxury. They are purely browsers that depend on high-growing vegetation for food, as well as cover, so they are much more likely to be found in shrubland habitats rather than wide-open savannas.

Their grayish coat has 6 to 10 white torso stripes which help them blend seamlessly into their surroundings. Their suspicious and secretive nature adds to their camouflage. At the first sign of danger, they simply melt into the landscape without a sound, hoping their disguise will offer all the protection they need. For this reason, they are often referred to as the grey ghost of Africa. Only when eye contact is made, a sure sign their gig is up, will they burst forth, fleeing from danger.

The elusive antelopes include two species, the lesser kudu and the greater kudu (with numerous subspecies), each varying slightly in looks and pre-ferred habitat. The greater kudu is widespread throughout the woodland areas of southern Africa and, therefore, the kind we saw in this part of Tanzania.

According to the International Union for Conservation (IUCN), the greater kudu is listed as "Least Concern" and the lesser kudu is listed as "Near Threatened." Even with fairly secure populations, these antelopes still face a host of threats. Like most wildlife, they are losing habitat due to agriculture and the destruction of woodlands as more people need wood for fueling their fires or charcoal (an essential fuel source in sub-Saharan African countries). Unlike some species that adapt more easily, the grey ghosts do not survive well in open fields or farmland. The antelope's meat is also a preferred source of bushmeat, causing many to fall victim to the snares of poachers.

Kudu are also vulnerable to cattle-borne diseases. In the 1890s, the great rinderpest epidemic --a deadly virus affecting ruminants, especially cattle--swept through Africa. Soon the devastating disease spread from domestic stock to the hoofed wild species living close to them.

The rinderpest epidemic coupled with pleura-pneumonia didn't dis-criminate. Domestic or wild, it mattered not. According to Africa Geo-graphic, hoofed animals suffered nearly a 90 percent mortality rate dur-ing the outbreak, effectively gutting the *tandala* population of East and

Southern Africa.[1] Since then, populations have largely recovered but as humans expand into wilderness areas, so does the number of livestock and, therefore, the potential carriers of the disease.

Fortunately, by being located on the 540 square miles of Hilary's hunting grounds, the animals we saw were safeguarded from the threat of human encroachment and all that follows. Our eyes were constantly scanning for their magnificent spiral horns--not an easy task as they tend to seek wooded thickets during the midday heat.

Moments after Mgogo spotted the ear, we were in our serpentine formation slinking from scrub tree to scrub tree until we were facing the grove where the elegant antelope was hidden 150 yards away. Peeking through the branches, we could see the bull's entire body, in all its splendor, along with horns that seemingly curled to the heavens.

While Raphael peered through his binoculars, Mgogo placed the shooting sticks in position. This tripod arrangement creates a rest for the rifle's forearm while allowing its legs to be adjusted wider or narrower, thereby varying its height. The simple piece of equipment helps with stability and, therefore, accuracy. As an extra precaution, I took position slightly behind Rick, allowing him to rest his shooting elbow on my left shoulder for even more stability.

Rick, Rod, and Sue had sighted in their rifles within hours of our arrival, a standard procedure in Africa. Not only were the weapons checked for accuracy, but it also allowed the PHs to judge their clients' abilities—all necessary to ensure an accurate shot, causing the animal the least amount of suffering possible. Still, as an ethical hunter, Rick wasn't above using every trick in the book. That included using my shoulder as support.

Rick and me demonstrating the shooting sticks.

With Rick dead-focused on the target and me holding my breath so as not to screw up his shot, we waited anxiously for Raphael to give the okay. A few seconds ticked by. Nothing. We didn't budge. A few more seconds. Still nothing. Five more seconds--which felt like minutes--we remained rooted to the spot, our eyes glued to the quarry.

Then, unexpectedly, Raphael lowered his binoculars and shook his head, "No. He is not old enough."

Just like that, the hunt was over.

Rick and I looked at each other in confusion. Apparently, the horns--while absolutely dazzling--were *only* about 48 inches long, a couple inches shy of what he considered to be a legal bull. Believe me, when deer and elk antlers make up your wheelhouse, the sight of 4-foot-long horns spiraling into the sky will take your breath away. In our book, that was honking *huge*. Yet, come to find out, mature kudu can grow horns reaching well over 50 inches long. Thus, that bull still had a few years before he was past his prime.

It still boggles my mind that Raphael, through binoculars from 150 yards away, could determine an almost exact measurement. Apparently, it takes six years to complete two full twists of the horns. In addition, males have a small beard that turns darker with age.

As the saying goes, close but no cigar. You might think we were bummed, but the exact opposite was true. It was proof, bar none, that only aged bulls were targeted; the welfare of the species was put above a client's desire. *That* is the key to resource management.

It was also a testament to the importance of the PH. No amount of studying African game, as Rick had done in preparation, can replace a lifetime of experience. Stepping from America into the African bush felt like we had entered another world. There were different customs, laws, political systems, languages, foods, wildlife, and dangers. While all these differences are what make the experience so amazing, it is also why we depended on Raphael's wisdom and guidance to usher us through that altered universe. Hopefully, it was a universe that would offer up another opportunity for the grey ghost of Africa--one whose spiral silhouette curled just a bit further into the heavens.

5
THE DARK SIDE

Where there had been flatlands for miles upon miles, a blip in the distance jutted above the landscape. Fascinated, I watched as *Chui* Rock grew into a mountainous tower of stone. The fused-together boulders, probably 100 feet high by 300 feet long, protruded above the savanna like a skyscraper sitting amidst the corn fields of Iowa. Its perimeter was fringed with piles of rocks splintered off from the main structure eons ago, creating oodles of nooks and crannies. The perfect hiding spots for leopards, the rock's namesake.

Chui Rock

Chui Rock's monstrous size was not only a feast for the eyes, but its shade also offered a luxurious break from the scorching sun as we skirted its base. As soon as we left the shadowy wonder, however, we were again struck by the sun's brutal assault, as well as reminded of the darker side of Africa.

Less than 100 feet away, massive sun-bleached bones dotted the ground. Stopping to investigate, we needed no explanation for which species they belonged to. Only an elephant had such Jurassic-sized bones. Time had allowed critters to carry off or consume everything but large chunks of *tembo's* skeletal remains.

Though any evidence of the pachyderm's cause of death was long gone, the lack of tusks was as telling as any words.

"*Jangilis,*" Raphael stated. Poachers.

Lilian with part of the elephant skull.

Masimba Camp had ended the previous hunting season with no bones littering the base of *Chui* Rock. Therefore, sometime during the off-season, the elephant lost its life.

Although the thoughts of any animal dying at the hands of poachers shook me to the core, the bones opened a dialogue, one which opened my eyes, making me aware of *all* facets of poaching--not just the ones making the headlines in the news and social media.

Before our trip, my concept of poaching, *ujangili,* revolved mainly around elephants slaughtered for their tusks or rhinos mutilated for their horns, then sold on the black market by evil crime syndicates for megabucks. While that type of poaching is a horrible reality, I soon learned that killing prized species for their money parts is just the tip of the iceberg.

Wood poaching caught me totally off guard. Rural Africans cook largely over open flames, requiring firewood as fuel. In addition, charcoal, because of its convenient format and reasonable price, is the main source of fuel in urban areas throughout sub-Saharan Africa. Yet, much of the firewood and wood for making charcoal is harvested illegally by hundreds of thousands of separate small-scale producers.

There are large-scale operators as well. Armed loggers enter the forests at night, cut both protected and non-protected species and transfer the profits to organized crime syndicates. According to the report "Combating Poaching and Illegal Logging in Tanzania Voices of the Rangers" nearly 1544 square miles of forest disappear every year from Tanzania, the fifth highest annual loss of forest in the world.[1] Illegal logging accounts for as much as 96 percent of that figure. Logging, both legal and illegal, is occurring at unsustainable rates.

Typically, large-scale illegal loggers are armed, making it extremely hard for local unarmed forest rangers to confront them. Only wildlife rangers, game scouts like Lilian, have permits to carry guns; and, unfortunately, they are not always available to help the local rangers. Sometimes only a handful of enforcers, with limited access to vehicles, are responsible for the protection of vast forests. With resources spread so thin, illegal logging goes on largely unchallenged.

It is perfectly legal to harvest wood, subject to restrictions, *if* a permit is obtained. Getting permits takes time and money, both of which poverty-stricken people don't have or aren't willing to part with. Estimates suggest that 80 percent of all charcoal production is done illegally and is ultimately responsible for about 40 to 60 percent of Tanzania's deforestation. With the country's rapidly growing population, the strain on forests will only continue to increase unless other methods are found to fuel local households.

Honey poaching is another illegal activity that wouldn't have crossed my mind in a million years. Again, just like wood, harvesting the golden treat is legal *if* a permit is obtained and sustainable methods are used; but again, permits take time and money that many villagers can't afford or won't pay.

You might wonder as I did, *what does it hurt to take a little honey? It's renewable, right?* Well, it turns out that trees are often damaged or destroyed in the process. Poachers must get in and out quickly so as not to get caught. That sometimes means cutting down trees, even those vital to the ecosystem.

The Baobab tree, also known as the "Tree of Life," is a prime example. The magnificent life-sustaining specimens can be thousands of years old, which filled me with awe each time we saw one. Imagine my horror when Lilian explained that honeybees often nest in their crevices, sometimes making them collateral damage of honey poaching.

Bushmeat poaching is another type of illegal killing that I never knew existed. Bushmeat is a catchall phrase for the meat of wild animals, most often referring to African species.

Although the phrase was new to me, the concept itself was not. The African people have long hunted bats, monkeys, rats, snakes, antelopes, and other wild creatures for food. Smoked, dried, or cooked, the meat provides a valuable source of protein for people in rural communities where raising domesticated livestock is too expensive or impractical. In addition, it serves as an important source of income in places that offer few alternatives. My American ancestors did the same. The wildlife may have differed, but the concept was the same.

In the past, Africa's vast animal resources could sustain subsistence hunting. Now, however, it has risen to unsustainable levels due in part to expanding human populations, increased demand for protein, new roads for logging and mining making wild country easier to access, and a growing demand for bushmeat in urban markets. According to the 2019 National Geographic article "What is Bushmeat?" by Jani Hall, conservation experts claim that bushmeat poaching is "considered one of the most immediate threats to African wildlife."[2]

Poaching for bushmeat not only destroys the prey species but the predators that depend on them as well. Especially concerning is the large-scale commercial hunting of slower-breeding animals like apes and monkeys who can't recover as quickly as faster-producing ones.

Nowadays, there are two distinct types of bushmeat poachers: those who kill to put food on their table and those who kill for profit. In many parts of Africa, locals are protein deprived which leads to small-scale subsistence poaching. But the more nefarious brand of poaching stems from a huge demand for the commercial bushmeat trade, most of which is sold at bustling rural markets, far removed from the watchful eye of government authorities.

Honey, wood, charcoal, and bushmeat poaching may seem fairly harmless since they don't directly involve the iconic species that people tend to get emotionally attached to, but, that thinking is dead wrong. Wood and honey poaching is wreaking havoc on wild habitats, and the thriving bushmeat trade is destroying prey that carnivores feed on. Anything that alters or destroys balanced ecosystems, ultimately, is far deadlier than any rifle, snare, or poison.

We also mustn't overlook the money factor. The government loses millions of dollars each year from fees that could be generated from well-managed legal activities while, at the same time, having to spend millions on anti-poaching efforts.

Just as significant is the inhumane way in which many victims of bushmeat poaching die. Few rural Africans can afford or even have access to guns, but when they do, they are typically substandard models using crude handmade bullets. Low-quality weapons and inferior ammunition are much more prone to injuring animals, rather than killing them quickly and mercifully. For those having no access to firearms, the killing of animals typically involves the use of primitive snares made from easily accessible wire. They are cheap, effective, and work while the poacher is away.

The simple handmade snares used predominantly in Africa, however, can be brutal, often causing deaths that are long drawn-out affairs. Victims lucky enough to be ensnared by the neck may die fairly quickly of asphyxiation. Others caught by a leg may be forced to endure hours or even days of trauma.

The bushmeat poacher's snares and traps also maim and destroy indiscriminately. Any species. Young or old. Male or female. Nursing, raising young, or pregnant. They don't kill only a *few* allotted males past their breeding age, no longer spreading their genes. The loops of wire are equal opportunity death traps, killing whatever creatures chance upon them with no regard for healthy quotas, species protection, or the law.

Game scouts holding snares removed from the bush.

© Tony Bynam, Shepherds of wildlife

To heighten the tragedy of such deaths, most small-scale poachers operate on foot or bicycles, allowing them to carry only what fits in their packs, mainly prime cuts of meat or valuable parts. Often, the rest is left to rot on the savanna. Illegal killers also sometimes fail to retrieve a carcass altogether, or don't recover it promptly. While a rotting carcass may be good for the scavengers, it does nothing to help feed hungry people.

It must be noted that all trapping should not be thrown under the bus. Trapping in other parts of the world, like hunting, has evolved over the years. Legalized and well-managed trapping is intended to maintain and enhance wildlife, and therefore, follows strict regulations, quotas, and humane parameters. The newer devices are designed to be quick and efficient so that when used skillfully in the hands of educated trappers, few non-targeted animals become ensnared. Not only is this the right thing to do for wildlife, but it also increases the trapper's efficiency. Simply put, tightly controlled trapping can be the solution to wildlife management problems, not the problem.

Lilian's knowledge of poachers shot down another stereotype of mine: all poachers are dangerous, evil, criminal types. As you've probably figured out by now, that is not the case at all. Many poachers are ill-trained, poverty-stricken, food-deficient villagers, desperate to feed their families. Sadly, it makes perfect sense that food-deprived people would turn to whatever wild creatures are available for money and food to feed their families.

In addition, rural people often kill dangerous, destructive beasts just to be rid of them, *without* selling anything. Human-wildlife conflict is a huge issue in rural areas. Predators and supersized herbivores can be deadly, unpredictable, and ruinous. Lions, leopards, and other carnivores kill livestock while elephants frequently destroy crops, water systems, and infrastructure, all of which the people need to survive. Neither are humans home-free. Hundreds of people die each year while trying to protect their livelihoods or simply by being in the wrong place at the wrong time. Therefore, killing such injurious species is done strictly in retribution for previous losses and to prevent future deaths and damage.

When animals are eliminated for these reasons, poison is often the method of choice. In fact, according to Lilian, poison is probably the most common tactic, especially for lions and leopards. It is, by far, the easiest, cheapest, and safest method to destroy dangerous carnivores. Simply place toxins in a hunk of meat and let the predators feast. Easy peasy. Predators are no longer killing livestock or threatening native people.

While any illegal slaughter is dreadful, poison is the gift that keeps on giving, or rather, keeps on taking. Toxins kill and keep on killing. Anything and everything eating the tainted food will die, including secondary species (mamals, birds, reptiles, and insects who feed upon any beings killed by the poison).

Thinking of the piles of bones on the ground near *Chui* Rock, my thoughts returned to elephants. They, too, are sometimes killed with poisons. After all, elephant poaching has little to do with the thousands of pounds of protein their bodies could offer a poor community; it is done almost exclusively for their magnificent ivory tusks. The chunks of white gold are worth close to $1500 a pound. With each tusk weighing from 10 to 100 pounds, that is a lot of incentive. Again, poachers don't just target old males with large tusks. Any elephant sporting ivory is fair game.

One-third of an elephant's tusks are hidden from view, embedded deep in its head. Therefore, simply cutting off the exposed ivory is not enough. Poachers must hack deep into the elephants' faces, using primitive machetes or axes, to remove the entire prize. Once that is accomplished, the rest of the pachyderm is typically left to rot. Depending on the method of extermination, snare or poison, the carcass can either be a smorgasbord for the scavengers or a mass slaughter, while again doing nothing to help food-deprived people. One can only hope that the elephant victims are dead before the mutilation begins.

The last couple of decades has been brutal on the colossal beasts. According to the July 2019 CNN article "African Elephant Poaching has Declined, but Study Warns They Are Still Vulnerable", sub-Saharan Africa lost more than 100,000 elephants between 2006 and 2015, the worst poaching surge since the 1980s.[3] Most scientists believe the crisis began in 2005 with the booming Chinese economy, which produced significant growth in the number of middle-class Asian citizens, a society that has long treasured carved ivory. The two things together were a recipe for disaster.

The illegal slaughter peaked in 2011 when 10 percent of all elephants fell to poaching. By 2014, the continental population of elephants had dropped by almost a third. Tanzania was hit hard too. Between 2009 and 2014 their elephant population dropped by 60 percent, during a wave of well-organized, large-scale commercial poaching.

In response, Tanzania developed a strategy of intelligence-led investigations, including a National Taskforce on Anti-Poaching geared at identifying, arresting, and prosecuting major players to disrupt the trafficking networks. It has also strengthened wildlife laws and sentences along with enlisting approximately 2,000 rangers like Lilian and another 2,000 unarmed forest rangers.

Fortunately, according to the article above, the number of elephants falling to poaching has decreased significantly since then. Aside from anti-poaching efforts, many conservation groups credit the Chinese government's 2017 ban on the ivory trade for the decline. Others say that the ivory ban created a Catch-22 so to speak; prohibiting trade also drove the value of ivory up.

Typical for all commodities, legal or illegal, supply and demand factors in. Placing a higher value on ivory just provides more incentive for illegal harvesting of the prized material. Many scientists and conservationists fear that the large decline in elephant poaching may be due more to China's economic slowdown than to the ban itself. Either way, there is no time to be complacent. Any elephant found rotting on the savanna with its tusks hacked off its body is one too many.

With Lilian as our game scout, I was privy to understanding some of the challenges and hardships the wildlife rangers face. In Tanzania, for instance, law enforcement officers are tasked with protecting areas so vast that it would make your head spin. Confronted with such large expanses of wilderness, while tackling so many different types of poaching, resources are stretched to the max.

In addition, resources that many law enforcement agencies take for granted are very limited, including even the most basic of tools: GPS, maps, radios, and sufficient ammunition. Higher priced items are in even shorter supply. For example, many patrols are performed on foot due to an insufficient number of off-road vehicles.

Toyota Land Cruisers, the safari vehicles we rode in each day, are perfect for the task. Nevertheless, their purchase, along with the equipment and maintenance necessary to operate in such rugged conditions, is very expensive. Plus, even the best vehicles struggle to navigate the water-ravaged terrain during the rainy season.

Sustainable salaries are also essential to keeping rangers. Without adequate incomes, some individuals may be tempted to jump ship, entering instead into more profitable illegal activities.

Wildlife rangers must also spend significant amounts of time away from their families. Poaching patrols are typically 15 days long. Not only do they leave their loved ones behind, but they must also tackle all the harshness that bush Africa can muster. Heat. Insects. Mud. Rough terrain. Deadly reptiles. Unpredictable beasts. Sleeping on the ground or in a tent. No facilities. No cushy comforts. *Masimba* Camp by comparison was a paradise.

Aside from the basic dangers, inconveniences, and discomfort, one must not forget about the poachers themselves. While the majority of non-commercial poachers rarely have access to guns, the high-stake poachers do. Elephant, rhino, and commercial bushmeat poachers are typically backed by crime syndicates, giving them access to weaponry. While many are untrained and don't put up much of a fight, others are more deadly. According to the 2019 National Geographic article "Poaching Animals, Explained," nearly 600 African rangers were gunned down between 2009 and 2016.[4]

With such vast patrol areas, inadequate resources, and limited personnel, Lilian explained that patrols must focus on preventing crimes where criminals are most likely to be prosecuted. In other words, offenders need to be caught and arrested while they are in the field. Any disruption to poaching is extremely valuable; the more people caught and held responsible, the more reluctant others are to participate. A key tactic is to target poaching hot spots.

Lilian, the year before we met, had been hiding in one of those hot spots along with six other rangers. For tension-filled hours they waited in ambush behind a dense thicket, having no idea what was in store for them. Eventually, the illegal killers returned, armed with a submachine gun and a muzzleloader. On that day, luck was on their side; the culprits were ill-trained. After a short firefight where one poacher was shot in the leg, the offenders gave up. No law enforcement officers were injured and all three *jangilis* were arrested successfully.

Rhino poaching is another high-dollar target that is prone to having skilled, well-armed poachers--compliments of the kingpins and criminal masterminds running the illegal wildlife trafficking trade. Unless you live under a rock, you are well aware that the rhino's unique horns are coveted by some Asian cultures for their supposed medicinal qualities. They are used for curing cancer, fevers, arthritis, gout, headaches, hallucinations, high blood pressure, snakebite, hangovers, impotence and even possession by spirits.

Yet, all of this is just a fallacy. They have no proven medicinal qualities whatsoever. The so-called horns are not even true horns; they are keratin, the substance of our human hair and fingernails. In other words, chewing on your fingernails would be just as effective for curing cancer. Unfortunately, changing over 3,000 years of widespread, deep-rooted beliefs is no easy task.

There are only two species of these prehistoric-looking pachyderms living in Africa today: the White rhino and the Black rhino, both having the coveted distinctive duo horns. The White rhino stands up to 6 feet tall, weighing up to 4,000 pounds. These big guys are actually much calmer and more sociable than their smaller relatives and, therefore, typically live in small territorial groups. Through conservation efforts, largely driven by South Africa's vibrant trophy hunting market, the White rhino population has grown to approximately 18,000 individuals, allowing the IUCN to upgrade their conservation status to "Near Threatened." While that in itself sounds depressing, it helps when you understand that until 1895, they were thought to be extinct. Then miraculously, 100 individuals were discovered in a remote part of South Africa, allowing a new start.

Although Black rhinos are smaller than their bulkier relatives, they are still no slouches. Nevertheless, they do seem to have a small-man complex. Black rhinos, weighing in closer to 3,000 pounds, are much more aggressive, as well as solitary. Rarely are they found with other rhinos, other than their calves or for breeding purposes.

Their eating habits are also quite different. Black rhinos are mainly browsers and, therefore, have a more pointed upper lip allowing them to grasp leaves and shrubs. White rhinos, on the other hand, are grazers whose lips are squared, allowing them to best access the grasses.

Between the 1970s and 1995, Black rhino populations declined from 70,000 animals to only 2,410. Thanks to persistent conservation efforts across Africa, their numbers have risen to approximately 5,500 individuals. Just as importantly, their geographic range has increased to include areas where they previously roamed. Still, the IUCN lists the Black rhino as "Critically Endangered."

Similar to elephant poaching, the current rhino crisis began in the mid-2000s when Asian economies began to thrive. When the middle class grew, so too did the demand for rhino horns. The basic laws of supply and demand entered the arena. The more it was sought-after, the pricier it became—making it more valuable than its weight in gold. In fact, two to three times its weight in gold.

To make matters worse, its high price soon made it attractive as a status symbol and a cocaine-like party drug by wealthy individuals. With such astronomical value attached to it, criminal syndicates became involved, causing poaching to skyrocket. Crime organizations can use high-tech equipment and employ local populations to track down and kill rhinos.

Watching African wildlife and anti-poaching television programs will leave you stunned with horrific scenes of grotesquely distorted creatures entangled in primitive snares, yet little compares to the hollow, mutilated face of a rhino who has had its horns ruthlessly hacked off, oftentimes while it is still very much alive.

Even poachers with access to bullets use as few as possible. The sound of a gunshot is distinctive and telling. The first one will get your attention, alerting any nearby authorities or law-abiding hunters. The second shot will give a pretty good indication of where it is coming from. The poachers cannot have that. In addition, ammunition is a precious commodity to the local people who are typically hired for these boots-on-the-ground atrocities. High-quality ammunition can be extremely expensive on the black market. One bullet may disable a huge mamal, but it doesn't always end life instantly. Therefore, to lessen the risk of being caught and to save the price of a cartridge, poachers will remove the horn while the wounded beast is still thrashing.

At a seminar I attended, a mutilated rhino, with a gaping bloody hole where its horns had been, was displayed on the screen in what I *thought* was a photo. While the scene sickened me, it's sad to say that I wasn't shocked by the gruesome picture. During my research, I'd seen the mangled, de-horned images of *dead* rhinos before. While focusing on the rhino, its mutilated head suddenly swung back and forth. It was *not* a picture. It was a video of a hacked-up rhinoceros struggling in agony. Still very much alive!

The shocking scene caused me to gasp out loud, as did most everyone in the room. Through tear-clouded eyes, I could barely make out the next parts of the presentation.

Fighting rhino poaching is extremely expensive. The national parks, private landowners, or countries that have the money are using helicopters, dogs, and even high-tech mediums like artificial intelligence, drones, and surveillance platforms. Even with all the technology, law enforcement officers have to work hard to stay one step ahead of the higher-stake poachers. Some countries have started programs to hire reformed rural poachers to help in the fight, essentially turning poachers into gamekeepers. This technique offers them an income and a purpose. In addition, they know the poacher's mind, offering great input on how to best combat them.

Protecting rhinos on private land is now very expensive for the landowners since it is not covered by governments, charitable organizations, or park income. This is troubling because the largest percentage of rhinos live on private ranches, putting many rhinos in serious peril.

Recently, I watched Carter's W.A.R. (Wild Animal Response) episode "At All Costs" in which a small rancher, relatively speaking, lacked the funds and resources to protect the 19 rhinos living on his property. He made the difficult decision to send them to a large game farm that had the funds available to protect rhinos around the clock with armed guards. The small rancher hated giving up his beloved charges, but he recognized that it was their best chance of survival.

The transfer of the 4,000-pound pachyderms was quite an undertaking. Each was rounded up, darted with a tranquilizer, attended to by veterinarians, and transported over 600 miles to their new refuge. The operation was not only a logistical nightmare, but it was also a high-risk endeavor kept as secretive as a special-ops mission. The rhino convoy made the trek in the dead of night accompanied by the staff, veterinarians, wildlife officials, and a mass of armed escorts. That an animal, because of the horns on its head, had to be guarded like it was a convoy of gold bullion is reprehensible.

Some sanctuaries have resorted to cutting the rhino's horns back to the nubs to make them less valuable to poachers. While the process is painless for the rhino, being that the horn is nothing more than fingernail-like material, it is an expensive and risky undertaking. Anytime an animal, especially such a massive one, is tranquilized in the wild there is a medical threat to its life. Plus, the horn, which regenerates itself like fingernails, has to be removed about every 18 months. In addition, since part of the rhino's horn is buried in the skull, dehorned ones are still at risk.

Many traditional Chinese medicine experts have joined the fight by offering alternative medical treatments, such as ground buffalo horn. China also removed rhino horn as an ingredient in traditional Chinese medicine, as well as officially banned the international rhinoceros trade in 1993. Still, altering such long-entrenched views is a difficult task.

Due to anti-poaching and dehorning strategies, as well as other factors, rhino poaching has decreased slightly since its peak in 2015. Still, estimates suggest that two and a half rhinos are poached every single day. Even with these losses, the global rhino population is increasing, but only minimally.

While this is encouraging, many conservationists are afraid to get too relaxed. These individuals feel that the decrease in poaching is more a result of the slowdown in Asian economies, not so much the strategies listed above. They fear that when the Chinese and Vietnamese economies rebound, so too will the demand for rhino horns. Others feel that the reduction in rhino poaching can be attributed to having fewer rhinos in general, thereby making them harder to find and more difficult to poach. Either way, it is no time to breathe a sigh of relief.

Interestingly, even though selling rhino horn is illegal, it is *not illegal* to cut off a rhino's horn, as long as you have a permit. Every couple of years, many South African, Namibian, and Zimbabwean ranchers painlessly cut their rhinos' horns back, storing them in bank vaults hoping that someday it will become legal to sell the horn again. Many conservationists even advocate for legalizing the trade in rhino horn, being that it is a sustainable resource. These people believe that legal, well-documented, replenishable horn will flood the market, thereby driving its value down like any supply and demand market. The rhino horn would then be less valuable and less tempting to poach. Others argue that legalizing the trade will just make matters worse.

Like most legislation regarding the wildlife industry, rhino horn is a controversial topic. Hopefully, well-informed wildlife industry and government experts will be allowed to make the difficult decisions based on scientific evidence, facts, and statistics--not emotion.

One thing is very clear. It will take a mix of strategies to solve the rhino poaching problem: well-trained and well-equipped rangers, secure habitat, rhino monitoring, education about their lack of medicinal qualities, education for locals, and management to maintain genetic diversity. According to Save the Rhino International, the well-being of the African people also cannot be excluded: "Making sure that the communities living near rhino habitats see and feel the benefits of conservation is another critical factor in preventing people from turning to poaching or encroaching on rhino habitat."

This brings us back to the human condition. You can bet your bottom dollar that the head honchos in the crime syndicate aren't the ones hiking through the blistering, Tsetse-fly-infested savanna risking life, limb and imprisonment. They hire desperate local people and sometimes game department officials to do their bidding while operating the black market from afar. It is the local, destitute people who are typically arrested, leaving the masterminds and their networks safe to operate again.

The small-time accomplices who were caught and interviewed often-times had no idea of the true value of the rhinos' horns or even that rhinos were an endangered species. In their tiny corner of the world, it was all about putting food on the table and surviving. Newspaper headlines, the market for rhino horn, or the rhinos' IUCN status were irrelevant to them. The money they were paid was huge by African standards but tiny when compared to the horns' worth on the black market.

The famous line "it takes a village" comes into play. The struggling cattle farmer might as well talk to the man on the moon as find an affluent buyer across the world. The ivory from a slaughtered elephant or rhino does not transform into a carved figurine or presumed medicine with a simple swipe of a magic wand. It takes people. Plenty of people. Once an animal is poached, it must be processed, stored, transported, and sold--multiple times. In areas as vast and remote as Africa, that is not easy, especially when much of the contraband is supersized.

Poaching, quite simply, cannot be done in isolation. It takes just one person *not* turning a blind eye to stop poaching in its tracks. Still, turning friends and relatives in is not easy, especially when the local people and their existence have been largely disregarded when it comes to policy-making.

That is why so many conservationists who truly understand the problem recognize that improving the lives of the local people and providing a benefit to them for protecting wildlife is the best defense against illegal activities. Plain and simple: they are the people who most often suffer from the costs—physically, emotionally, and financially--from living with such large dangerous animals. Yet, they receive little, if any, advantage from the coexistence. Living with lions, leopards, elephants, and hyenas in your backyard is a far cry from squirrels, raccoons, bats, and coyotes.

Severin Hauenstein, a biologist from Germany's University of Freiburg, discovered this as well. He had assumed that elephant poaching would be worse the further it was from anti-poaching posts. After crunching the data, however, he and his colleagues were surprised to find no correlation whatsoever. This led them to compare economic, social, and political factors instead. In the 2019 National Geographic article "Where Humans Suffer, So Do Elephants," he asserts that poverty and corruption, in that order, had the biggest impact on higher poaching rates--both of which typically go hand in hand.[5] Adequate law enforcement came in third.

Therefore, while anti-poaching enforcement is important, it is even more critical to focus on elevating the human condition.

According to the article, there are many strategies and projects in place to alleviate poverty. The problem is, many of these tactics create a rock-in-a-hard place situation which sometimes sabotages conservation goals. For instance, if you place water, education, or health services right next to wilderness areas, it leads to pressure on the wild habitat. If you build capacity for livestock and agriculture, you increase the risk of human-wildlife conflict. Other ideas, of course, include tourism, both through photographic safari and through tightly managed big-game hunting.

The correlation between hunting tourism and diminished poaching is supported by Marina Lamprecht--a Namibian writer, conservationist, public speaker, and owner of Hunters Namibia Safaris--who was kind enough to speak with me after one of her seminars. With the meat provided by their clients, they provide a protein-rich meal daily to over 260 local school children. For many students, it is their only protein for the entire day. Because of the connections and benefits provided to the local people, she insisted that poaching on their 80-square miles of privately-owned land was virtually non-existent: "Not a single footprint on our property goes by without me being notified. Poachers simply will not attempt to operate on our land because the locals would report them."

Sharing the meat of harvested game with local people is a central component of legalized hunting throughout Africa. Unlike in the States, it is impossible to process the meat and get it into a freezer in a timely fashion. Therefore, rarely is any brought home. Instead, it is used to feed villagers, thereby providing a direct benefit to the people who must live with the animals.

Although Rick had yet to harvest anything when we came across the elephant bones, the practice was already evident at *Masimba* Camp. With the nearest village four hours away and no refrigeration, Sue's zebra had been cut into strips to hang like bright red socks on a clothesline. The sun's rays soon turned the rows of suspended meat into dried jerky, easily stored for later use.

In our many discussions about poaching, Lilian also informed me of something else I had never considered: legalized hunting greatly curtails poaching. Poaching in hunting concessions is just too risky. As noted, all

foreign hunters must be accompanied by professional hunters and government game scouts when on government-owned land. Not only are such
men and women armed, but they also travel on safari vehicles crisscrossing
vast amounts of terrain daily, whereas most small-time bushmeat poachers
are on foot and unarmed. If I were a poacher, you can bet your sweet bippy
I'd think twice before operating in areas where so many stewards of wildlife
would be cruising.

While exploring the bleached elephant bones at *Chui* Rock was distressing,
it set the stage for understanding. Like many aspects of Africa, the soaring
landmark stirred conflicting emotions. In one sense, it became like an old
familiar friend, a presence to seek in the skyline as we meandered through
the reserve. Yet, it also served as a vivid reminder of the complexities of
wildlife preservation in a harsh land, a bitter reminder of greed, ugliness,
and cruelty. Still, you can't acknowledge such grim deeds without also recognizing the face of poverty. Food-insecurity. Danger. Frustration. Anger.
Misery. Desperation. Hopelessness.

Ultimately, *Chui* Rock, the poached elephant bones, and all that I
learned as a result led me to see well-managed hunting in a different light.
Hunting's success is statistically well documented. My emotions regarding
the hunting of prized species overrode those truths. Gradually, my heart
began to understand. Using animals as a renewable resource helps provide money, food, and jobs for local people, thereby elevating the human
condition. Tourism--consumptive and non-consumptive--is critical to the
African people, wildlife preservation, and anti-poaching efforts. Attacking
poaching without attacking its underlying causes is a losing battle, one that
Africa's wild creatures cannot afford for us to lose.

6
THE WIDOWMAKER

Racing through the mixed savanna scrublands, I dodged acacia trees and thorn-covered bushes, trying desperately to stay on Mgogo's heels. Raphael and Rick were somewhere ahead of us. Whether it was 10 feet or 10 yards was lost on me. Keeping my eyes glued to the ground, I was looking for snakes while trying to stay upright and keeping my peripheral vision locked on my human lifeline. Although I couldn't see Abdalah or Lilian, the rustle of parched grasses told me they were trailing close behind. The previous day's slow, deliberate games of Follow-the-Leader were gone, replaced without warning by an urgent speedy version.

Running has never been my thing. Ever. Ever. Ever. Short legs on a 5'3" frame are not the best asset for sprinting the 100-yard dash. My body was ill-equipped to keep up a blood-pumping, air-sucking pace for any length of time. Luckily, adrenaline and fright provided a little extra oomph. There was such urgency, but I was clueless as to why.

Everything had happened so fast. Only 20 minutes earlier, amid the typical fanfare of parting encouragement, we pulled away from *Masimba* Camp and settled in for another jarring drive through pitted countryside. Not only was the morning's breakfast still parked in my stomach like a freight train, but I was combatting another relatively sleepless night. We had again been haunted by the hyenas' eerie vocals and *Simba's* blood-curdling serenades. Restless nights in the bush seemed to be par for the course.

My food-induced, sleep-deprived stupor was shattered when Raphael and Mgogo pointed excitedly, rattled something off in Swahili, and pounded on the cab window. As soon as Mike stopped, everyone erupted from the vehicle like it was about to explode. Adrenaline permeated the air as Raphael, Rick, and Lilian grabbed their rifles and Mgogo seized the shooting sticks. Gawking in confusion, I followed suit and scrambled to the ground. Yet, I had seen nothing!

Before I could make sense of anything, we were dashing through the brush. The steady, carefully placed steps of the previous day's pursuits had given me a sense of security, especially when it came to avoiding snakes. At this reckless pace, however, thoughts of sluggish puff adders or black mambas unable to make a speedy exit filled my head and provided an incentive to stay on Mgogo's heels.

Just when I was about to keel over, we caught up to Raphael and Rick. They were crouching behind a cluster of trees peering through a hole in the branches. Following their gaze, I saw them. Hundreds of them. Cape buffalo in a long, strung-out formation barreling across the savanna only a few hundred yards in front of us.

It was like a scene from a cowboy movie. Instead of familiar-looking cattle, the charging bovines resembled fiercer versions of black Angus bulls, only with massive, terrifying horns. Hundreds of hooves kicked up clouds of dust as the ground trembled under our feet. Grunts, bawls, and bleats rose above the thunderous roar. Somehow, during the mad dash, this clamor had escaped me.

After a moment, we returned to the previous day's slower, more meticulous game of Follow-the-Leader, advancing tree to tree, 10 to 20 yards at a time. Adrenaline, disbelief, and blind obedience worked together propelling me forward, still on Mgogo's heels.

As the distance dwindled, stories of the Cape buffalo's ferocity and cunning came flooding back to me. Cape buffalo--aka *nyati, mbogo, narri, inyati, dagga* boy, 'Black Death', or 'Widowmaker'--earned its designation as *dangerous game* and was placed among *The Big Five* by living up to the requirements of that exclusive club. Responsible for killing an estimated 200 people a year, these black brutes are every bit as deadly as lions, leopards, rhinos, and elephants.

Nyati have few weak points. They are masses of pure muscle, weighing close to a ton, with tank-like chests, barrel-sized necks, and stout powerful legs equipped with sharp hooves. This burly animal is capable of pulverizing any critter unlucky enough to fall under its wrath. In addition, their massive, curved horns fuse in the center of their foreheads, forming a rock-hard shield referred to as a *boss*, creating an excellent ramming instrument. From the boss, each horn dips down, then curls upward into a half circle on each side. Both the boss and the tips make excellent weapons, one for crushing an adversary, the other for disemboweling him, whatever strikes their fancy. The buffalo's brawn and sturdy horns don't hinder its speed or maneuverability as one might think. They are also fast and athletic. Unlike many species, the buffalo is also blessed with the trifecta of outstanding senses--hearing, sight, and smell.

Cape buffalo

Left to their own devices, Cape buffalo are peaceful enough, but, once annoyed, they are the quintessential example of Dr. Jekyll and Mr. Hyde. Their tendency to flip from a calm grazing animal to a relentless, cunning, bad-tempered opponent with high preservationist instincts is probably even more lethal than their arsenal of weapons. This inclination to defend themselves extends to the rest of the herd as well. One bleep from a calf in danger will have the entire herd running to its defense and forming an impenetrable barrier of angry, black-horned bovines.

YouTube is a great place to witness this phenomenon. I once watched as four lionesses pounced on a calf, rolling it into a river. As the little guy struggled frantically in the water against the attackers, the calf's mother vanished from the screen. The calf was then grabbed by two large crocodiles initiating a tug of war between predators. Still, no sign of the calf's mama. Then in a united burst of effort, the lions pulled the calf from the crocs' mouths, dragging the poor thing back onto dry land. Still, no mama.

The bleating calf seemed doomed. Then low and behold, an entire mob of buffalo materialized from the side of the video. Pressing their tank-like chests shoulder to shoulder, forming a wall of black, they advanced on their adversaries and attacked. The lions were forced into defense, dodging the massive horns and pounding hooves. While distracted, the calf floundered to its feet and scrambled into the safety of the herd.

Another clip showed a lioness's jaws clamped onto the tailbone of a downed buffalo. The prone victim barely struggled, seemingly immobilized in pain. Suddenly, a lone buffalo came charging to the scene, dipping its head to one side, hooking the lioness with its horn, and flipping her 15 feet into the air like she was a 10-pound pussycat, not a 280-pound killing machine.

In admiration, dread, and sometimes tears, I watched as mobs of bulk returned time and time again to take on whole prides of lions to rescue one of their own. A lion's blunder could cause him to be gored, trampled, or crushed by the *Nyati's* extensive weaponry.

The Cape buffalo's solidarity, courage, and chivalrous behavior isn't restricted to four-legged predators. Its tendency to rescue or counterattack applies to two-legged carnivores as well. In 2018, Claude Kleynhans, a professional hunter in South Africa, was killed when he was loading the carcass of a buffalo that had just been harvested. Without warning another *dagga boy* burst from the bush, rammed the unsuspecting hunter in the groin, and gouged his femoral artery, killing the PH.

Normally, Cape buffalo will try to avoid people. When surprised or in a compromised position, however, the horned bulldozers would rather fight than flee like most prey animals, especially lone *dagga boys* who are lacking the security of the herd. Essentially, they charge first and ask questions later.

Cape buffalo are deadly under normal circumstances. When wounded, they are an even more terrifying force to reckon with. Injured and enraged, their strong survival instincts kick into overdrive, providing enough adrenaline to sink a small battleship. A maimed *Nyati* will fight until the bitter end, often counterattacking in planned assaults.

This tendency to seek revenge, along with its resistance to dying, is what sparks so much anxiety and fear over injured buffalo. It is also why PHs take great pains to position hunters allowing for a clean shot the first time. It is their responsibility to terminate an injured animal, not only to end its suffering but to eliminate its threat to the hunting party, as well as any locals who cross its path.

Even taking precautions, the adrenaline and anxiety of hunting big game can cause the most seasoned hunter to misplace a shot--a mistake that many PHs have paid the ultimate price for. In one such incident, a PH had tracked an injured bull for three days. On the third day, the *Nyati* charged from the undergrowth, catching the PH unaware. Using his horns, the bull first launched him in the air and then pummeled him to death.

Andrew, one of Hilary's PHs, experienced a Cape buffalo's cunning and revenge-seeking mission firsthand. After one of his clients wounded a bull, Andrew sent the hunter and his daughter back to the safety of the vehicle. While tracking the tormented bovine, he expected it to hide in the thick brush and burst forth, a typical scenario. Instead, the bull circled, hid behind a massive termite mound and—in one last-ditch effort--stormed at him from behind. Thankfully, Andrew's quick reaction ended its rage before it reached him.

This attack-is-the-best-defense strategy, along with their brute strength, is why Cape buffalo earned their nicknames *Black Death* and *Widowmaker*. While species such as hippos, crocodiles, lions, and elephants kill more people each year overall, Cape buffalo kill more *hunters*.

Locals say the buffalo *will kill you twice just to make certain*. Another mantra is: *Buffalo never forgive. They will find you.* In the book "Horn of the Hunter," Robert Ruark famously writes "...they look at you like you owe them money." He goes on to say "...the reason my friend *Mbogo* is generally rated as the toughest piece of all the African furniture is that he is a single-minded type. You got to kill him to discourage him." In another passage, Ruark advises that the buffalo "...delights to dance on your carcass until there is nothing much around but spatters of blood and tatters of flesh."

Paradoxically, the very qualities that make these notorious beasts so deadly are also what prompts them to be one of the most revered, esteemed, and admired species of Africa. How can anyone not respect and appreciate a being whose survival instincts are so powerful for itself and its herd that it will fight with every ounce of its vitality, whether taking on an entire pride of lions or two-legged predators with rifles? Still, this reverence for the Cape buffalo must also be accompanied by a healthy dose of fear.

As hundreds of forceful strides battered the earth just 200 yards away, stories of the buffalo's ferocity flooded my brain. Dread filled my innards as the distance between us shrank. The fear, a primal ancient fear, was unlike any from our civilized world. My lizard brain, that part of me responsible for survival instincts, kicked in, driving me forward.

At my core, I knew that the safest place for me to be was in the shadows of the men and woman I was with. I trusted the calm, cool strength of my husband, and even after such a short time, I had complete faith in the skills of Raphael and Mgogo. Lilian, too, was close behind with her AK47, a rifle meant for poachers but nonetheless capable of other uses.

After darting forward a few more times Raphael suddenly stopped. Mgogo set up the shooting sticks. Rick rested his gun in the cradle of the tripod, placed his arm on my shoulder for stability, peered through the scope of his rifle, and put his finger lightly on the trigger.

At 140 yards, we were further than the preferred shooting distance. Apparently, Raphael felt comfortable with Rick's accuracy at that range. Typical of all African hunts, a portion of the first afternoon had been spent at target practice sighting in guns, allowing PHs to judge their client's abilities—a critical factor when assessing hunting's logistics.

By the time Rick was on the shooting sticks and we were in position, nearly three-quarters of the herd had passed by. The flurry of pursuit was replaced by a waiting game. For the first time since exploding out of the vehicle, I stood utterly motionless gazing in wonderment as the mesmerizing scene played out in front of me.

Buffalo after buffalo pounded by. Some were in bunches, some scattered, some hugging the fringes of the herd, with calves seemingly nestled in the middle. The irregular ribbon of supersized bovine spread out for hundreds of yards across the savanna. Except for the calves, they all looked like carbon copies of each other: huge black brutes with massive, curled horns. Horns that from an untrained eye all looked the same. I couldn't tell a cow from a bull, a young bull from an old bull.

Like the kudu, Rick didn't have the skill to judge African species. It was totally up to Raphael to find a mature shootable bull amid this hornet's nest of galloping *Nyati*. As they continued to stream by, over and over I thought to myself, "*What's wrong with that one?*" or "*How about this guy?*"

You must remember, we sacrificed a lot to pay for our trip. The previous day's 13 hours of dodging elephant potholes, tracking the old *dagga boy*, and stalking multiple species with no success were in the back of my mind. Although those experiences had been worth every penny, I knew the opportunity to hunt Cape buffalo had been Rick's dream since picking up his first safari magazine at 8 years old.

Loving someone means that their dreams also become your dreams. And so even as a non-hunter with reservations about hunting certain species in Africa, I desperately wanted Rick to fulfill his long-awaited quest.

Another tank-like black blur stormed by. Then another. And another. As the tail end of the stampeding buffalo herd came into view, the conversation inside my brain switched from subdued questioning of each buffalo's merits to urgently screaming, "*What's wrong with that one?!*" Then, finally, my unspoken shriek was answered when Raphael pointed to the very last bull, a straggler 15 yards behind the moving mass of blackness.

"That one," he whispered.

Unexpectedly, another thought entered my brain. What if I flinched as Rick was ready to pull the trigger? With his elbow resting on my shoulder, I would screw up his shot. Instantly, I squeezed my eyes shut. I figured if I couldn't see, I wouldn't react instinctively, possibly sabotaging the shot.

On too many occasions in the past, calm had eluded me. While living in Alaska, where Rick and I met, each of our hikes included trailhead postings warning '*Stay calm during a bear encounter. Do not run!*' Detailed instructions followed, primarily urging hikers to play dead if attacked by a brown bear and fight like hell if attacked by a black bear. Brown bears normally leave after the perceived threat is over, but a black bear will eat you.

Well, believe me, even with these tidbits of information firmly implanted in my brain, remaining calm is easier said than done. When spotting a bear from a distance, no problem, but flash a blackish blob 20 feet from me and I sprint. Fortunately, my 100-yard dashes were typically the result of friendly black labs rounding a corner. Not bears.

Anyway, I certainly did not want my instincts to be responsible for wounding *any* animal, let alone one nicknamed *Widowmaker* and *Black Death*. Also, as much as I hate to admit it, the thought of a $3,000 trigger pull crossed my mind. Wounding a *nyati*, whether it was recovered or not, would mean dishing out the Cape buffalo's trophy fee and Rick losing the chance to harvest that species. Consequently, keeping my eyes shut seemed to be the best course of action.

Meanwhile, unbeknownst to me, the targeted buffalo spotted us, pivoted, and charged in our direction. I was, therefore, blissfully unaware that almost 1,500 pounds of disgruntled muscle was barreling straight at us.

Suddenly, I heard Raphael yell, "Shoot. Now!"

An instant later, the *Boom!* reverberated through my entire being. My eyes impulsively opened to see a cloud of dust and the blur of thrashing horns turning towards the receding herd. A second later, we were all running across the savanna in pursuit. I had no idea if Rick had hit the buffalo or not.

Sixty yards later, everyone slowed. There he was: *nyati*, lying motionless and sprawled out on the ground in front of us. Tension and vigilance pervaded the air as Raphael gestured for us to stop. Although the buffalo appeared lifeless, he instructed Rick to fire one more bullet into its spine, an insurance shot. This preventative measure was common practice for buffalo because of their reputation for retribution and refusal to die.

Even after the insurance shot, Raphael signaled for everyone to stay back while he approached the motionless mass as if it might explode at any minute. Using the long shooting sticks, he gently prodded the bull for any signs of life. Satisfied, he finally relaxed.

Our whole entourage breathed a sigh of relief as worry and caution were replaced by excitement and awe. Gazing at the magnificent buffalo lying on the grass, Rick and I clung to each other as tears streamed down my face. Rick's eyes, too, were glistening with sentiment.

Tears are peculiar. They convey a whole host of emotions. There were, of course, tears of joy. After over 40 years of dreaming about it, Rick had hunted a Cape buffalo in the wilds of Tanzania. But the tears entailed other things as well. Remorse. Regret. Sorrow. Thankfulness. Awe. Excitement. Relief. Wonder. Loss. Even disappointment that the hunt was over.

While these conflicting sentiments are a part of any successful hunt, there was a whole other dimension to our emotions in Africa. Rick was, after all, harvesting species that we had both loved and idolized for decades.

The logical part of my brain may understand the significance of well-managed hunting, but my heart still grieves for the sacrifice of any once vibrant animal. As a little girl, it was difficult to get through even one *Lassie* episode without tears streaming down my face, giving my brothers plenty of opportunities for teasing. With tears filling my eyes, I'd lash back at them. "I can't help it if you don't have any feelings." The *boys* were always acting tough, just like little boys do.

Yet, they weren't as hard-hearted as they pretended to be.

I found this out at my Grandma's river camp. As kids, we loved to fish, but instead of eating them, we preferred putting them in our kiddie pool to watch them swim. Then, before leaving, Dad would toss them back into the river to go about their business. When I was about 8 years old, we were staying overnight and decided the fish might enjoy a sleepover as well. It was a bad idea. We woke up to find our water sanctuary startlingly void of catfish. Instead, scads of raccoon prints marked the ground. Unwittingly, we had created an easy feast for multiple black-eyed bandits.

To this day, I can picture us standing in a circle around that empty pool, shocked and devastated. Bawling hysterically, I cried, "We're murderers! We're murderers! We killed them!"

My brothers didn't lose it as I did, but for once, they were dead silent. They, too, felt wretched. I'll never forget that day: maybe because it was my first experience with death; maybe because I felt responsible; maybe because I was so struck by the sorrow in the faces of my normally macho rambunctious brothers, the soon-to-be hunters.

While I, of course, can't speak for all hunters, most of the ones I know love, respect, and admire the very animals that are sacrificed. That is hunting's great paradox. For although a hunter is proud, happy, and relieved to fulfill his quest, he is also deeply saddened by his prey's death. Rick, like me, is torn with conflicting emotions when the bullet hits its mark.

Rick explains: "It is the *hunting* that I love, not the *killing*."

Rick had seen enough death in the army. As a captain of a Cobra helicopter gunship, he flew many missions in Somalia in the 1990s when America was battling the warlords and the infamous *Black Hawk Down* incident occurred. He was a part of all that. It wasn't just buildings that his weapons annihilated. While killing is absolutely part of the hunting process, he has *no* desire to kill for the sake of killing.

This odd mixture of feelings isn't unique to Rick. If asked, most ethical hunters admit to the same type of sentiment. They kill to have hunted, not hunted to kill. That may be difficult for many people to understand, but there is a huge difference. In a podcast with Joe Rogan, Corey Knowlton put it this way: "If I just wanted to kill things, I would work at a chicken plant where I could kill thousands of animals a day."

Hunting, that primal urge to test one's abilities, provide for one's family, and to do so in the wilderness was ingrained in Rick from the time he was a little tyke growing up on his family's ranch.

His Granddad Verl taught him to hunt deer to put meat on their table. His Grandma Alice lit up each time he presented her with a steelhead he'd caught in the river below their house. At age 12, he and his sister raised rabbits for food and sold their meat to the local food co-op. At about the same time, he learned how to hunt small vermin and trap coyotes, lessening the predation of newborn cattle.

Their small ranch was like many small spreads throughout the country—land rich and money poor. Those activities weren't just done for the fun of it; the meat, income, and predator control helped sustain life in their little piece of the world.

Although Rick is a principled hunter, that's not to say he didn't have transgressions along the way. It's all a part of learning. At age five he shot one of their cattle in the backside with his BB gun. His Grandpa Verl never raised his voice. He simply forced Rick to watch as he methodically dug each pellet from the cow, while lamenting about the pain the poor old gal was experiencing.

Rick worshipped his Granddad. He insists he'd rather have been beaten with a 2' x 4' than listen to the disappointment in his Granddad's voice. That lesson is as ingrained in Rick as those BBs were in that cow's rump. Never again did he shoot at a living thing just for the fun of it.

Growing up on the ranch offers exposure to death that most of us can't comprehend, including me. Regularly, calves and other livestock are lost at birth, to disease, or as a result of predators.

My first time at the ranch, it was calving season. Rick's sister, Bobbi, and I were riding the upper pasture checking the cattle. We found a mama cow down in a draw with her entire back side ripped open from a coyote or mountain lion. The dead calf was lying on the ground beside her. Knowing we had to get the cow to the barn for doctoring, Bobbi decided we'd use the dead calf to lure the grieving mama.

Not all horses are fond of carrying dead animals on their backs. As a novice, I'd been given Baron, a ranch-savvy, trustworthy mountain horse; it was therefore decided that the calf had to go with me. We draped the tiny bovine across Baron's neck in front of my saddle and headed out of the canyon. Carrying that limp, lifeless calf essentially on my lap while its mutilated mama slogged behind in mourning pierced my heart.

By the time we got to the barn, tears streamed down my face. Betty, Rick's Mom, came darting toward us shouting, "What's wrong? What's wrong?"

Through sniffles and tears, I sniveled "Th-th-the calf is deaaadd."

Instantly, Betty relaxed. She wasn't used to having a tenderhearted newcomer around. That didn't mean she didn't care about the calf or the injured cow. The cattle were not only their livelihood, they were precious animals. Each had a name. They knew which ones were good mothers and might adopt an orphaned calf. They knew which ones were ornery and, therefore, to be wary of when doctoring their newborns. They knew each cow's history, past ailments, and age. Yet, loss of life on a ranch is a brutal reality.

Some deaths, even on a ranch, are more tragic than others. Some are never forgotten. Rick wasn't even a teenager when learning that lesson.

While riding horses to move cattle on the steep bluffs above the Salmon River, one of the horses stumbled on the narrow trail, lost its balance, and rolled hundreds of feet down the almost vertical canyon. With three broken legs, they could do nothing for the gelding but put it out of its misery. At 12 years old, Rick was the only one agile enough to maneuver down the steep slope to get to the horse. Equipped with only a knife, he had to cut the jugular vein of an animal he loved.

Horses aren't simply livestock or beasts of burden for Rick's family. They are cherished members of their family. Having to put down that horse was a gruesome task that still haunts him. Death isn't easy, but sometimes it is necessary.

It is the same for hunting. These conflicting emotions associated with hunting may be hard to fathom for people who aren't familiar with it, but hunters, and people like me who understand its place in our society, desperately want the animals to flourish, remain wild, and survive in their natural environments.

After Rick and I regained our composure from his harvest of the Cape buffalo, hugs and congratulations were offered all around. We knelt next to the massive, now lifeless *nyati* in admiration and wonder as we whispered our thanks for his sacrifice. We did this not in any type of official or organized way, just a heartfelt thank you to an incredible creature for its sacrifice. The crew did the same, each in their own way, depending on their tribal or religious customs.

Rick with the Cape buffalo moments after it died.

Rick's first bullet hit the old buffalo in a frontal shot to the heart as it charged toward us. Adrenaline alone had allowed the magnificent bull with 43-inch horns to cover the 60 yards to where he lay.

While absorbed in our thoughts, the rest of our party was already busy. Our location had been radioed to Mike and soon the vehicle came zigzagging through the trees and creeping over the savanna floor to rest beside the buffalo. While it is customary not to take vehicles off-road to hunt, you are allowed to use them for retrieving a harvest.

Only minutes later, Hilary and more staff members showed up in another Land Cruiser. Being only a few miles from camp, Raphael had radioed them so they, too, could join in the celebration, as well as the work. In the retelling, amid another round of hugs and congratulations, I mentioned that I had shut my eyes and therefore had no idea the bull had charged.

Raphael looked at me intensely, then implored in his calm serious manner, "Sue, please keep your eyes open."

The look on his face spoke much louder than any words could have. Lesson learned. My eyes would stay open.

The good-natured banter also led to an answer regarding the earlier all-consuming question: *What's wrong with that one?* Although the Cape buffalo all looked the same to me, there were subtle differences in the huge beasts *if* you knew what you were looking for. Both sexes do have horns but only the males' fuse on their foreheads creating the boss, or ramming instrument, as I mentioned earlier. Their horns are also much larger than the females'. Therefore, picking out the males was easy. Well, easy for Tanzanians.

Distinguishing the old males from the younger males was where it got dicey. The bosses of the older bulls were larger, bone hard, and had a dullness to them. The younger bulls had bosses that were slightly smaller, shinier, and not completely solidified yet. The fact that anybody could distinguish these slight variations from over a hundred yards away while they were in stampede mode, was dumbfounding.

Still, the primary reason that Raphael made Rick wait, and wait, and wait, until most of the herd had gone by was that the oldest, and therefore, the lowest-ranking bulls are typically located at the back of the herd. Cape buffalo have a strong hierarchy. The low-ranking bulls that are no longer breeding or contributing to the gene pool are forced to bring up the rear until they are kicked out of the herd altogether to become *dagga boys*.

Animals forced to the rear of such a mob not only get inferior grazing, but they are also more at risk from predators. The high-ranking, dominant breeding bulls, on the other hand, travel front and center, essentially the safest spot, while also having access to unsullied premium grasses. Finally, I knew the answer to "*what's wrong with that one?*"

The next hour was a flurry of activity. Mgogo took the lead with most of the staff working alongside him to process the buffalo.

Typically, we would jump in to help, but it was obvious that the staff didn't need newbies getting in the way, especially since Hilary had brought the extra men. In addition, we were still familiarizing ourselves with this whole alien world and our place in it, so to speak.

Lilian, too, was still gauging her place among the staff. The Tanzanian game scouts are employees of the government, not of any particular outfitting business. Along with ensuring all hunts are legal, their duties include recording each harvested animal's age, size, health, and location where it was killed. Lilian and Nikko, also known as Mriru, the game scout assigned to Rod and Sue, arrived at camp the same day we did. Like us, they knew no one. I'm assuming this is by design. It makes sense that wildlife officials shouldn't get too cozy with the outfitters they are monitoring.

Lilian recording buffalo data for the Tanzanian government.

Standing around like a bump on a log is not really in my nature, so I gravitated toward Lilian who also seemed a little lost. We immediately clicked.

On top of being a warm intelligent young woman with a great sense of humor, her free-flowing command of the English language allowed for easy conversations, a blessing I will treasure forever. Nikko, who accompanied Rod and Sue, also spoke English along with his native tongue and Swahili. His English, however, was less fluent than Lilian's, making conversations more difficult.

As far as I was concerned, we hit the mega lottery when Lilian was assigned to us. Not only did we become fast friends, but she also became my private tutor.

Teaching, even informally, is in Lilian's blood. While saving money for college, she taught younger children at a local school. Once she had enough funds, she attended the College of African Wildlife Management, also known as Mweka College, where she attained her Wildlife Management

Technician Certificate. After completing that, she spent a year and a half as a volunteer at the Malihai Clubs of Tanzania, an organization that trains and educates the community in nature, wildlife, and environmental conservation.

Though she wanted to continue her education in Wildlife Management and become a lecturer, money became an issue, forcing her back into the workforce. The Tanzanian government requires all game scouts to have some college education and therefore, this job was a perfect fit for her skill sets.

Being exposed to such a vastly altered world opened my 54-year-old eyes to the zillions of things that I *didn't* know. Fortunately, Lilian jumped on the "educate Sue bandwagon" and soon I was learning all kinds of stuff, including snippets of Swahili.

As the only female who was not a client, Lilian was definitely immersed in a man's world.

Being a woman outnumbered by men wasn't an issue in itself. *That* I was used to. Aside from growing up in a male-dominated household, I'd spent 10 years working in a Pennsylvania steel mill where at least 95 percent of the employees were men. In the '80s, many people considered that gutsy, but I had no trouble relating to the mostly male workforce. Work hard, you earn their respect. Period.

What I could *not* begin to relate to were the actual tasks required of her. No way. While in the mill, I'd had tons of safety gear to keep me fairly insulated from harm: a hard hat, steel-toed boots, geeky safety glasses, steel mesh wristlets, etc. As long as you follow safety procedures, the days of being lassoed and mutilated in a spool of razor-sharp scrap metal were mostly gone.

Working in a grungy, mechanical, potentially hazardous world that repelled most women instilled a certain amount of pride in me. But geez, my accomplishments in a masculine world were nothing compared to Lilian's.

She was toting a machine gun, chasing down poachers, crossing flooded rivers in the rainy season, battling Tsetse-flies daily, and ending each grueling day by bathing from a bucket of murky water and crawling into a bedroll tossed onto the hard ground with only tent fabric to shield her from the things that go bump in the night. Her courage at only 23 years old was beyond me.

At the time, I didn't appreciate the full extent of it. Without getting too deep, let's just say that in large parts of Africa, women do not enjoy the same basic human rights or privileges--including education and work opportunities--that many of us take for granted. None of this was apparent at *Masimba* Camp. It wasn't until recently when talking to a filmmaker of African documentaries, that I learned how exceptional it was to have a female game scout.

While I was visiting with Lilian, the crew sliced the buffalo carcass in two, front quarters and hindquarters; six-foot tree limbs were positioned on the ground; and each half of the meat was placed on top. Standing on both sides, the men then used the branches to hoist the 700-pound slabs into the cargo hold. The entire buffalo, amid plenty of grunts and a lot of finesse, was somehow crammed into an area the size of a small kitchen table. Even the entrails were taken; tripe, the stomach's muscle lining, was considered a delicacy among the staff.

Loading the buffalo.

Once there was nothing left of the *nyati* lying on the ground, it was time to part ways. Our crew took off in the direction we had headed almost two hours earlier. Hilary and his crew took the Land Cruiser, slumping with the burden of 1,400 pounds of buffalo, back to *Masimba* Camp where Emilian, Hilary's brother, would perform his magic. As a skinner, it was his job to meticulously remove the skin and transform the carcass into usable meat.

Rick and I marveled at the efficiency in loading the cumbersome beast. While their efforts may not seem like a big deal to those unfamiliar with hunting, believe me when I say it *was* a big honking deal.

In Idaho, most hunting is done in steep rugged wilderness where access to vehicles of any kind is few and far between. Typically, an elk has to be gutted, quartered, and packed out in a pack frame or, if you're lucky, on the back of a horse or mule. Without stock animals or several strong backs, that involves multiple trips. It is a tedious labor-intensive process taking many hours, depending on the elk's location, weather conditions, distance from the road, helping hands, mode of transport, and umpteen other factors. Any hunter will tell you that the *real* work begins after the shot is fired.

Although part of me had been fascinated with the staff's competent preparation and loading of the buffalo, it was great having Lilian as a distraction. Dressing a harvested animal is part of the process. In fact, it is the most fundamental reason for the kill. That doesn't mean it isn't heart-rending to watch an animal being transformed from a magnificent, spirited creature into a form of nourishment. I accept it, but I will never get used to it.

Growing up in a hunting family as I did, our freezer was full of deer burgers; deer jerky hung in the root cellar, and the deer's back strap (similar to filet mignon) sautéed in butter and onion was considered a special treat. Heck, until I moved out of the house, I doubt I ever ate spaghetti sauce made with anything other than deer meat.

During spring and fall, life in our house largely revolved around hunting and fishing seasons. That hasn't changed. My family's passion for hunting grew as my brothers became fathers themselves, sharing their love of hunting and the outdoors with their children. Typically, hunting is a family affair, a tradition passed down from generation to generation.

Even my dad, who had both legs amputated above the knees in his 70s, still hunted until almost the end. At 85 years old and legless, his version varied from most hunters. Still, he took it seriously. Just ask the neighbors. Dad was a take-charge kind of guy who took it upon himself to eliminate the groundhogs wreaking havoc upon their gardens. He would go barreling through their backyards in his electric wheelchair with his rifle lying across his lap. Knowing my dad, he never even asked permission. He just assumed the neighbors wanted the pesky groundhogs gone. Apparently, he was right because an abundance of fresh vegetables showed up on Mom and Dad's porch almost every day in the summer months.

Even the young in our family are diehard outdoorsmen. When visiting my parents a few years back, my nephew stayed with us for a week. Mysteriously, the TV remote control kept disappearing with the TV conveniently stuck on the hunting channel. At only 8 years old, that little turd was already obsessed with hunting. When we figured out that Cooper was hiding the remote, Dad's all-bark-and-no-bite thunderous voice put an end to his little scheme.

Two days later, he was desperate to go *hunting* with his BB gun, but all my brothers were busy. Not only was I not a hunter, but it was also a nasty, cold, drizzly day. For hours, I distracted him with games and movies. In the late afternoon, just when I thought I was in the clear, his sweet little voice pleaded, "Aunt Susie, isn't it time to go hunting yet?"

I caved. We layered on clothes, donned raincoats, and took off with his BB gun into the neighbor's cornfield. For Cooper, walking through six-foot-high cornstalks was like traversing a jungle. I wasn't worried about bumping into the prey; walking noiselessly through a tangled maze isn't easy. Any critters hanging around were long gone. Still, we stealthily weaved in and out of that cold dripping wet sea of green for over an hour scanning for hoofprints or any sign of wildlife. Eventually, he was satisfied with the *hunt* and agreed to give it up for the day.

Certainly, hunting is a tradition in our family, as well as our community. Still, it goes much deeper. Unlike some of us, hunters are drawn to that primal instinct to hunt. An instinct that has been embedded in mankind since primitive times and generally passed down from generation to generation.

Although hunting permeated my entire life growing up, I never went with Dad and the boys. Therefore, I was never present for the kill or the initial processing. Not only did I not want to be a part of all that, but I also had no desire to wake at 4 a.m., tromp miles through nasty weather, or sit motionless for hours in bone-chilling treestands. By the time I saw the deer, their essence was gone. Seeing them as carcasses or slabs of meat waiting to be cut up and wrapped was easier than seeing them as once living, breathing, beautiful creatures. The meat was an understandable necessity of life. With much of the emotion taken out of it, it was easier for me to accept.

Once I met Rick everything changed.

When my first marriage ended, so did my career at the steel mill. Needing a change, I quit my job and moved to Anchorage with my sister. Lo and behold, I got my dream job as a flight attendant for a small Alaskan airline. My hard hat, safety glasses, and the grimy insides of a steel mill were traded in for a uniform, a set of wings, and views of snow-covered mountains, rugged shorelines, and the Northern Lights.

After Rick's eight years as an Army Cobra helicopter pilot, he too had moved to Alaska to pursue a career flying fixed-wing aircraft. Although we worked for the same airline, he was stationed in the remote village of Bethel as a bush pilot. Ultimately, our paths crossed. The rest is pretty much history.

Within a few months of dating, our hiking and outdoor adventures expanded to me going with him on hunts as well. Although I originally wasn't thrilled about it, my resistance ultimately melted. Rick was pretty handsome after all. Besides, it gave me the chance to experience parts of Alaska that I would never have seen on my own.

Our first hunt together is a vivid memory that neither of us will ever forget. Rick had drawn a Kenai Peninsula caribou tag. For months I had been taunted by a beautiful alpine hike to an abandoned gold mine in Hope, Alaska, where, according to my hiking book, *the elusive Kenai caribou herd* could often be spotted. Jumping at the opportunity, I showed the hike description to Rick who decided it was a good place to start.

After a two-hour drive, we turned onto a bumpy dirt road leading 10 slow miles up the valley. As we gained elevation, the road morphed into essentially a goat trail until we could go no further. From our spot at the head of the basin, we could see the whole sweeping vista below us with mountains surrounding us on three sides. It was the perfect place to set up camp and start the hike in the morning. Or so we thought.

The basin created a wind tunnel that made putting up our tent an exercise in futility. Still, we tried. The wind whipped the tent uncontrollably, with me trying to hold it as it wrapped around my body, while Rick drove stakes into the ground. During this whirlwind of activity Rick suddenly stopped.

"Caribou!" he yelled above the sound of fabric flapping in the wind while pointing to the valley below.

The very valley we had just driven through. That *elusive Kenai caribou herd* was grazing its way right to us.

All work on the tent halted. We watched the herd gain ground and close the miles between us. Sticking out like a sore thumb was a bull limping on an injured leg. His struggle broke my heart. If a caribou had to be sacrificed, it should be him. Although Rick worried that the wounded animal's meat would be infected or compromised, he agreed it must be put out of its misery.

A few minutes later, Rick shot the injured bull. The rest of the herd milled around in confusion for a few moments as tears streamed down my face. Not only had it been the first kill I ever witnessed, but I had also been an accomplice.

The caribou died within moments; Rick eliminated the long tortuous death of a wounded animal. Still, being present for the harvest is different than seeing it hanging lifeless as a slab of meat or on a plate as grilled steak.

My sobbing eased into silent tears as Rick processed the caribou and divided it into quarters we could carry. It's not a pretty process. Gutting. Slicing. Skinning. Sawing through bone with a bone saw. With tears trickling down my cheeks, I mechanically performed each small task that Rick asked of me, "Hold this leg. Grab my knife. Pull here."

After seeing plenty of deer carcasses over the years in Pennsylvania, that was the first time I was present for the arduous and gruesome task that accompanies a successful hunt. It was a devastating process to watch, especially the first time.

With a carcass and its entrails less than 50 yards from our partially set-up tent, nestled smack dab in the middle of brown bear country, I insisted that we pull up stakes and head home.

Alaskan brown bears are essentially grizzlies, but much brawnier versions. Since they live along Alaska's coastlines feeding on plenty of salmon, they tend to get much bigger than their inland relatives. Alaska's brown bears are notorious for identifying rifle shots as a call to dinner. Not wanting to become the evening meal, we tore down our partially completed camp, loaded the caribou carcass, and wormed our way back down the mountain in the dead of night.

Again, contradictions came into play. As traumatic as that first hunt was, it was also wondrous. Battling the whirling winds of a high alpine meadow in the spectacular mountain peaks of the Kenai Peninsula just hours before dusk, we'd been blessed with watching a whole herd of caribou in their natural environment meandering their way up the valley, a sight I'd have been far less likely to witness on a fair-weather afternoon hike.

Rick also had spared an injured bull a gruesome death, filled our freezer with meat, and helped manage the herd's population. In addition, the fee for the caribou tag went toward wildlife conservation while we indulged in the uncertainty and intrigue of the wilderness. Like Rick, I did not like the actual kill, but somehow, I found myself reveling in the overall experience.

That *elusive Kenai caribou* came drifting back to me as we jostled through the African savanna. For a moment, I was transported to another time and place. My actions and feelings have changed significantly since then. I still shed tears each time a bullet hits its mark, but I don't bawl like a baby anymore, at least not normally.

The truth is, some deaths hit me harder than others. I'm not sure why. I can't quite put my finger on it. Maybe it is the type of animal, the situation, or how it is killed. One thing that is certain, the conflicting emotions are *always* present.

A few minutes later, I was roused from my reverie when Raphael spotted a sable in the distance. Off we went on another stalk. Only that time, it was slow and steady in the familiar Follow-the-Leader linear formation. Before long, the sable got the slip on us. An hour later, Mgogo spotted a roan's horn protruding from a thicket a mile away. Okay. So, I'm exaggerating a bit. Anyway, after another short excursion, Mr. Roan also eluded us.

A bit later Raphael spotted a mature oribi bedded down under a lone shade tree. Oribis are small antelopes standing fewer than 26-inches high at the shoulder and weighing less than 50 pounds. It has delicate features with a long neck and limbs. Their yellowish-brown coat contains touches of white, allowing them to blend perfectly with the scorched grasses of the savanna. The little guy was smart enough to seek cover from the afternoon sun's merciless assault. Something we should have been clever enough to do.

We'd already seen quite a few oribi but typically they darted off, offering little more than a view of their rumps. Those little buggers are fast. Typically, they travel in small herds of four members or less, but that guy was by himself. Since only males possess horns, it was obviously a male. Still, we had to get close enough for Raphael to determine if he was old enough to harvest.

Oribi

The wind worked for us as we crept forward in our normal fashion hiding behind high grasses and eventually one of the ginormous termite mounds dotting the landscape. Upon getting a good view of the oribi's straight, narrow horns, Raphael gave the go-ahead. At about 120 yards, Rick and I simulated the same shooting position that we had used for the *nyati*. This time I kept my eyes open. The beautiful compact antelope never moved. Abruptly, it was over.

Our crew was exceptionally excited. As far as oribis go, he was a really old buck with horns over six inches long. Even though I had complete faith in their expertise, it was difficult to reconcile the fact that the fawn-sized creature was an aged male. My subconscious screamed in torment that he was just a baby starting his life, not an animal at the end of its lifespan whose sacrifice would help the species overall. It's amazing how our entrenched notions can play havoc on common sense, no matter what the facts are.

After offering our thanks to the oribi, the small antelope was easily picked up and gently placed in the cargo hold. A far cry from loading the Cape buffalo.

Raphael then took inspiration from the oribi, deciding that shade was a good idea. After another few miles in the relentless sun, we found shelter among a cluster of trees and set up for lunch. For us, it was pretty much a repeat of the day before, only we took a cue from Rod and Sue and placed a tarp on the ground for a nap. While I wasn't quite the walking zombie of the day before, it still felt like heaven to sprawl out, luxuriating in the magnificent shade.

As we lounged, the staff busied themselves preparing lunch. At first, I assumed they were making mielie meal like they did the day before. Soon, I recognized something was different. Curiosity again got the best of me. Peeling my sweaty body off our makeshift bed, I went to investigate.

The oribi, or parts of him, were roasting on an improvised spit over open flames; no *ugali* for lunch that day. Although they offered us some of the skewered meat, I passed, partly because I'd already gobbled up our Americanized lunch and partly because I was still picturing the oribi as Bambi.

Even with reservations about eating the critter myself, it was oddly comforting to see the cycle of life put into play almost immediately. The oribi's sacrifice was not in vain.

After lunch and a little siesta, we tackled the blazing sun for another five hours while adding four more rounds to our tally of zebra stalking. Finally, at dusk, we arrived back at camp to the normal fanfare of greetings and excitement that accompanied each day's return. Sue had harvested a beautiful mature sable, the primary species she sought, so spirits were high. Rod too had harvested an oribi about the same age as Rick's.

Although we had expected our dinner might include the Cape buffalo that Rick harvested in the morning, we were at a loss for words when it arrived. Amid the broth in my soup was a large chunk of buffalo tail. Tidbits of meat were nestled between a framework of bones. Who knew that tails had bones? I sure didn't.

We looked at each other wide-eyed, then dipped our spoons in the broth and hesitantly took a sip. Gaping in complete astonishment, all four of us dove in wholeheartedly. The soup was utter bliss. After our bowls were practically licked clean, Sue's sable made it to the table in the form of lean and delicious grilled steaks.

After our meal, I shocked the whole lot of them, thanks to Lilian's tutoring, when I casually, but a little awkwardly, stated, *"Asante kwa tamu chakula."* Thank you for the delicious food. The enthusiastic reaction and beaming smiles of our Tanzanian hosts were even yummier than the buffalo-tail soup.

After dinner, Rod, Sue, Rick, and I took another chance sitting by the fire on the makeshift patio. We were pleased to find that the bats were dining in a different restaurant for the evening. Not having to dodge plunging excrement allowed me to reflect a bit.

What a day it had been: watching a herd of stampeding Cape buffalo; Rick fulfilling one of his life-long dreams; a nap under the shade trees as fresh oribi was barbecued on a spit; Swahili lessons; stalking multiple animals; and a fabulous dinner with lively conversation. Last, but not least, who could forget a huge chunk of buffalo tail creating a mouth-watering soup? The entire day was unforgettable.

Splat. Plop. The bats were back. Apparently, the main course was over, and dessert was being served under the canopy of the patio tree. It seemed the perfect time to call it a day. Who knew what the next day would bring? *Lala Salama.* Sleep well.

7
ANGRY LITTLE DEVILS

Whack! Mgogo struck me across the back with a leafed branch. Seconds later, Abdalah, using a bough of his own, swatted my right shoulder. Next, one of them hit me across the left side. On the bench seat across from me, Rick was receiving a similar walloping. Over and over, our trackers slapped us with the foliage they had snagged from a passing tree. The whipping initially caught us off guard. Quickly, however, we welcomed it; the swats kept the miniature vampires from latching onto our backs while we waged our battle from the front.

One second we had been motoring along rather comfortably, the next we were swarmed by an army of the blood-sucking Tsetse-flies. "Angry little devils," as Lilian liked to call them, didn't do them justice on that occasion. The *ndorobo* were at war.

Up until that point, the day had been pretty normal: we'd enjoyed multiple animal sightings; stalked a sable before losing him in the long grass; and tracked a waterbuck until he crossed into the national park. As far as Tsetse-flies go, most of the day had been pretty uneventful, just a few minor skirmishes. Definitely, nothing to get our panties in a twist about. Then, just before dusk, all hell broke loose.

Each of us was fighting with all we had. Slapping. Swatting. Shaking. Jerking. Stomping. One glance into the Land Cruiser's cab told me that Mike and Lilian hadn't escaped the assault. The flies appeared so swiftly that they had no time to roll up the windows.

It was a repeat of our day one. Again, there was no such thing as each man or woman for themselves. Everyone took it upon themselves to defend each other, even if that meant pummeling clients with branches. Clearly, the honeymoon period of our new friendship was over, otherwise, whacking guests willy-nilly might not have been such a grand idea.

Unlike our first experience with the *ndorobo*, we were outfitted in Tsetse-fly armor from head to toe. Still, it was not enough. Any single layer of fabric was pierced like a hot knife slicing through butter. The *Maasai* blankets Hilary gifted us the first day, folded in quarters, provided a barrier too thick for little devils to penetrate, offering at least some relief for our legs.

With seven sets of extremities thrashing erratically we looked like spasmodic crazy people, or better yet, like Elaine from the sitcom "Seinfeld" performing her deranged dance moves. Legs kicking. Arms thrashing. Heads jerking. Suddenly Rick and I simultaneously burst into laughter. The entire scene was hysterical.

Me trying to protect myself from the Tsetse flies.

Apparently, the bloodsuckers didn't like being laughed at. Within minutes they vanished. Like a steak in a dog pound, they were completely and utterly gone. In reality, their retreat probably had more to do with the time of day. Unlike most demons, which tend to lurk at night, Tsetse-flies are just the opposite. Sunset brings relief. Like magic, the little tormentors evaporated into thin air.

The attack was by far the worst we'd experienced during our entire Tanzanian stay, far more wicked than the first day when we were caught unprepared and ill-equipped. Rick and I, therefore, dubbed the assault: "The Day of the *Ndorobo*."

The bayonet-equipped insects, 31 varieties to be exact, are a part of life in the bush of Tanzania. Since each species has a slightly different preference in acquiring their daily quota of plasma, each day and each battle was a whole new ballgame. Although they *supposedly* prefer woodlands and brushy areas, the attacks seemed random to us, happening at any time and in any habitat. Sometimes we were hit by a small squad. Other times by a few platoons. Once in a while, a battalion of the piercing soldiers would be on the rampage.

Although the nasty insects are related to the common housefly, their piercing instruments make them 100 times nastier. People aren't their only victims. Animals, domestic and wild, are also targets.

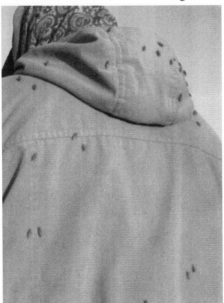

Raphael covered in Tsetse flies.

Female Tsetse-flies live up to four months while males live only one to three weeks. The difference in life spans may seem inconsequential until you learn that they also have different feeding preferences. Females prefer larger four-legged victims while their counterparts prefer humans. Lilian believes that the male's shorter lifespan is no coincidence; God allowed this so that her people wouldn't "be tortured for a longer period of time".

Ndorobo are not only blood-thirsty insects, they are the carriers of the deadly disease African trypanosomiasis (known as *sleeping sickness*). It isn't as well-known as malaria, yellow fever, and the West Nile virus which are carried by mosquitoes, but it is just as deadly. The flies carry the microscopic parasite from infected animals to non-infected ones. Within a few weeks, the victim displays signs of fatigue, headaches, muscle aches, and high fever. Over time, the parasite attacks the central nervous system resulting in sleep disorders, psychiatric conditions, seizures, comas, and eventually, death. Fortunately, only six varieties of Tsetse-flies transmit the sleeping sickness to people.

Knowing the fly's potential puts the fight against the tormentors in a whole new context. It's one thing to suffer the pain, but a different matter entirely to realize a deadly disease can be a part of the bargain. Trypanosomiasis has no vaccine; the only way to escape the possibility of getting the disease is to avoid getting bitten in the first place. From what we experienced, if you are in a Tsetse-fly zone, there is about a snowball's chance in hell of that happening.

We were already following the obvious recommendations: we wore medium-weight, long-sleeved shirts and pants *supposedly* too thick to bite through; we carried leather gloves and mosquito nets for when they attacked; we fought with an arsenal of insect repellents; and our clothes were neutral tones since they are drawn to bright, dark, and metallic colors. It's no accident this is one of the reasons safari guides wear khaki. Our efforts seemed about as effective as herding cats. The little buggers were persistent and superb at pinpointing any weak points in the armor.

For some reason, Tsetse-flies are especially attracted to moving vehicles. The Center for Disease Control (CDC) recommends thoroughly checking a vehicle before entering to make sure there are no miniature hitchhikers. If it wasn't such a deadly disease, that tidbit of information would be almost laughable. Most safaris are geared around wide-open vehicles. Plus, Mike and Lilian, without open windows in a sunbaked, non-air-conditioned cab, would have been roasted alive. Other recommendations suggest scheduling walking safaris in the early mornings or late afternoons when the flies are less active, as well as sleeping in air-conditioned rooms with the windows closed. Again, none of which was plausible at *Masimba* Camp.

Over the years, many methods have been used in attempts to wipe out the *ndorobo*: woodlands were cleared; the brush was periodically burned; and wild game was systematically destroyed. Yes, you read correctly. In the past, mass slaughter of wildlife was used as a primary method to control the fly: kill the food source, kill the fly. Thankfully, that school of thought has been replaced by more modern approaches.

Before anyone crosses Africa off their bucket list, don't worry. It's not as bad as it sounds. Tsetse flies no longer exist throughout the whole of Africa. This century's control measures have eradicated them in many places, including national parks, while bringing the disease largely under control. Plus, even when bitten, there is less than a 0.01 percent chance of getting the disease. In 2018, for instance, there were only 977 new cases reported. Even though there are still no vaccines, there are now better ways to diagnose the sickness and treat it successfully. Most general tourists truly have little to fear. Rural farmers, herdsmen, hunters, and fishermen having long-term exposure to Tsetse-fly zones are the people most at risk.

Although sleeping sickness in humans is largely contained, that is not the case with animal trypanosomiasis. The sleeping sickness has a devastating effect on livestock, especially cattle and horses. Medicines are expensive and often don't work anyway. Consequently, raising cattle and other farm animals in Tsetse-fly-infected regions is next to impossible. Those willing to try are plagued by sickness and death, losing approximately 3 million cattle each year throughout Africa.

The flies are prevalent in 36 sub-Saharan countries spanning an area of approximately 10 million square kilometers. That is a massive expanse of land rendered useless for raising domestic stock or growing crops where stock animals are needed to plow fields. The *ndorobo* are considered one of *the* most influential creatures on the entire African continent. In fact, the presence of the disease-carrying insect is one of the primary causes of poverty in Africa. Of the 36 countries affected, 30 are ranked as low-income, food-deprived nations.

Historically, the widespread presence of Tsetse-flies largely inhibited human settlement throughout parts of Africa. With eradication techniques, many areas have been opened for settlement (or resettlement) and livestock production and agriculture have been initiated. Undoubtedly, this is a good thing for the rural people living in poverty-stricken and malnourished nations.

Unfortunately, the successful extermination of the disease-ridden insect is a double-edged sword. The Tsetse fly's existence, and the devastating effect it has on farm animals, is ultimately the reason such large tracts of wild habitat remain in Africa. Without the bloodsuckers and the disease they carry, more wildlands would already have been converted to growing crops and domestic ranching. Although wild game is susceptible to the disease, they are far less vulnerable than cattle and horses. The Tsetse-fly-infested areas are the last stronghold for much of Africa's wildlife.

Learning of the *ndorobo*'s role in keeping large tracts of wilderness intact, I find myself, again, burdened with conflicting emotions. My heart goes out to the people of Africa whose lives are adversely affected by them. Yet, I am also grateful that their existence preserved habitat for the continent's fauna.

It is simply frightening to think of what Africa would look like today if the Tsetse fly, with all its nastiness, had never existed. Would it be like America, mainly a patchwork of fenced pastures and cultivated strips of land? What would be left of the majestic species: elephants, lions, zebras, Cape buffalo, and so many others? I have no idea. Doubtfully, anyone does. Even so, one thing cannot be contested, a Tsetse-fly-free Africa would not be the Africa we know today.

As the battalion of blood-sucking soldiers assaulted us that afternoon, all I knew was that Tsetse-flies caused incredible pain. I knew nothing of the sleeping sickness. All our gear was aimed at preventing discomfort, not disease prevention. Other than resembling an oversized pin cushion when the afternoon was over, we survived basically unscathed.

The next morning, we were barely out of camp when the relentless critters struck again. Thankfully, after a brief battle, we passed through the infested area. After distancing ourselves from the skirmish, Raphael suddenly directed Mike to stop. Along the pitted track he had spotted a huge pile of dried elephant dung. A short burst of Swahili sent Mgogo jumping down to gather the remnants of *tembo's* dinner, place it in a tin bowl, and light the dehydrated plant remains on fire, allowing it to smolder. Soon the pungent smell of plant-based manure was wafting through the air. As we watched in fascination, Mgogo brought the slightly odorous simmering mixture aboard the vehicle.

Lo and behold, smoking-elephant dung makes a natural non-polluting mosquito and Tsetse-fly repellent! We were dumbfounded. The question burning in my brain became: *Why on earth did they wait so long to pull that rabbit out of the hat?* When asked, Raphael explained that not all clients were thrilled to be doused with smoldering excrement.

For sure, not everyone would welcome that weapon, but it was definitely right up our alley. On a ranch, manure is just a part of daily life. For Pete's sake, it's basically just plant matter. Well, mostly. Heck, I would have rolled in the stuff if it meant keeping those bloodsuckers off me.

Abdalah burning elephant dung to ward off the Tsetse flies
with Mgogo collecting more in the background.

From that day forward, burning clumps of elephant muck became a regular part of our Tsetse-fly arsenal. There was no shortage of the stuff. Amazingly, adult elephants can let loose up to 300 pounds of dung every day. Now that is a pile of poop. The simmering doo-doo didn't keep the itty-bitty carnivores completely at bay, but it most definitely helped. Thankfully, "The Day of the *Ndorobo*" was never repeated on the remainder of this safari.

Even though the torment of the angry little devils will never be forgotten, I now recognize their contribution to preserving large tracts of wilderness and therefore look at them with new eyes. No longer do I see them *only* as instruments of pain. Instead, they are miniature warriors doing battle to preserve the wild creatures of the continent. In my extremely biased opinion, Africa and its dazzling array of species is God's masterpiece. Maybe the Tsetse-fly was put on earth as one of the Creator's tiny defense mechanisms.

I, for one, am willing to take my 0.01 percent chance of contracting the disease if it means preserving wildlife habitat. Yet, I make this profound statement while writing this book plopped on my cushioned chair in my secure Tsetse-fly-free home--one that has a refrigerator full of food with cattle grazing just outside in pastures free of Africa's sleeping sickness. Pretty egotistical, for sure.

8
Never Say Never

B arely had the orange hues of sunrise disappeared before I found myself in another intense game of Follow-the-Leader. The first few hours after daybreak, before the sun's rays were hot enough to scald a lizard, was prime time for wildlife to be on the move. My get-up-and-go, however, had yet to kick in before a herd of our striped nemeses had *once more* been spotted.

As I darted from tree to tree, I couldn't help thinking, "Zebras? Again, for the umpteenth time? More specifically, how could a horse-like animal be so difficult to hunt?"

Zebras, with their dazzling black and white stripes, are glorious fixtures of the African landscape, celebrated the world over for their striking appearance and horse-like features. Rungwa West was no different; it was jam-packed with herds of the equines.

Spotting them was a cinch. Even from a distance, their vibrant contrasting colors caught our eyes immediately. Still, that did *not* make them easy to get close to. Who could have imagined that an exotic species related to horses would dodge us time and time again? Certainly not me.

Horses are, after all, an integral part of ranch life. Idaho's steep brushy terrain makes horses crucial for checking cattle, driving them to different pastures, and various other ranch duties. Once chores are complete, Rick's family jumps into their saddles for local competitions, trail riding, and hunting in the backcountry. Horses are not just work animals; they are beloved pets.

Therefore, you can imagine my shock when learning that Rick wanted to hunt zebras. It was simply impossible to wrap my head around. Zebras were just too similar to the horses on the ranch; remove a zebra's stripes and they could be Dreamer, Sugar, Cowboy, or Butterscotch. It just didn't seem right. It was also hard to visualize *fair chase* coming into play. Surely, harvesting a zebra would not offer much of a challenge. How would that be *hunting*?

Rick countered my opposition with assurances that zebras are wild game, *not* pets. They need to be managed just like all wild species. Zebras are voracious eaters whose long teeth allow them to eat the coarse long grasses. Their overpopulation can wipe out food sources for wildlife who depend on the same type of feed. Also, as grass eaters, they compete directly with livestock.

As I dashed from scrub tree to scrub tree for the hundredth time, I began to rethink my original opinion of zebras. Truly, they were as wild as any creatures we had seen in Tanzania. At the mere glimpse of our vehicle, they turned tail, leaving nothing but a cloud of dust.

Spotting them from a distance was crucial so that the Land Cruiser could be hidden behind trees or a termite mound. We'd then scramble out of the vehicle to begin our synchronized Follow-the-Leader in the hopes of getting within range of the wary beasts.

Hartebeests, or *kongoni*, also greatly hampered our efforts. These medium-sized antelopes weighing about 350 pounds have a symbiotic relationship with the zebra. Other than having beautiful reddish-brown hides, they were short in the looks department. Both sexes of the Lichtenstein hartebeest have long rectangular heads, pointed ears, and curvy, ringed horns. The combination of odd-looking horns sprouting from odd-looking heads creates a face that only a mother could love. Their body, too, is rather ungainly, consisting of a short neck, hump on their back, and unusually long legs. Every single species of antelope I experienced in Tanzania, whether it weighed 20 pounds or 1,600 pounds, was graceful, beautiful, and elegant looking. The hartebeest, looking like he was made from a bag of mismatched parts, was the exception to that rule to me.

Hartebeest

What the *kongoni* lacked in good looks, they made up for in eyesight and intelligence. Because of their elongated faces, their eyes are positioned high on their heads, allowing them to survey their surroundings while grazing. From the bag of mismatched parts, the hartebeest also scored a highly developed brain making them remarkably alert, cautious, and savvy enough to use their vision to the best advantage. A sentry is always posted at an elevated position, often on a jumbo termite mound, playing King of the Hill, so to speak. This lookout allows the sentinel to continually scan for danger while the rest of the herd grazes peacefully. At any sign of a threat, the appointed guard lets out a sneeze-like snort, alerting the herd to make like dust in the wind. Along with excellent eyesight and intelligence, the *kongoni* has a superior sense of smell, but its hearing is slightly lacking.

The zebra, on the other hand, is blessed with the trifecta of great senses: hearing, smell, and sight. Like horses, they can rotate their ears to pinpoint and decipher sounds. Yet, the zebras' ears are rounder and much larger, allowing them even better hearing. Zebras also have keen eyesight, both day and night. Also, while most animals are color blind, zebras are not. With eyes on the side of their heads like most prey species, they have a wide field of vision for spotting intruders. At any sign of danger, a loud bray sends the herd bolting. *Punda milia,* at 35 mph, aren't as fast as their domestic relatives, but they have much more stamina, allowing them to run for long distances. They also tend to run in zigzag patterns to outmaneuver predators.

Their vivid stripes aren't simply visual treats, they also work as weapons against predators. When the herd is in motion, often referred to as "motion dazzle," the confusing mass of shifting black and white makes it extremely difficult for a predator to pick out just one individual target. Owing to their distinctive stripes and this unique phenomenon, a group of zebras is often called a *dazzle*.

In Africa, the buddy system is a great strategy. With the hartebeest and zebra hanging out together, they can use the strengths of both species while also having additional sets of eyes, ears, and noses. Just as significantly, it benefits their bellies. As noted, zebras tend to eat the longer grasses; hartebeests, on the other hand, prefer shorter cropped grasses. This arrangement allows both to feed without being in direct competition with each other, a win-win for both species.

For us, not so much. The partnership was a definite pitfall. The hartebeests' posted sentries' alert, cautious nature, and additional sets of eyes made it twice as hard to get near zebras, especially when six people were dashing from one feeble tree to the next. Once either group of animals sounded the alarm, it was game over.

Rick, Raphael, and Mgogo glassing zebra in the distance.

Zebra, as well as all prey on the savanna, were also greatly aided by birds. Specifically, the Guinea fowl. You've probably seen a version of them throughout America. The speckled chicken-sized bird is highly prized for eating ticks. Lots of them. At least, that's the case in western Pennsylvania where deer ticks carry Lyme disease in epidemic proportions. There are tons of the birds pecking around my brother's neighborhood constantly scrounging for ticks and other insects. Imagine my shock upon seeing the familiar bird on safari. It had never occurred to me that the birds were native to Africa.

Thanks to grazers' bodily functions, Guinea fowl also have a symbiotic relationship with these species. What goes in one end eventually comes out the other. The resulting piles of dung attract a host of insects creating the perfect place for the noisy tattletales to feed.

The clucking, chattering feathered friends aren't so friendly. With posses of up to 50 birds, their eyes constantly dart around, strategically providing them with a 360-degree view. We'd just get close enough for Raphael to pull out his binoculars and, voila, a flock of the high-pitched squawkers would sound their deafening alarm. If they were in the vicinity the gig was up.

Sue had somehow overcome all the clacking birds and vigilant four-legged informants on the very first day, but our experience was much different. We had already stalked zebras seven times. Each time ended with another story to tell and thousands of steps on my Fitbit. Sometimes, the *punda milia* got a whiff of us. Other times, the hartebeest spotted us. More than once, the noisy cluckers sounded the alarm. A few times, our jaunt ended with the discovery that the zebra herd was an untouchable harem.

A harem is a group of mares, their foals, and a dominant male; harvesting that breeding stallion, however, is off limits. Since hunters must target older post-reproductive males, they can only hunt males who are on their own or within a bachelor group. A bachelor herd, as the name suggests, is a group of males either too young, too old, or too timid to gather a harem of their own. Having said that, distinguishing a bachelor herd from a harem from a distance was a bit tricky.

Pursuing the exasperating equines so many times filled me with new-found awareness. The horses we are familiar with today have been altered quite a bit during their 5,000 years of domestication and selective breeding. They have been the friends and workhorses of man, pulling carts, plowing fields, and carrying us on their backs in war, leisure, and competition. Horses have, therefore, become more attached to man and the comforts they can provide.

Punda milia have no such inclination. Domesticating zebras has been attempted multiple times, especially in the late 1800s and early 1900s when European powers were vying for control of African territories. Horses, the main way of transporting people and supplies before vehicles, were essentially useless in large parts of Africa thanks to the ever-present Tsetse fly and the deadly disease it carries. As mentioned previously, trypanosomiasis or "tryps" is especially deadly to horses. Therefore, they are not an option for use in the *fly zones*. This fact greatly curtailed European conquest, dominance, influence, and development of the continent.

The efforts to tame zebras never amounted to anything sustainable. Time and time again, their extremely aggressive nature proved that domestication was simply not in the cards.

Zebras evolved in a place where large carnivores are their main predators. Their acute senses and alertness enable them to flee when danger exists. Along with their *flight* response is a powerful *fight* response. A zebra doesn't just kick randomly. It looks between its legs, aims precisely at its target, and kicks violently with both hind legs. A powerful, well-placed blow to the head can kill a lion instantly or break its jaw causing a slow excruciating death by starvation. Zebras are also savage biters. Their long teeth, perfect for grazing the savannas, double as lethal weapons.

Their lack of trainability doesn't end there. There is a strict hierarchy that is strongly enforced. The dominant female assumes the best grazing rights, in other words, the position at the front of the herd. Subsequent mares follow behind according to their ranking in the pecking order. Their offspring follow the position of their mothers with some exceptions to tag along with other foals.

Breaking the entrenched ranking can lead to the lower-ranking animals being ferociously attacked. The stallion leads the chain of command and can go wherever he wants. Usually, he brings up the rear or patrols the flanks on the lookout for predators or males wishing to steal his ladies.

Horses, too, have a definite hierarchy using these same methods. Still, their response has been tempered by thousands of years of domestication.

The savage, seemingly barbaric, pecking order within zebra populations makes domestication extra hazardous. Once, in the 1980s, officials were attempting to relocate a herd of zebras in Zimbabwe. Sixteen individuals were loaded into a truck. Upon arrival at their destination, only one zebra remained alive. With their hierarchy askew, they had viciously battled, effectively kicking and biting each other to death.

Zebras are also known to participate in infanticide. This occurs potentially when a new male assumes control of a harem. Killing the competitor's offspring will force the mares into estrus, thereby allowing the newcomer to sire his offspring. For the same reason, a new stallion may also repeatedly mount a pregnant female causing her to abort the opponent's unborn foal.

It's difficult to accept such fierce savage-like behavior in a cherished species that we equate with our beloved horses. Seeing the distressing reality play out on YouTube will offer a new perspective.

Tourists got more than they bargained for when they videoed a stallion attempting to drown a foal. Clasping the baby's neck in his mouth, the male held it underwater while kneeling on its torso, pinning it to the ground. When the colt's mama saw her offspring struggling desperately to break free, she darted over to challenge the stallion. With the stallion distracted temporarily, the foal gasped a breath of air. A few seconds later, the stallion again grabbed the foal's head, holding it underwater. The female again distracted the male, allowing the baby to leap up and tear across the savanna. With the stallion hot on its heels, both disappeared from the screen before the video cut off. Although the baby's fate will never be known, the optimistic part of me chose to believe that it survived. How can you not root for the underdog?

It's hard to accept that such beautiful peaceful-looking animals are capable of such cruelty, even to their own kind, but one must recognize that this practice is nature's way of ensuring the overall survival of the species, brutal or not.

Our eighth zebra pursuit came to a sudden stop behind a small outcropping of trees. In front of us was a clear view of the herd. Finally, no hartebeests on patrol; and no Guinea fowl policing the premises. The wind was in our favor, keeping the zebra from catching a whiff of us. Most importantly, it was a bachelor herd. With the probability of an old male being in the mix, we slowly stalked forward until we reached a bush 200 yards from the zebra.

To me, the zebras all looked pretty much the same. Raphael and even Rick, from so many years around horses, could read the minute differences. Old stallions have a very pronounced rounded bottom jaw. In Africa, where brutal fights for dominance are ongoing, scars are another great indication of age.

Rick and I assumed our usual position on the shooting sticks waiting for Raphael to point out the targeted male. Seconds later, it was over. The *punda milia* slumped to the ground as the rest of the herd bolted across the grasslands. There was no suffering. No slow wasting away of flesh. No getting eaten alive by *Simba* or *Fisi* as the old boy weakened. His part in the cycle of life had been fulfilled.

As I looked down at the lifeless zebra, the gamut of emotions materialized. Surprisingly, however, it did not hit me with the impact I expected. Tears glistened in my eyes, but its death did not bring me to the level of heartache and emotional turmoil that I had anticipated, no more so than any other creature.

My reaction, or lack of reaction, confused me. When trying to make sense of it, I concluded that I had come to appreciate the zebra's true wildness. They aren't horses. Nor are they pets. They are wild animals and, therefore, need to be managed as such. I also began to recognize that my emotional attachment to zebras didn't make them any different or more special than other species.

Rick had tried to convince me of all this, but no amount of persuasion could have convinced me more than experiencing their untamed spirit firsthand. Not only had I opposed hunting zebras because of their horse-like qualities but I felt hunting one would be like taking candy from a baby. I was wrong on both accounts.

I was used to Rick's elk hunts. Most often, they were grueling affairs that pushed our bodies to extremes. When all the sore muscles, exhaustion, and exposure to the elements paid off, it wasn't just Rick who felt relief and accomplishment; I felt it as well. It may have been his bullet or arrow that hit its mark but I was a part of the journey, one that helped me to understand the lure of hunting beyond the meat and its benefits to conservation. While the zebra hunt so far was nowhere near as punishing as those elk hunts, the same concept applied.

It, therefore, seemed no accident that the zebra became our greatest nemesis. It was utterly clear to me that forces were set in motion, on eight separate stalks, to open my eyes to the reality of zebras--not the myth nor my predisposed emotionally motivated perspective.

While expressing our thanks to the stallion--each of us in our own way--Mike brought the vehicle to our location and backed it within feet of the zebra. In bewilderment, I watched as Mgogo and Abdalah dug holes almost a foot deep behind each rear tire. Mike then backed up the vehicle, allowing the back tires to slide into the pits, effectively lowering the cargo hold just off the ground. As they cut a sturdy branch from a tree, the light bulb finally went off in my head. The entire zebra would be loaded whole. No processing. No halving. No quartering.

Using a branch to load the whole zebra on the
vehicle with its tires lowered into holes.

Plains zebras can weigh between 500-800 pounds. Since the zebra was a male, I'm assuming he was at the higher end of that range. That's a huge hunk of flesh to lift in one piece. Like the buffalo, the branch was placed under the zebra's body so the ends could be used to lift. Everyone pitched in, two people lifting from the vehicle while the rest lifted from below. Within minutes, the full-grown zebra was in the cargo hold.

We had yet to get over the novelty of loading such extremely large game whole, without the need for quartering, backpacks, pack-saddles, multiple trips, aching legs, and hours of backbreaking effort. As soon as we reached *Masimba* Camp, the *punda milia* would fall into the skilled hands of Emilian and his helpers, transforming the lifeless form into usable protein, and eliminating another aspect of our typical Idaho hunts. Not having to participate in the arduous, but necessary, task while in Africa was a huge treat.

As we pulled into *Masimba* Camp amid the typical fanfare of greetings, the sight of the skinning shed caused the gears in my head to start turning. Dinner each night included meat from a harvested animal. Did that mean zebra for dinner?

The realization slapped me across the face. You don't have to be a rocket scientist to guess that my initial opposition to shooting a zebra extended to the idea of eating one. Even recognizing the value of the zebra's sacrifice, the thoughts of putting horse-like flesh in my mouth made me want to gag.

Do not fear, sanity prevailed. With a protein bar in my bag and evening meals that always included Moses' soup, there was zero chance I'd starve.

While waiting for dinner, Rod, Sue, Rick, and I decided to try a new strategy to combat the nightly bombardment of bat feces. Having a few cocktails on the patio *before* dinner instead of *after* dinner might avoid a shower from the flying mammals. Weren't we the clever ones? It only took us three days to figure that out.

While enjoying the lack of bat droppings in our drinks, Joel showed up with a plate of skewered *punda milia* roasted over open flames. I'm not sure if it was the joy of not having to dodge bats, the fact that I was famished, or if I'd had one too many guano-free cocktails that prompted me to taste. Whatever the reason, I was hooked at first bite.

Each charbroiled piece of zebra was a mouthwatering burst of flavor so tender it practically melted in my mouth. Unbelievably, zebra was my favorite protein of our entire Africa trip; hands down.

If I hadn't tasted it myself, I would never have believed it. Another lesson learned: *never* say never. My opinion on hunting zebras evolved over a few days. Then my taste buds joined the revolution. You know that saying "I'm so hungry I could eat a horse"? Well, I did.

9

My Eyes Are Open

After a few days in the bush, eating lunch without having to shoo Tsetse flies away or having sweat dripping down my back felt like absolute heaven. Even during midday, the *mesi's* cozy structure maintained a temperature that was *almost* comfortable, thanks to a seemingly unending breeze. Granted, it was still hot, just not sweat-lathering, debilitating hot. Escaping the jouncing broiler pit on wheels during the sizzling part of the day was a welcome change. One that Hilary thought we needed.

Every day up until that point we had pounded the bush from sunrise to sunset leaving little time or energy to explore camp. After our long days, our primary focus had been: shower, food, bed. How these luxuries were possible in the bush of Tanzania had barely crossed our minds. That ended abruptly after our relaxing, blissfully oblivious lunchtime when Joel and Michael proudly took us on an official tour of *Masimba* Camp.

Since water, or *maji*, is the life and blood of any encampment, we were first escorted to the camp's water supply. In the dried-up riverbed 30 yards behind our tent was a crater about the size of a washtub filled with murky liquid. I'm not sure what I expected as a water source in such a parched land, but it was not the mudhole of my youth.

Essentially, the entire camp's non-drinkable water came from a pit resembling the one I'd spent hours in making mud pies as a kid. Upon closer inspection, I was relieved to find that the sandy riverbed made the water cloudy but still relatively clean. Water was scooped out of the hole with a small container and then dumped into 5-gallon buckets. As the water was removed, moisture from below the ground's surface seeped up to replace it.

Although the water exceeded the cleanliness of our childhood mud bog, I was pleased to learn that our drinking water came from bottled water instead of the pit in front of me. Which *maji* was used for cooking, I didn't think to ask. Who knows, maybe sand-filtered water was the secret ingredient of the fabulous soups we slurped down each night.

Joel (on left) and Michael showing Masimba Camp's water source.

We were stunned to learn that all the water for our toilet, sink, and shower came from that one tiny waterhole. Behind each of our bath huts was a 10-foot-high scaffold with a water cistern on top. Musa, Thomas, and others had to carry buckets of wate--scooped one coffee can at a time--up a crude ladder to dump it into those storage tanks. The miracle of gravity then allowed flushing toilets and running water. Although I had noticed the scaffolding previously, my mind was on sensory overload. Shamefully, it had never occurred to me how water managed to find its way into those tanks.

If the labor involved in furnishing a flushing toilet wasn't enough to put the guilt trip on a person, there was more; no hot-water fairy swished a magic wand, allowing us to have hot steamy showers. Water, scooped one small container at a time, had to be carried 30 yards, heated in a caldron over a wood fire until piping hot, put back into buckets, toted to the scaffolding, lugged up the precarious-looking ladder, and dumped in the reservoir. Ta-da! Hot showers.

Let me tell you. Having our eyes opened to the effort and logistics required for something we utterly took for granted in the States made us rethink things a bit. One of those "things" was our elimination habits. We adopted the concept: *When it's yellow, let it mellow. If it's brown, flush it down*. Surprisingly, this concept was not new to us.

Water tank and scaffold

When Rick transitioned from Army helicopter pilot to civilian fixed-wing aircraft, his job with Era Aviation took him to Bethel, Alaska, the hub for flying to remote native villages along the Bering Sea. It was a great place to accrue tons of flight hours while learning to fly in butt-puckering weather conditions. Landing on unpaved icy runways with major crosswinds, often lighted by an ATV's headlights, creates a great pilot; but living there was dismal. Bethel, nicknamed the *armpit of America* by the pilots, was a dreary, blustery and frigid place in the middle

of the tundra. Because of the permafrost, all dwellings and infrastructure, including water and sewage, had to be positioned on stilts, keeping them off the permanently frozen ground.

Rick shared a house with eight other struggling young pilots with a 1,000-gallon water tank of water to last an entire week. That was for showers, dishes, cooking, and toilets. Such strong water rationing meant toilets were flushed only when necessary. Hence, *when it's yellow, let it mellow*. Since I visited the flophouse from time to time, I was privy to the practice. We adopted the same rules for *Masimba* Camp. It was ludicrous to make anyone climb up that scaffold any more than necessary.

Even after learning about the effort that it took for us to have a shower, though, we just couldn't resort to the PTA baths of our elk camps. Already, they had spoiled us with flowing water to wash away the day's sweat and filth, making it hard to go back to a washcloth and a pail of water. We did revert to Rick's Bethel days. Showers became short and sweet, not-long drawn-out luxurious affairs. We also limited ourselves to one shower a day. Max. No morning wake-up showers. No afternoon cooling showers.

Just one quick shower before dinner to remove the day's accumulation of grunge.

The laundry room was next on the tour. Michael, our tent attendant, had a small area set up under a shade tree near the waterhole with several tubs placed on the ground: one for washing, one for rinsing, and one for him to sit on. Each day, he sat atop that chunk of plastic to hand wash our safari clothes, then strung them on a clothesline to dry--including our underwear, as mortifying as it was.

Musa (left) and Michael at the clothes washing station.

While still cringing at the thought of him washing our skivvies by hand, we moved the tour to his ironing board located near the cooking area. A piece of wood was elevated off the ground and covered with a blanket. The iron was a heavy, antique-looking affair, filled with hot coals from the fire.

Seeing the labor that it took for such an unnecessary task made me want to shudder. Still, no amount of persuasion could convince Michael to skip the ironing. Come hell or high water, we were going to look spiffy as we dodged elephant potholes and crept through the clusters of long grass.

I've already mentioned the care Michael gave to our tents. How, in sandy terrain, he kept every spec of dirt out of our sleeping quarters is a mystery in itself. Even better than the cleanliness was the lack of bugs. Never once, in 21 days, did we spot even one creepy crawly in our *hema*. No ants. No Tsetse-flies. No spiders. It was an absolute miracle in a world containing a bajillion insects, many of which are poisonous.

Aside from his daily chores, Michael went above and beyond. One evening I came back to find an extra blanket neatly folded and placed on my pillow. Before breakfast, I told Rick that I was a bit chilly during the night. I only mentioned it because, after being hot all day, it surprised me. Michael must have overheard, either that or his skills included mind reading. Anyway, that night the extra blanket mysteriously showed up on my bed. This may seem a trivial thing, but such genuine kindness and attention to detail touched my heart.

Next on the tour was where the edible magic happened. At least it seemed like magic. The quality of food that Moses and Kaumba produced in a kitchen with no electricity, no fancy gadgets, and limited ingredients was simply mystifying. In reality, the kitchen was open sky with a nearby thatched shade shelter. The center of the space contained a huge, rectangular, home-fashioned barbecue pit with partitions, allowing items to be boiled or charbroiled at different temperatures. There was even a version of an oven: a covered pot nestled in a bed of hot coals with more glowing embers piled on top. This Dutch oven-like setup produced fresh bread, pies, cobblers, and even cake.

A 7-foot-tall thatched fence surrounded the perimeter of the area to deter critters from easy access. A few yards away from the fires was a partially enclosed grass hut for storing all the produce and foodstuff that Hilary had purchased while in Arusha. (No gardens were grown at *Masimba* Camp to tempt four-legged opportunists.) The storage shelter also served as sleeping quarters for our chefs, providing another deterrent for fur-covered uninvited guests.

Cooking has never been my thing. The thought of coordinating and preparing dinners on wood-fired heat for 21 days, without the use of hamburger helper and instant scalloped potatoes, made my heart skip a few beats. Even the idea of making the grocery list made my head spin. It's not like you could just scoot down to the corner store for a gallon of milk. Although they had the use of a tiny refrigerator, thanks to the generator for a few hours each day, vegetables had to be used strategically. More perishable ones were used first and hardier ones were saved for the end of the three weeks.

Joel, Kaumba, and Moses showing the cooking area and barbecue.

After our eyes were opened to the planning, skill, and work it took to keep us fat and sassy, we headed off to the skinning shed where Emilian was an expert at a whole different kind of magic. The skin of the once beautiful animals had to be meticulously detached and preserved in a bed of salt; skulls placed in vats of boiling water to eliminate flesh; horns stowed on a scaffold to deter predators; and meat processed into usable form.

The skinning shed was built a little differently than the other huts. The walls were made of logs laced together, instead of grasses, forming a mostly impenetrable enclosure. I say *mostly* because the resident elephants could have easily shattered the log walls into toothpicks if they so wanted. But it wasn't those behemoths who longed for the booty inside, it was the lions, hyenas, and other carnivores who would relish a chance at a free meal. What predator wouldn't prefer already sliced and diced chow, rather than risking life and limb to tackle Mr. *Nyati's* thrashing horns or a zebra's lethal kick? The log barrier made entering a little more challenging.

One thing we learned quickly, there was no labor union at *Masimba* Camp. In my steel mill days, you got dirty looks if you tried to do a task not assigned to you. Not here. Each staff member had multiple talents and pitched in wherever and whenever help was needed. It shouldn't have surprised me to see Mgogo and a few others elbow deep in the zebra Rick had killed a few hours earlier. Just because we had a 3-hour lunch break didn't mean they did.

By the time we arrived at the skinning shed's shade shelter, Moses had already taken the zebra meat needed for upcoming meals. Unable to refrigerate the rest, it was cut into strips and strung up to dry, resembling red socks hanging on a network of clotheslines.

Zebra meat hanging up to dry.

It didn't occur to me to ask how the meat was divvied up at the end of the season. Maybe it was split evenly among everyone. Maybe each individual was responsible for his own. Maybe it was sent to villages. Since Mgogo had two wives, four children, and a small farm waiting for him to return, I had little doubt that much of Rick's *punda milia* would be feeding his family in the months ahead.

To deter lions, hyenas, and leopards, the area was kept as clean as possible with the fire burning all night long. The final hindrance was a 7-foot-high grass fence, like the kitchen's, built around part of the outside perimeter.

With meat draped everywhere, it was easy to see why so many precautions were taken to deter carnivores. Even so, there were plenty of creatures lurking around. One night, the camp's game camera captured 24 lions. This number is hard to fathom until you realize that Ruaha National Park contains 10 percent of the entire world's lion population. Still, I was hoping that number was a large exaggeration, or just one lion caught on camera *many* times, especially since our tent was only 100 yards away. Joel was nice enough to point out a large pile of lion scat 20 feet behind our tent earlier in the tour, a tidbit of information I could have done without.

Twenty yards from the skinning shed we stepped into a little shelter that was Anton's domain. He was in charge of the two sets of solar panels, one that powered the radio transmitters and another for the solar lights, as well as the ever-important generator. Without him, the miracle ice machine wouldn't have been spitting out those wonderful chunks of ice every day.

Not far from the generator was a larger shade pavilion where the staff hung out during any downtime. This was also where they cooked their meals, closely resembling what we'd seen them eating in the bush, mielie-meal accompanied with some type of meat or vegetable stew. That day, Zefania and Imma were grilling a special treat, the stomach lining from Rick's zebra. While tripe may be a delicacy to the staff, we were happy to live without that treat. Thank you, but no thank you.

Most staff slept in little bunks in their respective areas. For instance, Joel and Michael slept in beds in a partition attached to the dining hut. Moses and Kaumba slept in the cooking area. Emilian had his bunk in the skinning shed. The extra staff, as well as Lilian and Nikko, pitched their tents in the small clearing near the staff's shade shelter.

The sleeping arrangements came as a shock to me. Until the end of our tour, I had assumed the staff stayed in shelters similar to ours. Come to find out, only Hilary, the PHs, and clients had the swanky, zippered tents with bath facilities attached. The rest of the workers had no showers, flushing toilets, bug-free interiors, or screened windows allowing a breeze. Still, the thing that rattled me most was that the tent area was so close to the skinning shed. Call me crazy but sleeping within yards of a meat buffet with so many predators lurking about didn't seem like a grand plan.

*Zefania grilling tripe, the zebra's stomach
lining, for the staff.*

The staff lived like this at *Masimba* Camp for six to seven months, serving one set of clients after another until hunting season was over. When returning home to their families, the living arrangements for many weren't much different. Water was still in short supply, retrieved from manmade wells or rivers. Few people had indoor plumbing. Electricity, too, was scarce. Only about one-third of the Tanzanian population has access to electricity.

Grasping the staff's less-than-cushy and semi-vulnerable sleeping arrangements, as well as the backbreaking effort it took to keep four Americans happy, I felt overwhelmed with guilt. Upon arrival, we had been skeptical about the need for so many staff members. After all, we considered ourselves seasoned campers--not inexperienced and uninitiated people who couldn't squat in the bush or live with a little dirt under our fingernails.

Still, we took the most basic conveniences utterly for granted. Camping for us back home was a fun respite from busy lives and the trappings of civilization. Our PTA baths and squatting over a hole in the ground were something to endure for a week and joke about later. In much of Africa, it was not a vacation; it is a way of life.

Now, imagine this. You go on a camp tour. You see all the huts, grass fences, pavilions, and solar power stations that were built to accommodate you. You finally understand the effort involved in having clean clothes, showers, flushing toilets, and delicious meals. Then, just when all this sinks into your brain, you learn that the day after you leave it will all be destroyed. Kaput. Vamoose. Totally gone.

All the grass, scaffolding, huts, and anything burnable would be dragged to the riverbed and set aflame. Toilets, sinks, showers, bedding, pots and pans, the ice machine, solar panels, electric lines, the generator, and anything man-made would be hauled to Mgogo's village to be safely stored for the next hunting season.

Masimba Camp, our little slice of heaven, would revert to wildlands. The long-awaited rainy season would fill the rivers with hordes of crocodiles and loads of hippos; the rocky creek beds we crossed daily would be impassable, filled with torrents of water; and the parched cracked earth would be alive with green growth and mired in mud.

The thoughts of destroying *Masimba* Camp left me dumbfounded, pleading to know why.

"Poachers," Joel solemnly answered. "Ohhh, they're bad. They move in if the camp isn't destroyed." He went on to explain that *Masimba* Camp, sitting on the border of Ruaha National Park, is the perfect staging area to kill animals in the park, as well as in the game reserve in which we hunted legally.

It turns out that it is no accident that many national parks are bordered by hunting concessions. Hunting camps and the huge swath of land they encompass are laced with PHs, Tanzanian game scouts, trackers, plenty of staff, and tons of activity. All of this provides a sort of buffer zone between poachers and the wildlife in the park systems, creating a literal human shield of *legal* activity, making poaching far riskier. The practice may seem contradictory, but it saves an untold amount of wildlife from slow torturous deaths.

Hunters and outfitters despise poachers and their inhumane unselective practices. In turn, poachers fear hunters, encampments, and the law that accompanies them. Lilian, as a law enforcement officer, was required to carry that heavy machine gun at all times for a reason. Such a gun might not easily do the trick against an attacking animal, but its purpose was geared towards poachers, not wildlife.

A few years ago, Rod and Sue were hunting in Tanzania and poachers were spotted in the distance. As the men fled into the bush, they could see that at least one had a gun. The entire hunting party--minus Rod and

Sue--dashed after them in pursuit. Ultimately, the poachers got away when they disappeared into dense brush making it too dangerous to follow. It was a prime example of why poachers do not want to be anywhere near legalized hunting activities.

While Rod and Sue were asked to join the chase, they refused. Loathing poachers and shooting them are two different balls of wax. Some countries have tried, or still have, a controversial shoot-to-kill policy when it comes to poachers. According to Lilian, Tanzanian game scouts are directed to arrest poachers to give them their day in court. They are to shoot only those "who intend harm, have weapons, or if the situation makes it necessary."

Upon learning of the dismantling of our little piece of paradise--and why--my eyes watered with emotion.

"Ahhh, don't worry," Joel assured me. "As soon as the rainy season ends, the camp will be here again."

He explained that it would take 30 villagers approximately 30 days to rebuild the remote little paradise. All the supplies would be brought back; grasses would be cut and lashed together to make new roofs, walls, bunks, and fences. The *mesa*, bath shelters, kitchen area, skinning shed, and multiple shade shelters would be rebuilt; solar panels would be set up and electric wires restrung. In thirty days, the camp would be alive again, new and refreshed, ready for the next season.

Operating camp. Dismantling camp. Rebuilding camp. Such time and effort from *so* many people for us to enjoy Tanzania's remote magnificence in the relative luxury that we, as Americans, have come to expect. It was truly humbling. The more I learned, the larger my guilty conscience grew.

Just as the guilt felt like an elephant on my back, Joel continued, "Ahhh, don't worry. It is a very good thing."

Rebuilding the camp each year creates many jobs for villagers who, otherwise, had few employment opportunities. Plus, those working at camp during the hunting season enjoyed coveted well-paying jobs, relatively speaking, for many months of the year. In fact, most of the staff returned year after year. Jobs in the villages were few and far between with little earning potential. The workers at *Masimba* Camp made more money than most factory employees and day laborers in the cities. It's worth noting that in 2020, 80 percent of the total Tanzanian population lived on less than $3.20 a day.

The employment created by building and running this camp was just a tiny piece of the puzzle. Joel reminded us of the incidentals: the food and supplies purchased in Arusha; the airplane chartered to fly into the bush; the small airport that handled the charter, us, and supplies; the international airport with its dozens of workers; the hotels at each end of our stay; and the various drivers to shuffle us between destinations. You also can't visit such an amazing place without taking home mementos, souvenirs, and gifts. Then there were the animals to consider: hides and horns to be taken to Arusha where they would be treated with solvents and insecticides and prepared for shipment to the States. This all involved various shipping companies, government officials and customs agents.

Until Joel pointed all this out to us, I had never considered the trickle-down effect of our 23 days in the country and how it provided income for so many people.

At the tail end of our tour, while I was still processing Joel's information, Hilary showed up and chimed in. "You must understand. While your being here has provided money and jobs for many people, you have done something even more important than that. You have made the remote lands of Rungwa West very valuable. Lands that most non-hunting tourists will not pay to see."

Seeing my rather clueless expression, he went on to explain that most non-hunting tourists want to see gobs of wildlife in a relatively small area, with sweeping vistas and majestic scenery as a bonus. In addition, most travelers want their destinations to be reasonably priced and easy to get to while offering plenty of hotels, restaurants, and other tourist activities along the way. They also don't want to deal with Tsetse-flies.

The wheels in my brain started turning. It was true--Rungwa West had *none* of that. The remote section of Tanzania that we traveled to was spectacular because it *was* Africa; but its scenery, animal concentrations, and lodgings were humble compared to other well-known tourist destinations.

The dry, flat scrublands that carpet the terrain during the dry summer months change into an almost impenetrable waterlogged landscape during the wet season, evident from the multitude of water-gouged ravines, oven-baked elephant potholes, and pictures Lilian shared of hazardous creek crossings during anti-poaching operations. We bobbed along the rough trails, exposed to the elements, for sometimes 12 hours a day crisscrossing the 540 square miles of Rungwa West Game Reserve. Some days were enough to suck the life out of you. Still, I came to appreciate the bobblehead safaris as part of the adventure. Not all people would agree with my line of thinking.

Since we were in a hunting concession, not a national park, animals rarely stuck around to pose for the camera. The wildlife in such isolated areas wasn't accustomed to an endless parade of tourists driving by. We enjoyed most species in fleeting moments or from a distance. My pictures, typically snapshots of hindquarters melting into the bush or dots on the horizon, attest to that fact. Even a six-ton elephant, amazingly, can somehow vanish within moments.

Also, to take pictures of animals--even the ones willing to stand still--one must be able to *see* them. Period. Not all of Africa is a wide-open savanna, allowing animals to be easily visible. Large parts are forested, have dense brush, or involve terrain that can't be navigated in a safari vehicle. Plus, not all areas have the favored species that people expect to see when they travel across the globe.

Sleeping arrangements were also something that tourists must consider. The idea of sleeping on a cot behind a piece of fabric with lions roaring just outside is not for everyone. It had taken me only one night to fall in love with the ghostly compositions of "The African Symphony", as I came to call it; yet it would be a lie to say it wasn't also bone-chilling.

One must remember that comfort, and everything for that matter, is relative. Rick and I viewed *Masimba* Camp as a literal haven compared to our typical elk camp. I can't tell you how pampered I felt by the simple joy of a flushing toilet instead of an outhouse, a makeshift shower instead of a pan of hot water, and a zippered tent that small varmints couldn't slink into. There are many people, like me, who would love this arrangement.

Still, many others would view our little oasis as primitive and intolerable. Not everyone would be on board for standing on a dirt floor after stepping from the shower, scanning for snakes in the rafters while relieving yourself, sleeping behind anything other than solid secure walls, and having no choice of menu. They might prefer air-conditioning, swimming pools, afternoon massages, hairdryers, tourist activities, and access to a hospital.

One also cannot overlook the money factor. If it hadn't been for Rick's desire to hunt, we would never have justified the money for a chartered flight or the alternative, 16 punishing hours perched atop a pitching Land Cruiser. No way. Not when there are five national parks within three hours of Arusha, including the famous Ngorongoro Crater and Kilimanjaro National Park. Even the world-renowned Serengeti National Park is only eight hours from Arusha. For anyone on a budget wanting easy access, cushy lodgings, and breathtaking scenery with oodles of animals unafraid of people, those are great destinations. They were *exactly* where *I* would have gone--*if* I wasn't with hunters.

Rungwa West is not alone. There are huge chunks of Africa that simply cannot offer the checklist items that parks can offer.

Realizing all this, clarity overcame me. That is where well-managed hunting comes in. Hunters do not need, or even want, *any* of that. In fact, they want the exact opposite. They want remote unaltered wilderness where game remains wild. Heck, most hunters would sleep on a bed of nails in the middle of Timbuktu if they had to.

Hunting, by making wildlife valuable as a renewable resource, makes land that is unsuitable for general tourism extremely valuable. That in turn offers an incentive to keep the habitat in its natural state, ultimately protecting that habitat from human-related growth.

Africa's human population is booming. Estimates expect the continent's population to double by the year 2050. That means more and more stress will be put on the continent's limited resources as humans and their ways of life expand into areas once inhabited primarily by wild species. Wild habitat is being transformed into grazing lands, agricultural areas, mines, logging sites, wood for cooking fires, and infrastructure. Also, water, critical to wildlife populations, is being diverted for livestock, human households, crop irrigation, and other human-related endeavors. Population growth, and all that it entails, also leads to habitat fragmentation. Land is being carved up and split into smaller pieces thus reducing ranges and restricting movements for natural migrations. Not only does this affect genetic diversity, it often prevents animals from accessing water sources needed during droughts.

Habitat loss due to human expansion is, therefore, *the* most critical threat to *all* African species. Period. End of Story.

Everything clicked and I had my *aha* moment, so to speak. Hunting offered many benefits but, above all else, it protected vast chunks of habitat that non-hunting tourists had little interest in. Hunting made less impressive lands valuable and worth saving *without* transforming them in any way. The proof was in the pudding, smack dab in front of my face all along.

An aerial view of the Maswa Game Reserve boundary in
northern Tanzania showing the habitat protected from
human encroachment by hunting concessions. (2020)

This realization did not come to me from blindly believing everything
that our hosts had shared with us during the camp tour. It was because the
words made perfect sense. My mind *knew* it to be true. More than that, I
could *feel* it to be true, not just in my heart but deep down in my bones.
Not just figuratively but literally. Bouncing over pocked terrain through
a nondescript sun-scorched landscape with sweat running down my back
watching fur-covered butts disappear into the bush as Tsetse flies have their
way with me offered a kind of clarity that can't be read in a book.

Joel and Hilary hadn't been exaggerating the importance of hunting to their economy. Maybe they didn't even realize the full extent of it. Lilian later emailed me a paper written by Priya Miller in 2017 entitled, "The Economic Significance of Hunting Tourism in Tanzania."[1] Miller writes an in-depth study of the monetary value between the hunting industry and the tourism industry. Although she found that the hunting industry has room for improvement, she discovered that it essentially took 29 photo tourists to generate what one hunter produces.

Another study led by University of Zimbabwe researcher Peter Lindsey found that hunters spend 14 times more than ecotourists in Tanzania and 30 times more in Zimbabwe.[2] In addition, the money spent by photo tourists is highly localized. Much of their money goes directly to the business owners and a handful of businesses clustered around national parks whereas money spent on trophy fees goes directly to concession holders and local communities. Also, since hunting concessions are widely dispersed throughout the country, the money is spread throughout multiple communities. The study also found that many booking agents for ecotourism are based outside of Africa. Consequently, a large portion of the money from those enterprises never even makes it into the country. On the other hand, nearly 93 percent of hunting operations are based in Africa, so the money stays *in* Africa.

In a privately-owned protected area adjacent to Kruger National Park in South Africa the difference in income was staggering. According to the 2020 African Sustainable Conservation News article "Sustainability and the Funding of the Timbavati Private Nature Reserve," it took 24,000 tourists in 2016 to create less than a third of the income earned from the 46 hunters who visited during the same period.[3] That translates to 1,600 photo tourists to replace the income generated by one hunter. That is a mind-blowing number.

Numbers, of course, vary greatly from country to country and area to area, but there is little dispute that it takes far fewer hunters to generate the same income as scores of non-hunting tourists.

There are many reasons that hunting is more lucrative. The money paid to hunting outfitters is significantly larger than that of general tourism. A much larger staff is needed, like that of *Masimba* Camp's 21 people; the average stay for hunters is much longer than photo safaris; and there are multiple layers of legislative fees the government requires for hunters that don't exist for non-hunters. Still, the trophy fees associated with hunting are ultimately what makes hunting so much more profitable than other forms of tourism. Part of these payments goes to the outfitter and part to the government to fund conservation projects and the Ministry of Natural Resources and Tourism.

The environmental imprint of each type of tourism must also be considered. It takes fewer resources to accommodate one hunter compared to the equivalent of eco-tourists. To house, feed, and transport hundreds of tourists requires a huge number of supplies and raw materials. More lodges and hotels, often with fancy pools and plush amenities that the general tourists prefer, must be built. Ones like I pictured in my original dream of Africa. Also, ecotourists stay an average of one or two days at a place before moving on, thereby requiring new bedding each time they leave. The majority of hunters on the other hand prefer more rustic lodging, do not bounce from lodge to lodge, and stay much longer.

Eco-tourists usually book one or two game drives a day and expect to see a large amount of wildlife in a fairly short amount of time. This is not always sustainable in a natural environment. To accommodate the photo tourists, more roads and infrastructure must be constructed. Food and water must be supplied in a place that is lacking both. There is also waste material that must be dealt with. All of these needs and activities destroy wildlife habitat and create a larger carbon footprint on the land, instead of keeping it intact as hunting does.

It should also be recognized that studies have found that any lands where ecotourism *can* work are *already* being utilized.

Please don't misunderstand me. I am not criticizing general tourism or "non-consumptive" tourism as it is often referred to. It is critical for the economic well-being of the African people and the protection of huge tracts of animal habitat. It safeguards entirely different segments of land while offering a huge array of economic opportunities throughout the continent. I am just pointing out that no type of tourism doesn't consume valuable resources of some kind--whether land, water, minerals, or wildlife.

Even so, there are debates over which type of tourism is best for Africa. Some claim that the money brought in by ecotourism is greater overall. Others claim that the revenue brought in by each hunter through hunting tourism, or "consumptive" tourism, is much higher with much less impact on the environment. The thing is, both are largely true. The real question we must ask is, "Why does one have to be exclusive of the other?"

Tanzania and many other countries simply cannot afford to sacrifice the money generated by hunting tourism and the large tracts of habitat that it protects. They also can't afford the loss of money generated by ecotourism or the loss of habitat that national parks protect.

Africa one hundred percent needs *both*, without sacrificing one for the other. Conservation efforts are best served when both forms of tourism coexist peacefully and work together to preserve as much habitat as possible.

Knowing that *Masimba* Camp would be dismantled upon our departure still made me a little sad. On the flip side, I was happy that our little sanctuary would be returning to the resident elephants and many other creatures who added their beastly cries to the nightly symphony. No permanent structures had been built. No habitat had been destroyed. Our safari provided jobs for local Tanzanians as well as many others in the cities.

Masimba Camp might not be a paradise to everyone, but for Rick and me, it was already priceless. We were in the African bush after all: a place where the cries of lions, hippos, and hyenas filled the nights with foreboding and dread, but also with wonder and intrigue; a place that allowed us to immerse ourselves in nature, along with incredible beasts who remained wild and unfettered by fences.

Hunting also enabled us to build relationships with the locals, which would have been much more difficult from the seat of a safari vehicle packed with people moving from lodge to lodge every few days. Even after just a short time, I became attached to the staff. Not only did they readily share their culture and knowledge, but they also accepted us as friends. From their most grandiose deeds down to the most minute details, I was humbled by their efforts.

These bonds of friendship not only facilitated a comfortable, safe, once-in-a-lifetime experience in the Tanzanian bush, but they also opened my eyes to so many things, offering me a completely new perspective. Another level of knowing. A whole different way of being. One that allowed me to see *the big picture*, so to speak, when it came to hunting. The successful harvest of any animal would still bring about conflicting emotions. That would never go away. Even so, all my doubts about hunting's value in Africa completely vanished.

There simply aren't enough words to convey my gratitude and appreciation to our Tanzanian counterparts for opening their hearts to us and making the life-changing experience so remarkable. *Asante sana rafikas.* Thank you, my friends.

PERCEPTION VERSUS REALITY

L ying wide-eyed with grilled zebra digesting in my stomach, I couldn't help realizing that I was a bit of a hypocrite. Rick's zebra hunt and the challenge it presented blew my perception of the horse-like animal. Then I had the *aha* moment during the camp tour that made it utterly clear why hunting was so important in Africa. The weird thing is, I already recognized the merits of hunting in America. I knew our pay-for-play system of conservation worked. In fact, it not only worked, but it also excelled. Yet, I had come to Africa with resistance to hunting, largely based on preconceived notions.

The words of Theodore Roosevelt, our 26th President, came to me: "Wildlife and its habitat cannot speak, so we must and we will." These simple words essentially led to the preserved places of America that we know today, a place with wilderness areas, public lands, and ample wildlife. Much of which we came close to losing.

By the turn of the twentieth century, America's wild species were in a bad place. The country's rapid westward expansion, market hunting, trapping, and invasive species pushed many of the animals that we now take for granted, and sometimes considered a nuisance, to the brink of extinction. American bison came close to being completely wiped out, reduced to 300 individuals from a staggering 30-60 million. Bighorn sheep, elk, deer, and a host of other game weren't faring much better, existing at only a fraction of the numbers they enjoy today.

Roosevelt was not just a president, he was an avid hunter. In his quest to hunt America's big game he chronicled his hunting trips while lamenting the loss of species, habitat, and the effects of overgrazing on wildlands. At the time, this was unprecedented because most people still considered America's resources inexhaustible. Thankfully he, John Muir, and a few others had the foresight to see its impending destruction.

Roosevelt was a dynamic force who believed "the rights of the public to the natural resources outweigh private rights". During his presidency from 1901 to 1909, this philosophy set in motion legislation that protected nearly 230 million acres of public land; created the United States Forest Service; and established 150 national forests, 51 federal bird reserves, 4 national game preserves, 5 national parks, and 18 national monuments, effectively earning him the title of the "conservationist president".

While Roosevelt got the ball rolling with the creation of so many protected areas, 30 years later the Pittman-Robertson Act gave it momentum with an 11 percent excise tax on hunting arms and ammunition. This important tax--which has cumulatively generated over $12 billion to restore, manage, and conserve the resources initiated by Roosevelt--is almost entirely responsible for the resurgence of multiple species.

It's hard to fathom, but in 1900, according to the Rocky Mountain Elk Foundation, America had only half a million whitetail deer compared to 32 million today.[1] The story is the same for other wildlife: 100,000 turkeys grew to 7 million; 12,000 pronghorn antelope surged to over 1.1 million; 41,000 elk also grew to more than a million; ducks barely existed but now number over 44 million; and the bison population rose from that piddly 300 to over 385,000. With habitat protections for game species, the nongame species—including bald eagles--soared as well. These drastic increases were all achieved with, and because of, well-managed hunting.

Yet, because of the exotic nature of African animals and my emotional attachment to them, I resisted everything I knew about hunting's conservation benefits. It had taken several days, with real-life experiences, for my views to evolve. It made me consider another juncture in my life. A time when my beliefs and convictions, once viewed through real-world experiences, were challenged.

Growing up in Pennsylvania, where it was exciting to see a coyote, I was captivated by wolves. Their beauty, intelligence, tenderness towards their pack, and likeness to the domesticated dog also trigger affection, adoration, and glorification by large segments of society.

Not everyone agrees with that line of thinking. People living on the front lines with wolves, and dealing with their aftermath, tend to have a vastly different perspective. Instead, they view them as ravenous killers.

Such grossly differing views involving an animal treasured by many leaves little doubt they are the most polarizing creatures in all of America. Some people want wolves to have free rein with no management of any kind while others want them all dead.

As someone enchanted by wolves, I wrote countless letters to congressmen as instructed by wolf-advocacy groups, donated money, and supported the wolf's reintroduction into Yellowstone National Park. I wanted them to flourish with little personal care for the consequences. *Who cares about those ranchers losing sheep and cattle? They can be reimbursed. Right?*

Truly, I didn't want anyone to suffer but I was a naive young idealist being ruled by emotion and a romanticized view of the dog-like species. I wanted them free, wild, and everywhere.

Looking back, it was unjust of me to take that stance. My money at the time was earned working in a steel mill and my days off were spent water-skiing at my Grandma's river camp. Nevertheless, from my industrialized corner of the world, I championed a crusade that would have no effect whatsoever on me directly, without having done research to back up my position.

As the saying goes, *be careful what you wish for*. Who would have thought that 10 years after sending countless wolf reintroduction letters I'd be living smack dab in the middle of wolf country? Fate is a funny thing.

Just a few months after Rick and I were married, we moved back to the ranch so that Rick's 15-year-old daughter, Mandi, could live with us. That was the year 2000, five years after the first wolves were released into Yellowstone National Park and the state of Idaho. Not only had the reintroduction been a success, the wild canines were thriving.

When I first started going on hunting trips with Rick, the wolves had yet to take hold in the areas that we were familiar with. Rick's elk camp was only an hour's drive down forest service roads and then another six miles up an ATV trail to a small meadow on a ridge overlooking thousands of acres of forest. Once camp was reached, hiking boots were the mode of travel. Luckily, you could huff and puff your way to elk hotspots within five miles of the tent. The countryside was spectacular; the campfires toasty;

the food yummy; and the camaraderie priceless. My brothers, nephews, and friends were always a part of the equation.

Even in those days when there was a lot of elk, shooting one was rarely easy. By no means did purchasing an elk tag guarantee success--not by a long shot. It involved hiking miles and miles of steep country to scout multiple clear-cuts or open meadows. More often than not, my brothers traveled 3,200 miles from Pennsylvania to return home with no more than aching muscles, blisters, and stories to tell-- lots of stories.

Still, back then, elk were always at least part of the equation. The opportunity for a bull was on the next hillside cleared by logging, over the next ridge, or down the next ravine. Days were spent not only with sore muscles but filled with anticipation, exhilaration, and promise.

As years passed and the number of wolves increased, the elk population dwindled more and more until we were lucky to spot any at all. The last time Rick hunted that area, or tried to, I was with him. We climbed and descended mile after air-sucking mile scouting every clear-cut and meadow we could access during the week. We saw none of their telltale hoof prints or egg-shaped droppings. Instead, we saw large whitish, turd-shaped masses of matted hair, barely recognizable as feces. It was everywhere.

Wolves had overtaken the area. None of the scat was new. The elk were long gone and so, too, were the wolves. They'd moved on to greener pastures so to speak, leaving devastation in their wake. The only sign that elk had existed anywhere in those mountains was in the aged, fur-laced, dung littering the forest. It was devastating and heartbreaking to see what one exploding population of predators could do to a prey species.

That was our last time hunting in that area. To justify the work of setting up camp, as well as the torment and abuse to the body, there has to be at least some potential for success, to at least know the animals are there. *Somewhere.*

When I began joining Rick in Idaho's backcountry, another perception of mine was blown out of the water: the effect of clear-cut logging on the ecosystem, a practice that uniformly cuts down *all* trees in a section of forest. The environmental action alerts from my twenties showed closeups of barren mountainsides piled with logging debris but devoid of trees. The pictures looked like remnants of a war zone. You guessed it. More letters to congressmen and more donations to various organizations.

Imagine my shock when the very place we searched for elk were those clear-cut sections of forest, natural meadows, or fire-ravaged areas. Elk are grazers and browsers, essentially feeding on grasses and low-growing vegetation, both of which thrive on open lands which allow for new growth. Forests are necessary for cover but when they become too dense, the lack of sunlight eventually kills much of the vegetation, taking away a variety of food sources. Patches of open areas, at different phases of rebirth, offer elk and other wildlife a diverse healthy habitat where they can thrive. Never was this fact mentioned in the action alerts I had received.

Witnessing the immensity of Idaho's forests firsthand, it became clear that much of the information I had been fed in my twenties was only half of the story. The pictures were real, taken right after logging *before* the slash piles were burnt and new trees planted. What the pictures didn't show was the thousands of acres of remaining forests surrounding the small chunks of clear-cuts, a humongous puzzle, so to speak, with missing pieces scattered throughout, but, instead of a missing piece ruining a puzzle's beauty, it enhanced it with contrast and variety. Pictures showing *only* the closeups, not the vastness of trees surrounding each cleared piece of land, are distorted, effectively leaving an impression of devastation and destruction. These half-truths were highly successful in getting my support as well as my money.

Don't get me wrong. Environmental protection and regulations are absolutely necessary. Without them, it is scary to think of what our natural world might look like today. Facts, however, are often manipulated to appeal to various values, emotions, and attitudes. Usually, the truth lies somewhere in the middle. Too often, regulations are put in place, not for biological reasons but to appease special interest groups on both sides. Facts should decide policy, not emotions. Sentiment and passion can be easily manipulated. Their tactics certainly pulled at my heartstrings.

Originally, when legislation was passed to reintroduce wolves into Idaho, there was supposed to be a fixed amount. With the state's hands tied due to legislation, they were unable to manage the wolves' numbers causing their population to explode, decimating elk and other prey animals.

Some areas of Idaho were hit much harder than others, especially the more remote rugged areas where wolves thrive. In any zone that had a moderate to high wolf population, the elk populations declined sharply. Two of the zones are within an hour's drive of our home. According to the Idaho Fish and Game Department, the elk in the Lolo zone decreased from 16,054 elk in 1989 to 2,178 in 2010, a decrease of about 86 percent.[2]

To keep it fair and to look at both sides of the equation, one must recognize that wolves are not entirely to blame for the elk's drastic decline. The huge fires of 1910 and 1930 created hundreds of thousands of acres of prime habitat enabling them to thrive. As the forests replenished themselves, elk habitat shrank. Because of years of fire suppression, no new burn areas were created to replace the elk habitat lost as the forests regrew. Decreased logging also lowered the amount of new browsing habitat. Mother Nature, too, had her hand in the nasty business. Extremely harsh winters made survival even tougher. Lastly, wolves aren't the only predators that prey on elk. Bears and cougars also do their fair share of plundering prey species, especially the calves. Therefore, when the number of those predators increases, elk take another hit. As with most things, there is typically no one simple answer.

Even with all these factors in play, it is hard to ignore the fact that elk numbers plummeted drastically in the same period that wolves thrived. The numbers may be argued, but it is indisputable that *unmanaged* wolves do have a drastic impact on elk populations.

Adult wolves are 4 to 6 feet long, weighing over 100 pounds. They are lethal predators in their own right, but with a pack, they are killing machines. Elk aren't the only species to have suffered from the wolf's thriving populations. Moose were plentiful in Idaho when Rick was growing up. Now it's a rarity to get a glimpse of one of these lumbering giants. Deer have fared a bit better because they tend to live closer to civilization. Wolves avoid such places like the plague.

Ranchers have lost thousands of cattle and sheep over the years costing taxpayers millions of dollars in reimbursements. Many ranchers never receive any kind of compensation. The livestock in rural areas is often set loose to graze for months at a time before being rounded up in the fall. Finding and documenting wolf kills in such remote terrain, months after the fact, is about as feasible as herding cats.

Wolves don't kill only to eat. They are extremely territorial and adamant about slaughtering any canine-related rivals, including my Rags and your Fido if they have the opportunity. Hounds that spend lots of time in the woods are especially susceptible to being slain. Ranch dogs, or herding dogs, are also extremely at risk. These highly skilled cattle dogs are critical for rounding up cattle in steep rugged terrain or brushy areas that horses can't access. Friends of ours who work a large ranch across the river from us lost five cattle dogs to wolves in the 2019 season alone.

Hunting dogs. Ranching dogs. Pets. It doesn't matter to the wolf. Any of man's best friends found in the wilderness are goners. Since my Raga-muffin was always with us, even on hunts, that was a huge concern. Rags, a scruffy, curly-haired, lab-schnauzer mix who showed up on our doorstep the same month we moved to Idaho, didn't have a mean bone in his body. His gentle, loving nature made him a constant fixture at my side. He was also a constant source of amusement as he dove, dashed, and launched himself in unending, mostly unsuccessful, pursuits of chipmunks anytime we were in the woods. Still, when it came down to business, he crouched beside me waiting patiently for Rick to do his thing.

Not fans of rising at 'o-dark-thirty', Rags and I often skipped the morning hunt and cozied up in the tent until a sane hour. Later, I'd read a book by the fire while he'd chase furry-tailed tormentors around the woodpile. After a few hours, we'd venture out for a hike.

It was those days at camp when Rick and the guys were gone that convinced me that I needed to know how to handle a pistol. Just like hunting isn't my thing, neither are guns. While Rick encouraged me to practice shooting, it wasn't until the wolf problem and my concern for Rags that I relented. Wolves aren't prone to attacking people, but my devoted little buddy would have been destroyed in a New York minute. I had no desire to kill anything, but if it was to protect that mutt of mine, you can bet your bottom dollar I would have pulled the trigger.

Horses are another animal at risk in the backcountry. A few years ago, a man from our area was camping close to where we used to camp. His four horses were tethered to the horse trailer for the night while he slept. A commotion alerted him that wolves were attacking. One of the pregnant mares flipped over, breaking her neck in an attempt to escape. Two of the horses broke their halters and fled. After searching for over a week, the horses were never found. The man lost three horses and an unborn colt that night. For horse people, losing a horse is like losing a fur baby-- it's heartbreaking. No monetary reimbursement can replace the years of training and emotional attachment.

This man lost his horses only a few months before I found myself squatting above that hole in the ground with a packrat above my head and wolves howling in the distance. While it was chilling, figuratively and literally, we had little to fear. Wolves rarely attack humans. Even our mules had little to worry about. The donkey part of their nature assures they will fight, rather than flee. The sturdy, draft-size mules, nine of them, tethered to a high line allowing some freedom of movement, would have stomped, bit, and pummeled the attackers.

With that being said, the elk were not so fortunate. We spent a week hiking up and down steep slopes in frigid temperatures without seeing even one elk or any sign. Another elk-rich habitat had been decimated. We left dispirited and heartbroken, another hunting spot we have not returned to.

Once living in wolf country, it is easy to understand why wolves are so polarizing. Many ranchers, farmers, business owners, hunters, and locals who are directly experiencing the devastating effects of such destructive predators are on one side of the fence. Some of these people want every single wolf exterminated, never to return. They paint wolves as nothing but cold-blooded killers totally to blame for the decline in elk populations since they kill indiscriminately, wastefully, and excessively. Nothing will convince them that there are other factors in play as well.

On the other hand, wolf advocates make wolves out to be gentle loving canines, a romanticized unrealistic view presented by people who live far away from the effects of them. Many people, including me in my twenties, fight tooth and nail to protect that one species at the expense of all others, including humans and their livelihoods.

Many animal rights advocates support letting nature take its course. Unfortunately, it is too late for that. Man's meddling over the past centuries has created unnatural imbalances that can't be extinguished by simply taking our hands off the reins. Too much habitat has already been destroyed or altered and too many good-intentioned people want to transform the natural way of things and protect everything. This approach has given predacious species an unfair advantage. Consequently, unchecked predators--feral cats, coyotes, bears, cougars, raccoons, foxes, and many others--are drastically reducing prey populations throughout the Americas.

Four-legged predators, unlike well-managed hunting, don't specifically target males; they prefer the weakest and most vulnerable. Typically, that involves females and their young, the very animals critical to growing populations. The sacrifice of a few males by hunters still leaves plenty of males available for breeding purposes.

Looking back, it upsets me that I didn't look at the flip side or research the things I was fighting for. What right did I have to impose my sentiment on others, especially when it wasn't me who would feel the impact of my actions up close and personal? From a distance, with no skin in the game, I sat on my idealistic high horse with judgment and disapproval.

Eventually, my life experiences allowed me to look at things from both perspectives. I came to know the hard-working, salt-of-the-earth people whose lives were unfavorably affected by wolves.

That doesn't mean I, or *most* people in wolf country, want wolves totally gone. Absolutely not. Wolves *should* be a part of our wild areas, but so, too, should elk. The sound of the elk's bugling and mating ritual belongs in the forest as much as the wolves' vocal exhibitions. Both primal dialogues make the woodlands whole.

It's kind of funny when you think about it. My bond with people who I rallied against in my twenties is what allows me the opportunity to experience wolves in the wild. Huddled around a wood stove with hunters, I can appreciate the wolves' soulful howling as they call to each in their mournful-sounding dialogue. Just like the cries of the lions and hyenas, the wolves' haunting vocals are somehow beautiful, eerie, mesmerizing, and enlivening at the same time. You feel the echoes of their bestial cries deep in your core, reminding you of times long ago. Simpler times. Times when man and beast lived almost wholly as predator and prey.

Fortunately, after years of unbridled wolf population growth and the ensuing court battles, Congress finally delisted them from the endangered species list. This has enabled the Idaho Fish and Game Department to take over wolf management based on biological data, thereby giving elk a fighting chance.

In addition, the forest service is helping by creating more elk feeding grounds with the use of controlled burns and letting some wildfires burn unchecked. After years of frustration and hard times, there is promise; elk populations have started to rebound. Areas that were decimated a few years ago are showing signs of the majestic animals once again. Bull antler sheds are being found in parts of the mountains that hadn't seen them for years. Forests that were void of the bull's distinctive bugle are once more hearing the deep resounding trumpets, high-pitched squeals, and succession of grunts again.

As noted, the elk population's rally did not happen on its own. It took the time, expertise, and resources of the forest service and others to improve habitat and actively manage predators, including wolves. All of this came with a price tag which hunters had their hand in as well.

The money dished out by hunters for the taxes resulting from the Pittman-Robertson Act mentioned earlier is just the tip of the iceberg. Hunters must purchase licenses, tags, and permits in amounts that can range from just a few bucks to thousands of dollars, depending on the species, the state, and other factors. Currently, money generated from such means provides about 60 percent of the funding for state agencies that manage most of the wildlife in the United States.

When you add all the income from hunters' fees, taxes, and donations, you will find that they contribute billions with a B to help species recover, preserve and improve habitat, and ensure that state fish and wildlife agencies have the funds needed.

Unfortunately, there is one huge problem with the current model. Hunting participation is plummeting nationwide in large part due to the loss of the baby boomers, which currently make up roughly one-third of all hunters in our nation. Quite frankly, even though they still have the heart of a hunter, their bodies resist. Retiring their hunting boots also means no more buying licenses, tags, and sporting equipment at a time when the younger generation is not filling the gap.

The sharp decline in hunters, along with their vast amount of money spent, has caused funding to nosedive, leaving wildlife agencies scrambling to find new sources of income. Staff positions are being left vacant and programs are being drastically cut.

Countering hunting's downward trend is an increase in birdwatching, hiking, photography, canoeing, biking, and other outdoor pursuits, many of which use the same lands protected by the funding from hunting and fishing. The problem is, other than buying a park pass, there are no fees or taxes associated with these activities or any corresponding gear. Therefore, much less money is available for protecting wild areas.

Congress, state governments, and agencies are aware of the increasing deficits in wildlife management and are considering other avenues, including adding a general sales tax, taxing outdoor equipment, or finding a way to monetize other outdoor activities. In addition, wildlife agencies are searching for ways to stop or reverse the loss of hunters and the money that goes with them. Ideas include making hunting more accessible and targeting the locavore movement (people who wish to eat local, sustainable, ecologically conscious meat).

Not having access to lands previously available had a huge impact on Rick's hunting. As a young hunter, the majority of the local farmers and ranchers were eager to allow hunters on their property. It stabilized the herds of deer, elk, and bear while decreasing the loss of their crops and pastures. Over time, these same animals became far too valuable to allow locals to hunt for free. Most of Rick's old stomping grounds, for instance, are now leased to outfitters who charge fees for guided hunts. Species that used to be considered a nuisance have now become valuable assets.

Boom! Another *aha* moment. While I had come to understand the importance of hunting in Africa to protect Africa's habitat, I had yet to consider this part of the equation. Why wouldn't placing a monetary value on African animals work the same way, especially when the wildlife they deal with is far more destructive than deer, elk, bear, or wolves? No matter how damaging and dangerous our wildlife can be to humans and their activities, they don't hold a candle to the menace created by lions, leopards, hyenas, and elephants.

Placing a monetary value on such creatures--as well as zebras, antelopes, and other species competing for grazing lands--gives local people an incentive to coexist with wildlife.

Wild creatures being more valuable than crops and livestock is a crucial part of why wildlife in Africa recovered significantly from their lows at the turn of the century, especially in South Africa and Namibia which are made up primarily of sizable farms and ranches. Trying to raise livestock or grow crops in arid and carnivore-infested lands while keeping monstrous grazers, like elephants, at bay was a daunting task. An adult elephant alone can eat between 200-600 pounds of food a day. Imagine that oversized lawn mower whittling down your crops and trampling your fields.

After years of struggling, a few perceptive ranchers in South Africa realized that the very creatures they were battling, and often exterminating, could be the source of their income with minimal work. No more planting crops. No more tending livestock. No more harvesting and transporting to market. They just had to let nature take its course. The concept worked. Managing for wildlife preservation as well as species variety and enhancement replaced crop rotations and livestock care. Within years, game farms took over traditional farms, allowing animal populations to soar.

In 1964, when South African game ranches were mere fledglings, the country had about 575,000 head of wild animals countrywide.[3] In 2020, that number has grown to 24 million, some of which were brought back from the brink of extinction. Currently, there are approximately 10,000 privately owned ranches covering an estimated 52 million acres, most in marginal agricultural areas. To put it in perspective, that is three times more land than all of the parks and reserves combined. The South African conservation success story is based on private ownership of land and wildlife, and the use of "sustainable utilization". This essentially means wildlife species are managed in such a way to sustain their populations and habitat over time considering the socioeconomic needs of human populations.

Namibia, nicknamed "the conservation capital of Africa", is also a shining star.[4] Upon its independence in 1990, the government enacted landmark legislation that gave community members the power to benefit from the proceeds of its wildlife resources. Over 40 percent of Namibia's surface area--including over 70 community-run conservatories—is under active conservation management, utilizing both ecotourism and well-managed hunting tourism. Empowering the people to experience direct benefits from wildlife protection has paid dividends. Wildlife numbers there continue to climb even as the populations of other countries fall. Namibia, therefore, has the honor of being home to the largest mix of wild animals and endangered species in Africa, including the largest free-roaming populations of cheetah and Black rhino in the world.

To understand this fully, we need to look at the opposite end of the spectrum. Kenya is the poster child for a country that went to the other extreme. In 1977, all hunting in Kenya, aside from bird hunting, was eliminated. Even landowners, regardless of ethnicity, have no right to kill wildlife on their property. The 2018 Earth and Environment article "Dramatic Declines in Kenya's Wildlife Demand an Urgent Response," states that wildlife declined by 68 percent overall in under 40 years, along with a huge depletion of diversity.[5] Some species have plummeted as much as 88 percent, and many are severely threatened or endangered.

Because nearly 70 percent of Kenya's wildlife exists in private or community areas, it doesn't fall under the protection of game reserves and national parks. With no financial incentive to live with wildlife, the local people kill them when human-animal conflict occurs and, instead, introduce more and more domestic livestock. While wild populations tanked, the number of sheep and goats increased by more than 76 percent during that same 40-year span.

Advocates of the hunting ban argue that population growth and economic expansion is the primary reason for the stark decline in Kenya's animals. But that is the point! Since wild species on the private property offer no cash value for landowners, there is no reason to protect them. But they can earn an income from farming and livestock without dealing with the havoc, destruction, and added expenses of living with wild creatures.

In short, money talks. If wild animals are more valuable than the land and livestock, they flourish instead of perishing, no matter what country they are in. That includes the beloved horse-like zebra, elephant, leopard, and lion.

Umphh. Simba's earlier-than-normal cry jolted me back to the present, but instead of hearing only the lion's beastly grunt, my mind took me back to Idaho. I remembered the mournful melodies of wolves sending shivers up my spine, while simultaneously filling my heart with wonder. The thoughts of a forest void of their ghost-like presence and soulful howls are tragic. But I also remembered the consequences of their more savage side when paired with a lack of management.

Even with my past experiences, I had based my reluctance of hunting certain species on my emotional attachment to them, instead of respecting the views and management policies of the people who live alongside them.

Life is an unending series of twists and turns, allowing awareness in bits and pieces. My life's journey again offered me an opportunity to compare my perceptions against reality. Just as living in the heart of wolf country enabled my romanticized view to evolve into one that was more realistic, my views of Africa's wildlife evolved to become more practical. Its species are not animals from Disney movies. They are wild creatures surviving as nature intended, capable of gentleness as well as brutality. They deserve to be respected, loved, admired, and protected, but not idealized.

11
Honey, Put Your Shoes On

Through the haze of slumber, I felt Rick's hand grasp my shoulder. "Honey. Wake up," he whispered almost imperceptibly.

Something was different. More urgent. I could feel Rick's presence as he crouched beside me waiting for the fog to clear from my brain. Rolling over to face him, I found him sober faced. Not buoyant like typical safari mornings.

Once he had my full attention, he continued. "Honey, get up and put your shoes on. We might have to run."

Now *that* is a wake-up call you do not want to hear while sleeping, or trying to sleep, in the African bush, especially after a night of extra-lively beastly compositions. My drowsiness changed into alarmed confusion as I looked at him with huge question marks beaming from my eyes.

"Look out the window," he whispered.

Although it was pitch-dark, a small light near the solar panels provided a thin veil of illumination. Looking out the mesh opening beside his bed, all I saw was a blob--a big blob--more like a giant shadow. It was not the lion or hyena that I was fearing. The huge blob was a full-grown hippo only inches from our tent.

"Is it Willy?" I murmured. Willy was the resident male hippo who had just moved into the waterhole only yards from our tent.

"No, it's a mother and her calf. The calf is in front of her."

We had been warned, multiple times, that the most dangerous place to be in Africa is between a hippo and the water, the place where the jumbo-sized mamals feel all warm and fuzzy inside. Water is their safety zone. Blocking access to their refuge can, therefore, be extremely hazardous to your health. In addition, we were cautioned about their extremely protective nature when it came to their young. In short, unless we were ready to meet our

Maker, we should keep a respectable distance from any roly-poly mother-calf duos as well.

Avoiding both of these dangers, they assured us, was a piece of cake--just stay out of their way. While we were happy to heed their advice, they hadn't mentioned how to tackle the scenario we found ourselves in. Obviously, we weren't blocking the pair's passage to the hippo pool, but still, having 3,000 pounds of notoriously protective mama at arm's length was a bit troubling, to say the least.

We could hear the muffled snorts and grunts as the two hippos fed on the grasses just outside the tent. Yet, it was *almost* 5 a.m.--time to get up. Apparently, an animal capable of slicing you in two with one chomp of its giant mouth should not hinder your breakfast plans and, ultimately, delay the safari.

That was Rick's reasoning. He wanted to turn on the solar light so we could get dressed, but he wasn't sure how the motherly hippo would react. Consequently, we were to put our tennis shoes on and, at the moment of truth, be ready to sprint for our lives. Just in case.

I'm not kidding you. This was my typically bright husband's insane plan. Even worse, I blindly followed his instructions.

Quietly, we slipped into our sneakers and prepared for the fateful moment. Looking at me, he mouthed, "Are you ready?" I nodded consent. He flipped the switch, the light flickered on, and the mama hippo and her calf bolted toward their watery oasis. Crisis over. Rick would not be late for the daily safari!

The *Masimba* Camp resident hippos, or *kibokos*, were something we treasured, but *not* within inches of our tent. Their home in the pond of stagnant water may not look like much to humans, but to our jumbo-sized neighbors, it was life itself.

Hippopotamus, the Greek word for "water horse" or "river horse," is considered a semi-aquatic mamal that depends heavily, if not entirely, on water. Typically, hippos spend 19 to 20 hours a day lounging in their soupy sanctuaries. Originally, scientists believed hippos to be closely related to pigs, but more recent DNA analysis shows they are more closely related to dolphins, porpoises, and whales. Underwater recordings of hippos even show complex vocalizations that mimic that of their oceanic relatives.

While they may communicate similarly to their ocean-dwelling kin, there is one giant difference between the two. *Kibokos* don't swim. They sink to the bottom and use their stubby legs to propel themselves forward, giving the *perception* that they are swimming.

Still, like dolphins, hippos depend wholeheartedly on water for survival. The rotund water lovers have no sweat glands. Plus, they have delicate skin, relatively speaking for such a robust creature. Soaking in water and mud is the only way to regulate their body temperature and protect their exterior from sunburn. Without the cooling effect of water, the hippos' skin would dry out, causing them to die a slow, agonizing death.

For an animal living in the sweltering heat of western Tanzania, this is not a good thing. Sometimes you just have to shake your head. It seems the Creator might have thought that through a bit more.

Anyway, the fact that a *kiboko* sanctuary existed just yards from *Masimba* Camp was wondrous. Watching the lounging giants from the safety of the rocky outcropping above was a huge treat. With each female averaging about 3,000 pounds and the large males weighing up to 6,000 pounds, their combined body mass took up a large chunk of real estate in what was left of the river.

I always visited the *kibokos* during midday, so most of their bodies were submerged, except for a few forced to lounge in shallower sections. For the hippos holding the deep spots, only their eyes, ears, and nostrils poked above the murky water. This enabled them to see, hear, and smell while still keeping their bodies cool and protected from the sun. I learned they also have impressive lungs, allowing them to stay underwater for up to five minutes at a time.

Usually, the ones I saw seemed fairly mellow. Periodically, their mouths would gape open into almost 3-foot-wide displays of teeth and gums, in what I thought were acts of boredom. Yet, it turns out the yawn-like spectacles were the hippos' way of posturing for dominance, basically saying *don't even think about it.*

Showing mouthfuls of lethal ivory gets the point across pretty readily. Their incisors and lower canines are laser sharp and up to a foot long, creating deadly sets of choppers. Adult hippos can bite down with a force of 2000 pounds per square inch, enough to slice a 10-foot crocodile or small boat completely in half.

Hippo pods typically average 10 to 20 individuals, echoing *Masimba* Camp's size. The herds have a hierarchical society with one dominant male acting as leader. The rest of its members consist of a dominant female, lower-ranking females, their young, and a few non-breeding submissive males. The breeding bulls are very protective of their little harem and they use their display of deadly ivory, as mentioned above, to warn off rivals, along with loud grunts and aggressive splashes in the water.

As long as younger males don't challenge the big guy, all is hunky-dory. If one chooses to test the hierarchical waters and puff his chest up a bit, so to speak, bitter battles can ensue. The same goes for any non-herd rivals who show up to challenge the top dog's dominance. Bulls will clash viciously for hours at a time, sometimes fighting to the death. According to the 2016 Real Wild documentary "The Dark Side of Hippos," scientists believe that only about 10 percent of male hippos succeed in mating, which they believe may be the reason for so much hostility in male hippo societies.[1]

On top of aggressive behavior between males, hippos in general are very territorial. In fact, they are regarded as one of *the* most territorially aggressive herbivores. The size of the chunk of water they consider their own depends largely on the body of water and food supply. Understandably, when there is plenty of water and a large food supply, the hippo world is a happier place. During the dry season and times of drought, tensions escalate dramatically as large numbers of *kiboko* are forced to congregate in limited pools of water, all fighting for the deepest channels that provide relief from the sun.

Typically, new hippos moving into an established pool aren't well received. The overcrowding disrupts the social order, ultimately causing even higher levels of aggression. Hippos are also notoriously short-tempered and being forced into closer proxmity with one another is a recipe for disaster. Fights can break out over minor infractions. A hippo startled by a bird landing on its back, for instance, can cause a chain reaction of hostility. While such scenarios typically don't produce fights that last long, a couple of seconds is enough to do a lot of damage to a young hippo caught in the crossfire, sometimes fatally injuring him.

Bulls driven from a waterhole entirely are often forced into risky situations. On National Geographic's *Africa's Deadliest*, I watched a male hippo being violently forced from multiple waterholes. Desperate for water, he finally found a hippo-free oversized puddle guarded by an entire pride of lions. Yet, that tiny piece of real estate was more important to him than any consequences. With power, persistence, and his mouth's deadly arsenal, he drove off the king of predators and took command of the life-saving water without dying in the process.

All had seemed fairly peaceful in *Masimba* Camp's reservoir. The sporadic chuffs, grunts, and snorts had given us no indication that trouble was brewing in paradise. Yet, all was not sunshine and roses.

A young male had apparently grown too big for his britches. Perceived as a threat to the dominant bull, the hippo was booted out of the liquid gold he had previously called home, instead taking up residence in the waterhole below our tent.

Fortunately, the ousted male showed no visible wounds. Still, without water, he was at risk of an even more agonizingly slow death. The oversized puddle barely contained enough water to cover half of his body, exposing his entire back and part of his torso to the blistering sun. Thankfully, Lilian assured us that there was enough water to keep him alive until the rainy season expected in just a few weeks.

While there were no formal introductions to our portly neighbor, we did as Americans do and gave him a name. Willy seemed to fit a hippo quite well. Lilian agreed.

Willy making his home in the puddle near our tent.

Here is the weird thing. The hippo's aggressive, territorial, and hierarchical nature typically applies only in the water. During the four to five hours spent grazing on land every evening, much of the grouchiness toward each other pauses. Essentially the social but moody beasts become calm loners. This solitary nature away from water may be necessary to ensure each individual has access to enough feed.

To maintain their massive bodies, each hippo must guzzle down up to 150 pounds of vegetation each night, traveling up to 6 miles to do so. Feeding solo also offers a break from being forced into tight quarters with family members all day long. Even if we love our family to pieces, we can *all* relate to that.

Knowing the hippos' deadly potential and thus, giving them plenty of room, we had zero problems. Not once did the bulky pachyderms show any hostile behavior toward us.

A visiting warthog couldn't say the same. One afternoon Joel was performing a chore along the riverbed as vervet monkeys and bushbuck drank from the puddle below the *mesi*. Seeing the spot occupied, a large warthog boar ambled nonchalantly toward Willy's newly claimed domain, apparently oblivious that there was a new sheriff in town. After being kicked out of his previous oasis, Willy was in no mood to share.

As the warthog unwittingly approached, the hippo launched from the water with his mouth gaping, weapons exposed. The startled warthog sprinted for its life, almost plowing Joel over in the process. Thankfully, the nimble-footed boar veered at the last moment. Still, he succeeded in scaring the bejeezus out of our entertaining host. The ruckus caused the whole horde of peacefully drinking visitors to explode in flight.

"Ohhh. It scared me. It scared me a lot," Joel admitted while telling us the tale.

Fortunately, Joel's little episode ended with nothing more than a near heart attack and a good story to tell. Nevertheless, accidents do happen. Sometimes people are just in the wrong place at the wrong time. Hippos may look like they'd be a cinch to outrun. Assuming that, however, could get you killed. Considering the mamals' immense size, they are extremely fast, capable of 30 mph bursts. How Rick thought we'd be able to out-sprint one is beyond me.

Because of the *kiboko's* tunnel vision regarding their watery sanctuaries, villagers often get into trouble when using the same well-worn paths as hippos. One of Lilian's friends was using such a trail, lined with thick brush on both sides, when a hippo decided feeding time was over. Upon seeing a human obstruction in his way, the hippo charged forward at full speed. Lilian's friend leaped into the thicket and thankfully escaped being steamrolled by the 30-mph bulldozer.

Willy grazing near our tent.

A few seconds of hesitation on the girl's part and she would now most likely be six feet under. The hippo was just trying to get to water. There was no malicious intent. Still, the young lady would have been just as dead--accident or not.

People who don't live with the chunky amphibious mamals are often clueless about the threat they pose. Hippos are often portrayed as cuddly stuffed animals wearing ballerina tutus. Reality is far different. As with so many living things, they are part Dr. Jekyll and part Mr. Hyde.

Like lions, zebras, and many other species, male hippos practice infanticide. If a new male takes control, he may kill infants to force their mothers into estrus sooner. My addiction to wildlife shows has allowed me to witness this unpleasant reality on multiple occasions. The documentary mentioned earlier was able to film an underwater battle for life and death. A hippo calf dashed skillfully along the bottom of the riverbed, completely underwater, while trying to outrun the attacking male. As swift as the calf was, the new bull was faster. He grabbed the baby in his jaws and within minutes it was over.

Although hippos are classified as herbivores they are known to eat meat as well. Sometimes even their own kind. Hippos of course aren't the only animals who engage in cannibalism. Nature is a dog-eat-dog world--sometimes literally.

You can't blame wildlife for doing what it takes to survive no matter how gruesome it may seem. The problem is, the unpredictable, sometimes short-tempered *kibokos* who tend to become very protective of their domain often turn their lethal tactics on humans as well, and sometimes not *just* by accident. Other than crocodiles, hippos kill more people each year than any other species. Most sources estimate that the docile-looking pachyderms are responsible for over 500 human deaths a year. Other sources estimate closer to 3,000.

In truth, it is hard to determine exactly how many people die each year from hippo attacks, or attacks from any wild resident for that matter. Not only are accurate records not a priority in the bush, many people simply go "missing", their remains never found. While encounters with any number of critters--lions, elephants, crocodiles, hippos, hyenas, snakes, leopards, or Cape buffalo--could lead to an untimely death, Africa's efficient recycling system ensures the evidence is short-lived. Hyenas, vultures, and other scavengers devour every morsel, including many of the bones. Any skeletal remains are carried off and scattered.

Most human deaths resulting from hippos are a consequence of human-wildlife conflict. Many rural villages, understandably, are nestled along riverbanks, allowing easy access to water for themselves as well as their crops and livestock. Many waterside communities also rely heavily on fish for sustenance, putting them directly in the line of fire of territorial hippos. *Kibokos* also aren't opposed to filling their vast stomachs with the crops planted conveniently within walking distance. The bulky herbivores can put quite a hurtin' on poor villagers' food sources. To combat this, local people often station nightly lookouts near their plantings to drive off hippos and other animals before damage is done.

The majority of the time, if hippos are given space, villagers can go about their business unmolested. For those who are the exception to the rule or encroach on hippo territory unknowingly, it is a gory death. With habitat shrinking and human populations growing, requiring more food and water, it is easy to see that the problem will continue to escalate.

Hundreds of hippos are shot each year to minimize conflict with humans, either in preventative measures or in retaliation. A while ago, I watched the 2016 Carter's W.A.R episode "Death in the Water," a great example of what is occurring all over Africa. Ivan Carter, a conservationist and wildlife investigator, journeyed to a stretch of the Zambezi River where a lot of people were living close to hippos. The two came into close contact with each other on a nightly basis.

During the episode, Carter met a man who had escaped with his life after a gruesome hippo attack while attending the funeral of another man who had not been so lucky. He investigated to determine what was contributing to the increased attacks. Ultimately, Carter discovered that the human-hippo conflict was because more people were living and fishing on that stretch of river than ever before.

While examining the problem, another death occurred in a nearby village. Carter was therefore summoned to shoot the "offender". After doing some dangerous experiments using himself as bait, he found no particular rogue hippo to blame for the attack. Still, the anguished villagers wanted a hippo dead. It didn't matter if it was *the* offending hippo or not. While Carter understood the struggles of the rural people living with the beefy animals, he refused to kill an innocent hippo just to appease them.

The episode had no happy ending. The grieving villagers berated and blamed him. He withdrew somber and disheartened, knowing that the predicament was not a hippo problem. It was a human problem--one that offered no easy solution. As Carter often puts it, "When there is conflict between humans and wildlife, wildlife ultimately suffers most."

Historically, the hippopotamus was widely distributed throughout sub-Saharan Africa. Human encroachment, however, has decimated their historic range. In three African countries, they have gone regionally extinct. The 125,000 to 148,000 hippos remaining in the wild are largely confined to protected areas. In just the last ten years alone, their population has decreased by up to 20 percent. The IUCN currently lists the hippo as Vulnerable to Extinction, one category away from Endangered.

For hippos, another factor comes into play. Water. Expanding agriculture is gobbling up much more water than in the past. Many wetlands are being converted into croplands and rivers and lakes are being redirected to agricultural areas. Decreasing water supplies is therefore considered one of the main threats to the future of hippos and other water-dependent species. This issue is not exclusive to Tanzania. The entire continent is in the same boat.

It's impossible to discuss the plight of aquatic animals and human-wildlife conflict without talking about our other water-loving neighbor at *Masimba* Camp, Freddy, the 4-foot-long crocodile who also lived in the waterhole below our tent.

Freddy was quite secretive. As a small version of the notorious Nile crocodile, he was barely visible in the muddied pool of water. Most of the time,
he was little more than glowing eyes under the gleam of a flashlight each
night before we went to bed. Once in a while, we'd see him basking in the
sun during our midday break, but it certainly wasn't a regular occurrence.
Freddy's elusive nature and small size made him no threat whatsoever.
That can't be said for his larger kinfolk, though, as Nile crocodiles are the
largest and most distributed crocodile species across Africa. The lakes and
rivers of Central and East Africa are known for having the most sizable
concentrations, as well as the biggest specimens. Tanzania is crawling with
the giant reptiles. Literally.

During our time in Rungwa West, Freddy was the camp's only crocodile.
Soon after we left, the rains would engulf the withered savanna, transforming the landscape into a waterlogged countryside. While the saturated
terrain and overflowing river channels made anti-poaching patrols like Lilian's problematic, it was a boon for wild species, especially the amphibians
and reptiles. As the rivers filled, the crocodiles would return from their
dry season sanctuaries--deep, isolated pools that retained water throughout
the year in the otherwise dry riverbeds. Soon *Masimba* Camp's dried-up
riverbed would be full of much more than just water.

Africa's largest crocodilian has absolutely no Dr. Jekyll in him. He is
all Mr. Hyde, but an even deadlier, more horrifying, prehistoric version.
Crocs can grow to 20 feet long and weigh up to 2,400 pounds during
their 70-plus-year lifespan. Fortunately, the death-dealing predators average closer to 12 feet long, weighing approximately 600 pounds. Still, that
is quite a package of pure terror.

Crocs don't start as monstrous beasts. It takes many years before they're
large enough to take down the wildebeests we see getting devoured each
year during the Great Migration in the Serengeti National Park. Young
crocodiles eat anything and everything they can fit in their mouths: fish,
birds, frogs, crustaceans, locusts, and carrion. As the crocodile grows, so
does its prey size. This is not only by choice, it's also a necessity--as their
size increases, their dexterity and maneuverability decrease.

Crocodiles can't easily chase down prey, consequently, they are ambush
hunters that prefer their prey to come to them. Their sheer patience is
extraordinary and could teach humans, including me, a thing or two.
They can wait hours, days, and even weeks for the suitable moment to

attack. Once a potential victim strays within striking range, the attack is sudden and unpredictable. Anything and everything, including humans who venture near water, are a potential meal. A croc will feed on anything that it can outswim, ambush, or overpower.

Life for the crocodiles is typically feast or famine, so when food is plentiful they gorge themselves, eating up to half of their body weight in one feeding. Fortunately, their metabolism is designed to store the energy from nearly all the food they consume for future use. This is one of the reasons that larger crocodiles can survive over a year without eating a meal. While this may be possible, it certainly isn't their first choice. Research says that the average croc eats about 50 full meals a year.

The extremely indiscriminate appetite of the reptiles also means they aren't squeamish about eating their own kind. Cannibalism is highly practiced in the crocodile world, basically applying the same principle to all potential prey: if they can kill it, they will eat it. Only smaller reproductive-age females are sometimes spared from this fate by male crocodiles for obvious reasons. This croc-on-croc behavior may help keep populations stable. It's also the main reason why like-sized reptiles tend to hang out together. Adult crocs don't eat each other because they are too large and too tough, and the resulting fight would end with massive wounds to both individuals.

Crocodiles are highly equipped for their gruesome pursuits. They have keen hearing, can remain underwater for over an hour at a time, and are capable of swimming up to 20 mph. Even more notable, they have 64-68 teeth that sink into flesh, allowing a grip that is almost impossible to loosen. Their jaws are powerful, capable of 5,000 pounds of pressure per square inch.

Though a crocs' teeth are lethal, they aren't designed for chewing their meals. Prey is typically drowned first, then torn into chunks to be eaten piece by piece. When groups are sharing a kill, they use each other as leverage, biting down hard, and then twisting their bodies, ripping off pieces of flesh in what is known as a "death roll." Any unconsumed meat is stashed in the water under logs or other obstacles to decompose for later use.

You might imagine that such antics would be pretty hard on dental equipment. Not to worry. If these conical weapons are lost, they are quickly replaced. According to Live Science, a crocodile can go through over

8,000 teeth in its lifetime. Interestingly, while their bite strength is 50 times greater than that of a human, they have minimal opening strength, meaning a croc's mouth can be held shut with a human hand or piece of duct tape.

It is no coincidence that crocodiles live in tropical climates. Like all reptiles, they are cold-blooded, gathering heat from their environment. To control their body thermostat, they bask in the sun when cool and seek shade or water when hot. Another way of keeping cool is to open their mouths in a process called mouth-gaping, similar to panting. Being cold-blooded, they don't need to use their energy to maintain their body temperature. This is part of the reason they don't need food as regularly as other types of animals. During colder months or long periods of drought, they hibernate or go dormant.

Although crocodilians are nocturnal, they do hunt by day as well. This also means that there is no *safe* time for humans to be in, on, or near the water wherever these indiscriminate eaters live--especially since crocodiles are one of the few species that have no aversion whatsoever to taking humans for food. When it comes to man-eaters there is one simple rule--the bigger they are, the more dangerous they are. Rural people have no choice but to face these risks since they need water for themselves, livestock, crops, and fishing.

Crocodiles are responsible for the most human deaths in Africa. There are several reasons for this. First of all, the most obvious is their incredible savagery, indiscriminate appetite, and lethal tools of the trade. Second, there are a *lot* of them, and they are distributed far and wide. Third, crocs can live near people without ever being detected.

Typical of statistics in Africa, a tally of crocodile deaths is tricky to gather. Again, aside from very poor reporting systems where births and deaths aren't even registered, too many rural Africans simply vanish. This is especially true of croc victims, thanks to the crocs' tendency to drown, drag, and stash their prey away from the scene of the crime. Unless another person is present to witness an attack, there is absolutely no trace left to tell the tale. Still, most sources suggest that between 1,000 to 2,500 unfortunate souls lose their lives to the prehistoric reptiles each year.

According to the 2019 article "When and Where do Nile Crocodiles Attack?" in The Conversation, 51 percent of crocodile victims are under the age of 15.[2] Not surprisingly, the younger the child, the more vulnerable they are. While attacks can occur anytime, the most common occurred while the victims were swimming, bathing, or fishing.

Once, when chatting with Raphael, the subject of my family's river camp came up and I mentioned my obsession with stand-up paddleboarding. Instantly, he snapped his head towards me. In disbelief, he demanded, "What about the crocodiles?"

The crocodile's lethal nature jumped into Raphael's mind the second I mentioned swimming in a river. Raphael sat fascinated as I explained to him that except for the southern tip of Florida, America had no crocodiles and that our smaller, less aggressive alligators, only found in the waterways of the southern United States, pose far less of a threat to humans. He just stared at me in disbelief as I told him of my water skiing adventures in the alligator-inhabited wetlands of Myrtle Beach, South Carolina, in my early twenties.

That simple conversation is the perfect example of two cultures living two different realities. The people of Africa must deal with the atrocities inflicted upon them by crocodiles. We, on the other hand, get to appreciate the crocodile's wonder and ancient ruthless quest for food from afar. Horrified, yet captivated, we watch the desperate struggle of a zebra trying to escape a crocodile's jaws on a National Geographic program. While it is admirable that most of society wishes to preserve the prehistoric carnivores, they must recognize the issues revolving around living among them.

The Nile crocodile is currently listed as Least Concern on the IUCN Conservation Status List. So far, they have proved to be the ultimate survivors, existing since Jurassic times. That doesn't mean they don't need diligent protection.

Alleviating retaliatory and preemptive killings of crocodiles may be a bit easier than other species. With crocs, there is no mystery as to where they will be lurking. They will always be within feet of the water's edge, not stalking domesticated livestock, eating and trampling crops, or destroying the livelihoods of local peoples. Villages can reduce their exposure to the deadly reptiles by digging wells in the villages, refraining from swimming in crocodile-infested waters, and changing their fishing habits. Much of this, of course, boils down to money and a lot of effort.

The danger of living with hippos can be mitigated as well. Constructing fences and digging ditches can help deter them from accessing farmlands.

One village, for example, voluntarily moved five miles away from the river to alleviate the conflict. While in many ways it made their life more difficult, it also resulted in far less conflict with wildlife. Again, it takes money and effort.

It won't come as a surprise to you that one way to earn money and offer an incentive to live with such creatures is through the harvest of a very few mature males or, in some cases, specific problem animals. You've heard of the *Big Five*: elephant, lion, leopard, Cape buffalo, and rhinoceros. Well, there is also something called the Dangerous Seven. Crocodiles and hippos, with their high body count and lethal attributes, are the additional members of that notorious group.

If there is no incentive for rural villagers to change their behaviors, allowing for a more peaceful coexistence with such lethal species, many may resort to the tried-and-true-method: "shoot, shovel, and shut up."

While it may be tempting to judge people harshly for such actions, it's not our children who are driven to the water's edge by the blistering sun, our families who must go to the water's edge to bathe or collect water, or our spouses who must fish in the pitch black of night to bring home the only protein available.

The fact that *Masimba* Camp was a safe spot, relatively speaking, for its human residents was no accident. They took extensive preventative measures to keep everyone safe and mitigate human-wildlife conflict. Food staples, other than meat, were purchased elsewhere. There was no farming, gardens, or crops for herbivores to trample and plunder. There was no livestock offering easy pickings for hungry predators. Edibles, hides, and horns were stored safely out of the reach of any opportunist scavengers. Thatched fences were built to protect certain areas and redirect four-legged visitors. Our bathroom huts butted up to our tents so that we didn't have to leave the safety of a shelter at night, thereby avoiding any conflicts with the nocturnal predators. Equally important, they educated us about the wild animals frequenting camp, while making sure we didn't unknowingly put ourselves in danger. The staff's watchful eyes redirected my naive pursuits on several occasions.

These deterrents and the manpower to accomplish all this did not appear out of thin air. It required money made available through hunting.

Until villages and rural communities have the funds needed to initiate alternate practices and take preventative measures to mitigate human-wildlife conflict, both humans and animals will suffer. May I again remind you of the words of Ivan Carter: "When there is conflict between humans and wildlife, wildlife ultimately suffers most."

As I headed to breakfast, a bellow coming from the hippo pool interrupted my train of thought. The sound reminded me of how fortunate I was to have an entire *kiboko* clan lounging just a few hundred yards away. For various reasons, I didn't always get to see them, but not a day went by without their highly recognizable vocals. Bellows, grunts, groans, roars, wheezes, growls, and chuffs pervaded the air, becoming a part of each night's primal masterpiece. For sure, the African Symphony was grander because hippos were a part of it, even if that meant waking up every single morning to: "Honey, put your shoes on."

Some of the hippos in the hippo pool.

12
A Place of Refuge

With eyes locked, we mirrored each other's movements. His head momentarily disappeared behind the branch until he peeked over the other side. In an exaggerated movement, I shifted my head to follow his gaze until his golden eyes were again fixed on mine. A few seconds later, we reversed our moves. Each time, his small black face disappeared briefly behind the large limb. I couldn't look away. The tiny relative had me captivated. Never in a million years could I have imagined that I'd be playing Hide-n-Seek with a wild primate, with a vervet monkey to be exact.

After the first few marathon days, we typically came back to *Masimba* Camp for lunch, a treat that allowed us to kick back and relax for a few hours before heading out on an afternoon safari. The dining hut's afternoon views, especially the frolicking long-tailed visitors, were a huge upgrade over swooping bats and flying excrement. In the heat of the day, the riverbed and two waterholes below the *mesi* were tiny oases that became a flurry of activity, allowing us to enjoy a smorgasbord of animals typically hidden from us after dark.

Vervet monkeys, *tumbilis*, were by far our most prominent visitors. Only minutes after we'd sat down, the spontaneous game of Hide-N-Seek had emerged. The curious delicate-looking monkeys have silver-grey bodies, black faces ringed with white fluffy fur and white eyebrows. Even large males only weigh about 17 pounds and grow to 24 inches long, not counting their tails; females are even smaller. Their size didn't diminish their curiosity, at least not the males. They flitted about bravely above our heads.

Most of the females kept their distance, hanging out in the trees across the riverbed when they weren't darting to and from the waterholes. Nearly all of them had babies latched underneath their bellies, holding on for dear life.

Originally I thought the females weren't interested in playing games because of their protective motherly instincts. While I'm sure that was part of it, I also learned that the monkeys were very likely two distinct groups. Most troops of vervet monkeys consist of 10-50 adult females and immature offspring. The males simply drop in to socialize and enjoy a little hanky-panky from time to time.

One might wonder how an African rookie like myself became such an expert at deciphering a vervet monkey's sex. Well, when it comes to *tumbilis*, you don't have to be the sharpest tack in the drawer. The family jewels are a brilliant turquoise blue accompanied by a bright red penis, essentially advertising their maleness like a flashing red and blue neon light. It might not surprise you to learn that they are often referred to as "blue-balled monkeys."

Vervet monkeys, male or female, are noisy little critters, capable of making 30 different alarm calls, each one distinctive for specific threats. No doubt, their cries made up part of the primal composition we listened to each night.

Every monkey within a matriarchal troop participates in the rearing of infants. With that being said, most of the mothering falls to the juvenile females who assume a lot of the parental duties. This enables the mother to reproduce sooner while simultaneously allowing the younger females to gain experience, ultimately making them better equipped to raise their own offspring.

Since *tumbilis* spend most of their time in the trees to avoid predators, their primary threats are leopards, eagles, pythons, and baboons. Around civilization, however, it is their eating habits that get them into trouble. While they eat mainly fruit, flowers, leaves, and insects, they are not opposed to an easy meal accomplished by raiding crops or stealing food when the opportunity arises. In some areas, this problem leads to annual slaughter by poison, traps, and guns, making them additional victims of human encroachment and shrinking ecosystems.

The injured bushbuck at the waterhole below the mesi.

(injury was on the opposite side)

There was no chance of that happening at *Masimba* Camp. The staff was diligent about keeping food tucked away, ensuring that temptation didn't turn the daily visitors into unwelcome guests. Besides, everything in the neighboring Ruaha National Park, as well as in the riverbed itself, was protected. Not that it needed to be. *Masimba* Camp not only offered us safety, shelter, and protection, it was a haven for wildlife as well. Without a word ever being said, there was an unspoken understanding that all wildlife in and around the encampment was off limits for hunting--even if it was on the game reserve side of the river.

While we loved and respected that concept, there was one animal in particular that made us question the rule. The first few afternoons at the *mesi,* a beautiful old bushbuck ram or *pongo* came to the waterhole with a huge festering wound on his side.

These elegant-looking antelopes closely resemble deer in size and appearance except they have white spots on their flanks, white socks, and straight horns with a slight twist. Unlike deer, they are very solitary. As browsers, they prefer forests and are rarely found in open terrain. The males go to great lengths to avoid each other. A fact that was supported by our experience. The reclusive ungulates mysteriously appeared from the thick brush, warily entered the riverbed to drink their fill, and were quickly swallowed up again by the forest. There was no dillydallying for those introverts.

The ewes are a little less antisocial, spending at least a few hours a day with their young. We spotted several at the waterhole at the same time. The need for moisture outweighed their natural shy tendencies for just a bit.

As much delight as we took in watching animals, seeing the nasty infected gash on the injured bushbuck was distressful. While we were clueless as to what caused the wound, there was little doubt that the antelope would die a slow torturous death.

Rick, Rod, or Sue would have ended the ram's suffering; but as it was, their hands were tied. Being that the animal was on the other side of that magical line--in the national park instead of the game reserve--meant it was off limits to human interference of any kind. Nature must be allowed to run its course, even if it seems inhumane.

This noninterference applies *even* when animals *could* be saved. The Grand Ruaha River, which typically flows year-round, is the main source of water for all creatures in the park during the dry season. Joel explained that the crucial life-giving river had been experiencing drastic decreases in water flow since 1993 when large-scale, water-intensive rice farms were developed along the riverbanks upstream from the park. Growing rice in those localities reportedly caused a 77 percent loss of all wetland surface area below the cultivated acreage. These sponge-like lands are what feed the river during the dry season. These wide-ranging farms are thought to be the primary cause of the sharp decline of the river.

In a river that previously offered much-needed water throughout the year, there are now sections that dry up completely for months at a time. This lack of water puts major stress on wild species, especially the hippos and other animals dependent on water submersion to survive. As a result of a particularly bad drought a few years before we arrived, hundreds of hippos died slow torturous deaths.

Joel's typical merriness left as he related the incident. While drilling water wells to save the pachyderms had been considered, ultimately, the proposals were rejected. Sound biology and environmentalism ruled against tampering with nature and its natural course of events. Park officials had to sit idly by as the lack of water killed off the weak.

The Tanzanian government has since formed a committee of ministers to address the issues facing the Grand Ruaha River. Hopefully, solutions for protecting this critical water source were found, enabling both human and wildlife populations to thrive.

Learning about so many hippo deaths was deeply troubling. Less than 300 yards away, the camp *kibokos* lounged in what was left of the Mzombe River. We witnessed the scarcity of the vital resource each time we stepped from our tent to see the puddles that clung to existence in the dried-up riverbed. Freddy and Willy made their home in one of those muddied pits of water. Yet, until then, I didn't recognize their full vulnerability.

While I was stressing over the plight of animals dependent on water, a large warthog or *ngiri* made his appearance. Like hippos, warthogs love to wallow in the mud to stay cool and coat their hide to protect against insects; but contrary to the hippo, they have adapted to living in a parched country. They amazingly can go several months without water if they have to. The opportunistic eaters have large rigid snouts that act like shovels for digging up water-laden tubers, roots, and bulbs. In addition, they eat grasses, bark, berries, and even carrion they chance upon, all of which allow them to get the moisture they need from the food they eat. Because of their adaptability *ngiri* can thrive in many conditions, even when displaced by humans.

At *Masimba* Camp, neither was an issue. The two-legged residents enjoyed sharing the camp with the butt-ugly visitors. There is no polite way to say it: like the hartebeest, this haggard-looking species is drastically short in the looks department. Still, while they won't be winning any beauty contests, their hideous faces also somehow make them cute as a button.

Warthogs, as one might guess, are relatives of the pig family and therefore, resemble them in many ways. Their name understandably comes from the cone-shaped wart-like growths protruding from their faces.

Males have four of these fleshy nodules, each up to four inches long. The unsightly growths serve as a form of armor to ward off blows to their face from the pointy tusks of other boars during fights over territory or breeding rights. Like most females, the sows are more sensible, typically not fighting one another. Consequently, they have only two warts, much smaller than those of the males.

Warthogs

Male *ngiri* grow to almost 5 feet long, 33 inches high, and weigh between 120-250 pounds. Females are slightly smaller. To add to their already odd appearance, warthogs are mostly bald except for sparse clusters of hair sprouting willy-nilly on their bodies and a dark shaggy mane running down their neck and back. Essentially, every day for the *ngiri* is a bad hair day. By far their most bizarre-looking attribute is the two pairs of tusks. Like elephants, about one-third of their tusks are embedded in their skulls, leaving up to 10 inches protruding from their lips, forming a half circle on each side. To top off all these outlandish features, warthogs have a long narrow tail with a tuft of hair attached to its end. When danger is perceived, the tail pops straight up into the air like a flagpole.

Female warthogs and their young travel in matriarchal groups called sounders. Boars may travel solo or in small bachelor groups. At the *mesi's* waterhole, only boars seemed to make an appearance. The cautious mamas and their babies stayed clear. These pig-like families were often spotted on our daily wanderings. Inevitably, our appearance sent their tails shooting into the air, broadcasting their alarm. I hate to admit that I took such joy in the fear of another living thing, but I did. The parade of hoisted tails cracked me up every time.

Warthogs have good reason to worry. Lions, leopards, hyenas, crocodiles, wild dogs, cheetahs, and eagles all have a hankering for juicy pork steaks. Although their ghastly appearance and intimidating fangs make them look quite savage, their facade doesn't intimidate predators. Their best tactic is to flee, not fight. Fortunately, they are speedy little buggers. Because their legs are quite a bit longer than their domestic relatives, they can dash 30 mph across the savanna.

If their speed fails them, those razor-sharp tusks on the bottom jaw become lethal weapons. When retreating into their burrows, they tuck their piglets in behind them and back into their holes positioned for an attack. Each time they exit their dens, they spring forth like their life depends on it because, quite frankly, it does.

While *Masimba* Camp was a place of refuge for any nearby wildlife, there were a few times their devotion to coexisting with wild things threw me for a loop.

You may remember that I *hate* mice. Not just a little bit. I have a completely irrational, over-the-top, aversion to the beady-eyed varmints. I'm ashamed to say that my idiocy, and the language gap, had me pleading for the death of an innocent creature. Thankfully, Michael stood up to my lunacy.

Before you think I'm evil, let me explain. Days earlier, a mouse had scrambled up Rick's leg while he was sitting on the porcelain throne, causing him to kick wildly. His knee-jerk reaction sent the tailed rodent sailing through the air, striking me in the stomach before dropping to the ground and scampering away.

Knowing Africa's host of unsavory characters, many of which feed on mice, it was already nerve-racking enough going into the makeshift bathroom. Therefore, a mouse on the premises kept me in an even greater state of terror. For days, the mouse tormented me with surprise appearances: while I was brushing my teeth, on the toilet, and twice while in the shower. Each sighting sent me into a frenzied Irish jig while trying to keep from screaming. Crying *wolf* in Africa is not a good idea. My next scream could indicate a black mamba or something that truly mattered and I wanted help to come when needed.

During daylight hours the solar lights were off, allowing only natural light to seep into the hut. The shelter took on an eerie grayness interspersed with shadows. One afternoon when entering the dim setting I was stopped dead in my tracks by my whiskered nemesis, which in the murky light appeared as a brown blurry blob. Instead of dashing out of sight, the blob stood his ground, never even trying to flee.

In a tizzy, I dashed out of the bathroom looking for someone, anyone, capable of ridding our bathroom of that miniature tormentor. Michael heard my yelping and came running to my rescue. In an emotional frenzy,

I informed him that the mouse was back and wouldn't leave. "You have to kill it!" I pleaded.

Instantly, he darted into the bathroom while I waited anxiously outside the tent. A minute passed but there were no sounds of chaos or commotion, to indicate the pursuit of the notoriously fast rodent. Finally, Michael hesitantly came back out with a troubled look on his face. "*Chura*. I can't kill it." He implored. "*Chura* is protected by the National Park. It's illegal to kill."

Still irrational, I begged him to forget the National Park. Surely, a mouse didn't matter. Besides, the boundary of the park was the riverbed, not our tent. I'm not proud that my emotions led me to make such a lethal appeal; but, in truth, I wanted that mouse gone.

After a few frantic minutes, Michael finally got it through my thick skull that the *chura* was a frog. Not a mouse. Typical of my foolishness when it comes to mice, my imagination had taken over the instant I saw the blurry blob nestled in the shadowy gloom. Instead of investigating, I tore out of the bathroom like a bat out of hell.

Chura. Lilian had yet to teach me that little tidbit of Swahili. *Panya*, meaning mouse, also hadn't come up. I had asked Michael to kill a frog!

Fortunately, Michael stood his ground, refusing to kill the so-called mouse even though I was visibly upset and begging him to do so. Again, the incident may not *seem* like a big deal but, in reality, it was incredibly admirable. I was a distraught client who'd paid considerable money to be there and requested the removal of a varmint that caused me great distress and torment. Some hosts may have caved and done the deed to keep a guest happy. Not Michael. He refused my desperate pleas even though it troubled him to do so.

The incident was also a great lesson on how miscommunication can get you in a pickle, especially between different cultures and languages. It took several minutes of verbal relays before I calmed down enough to comprehend that we were talking about two different critters. Certainly, I didn't want a pocket-sized amphibian dead because it strayed into our bathroom. A mouse. Absolutely.

Mysteriously, after the *chura* debacle, the original *panya* never showed his beady little eyes again. Maybe before he had another chance to torment me, a black mamba made a lunch of him. Maybe he figured the antics of a crazy woman weren't worth the risk. I prefer to think the latter.

Frogs weren't the only guests who proved *Masimba* Camp's commitment to wildlife. When we showed up at the *mesi* one afternoon, one of the supersized African bats or *popo* was hanging from the rafter above the dining table. Apparently, snoozing close to his food source seemed like a great idea.

In my book, bats and mice rank almost equal in nastiness. The flying rodent-looking creatures swooping through my childhood home terrorized me one too many times. Thus, as beneficial as bats are to the environment, I wasn't thrilled about one, literally, hanging out with us.

Again, even knowing my unease, the staff made it clear that the bat was off-limits. Of course, I didn't want it killed; I just wanted it shooed away. Surely, Africa was big enough for Mr. *Popo* to find other sleeping arrangements. However, when it became clear that our hosts were struggling with how to keep me happy without bothering the bat, I forced myself to cowgirl up and hide my irrational fear.

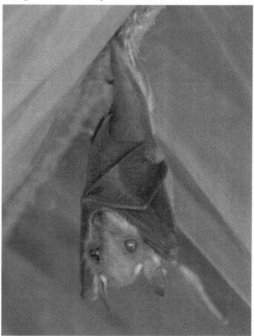

The bat, or popo, that slept in the dining hut
for a few days.

The saving grace was that the *popo* wasn't darting around under my feet like my tiny four-legged nemesis. Also, believe it or not, its face--with big eyes and long pointy ears--slightly resembled that of a Chihuahua puppy. It was actually a tiny bit cute. Still, it *was* a bat--a big bat. Just because it wasn't nearly as mousey looking or ugly as the bats I was familiar with at home didn't mean I was jumping for joy.

Unfortunately, Mr. *Popo* took a liking to his new digs. The next afternoon, there he was again. Hanging. Same spot. Dozing like he didn't have a care in the world. Since he slept utterly motionless, I even got brave enough to take a picture. Still, it was unsettling to keep an eye on *popo* while simultaneously reading a book or playing Hide-n-Seek with the *tumbilis*.

Thankfully, on the third afternoon, there was no bat. After he had taken off that second night, Joel and Michael fashioned a layer of plastic below the rafter where the bat had been roosting, thereby blocking its return. Without ever laying a finger on Mr. *Popo* or even disturbing him in the slightest, they found a way to redirect his sleeping habits and keep him out of the *mesi*. It doesn't take much to impress me because, again, I thought the concern for the bat was pretty spectacular.

The fact that our temporary home was a safe space for wild creatures filled me with joy. Even Freddy, who I rarely saw, made my heart happy. In some places, the threat caused by his continued growth may have led to his extermination, but not here. Willy, too, was such a treat for me. Although our chunky, sometimes grouchy, neighbor's presence meant we had to be extra careful, I loved that he adopted our waterhole. It made *Masimba* Camp just that much more special somehow.

While the whole of *Masimba* Camp offered wild creatures a safe haven, our tents became our little port in the storm, not only at night but sometimes in the afternoons as well. Midday naps became a common theme for Rick, Rod, and Sue. *Simba's* middle-of-the-night wake-up calls, zero-dark-thirty breakfasts, miles of stalking and tracking, and hours jostling in the Land Cruiser under the hot sun whipped our butts.

The tents didn't enjoy the natural breeze that the *mesi* offered but my companions found a tiny way around that. Miniature 8-inch battery-operated fans were one of the essential items brought from America thanks to Rod and Sue having a few safaris under their belts.

Rod developed the best system to take advantage of his itty-bitty wind machine. He plopped the device right on the middle of his chest aiming it directly at his face from only 10 inches away. Yet, after mocking his technique, both she and Rick stole his strategy.

As dog-tired as I was, I rarely joined them napping. *Places to go, people to see, and things to do* has always been one of my mottos. While I tried getting some shuteye a few times, all I ended up doing was laying there wondering what I was missing at the *mesi*. What stories might Joel tell? Was Mr. *Ngiri* rolling in the mud? Were the *tumbilis* willing to play Hide-n-Seek? I couldn't take it. Within minutes, curiosity trumped exhaustion; I didn't want to miss one second of any monkey business--two-legged or four-legged.

Masimba Camp's remoteness, as well as its butting up against a national park, ensured there was no lack of activity within the little oasis we temporarily called home. Wildlife of all shapes and sizes existed within its boundaries, allowing special moments and priceless viewing opportunities.

Even so, the memory I hold dearest to my heart, filling me with joy and hope, is the staff's love and respect for all creatures--not only the charismatic species but the distasteful and uninspiring as well. Winged, tailed, waterlogged, fanged, hoofed, butt-ugly, majestic, itty-bitty, or hulking--it mattered not. *Masimba* Camp was a refuge for all living beings, including us.

I Like Him, I Like Him a Lot

13

The dining hut was not only the perfect place to enjoy viewing wildlife, but it was also a gathering place to build friendships and experience people of different cultures in a foreign land. Whether hosting intimate discussions or spirited dinner conversations, the *mesi* was the core location of countless memories, essentially making it the heart of *Masimba* Camp. With that said, Joel, the camp manager, was the blood that kept that heart beating.

As camp host, anytime any of us were in the dining hut, he was in the dining hut. Lord forbid we might need a glass of water and have to pour it ourselves. Also, since he knew all the hazards to look out for, it was likely that his nearness was for our safety. No matter the reason, Joel was much more than Hilary's head honcho. In our eyes, he was the icing on the cake, *Masimba* Camp's "secret sauce," so to speak.

Hilary and Joel had been working together for over 31 years, starting when Hilary first became a PH. Then, in 2005, when Hilary started his own safari business, Joel was chosen to manage this little piece of paradise.

Although some people are better enjoyed in small doses, Joel was *not* one of them. We absolutely could not get enough of his exuberant personality or his knowledge of Tanzania. His anecdotes had us clinging to every word while riding an emotional roller coaster. Amazingly, his tales weren't meant to generate such drastic reactions; he was just, in a matter-of-fact way, telling the stories of his life.

As you may imagine, my fear of the deadly snakes, especially black mambas, or *koboko*, still dominated my thoughts at that point. Consequently, over the first few days, I anxiously asked the English-speaking staff if they knew anyone *personally* who had been killed by one of the deadly serpents. Raphael didn't know anyone; neither did Paul. Michael also was a nay. Hilary too was a nada. Heck, if all those Tanzanians didn't know anyone who'd died of a black mamba bite, maybe the danger had been largely exaggerated.

Then I made the mistake of asking Joel. Expecting to hear the same answer, my jaw dropped open when Joel casually remarked "Ahhh!! Yes. Bad snake. Black mamba bit my brother. He died in the field with the goats."

While helping his Dad tend to the family's livestock, his 10-year-old brother was struck by the lethal snake. Within just a few minutes of the bite, his sibling was dead. My heart was still in my mouth as Joel continued: "My brother was the oldest. Now I am the oldest of 35 brothers and sisters."

Two things in those statements blew me away. First, his very own brother had died from a black mamba bite. The object of my dread had stolen one of his very own family members. Second, Joel was the oldest of 35 siblings.

I'm not sure if our gasps and gaping mouths were a result of his brother's horrible demise or the inconceivable concept of having 35 siblings. Joel told the story so casually. His only emphasis was a few shoulder shrugs. It had happened so many years ago that he was just a young tike, leaving him few memories of his brother.

As we sat dumbfounded processing all the information, Joel's sober facial expression switched to one distorted in pain, recalling his run-in with a spitting cobra eight years back. While retrieving firewood, he had surprised a snake that was hidden in the woodpile. The startled cobra did what spitting cobras do; it spat venom onto Joel's face, causing temporary blindness, as well as numbness in his mouth.

"Ahhh, it hurt. It hurt bad." He lamented as he reflexively skewed his face in agony remembering the burning sensation.

Fortunately, this happened at one of Hilary's hunting camps that was close to a hospital, relatively speaking; therefore, they were able to get him treatment within hours.

Let me tell you, if some catastrophe happened at *Masimba* Camp, you might as well bend over and kiss your arse goodbye. Each village supposedly had a dispensary, including Mgogo's four hours away, but the treatments were very limited. The nearest actual hospital was about 200 slow, bumping, grinding miles away.

With Joel having access to a hospital and treatment, his sight improved each day--transitioning from blackness through a range of blues, yellows, and greens until his normal eyesight returned. The numbness in his mouth also eventually disappeared. After a four-day agonizing ordeal, he was released from the hospital presumably good as new but as he said, "Ohhh, it hurt. It hurt bad."

Joel's tales did not give me the warm fuzzy feeling I had been searching for. That was when I added cobras to my *dread* list. Thankfully, I was jolted from my stupor when discussions moved to Joel's other bombshell--thirty-five siblings! I breathed a small sigh of relief upon learning that Joel's father had five wives to obtain the large brood. Multiple wives are the norm in their cattle culture. The more cattle a man owns, the wealthier he is. Hence, more cattle. More wives. His Dad provided a home for each wife and her children, then he alternated between households.

In truth, Joel missed his true calling. He should have been a standup comedian. Watch out Howie Mandel; here comes Joel Hhoki. Unsurprisingly, some of Joel's favorite storylines involved his Dad. Each time that he spoke of him, his face beamed with pride and joy while informing us: "Ohhh, I like him. I like him a lot."

Five minutes later, he'd break out into another of his father's escapades while shaking his head in laughter. When he was done snickering, just in case there was any doubt whatsoever, he joyfully reminded us, "Ohhhh, I like him. I like him a lot."

We sat enthralled throughout all these proclamations of affection, listening to him explain that his Dad, now being quite old, was beginning to lose his memory. That can cause quite a few hiccups in a family with 5 wives, 35 children, and umpteen grandchildren. Heck, it would be hard to keep a clan like that straight if your memory was impeccable.

Anyway, from what we understood, his elderly father lived primarily with the youngest wife. Yet, he still liked to go visit the others. Joel was often enlisted to accompany him on these riveting visitations. With his Dad's powers of recall somewhat lacking, he couldn't remember his wives' names and constantly had to rely on Joel to keep him in the know and, consequently, out of the doghouse. Apparently asking, *hey, which wife are you?* doesn't go over so well in any culture. Joel would help keep him in line and then, out of the blue, his Dad would look at Joel blankly and say, "Hey, what's your name?"

Throughout all these adventures his Dad never went anywhere without his "little buddy." This constant companion of his was his talking stick, an 18-inch decorated staff used as a communication tool in many native cultures. During every story, Joel kept his own "little buddy" tucked under his arm as he paced jubilantly back and forth imitating his Dad's escapades. Grinning from ear to ear, Joel chuckled, "Ohhhh! I like him. I like him a lot."

Joel with his "little buddy" telling one of his stories.

The antics of these visits reminded me a lot of Abbott and Costello's famous baseball routine "*Who's on First. What's on Second*". It just kept circling as they traveled from home to home, wife to wife, child to child trying to figure out who was who and what was what. Feeling like we were an audience at an actual comedy show, we laughed hysterically at the father/son capers and learned beyond any shadow of a doubt that Joel emphatically liked his Dad. In fact, he liked him a lot. Other objects of his affection were his grandchildren. His son had three kids and his daughter had twin boys, the latter of which lived with him. At least that was the impression we got. While beaming like a lit-up Christmas tree, he proclaimed, "Ohhhhhh. They're funny. I like them, so I keep them." We never figured out if his daughter lived with Joel as well, or what the actual circumstances were. Elders are highly respected in Tanzanian culture so maybe he could choose to raise them if he wanted to. That was certainly how it appeared to us.

We were too enthralled with the toddlers' escapades and Joel's glee in recounting their antics to quiz him on it. There was no doubt in our minds that those tiny tots, along with his other grandchildren, held a special place in Joel's heart. Not only did he grin in obvious delight every time he talked about them, but he was also very vocal about it. You guessed it. Over and over, he declared: "Ohhhhh. I like them. I like them a lot."

Joel's family stories told us another thing. Tanzania is a country in transition. Approximately 40 percent of the population is Christian while 35 percent is Muslim. Many are clinging to their tribal cultures while some are moving forward with more modern lifestyles.

Even within Joel's family, there is a merging of cultures and beliefs. Joel, for instance, informed us that he only had one wife. "I'm educated," he said as he shook his head at the idea of having multiple wives, "one wife is enough."

Not all his brothers felt the same. Several had multiple wives with many children. As you might imagine, Joel didn't even know all of his nieces and nephews. Shaking his head and laughing, he admitted trying to convince his brothers to give up their cattle and change their way of life, but they would have none of it; they believed he was the crazy one.

It is easy to see why there are so many different ways of life within the same country. Tanzania is made up of roughly 120 ethnic tribes, most speaking their own languages. Seven of those tribes, with their own native tongue, were represented at *Masimba* Camp. Dialogue is made possible because most tribes also speak Swahili, the country's national language. The value of a common language cannot be sold short; it allows diverse

peoples to communicate effectively and work out their differences, helping
to make Tanzania a primarily peaceful nation.

Due to colonial rule in the past, many Tanzanians also speak English.
Most post-secondary education includes it along with their tribal languages. As a result, much of the population knows three or more languages. How impressive is that? In junior high school, I failed miserably
attempting to learn just one extra language.

When asked about village life, Joel explained that most typical villages
now have some type of solar power to operate lights and minimal ap-
pliances. A few lucky localities even have permanent electricity. Just like
Masimba Camp, most cooking is done outside over a wood fire. Running
water and sewer systems are pretty much nonexistent, but the government
has furnished many with a common well. This is a huge asset when other
water sources are loaded with deadly crocs and cranky hippos, as well as
require a hike through predator-infested lands. Larger cities and urban
areas like Arusha do have electricity, as well as other basic amenities.

The government owns all the land in Tanzania. Despite that, land in
the cities may be purchased from the authorities to build homes and
businesses. In the tribal lands, the government retains ownership of all
the landholdings. According to Joel, citizens are permitted to build and
maintain the ownership of dwellings on those grounds. If the government
appropriated the land for some reason, it must reimburse the villager for
the value of any structures.

Rural Tanzania is primarily a cattle culture and the grazing lands are
government owned as well. There are no fenced pastures and privately
owned ranches as is common in southern Africa, or like we are used to
in America. During the wet season when grasses are readily available close
to the villages, cattle are permitted to forage all day and then herded into
corrals (*kraals*) in the evenings. The stockades, typically made of thorn
branches, protect livestock from lions, hyenas, and other predators. During the dry season, most cattle herders become nomadic, moving with the
cattle wherever the water takes them.

Joel told us that the government is encouraging villagers to maintain
only ten or so cattle instead of hundreds or even thousands. With the
population growth, there is just not enough land for everyone to have the
number of livestock that was possible in the past.

As mentioned, Africa overall is growing by leaps and bounds. Tanzania is no different. It has one of the fastest growing populations in the world, jumping from 9 million people in 1961 to 57 million today. With their citizenry exploding, added pressure is being put on Tanzania's resources. Domesticated cattle have increased to roughly 35 million head, consuming resources also needed by wild species. Crops consume natural habitat, often without using efficient sustainable practices. All these things--unproductive farming methods, overgrazing, wood consumption, and dwindling water sources--can also lead to desertification.

In the past, there was enough land for both cattle and wild populations. For thousands of years, the animals coexisted rather easily in the vast ecosystems, each adding their unique contribution to the mix. It wasn't a problem until overgrazing and poor cattle management put too many cattle in too small of an area.

You can't talk about cattle and African culture in transition without talking about the Maasai people. While *Masimba* Camp had no ethnic Maasai as staff members, Joel and the others peppered us with stories and tales of these colorful people. They are one of Africa's most iconic tribes partly because of their distinctive customs and tribal dress and partly because they live so close to many of the park systems. As pastoralists whose society revolves heavily around cattle, they are highly nomadic people constantly in search of more resources.

Although they live side by side with wild creatures, the Maasai dislike eating wild game, relying almost exclusively on the meat, milk, and even the blood of their cattle. Once in a while, a goat or sheep is butchered for special occasions and ceremonies. Until recently, they largely resisted eating plant foods; but with dwindling cattle, they have been forced to rely on vegetables to supplement their meat intake.

Cattle are not only their livelihood; they are a major part of how the strictly patriarchal society measures its wealth. The number of children fathered is also significant. With that said, one asset without the other largely lessens a man's worth. For instance, a man who owns 50 head of cattle with multiple children is considered respectable. The more children and the more cattle, the richer a man is perceived to be. Interestingly, a man with over 200 head of cattle but no children or a man with 30 children but no cattle are both considered very poor men.

The Maasai have a reputation as fearsome warriors whose passage into manhood was historically marked by the killing of a male lion. Recognizing the lion's importance in the ecosystem, sacrificing female lions was prohibited unless they were posing a threat to livestock or human life. Nowadays, the killing of a lion is strongly discouraged or performed in a group instead of individually, thereby preserving as many lions as possible. Other alternatives allowing the ritual to take a new form are also being explored. This rite of passage is an elaborate ordeal up to eight months long, including circumcision using no anesthetic. To not dishonor himself, the participant must endure the trial of manhood in silence, without showing any expressions of pain.

Historically, the Maasai were also adept cattle rustlers who believed that God entrusted them with all the cattle on earth. Stealing cattle from other tribes was, in essence, only seizing what they believed to be rightfully theirs. They also had a strong aversion to slavery, never condoning it. As a result, most slave traders tended to avoid the fierce warrior societies of the Maasai people.

One nugget of information that got Sue's and my immediate attention was a nomadic warrior's right to stake claim to another man's dwelling for the night, including his wife, when he was traveling through a distant village. The visitor only had to plunge his sword into the ground in front of the chosen lodge. The male resident had to find another shelter for the night. Based on our biased Western perspective, the custom initially raised our hackles a bit until Joel informed us that the wife had the choice as to whether she offered more than just a meal and a bed to sleep in. Apparently, the custom helped ensure that the family tree had more than just a few branches.

Another interesting custom is how the Maasai handle death. When a person dies, there is virtually no ceremony. Their bodies are simply placed in the wilderness for the scavengers to consume. It is seen as a social disgrace if the body is rejected by the recyclers of the wild. Consequently, bodies are often drenched in fat and blood from a slaughtered animal as added enticement for hyenas and other opportunists. While this custom may seem shocking from our perspective, apparently the tradition stemmed from the belief that burying human remains was harmful to the soil.

Historically, the Maasai largely resisted government efforts to have them abandon their traditional nomadic lifestyle. Yet, as their rangelands are taken away, forbidden by national park systems, or encroached on by other tribes, it is proving to be increasingly difficult for their society to escape the influences of the modern world.

The Maasai of course are not alone. Africa is full of people and cultures with their feet planted in two different worlds, balancing the old with the new.

While the entire staff was wonderful, eager to share knowledge and to help us understand their truths and a world in transition, Joel's stories took us to another level. His anecdotes, combined with his infectious personality, shared pieces of his reality in a way that touched our souls. Mesmerized, we sat under a thatched roof in the wilds of Africa listening to life experiences that not only educated us but left us spellbound. Soaking up every word, we shuddered in fear, cringed in disbelief, or fought back tears. Most notably, however, tale after tale had us rolling in laughter. Joel was indeed the lifeblood of *Masimba* Camp.

My one true regret is that we didn't record Joel's impromptu afternoon entertainment. Nothing would bring a smile to my face quicker than listening to his stories over and over again while sharing his genius with the world. One thing is for certain: *Ohhhh. I like him. I like him a lot.*

14

THE HEART OF A HUNTER

Raphael lunged forward pounding on the cab window. Instantly, Mike slammed on the brakes. We'd been leisurely scanning for wildlife in clusters of trees and patches of savanna until the unexpected jolt brought us to attention. Raphael had spotted something. What that something was, we had no idea. While we were still sitting dumbstruck, the crew exploded into action. Raphael grabbed his rifle. Mgogo and Abdalah scrambled to the ground. Lilian jumped out of the cab. Only Mike remained fixed behind the steering wheel.

Somewhere amidst the activity, both Rick and I were sure we'd heard the word "dik-dik." Hearing this, we were perplexed by the sense of urgency. Briefly, we made eye contact silently asking the question: *So much intensity for an itty-bitty antelope?*

The dik-dik, or *digi-digi*, is a tiny little critter. Even a huge male weighs barely 15 pounds dripping wet. Among the smallest of the antelope species, the delicate creatures scarcely reach 16 inches tall and 25 inches long. They have grizzled gray-brown coats, pipestem legs, petite faces, pointy snouts, huge ears, and large eyes. Since their hind legs are much longer than their front, they remind me a little of a rabbit, lacking long floppy ears. Only males have short spiked horns, up to 3 inches long. Unlike many of the larger antelopes, *digi-digis* are monogamous and therefore tend to travel in pairs instead of herds.

While we had come across plenty of the dwarf-sized antelopes, I didn't really *see them* if you get my drift. The faithful teeny-weeny duos can bolt up to 26 mph. Therefore, they pretty much vaporized in front of our eyes. I never even came close to capturing a photo of one.

Rick's tag allowed him to hunt dik-dik, but they certainly weren't high on his priority list. Therefore, the crew's intensity seemed a little out of kilter for an animal half the size of a miniature goat. We were baffled, to say the least.

As soon as our boots hit the ground, Raphael sprinted past the vehicle with his gun readied. Mimicking Raphael, Rick did the same. Normally, Mgogo would have been next in line with me trailing, but everything happened so fast that I ended up sprinting directly behind Rick.

Dik-dik

Just when I was beginning to suck wind, Raphael halted abruptly causing Rick to almost plow him over. I in turn, almost plowed Rick over, looking like yet another slapstick comedy routine.

Mgogo plopped the shooting sticks down in front of us. Still confused, our eyes strained to find the dik-dik causing all the fuss.

Raphael pointed to the left and said, "Shoot!"

Rick and I had been looking for a pint-sized antelope sprouting oversized toothpicks for horns. Imagine our surprise when our gaze followed a pointed finger to three huge beasts scrambling to their feet from under a canopy of acacia trees. Those were *not* dik-diks! Almost under our noses, less than 15 yards away, were three Cape buffalo.

Seeing three massive *dagga* boys within ramming distance snapped us to attention pretty quickly. Assuming our shooting stance, Rick placed his rifle on the shooting sticks. This time, I took a deep breath and kept my eyes open: a lesson learned from the previous *nyati's* charge.

As the bulls fled, the one in the rear presented Rick with a broadside view. Rick placed the shot directly in the heart and 20 yards later, the bull crumbled to the ground. Rick and Raphael took off running towards the downed *dagga* boy with the rest of us in their wake. Once we were within a few yards, they slowed, approaching cautiously. The bull was perfectly still. Taking no chances, Raphael instructed Rick to fire the "insurance shot".

As Rick and I knelt to offer our gratitude and appreciation for this wondrous creature's sacrifice, Mgogo and Abdalah kept their eyes peeled for the two remaining buffalo, making sure they didn't circle back in retaliation.

With tears blurring our eyes, we gently stroked his warm body and studied him in awe. His once massive horns were broken off on each end making them small in comparison to other Cape buffalo. There was barely any hair left on his body. His frame was slighter in muscle than the younger bulls we had seen. Raphael opened the old buffalo's mouth to show us that his teeth had been ground down to almost nothing. He felt sure the buffalo was over 15 years old, which is ancient for a buffalo in the wild. This old boy had beaten the odds. He was a survivor.

Zefania, Mgogo, Rick, Lilian, Raphael, and Mike with the dagga boy.

As if that wasn't impressive enough, our eyes were drawn from his almost hairless face to the left side of his neck where Mgogo was reverently running his fingers across parallel scars. Four of them. Eight inches long. *Simba's* calling card.

This noble bull had survived a lion clinging to his back with razor-sharp claws digging into his flesh. The wounds weren't fresh. Time had healed them. Still, the marks told part of his story, a story that would now forever be a part of our story.

Because of the Cape buffalo's size and might, they have only three real enemies in the animal kingdom, lions, hyenas, and large crocodiles. Lions are their biggest nemeses by far. In some areas, these burly felines rely on the *nyati* for up to 40 percent of their diet. *Simba,* it seems, prefers buffalo steak over almost anything else on the menu. Unfortunately for the bovines, the prowling predators know the buffalos' routine.

Many species have adapted to the scarcity of water by consuming their moisture through green leaves, forage, or their prey. This allows them to go days without water. Cape buffalo are not so fortunate. They generally require about 10 gallons of water, twice a day. In other words, they need bucketloads of the wet stuff.

As the dry season progresses and the main rivers transform into ribbons of sporadic waterholes, it causes more dense concentrations of wildlife at fewer and fewer locations, a great advantage for lions searching for their favorite food source.

One lion against a lone buffalo would be a savage battle. Yet, rarely, do these deadly felines work alone. Often a lion will leap aboard the *nyati's* muscular back while others target the tendons of his back legs. Others will use their fangs to latch on to the base of the tail while piercing the buffalo's flanks with their sharp claws in an attempt to bring him down. Once the lions get the brute on the ground, it is much harder for him to use his horns and might to counterattack. Male lions, who are much larger and more muscular, will often use their powerful jaws to grab a buffalo by the throat, crushing the windpipe or suffocating them.

Since female lions make up most of the hunting parties, the powerful males are not always present to provide the more merciful death of asphyxiation. While the females do suffocate their victims once they are down, feasting on a large species like Cape buffalo sometimes begins while they are still very much alive. As soon as such a victim touches the ground, the tearing of flesh and viscera begins. Nature is a cruel master and, more often than not, spares no mercy.

Fortunately, even though Tanzania is a stronghold for lions, it also boasts a strong Cape buffalo population. Rick's 21-day hunting license allowed for the generous harvest of three buffalo.

The fact that Cape buffalo must be managed for *too much* growth is a very good thing, especially when you look at their history. They also suffered a 95 percent loss during the 1890s rinderpest epidemic which ravaged the wild ungulates and domestic cattle of east and southern Africa.

The buffalo's comeback has been quite extraordinary, largely due to well-managed hunting programs throughout Africa. Although the IUCN now estimates that the *nyati* population exceeds one million, maintaining the conservation status of Least Concern, it is still subject to the same threats as other wildlife. Diseases also still cause localized declines from time to time. In addition, their need for water makes them more susceptible to drought conditions.

Still, populations are not always spread evenly throughout. Some areas have too few while others have too many. To keep ecosystems in balance where hunting is restricted, drastic measures sometimes must be taken--although they are rarely talked about.

Culling, the process of managing wild populations by mass off-take is a strategy that occurs both in protected government-controlled areas as well as on private game ranches. Culling is different from hunting. The rules of fair chase aren't applicable in this scenario. It is simply about eliminating a specified number of a particular species as effectively and efficiently as possible.

Though the practice is inherently distasteful, there are justifiable reasons for it. Culling is used to save threatened species from excessively aggressive members of their own kind; prevent overgrazing and destruction of habitat due to overpopulation; and eliminate the threat of diseases. Drastic measures, no matter how gut-wrenching they may seem, must sometimes be taken to ensure the greater good for entire ecosystems. This is especially true when the population of one species is threatening the well-being of an entire habitat and the other wildlife living there as well.

When I arrived in Africa, I had no idea that the strategy was sometimes used in national parks throughout Africa, even in popular world-renowned places such as the Kruger National Park. Don English, a game ranger from Kruger, admitted that as protectors of wildlife, the rangers hate when culling is necessary but conceded that "sometimes you have to kill to conserve."

In 2016, Don was tasked with such a job. After shooting three buffalo from a helicopter, they landed to ensure the targets were not suffering. As he approached, a wounded buffalo attacked. The enraged beast used his massive horns to toss Don like a rag doll, then ground him into the dirt, breaking ribs and crushing organs. Ultimately, a fellow ranger ended the assault. Miraculously, Don survived, although it took him almost three years to recover.

The point is, culling is a necessary strategy that few people talk about. Not only is it an unpleasant process, but it is also expensive to boot. Helicopters. Game rangers. Vehicles. The list goes on and on. Controlling population sizes through selective hunting, on the other hand, provides income instead of costing money. Money that can be spent on other conservation and anti-poaching efforts.

Even though Tanzania's strong buffalo population allowed for the harvest of three *nyati* on Rick's hunting license, our intentions were for him to harvest only one. Never in a million years did we think he'd accomplish that goal on the second day of our safari. Nevertheless, after doing so, we discussed the possibility of another opportunity presenting itself and what to do if it did.

Call me crazy, but I love my husband. When we married, he knew that part of my heart was rooted in Pennsylvania and therefore supported me wholeheartedly any time life called me home: eight weeks for my Mom's back surgery; one month for my Dad's first leg amputation; four months for complications and his second leg removal; two month's when Mike was diagnosed with cancer; another two months after he died; and two more months after Dad's death. Yet each time I needed to be with family, Rick never blinked an eye.

Why is any of this relevant? Put simply, Rick has loved and supported me throughout our entire life together, even when it was inconvenient, costly, lonely, and stressful. When someone shows you that much devotion and understanding, it makes you love them even more. Their happiness becomes your happiness. If something is important to Rick, you better believe it is important to me. I wanted him to get the very most from his African hunting experience. If that meant a second or third Cape buffalo, so be it. We would find a way to pay for it, just like we found a way for me to be in Pennsylvania when my heart called me there.

It is still a mystery how Rick and I *both* confused the words that led to an itty-bitty antelope transforming into three burly Cape buffalo. Even so, the dik-dik turned *dagga*-boy holds a special place in my heart. Approximately 15 years of struggle for survival in a hostile world had worn his massive horns down to remnants of their previous glory. Time had stripped away most of his hair, ground away his teeth, and diminished his muscle.

It's hard to explain how emotional I get when thinking of that warrior buffalo. Somehow, the lion scars on his neck left a trace on me as well. When I look at those parallel streaks, I picture the buffalo's terror-stricken eyes as he struggled to break free. Tears form in my eyes as I imagine his painful bellowing as the lion's claws dug deeper. How did he break free? Did another buffalo come to his aid as I've seen on so many videos? Was he attacked while still a member of a herd or after he was forced to go it alone?

The fact that, ultimately, Rick ended the extraordinary bull's life filled me with heightened emotions. On the other hand, I also felt relief that the survivor died a quick death, rather than one of misery and torment. He would not waste away slowly from starvation when his teeth were ground down to nothing. He would not fall victim to a pack of hyenas or lions, possibly getting eaten alive.

His sacrifice also meant that his magnificence would live on. Others would see his rugged grandeur and know his story in the mounted memory that holds a place of honor in our home.

Preserving and mounting quarry is a grossly misunderstood practice that is looked at with disgust and disdain by a large segment of the population. Taxidermy, for some people, brings visions of horror movies, where serial killers are surrounded by distorted-looking lifeless creatures. Others denounce it as glorifying the kill, egotistical, or that some kind of sick pleasure is derived from it.

I can't speak for all hunters, but this is just not the case with the hunters that I know. Rick, my brothers, and our many hunting friends are far from perfect, but they certainly aren't axe murderers. Nor do they go around puffed up like a Thanksgiving turkey because a particular *trophy* is hanging on their wall.

Think of it this way. You have to be cuckoo for Cocoa Puffs to spend the money needed for gear and licenses, crawl out of bed at ungodly hours, trudge mile after mile through nasty weather and grueling terrain, or sit motionless for hours in a cramped tree stand in zero-degree temperatures, all while enduring frostbite, sunburn, aching muscles, and other physical abuse. Hunting is, most often, hard work with a good dose of misery mixed in. Doing all of that *just* for bragging rights and a trophy makes zero sense.

The word "trophy" itself is often misunderstood and misused. It holds such a negative connotation and doesn't foster the true intent behind the practice. Most hunters are proud and excited about a harvest because of the time and effort that went into it. Sure, they enjoy sharing their experiences, along with the pictures and mounted tributes. But that makes them human. Not monsters. Who doesn't enjoy sharing stories and important aspects of their life with friends and family?

With that said, it is easy to see how people can be put off by some of the pictures that make their rounds on the internet these days. In the past, images were shared with people who understood the blood, sweat, and tears that go into harvesting an animal. Nowadays, the photos--some of which are distasteful--show up on social media to be viewed by people who see *only* a dead creature with a person grinning from ear to ear.

It stands to reason that anyone who views these pictures as off-putting might feel the same about taxidermy and therefore, misinterpret its significance. Growing up in a hunting world, the practice seemed neither disgusting nor evil. It was normal. Still, I didn't totally *get* it. I viewed it as a silly waste of money using huge chunks of real estate on limited wall space. Quite simply, I shrugged my shoulders and figured: *Hey, whatever floats their boat.* I was just happy none of the mounts were hung on *my* walls.

Then I met Rick. Much to my dismay, his taxidermic memories soon filled the spaces between family photos. Most definitely, I was not a fan.

Decorating with a wildlife theme is pretty limiting. Not to mention, it's hard to create the right mood for yoga when a javelina--a pig-like species with razor-sharp tusks--scrutinizes your warrior pose. With limited wall space, the spare bedroom (also the workout room) became the resting place for the odd-looking varmint. Ohhhh! The things you do for love.

Although I wouldn't use the word love to describe how Rick feels about his taxidermy, his mounts are precious and irreplaceable to him. Just *how* precious hit home early in our marriage.

Our bathtub was often the scene of strategic planning sessions. One night after discussing our next fencing project, the smoke alarm in the kitchen went off. Dripping wet and naked, we darted to the kitchen thinking that I had put something on the stove and forgot about it (thanks to my prowess in the kitchen); but the stove was empty with no fire to be seen.

Beep. Beep. Beep. Beep. Suddenly, every alarm in the house blasted its warning. With a fire extinguisher in tow, we darted from room to room. Still, we could find no flames, only smoke billowing from every air vent. With no visible fire to fight, Rick called 911. We then split up, running to save our valuable possessions.

Dashing to the office, I grabbed my computer and began scooping up photo albums. *Many* photo albums, all pre-digital hard copies *before* iCloud. By the armful, I hauled albums into our front yard. Trip after trip. Although I heard Rick scrambling from room to room, even catching a glimpse of him once or twice, I paid absolutely no attention to what he was doing.

Finally, with the last load of photos in my arms, we bumped into each other. Looking at me wide-eyed, he exclaimed: "You better put some clothes on! The firemen are on their way."

Under my armload of memories, I was buck naked. Not one stitch of clothing on my entire body.

Barely had I reentered the living room, fully dressed, when the local volunteer firemen showed up. Moments later, more backup arrived. Mandi. Mandi's husband. Rick's sister. Her husband. Rick's mom. The neighbors. Word gets around fast in a small town. Really fast.

Still, there was no fire to be seen. Just as a fireman raised his axe to bust through the wall in our laundry room, another fireman, also an electrician (you gotta love our volunteer first responders), discovered that the furnace breaker had tripped. It turns out that a heat valve hadn't shut off, causing the particle board under our manufactured home to melt, filling the entire house with smoke.

Once the issue was found, all the doors and windows were opened to let out the smoke and our living room turned into an impromptu high school reunion. Amid the discussions of an award-winning rebound from a high school basketball game, I noticed that something seemed very different.

Gazing around, it hit me like a ton of bricks. All of Rick's taxidermy was gone. Alaskan Dall sheep. Idaho mule deer. Kansas Whitetail. Arizona Coues deer. For crying out loud, even that outlandish javelina-piggish-looking thing was missing! While I had been saving important documents and photo albums, he had also been saving priceless memories. As it turns out, "priceless" is in the eye of the beholder.

At that time, I hadn't been a part of the hunts that resulted in Rick's taxidermy. The animals on the walls were just that: animals on the walls. They were beautiful, but I didn't get all atwitter when I looked at them. It wasn't until I began going on hunts with Rick that I finally *got* it.

Preserving harvested game is essentially preserving the experience, transporting the participants back to those moments in time, to relive the hours, weeks, or even years of effort, challenge, joy, and camaraderie that went into harvesting such a splendid beast. The truth is, *no one* will appreciate a creature's essence as much as the person, or people, involved in the experience.

Still, while someone else's taxidermy may not trigger intense emotions within me, at least now I recognize that there *is* a unique story with vivid experiences and intense feelings behind each mounted memory.

Now, too, I see it another way. Taxidermy done right is beautiful. The men and women who recreate living things are true artists whose love, respect, and knowledge of wild species, along with their talent, enable them to create realistic representations. Their artistry not only pays tribute to an animal's existence but also allows its magnificence to live on long after death. Not just for us, but for others to enjoy or even learn from. People unable to experience creatures in the wild can see the animal's true majesty up close and personal, especially wildlife not native to the area. Recreating its wonder, in my view, is fundamentally paying an animal the ultimate respect.

While the heart of a hunter may be hard for many non-hunters to understand, one must recognize that we are all geared differently. Thank goodness. Imagine what a boring world we would live in if we were all the same.

My husband, and probably many hunters, need a purpose, a reason for being in the woods. Rick is just not into hiking for the sake of getting from point A to point B. I love heading up a trail to see what is at the other end, to escape civilization's trappings, and to see the sights and sounds of the wilderness. Rick will accompany me, to keep me happy, but his heart isn't in it. However, call the hike a scouting trip for new mule deer territory or elk habitat, and it is an entirely different ballgame. I admit that concept baffles me a bit.

Truth be told, we see many more wild things on his meandering jaunts than we do on my destination-driven hikes. Maybe it's because his jaunts are full of purpose but in a whole different way. He doesn't care if we get to a certain destination. The journey is different. One minute I can barely keep up with his determined stride while other times we are creeping along scrutinizing every inch of the forest. Other times, we sit for long periods, watching, seeing, and feeling.

Patience has never been my virtue. This type of maneuvering can be extremely difficult for me. Rick and I are just wired differently. Yet, as we sit like statues blending with the forest, we are rewarded by watching a doe nibble on shrubs nine feet away, a fisher scampering about looking for food, or a bear and her cubs rummaging through stumps on a hillside, all clueless that we are watching. Moments like those bring clarity to Rick's way of thinking.

Hunting takes skill, willpower, drive, patience, a knowledge of different species, and, of course, the right disposition. While some people like me do not feel that primal urge to hunt or test themselves in that way, others do. After all, it is a very real part of our ancestry. A primary reason that we didn't go the way of dinosaurs. For some, these aspects are deeply ingrained in their psyche.

In *Horn of the Hunter,* Robert Ruark put it this way: "deep in the guts of most men is buried the involuntary response to the hunter's horn, a prickle of the nape hairs, an acceleration of the pulse, an atavistic memory of his fathers, who killed first with stone, and then with club, and then with spear, and then with bow, and then with gun, and finally with formulae. How meek the man is of no importance; somewhere in the pigeon chest of the clerk is still the vestigial remnant of the hunter's heart; somewhere in his nostrils the half-forgotten smell of blood."

This all ties into another greatly misunderstood concept about hunting. The constant quest for bigger and better. This was another thing I shook my head at early on. I didn't understand why so much emphasis was placed on outdoing oneself. Since then, I've learned that, weirdly enough, it is precisely because of *the love of the hunt itself.*

Unless a hunter is only hunting for meat, the majority of hunters do not *kill* just to have killed. They kill to have *hunted.* In other words, they need a goal and a purpose to be pushing themselves to the limits. Looking for the big one gives them that purpose. Shooting just any buck in rural Pennsylvania for instance is not that difficult, relatively speaking of course. After all, there are more than enough of them around. If hunters want to fill their tags for meat only, they can typically do so in a host of 4 a.m. mornings.

On the other hand, the search for a mature buck is entirely different. My brothers may hunt all season and never bring home a big buck. It's not because they didn't see any antlered deer or have multiple opportunities. It's because they passed up many young males. The hunt for the *big one* still gives them an objective and aspiration. It provides a reason to be in the woods, to get up at ungodly hours on their days off, to test themselves, and to gather with family and friends to share stories and experiences. If they get the big one, all the better. Excitement and celebration ensue after all the early hours, hard work, and dedication pay off. If they don't get the big one, they are still able to do what they love without pulling the trigger.

Their quest to be in the woods, without feeling the need to harvest each time, is also why many hunters choose more and more challenging ways of hunting. Meat is always used, but it is no longer necessary for survival. Most hunters can now be more selective. Like everyone and society in general, hunters are constantly evolving.

They may start as young rifle hunters excited to make any legal kill. As they become more and more skilled, they become choosier about their quarry or they make the pursuits more challenging. This often involves converting to a bow or muzzleloader, both of which require different skills, as well as the need to get much closer to prey without being detected. Getting near four-legged beings without being spotted is no easy task.

Surprisingly, this concept of being very choosy about the game harvested, essentially selective hunting, is often vilified by a segment of the population. They have instead adopted the term "trophy hunting" as the catch-all phrase for condemning any type of hunting that they disapprove of. This go-to term has become synonymous with portraying hunters as evil people only interested in covering their walls with heads, horns, and hides.

Yet, many of these same people view hunting for sustenance as okay. When the facts are examined, this is crazy. First of all, selective hunters still use all the meat that is harvested, so they too *are meat hunters.* Even so, they are vilified for passing up oodles of smaller less-mature game in their quest to harvest only mature males, thereby allowing young ones to fulfill their life cycle.

Dwight Van Brunt, the author of *Born a Hunter*, in a recent email, put it to me this way:

> The term 'trophy hunter' seems to be the apex of most hunting arguments. While the vast majority of Americans at least accept hunting (meaning meat hunting), something over 90 percent oppose trophy hunting. To me, a self-identified and hopelessly dedicated trophy hunter, it means that I will only take an animal that is outstanding from a trophy perspective. It also means that I actually take far fewer animals in total, frequently don't shoot, take a very few old animals and spend a great deal of time and money in the process. I hunt deer at least 30 days/year, hard, and have taken exactly one deer in the last dozen years. Do I care? Not in the slightest. Finally, the meat of every edible animal has been recovered and utilized.

Think about the reality of selective hunting for a second. Wild species do not grow to a ripe old age without a healthy dose of smarts, along with a lot of luck. Just like us, years of experience teach them a thing or two. Also, since nature takes its toll on wild species, aged animals are fewer and farther between. Therefore, hunting wiser game, much shorter in supply, creates a much greater challenge for hunters. The large amount of money, time, and torment involved in hunting such clever specimens often ends with hunters coming home empty-handed, just as Dwight noted above.

In addition, selective hunters actually use much more of the harvest than subsistence hunters. The meat, skull, horns, and hide are all utilized. Meat hunters take *only* the meat. Period. End of sentence. That means large portions of a carcass goes to waste, simply left behind to rot on the bottom of a canyon somewhere or become food for scavengers.

Don't misunderstand me. I support subsistence hunting. Wild game has been part of my diet my entire life. It just seems unfair to crucify selective hunters--who also use the meat--just because they choose to retain a creature's essence as well.

One also must ask what specifically denotes a trophy. The term is completely relative; it depends on a person's perspective and life experiences. I can guarantee you that my stepdaughter's first mule deer or my nephew's first spike elk was as memorable to them as anyone else's record-book animal. The game Rick harvested in Africa may be what the anti-hunting crowd considers *trophies*, but none were trophies in the sense of setting records for the record books, even though they were aged males. The scar-ravaged *dagga* boy with its short broken-off horns, for instance, was no trophy by any official standards. Despite that, he was spectacular in our eyes.

As noted earlier, hunting is very often a family affair, building strong bonds and passing down traditions and knowledge from generation to generation. Most hunters, more than anything else in life, look forward to teaching their children to hunt. Spending hours and hours together in the woods. Sharing the same experiences. No electronics. No cell phones. Those moments are priceless, especially in today's world.

Some of Rick's favorite memories with his daughter Mandi and his nieces revolve around hunting. They still laugh about Mandi's moose hunt, where Mr. Bullwinkle, who they had been stalking for hours, circled back to play ring-around-the-rosy with their ATV, essentially thumbing his nose at them.

The first time Rick's nieces went hunting without him is now a famed family story. The girls are dead-accurate shots, thanks to lots of target practice. Upon their first successful solo hunt, they found themselves with a conundrum; Rick had taught them to gut, skin, and process a deer but had always been there to assist. Lacking confidence on their own, they didn't skip a beat. They googled it. Voila, instant video tutelage. Although it wasn't pretty and took hours longer than it should have, they got 'er done. Proud as peacocks, they gifted the backstrap, the prime piece of meat, to Betty. Instead of Rick's Mom receiving it in one large oblong chunk, however, it arrived as tiny chunks in a large bowl.

One of Harper's first fishing trips, at age seven, is forever planted in our brains, not only because of her excitement upon catching each fish but for her words afterward. On the way home, we stopped at the local gas station to use the restroom. While washing our hands, Harper looked up at a random lady standing beside us and proudly declared: "I just caught fish for my family so we could eat. I'm a provider." My heart just about melted on the spot.

It takes a lot of time and energy to teach novice hunters how to be good hunters, but it is something that most hunters truly enjoy. Sharing their passion with the people they love, or with anyone showing an eagerness to learn, is part of the whole hunting culture. That means there are many times that hunters spend countless hours holed up in a tree stand or hiking for umpteen miles alongside beginners, knowing that if a target presents itself, it is for the young hunter. Not themselves.

The camaraderie that unites families through hunting extends to fellow hunters as well. During a Pennsylvania archery season, my Dad's friend shot a bear behind our house in the last light of day. When darkness made tracking the injured bear too difficult and dangerous, he had to stop. Harvesting a bear with an arrow is a big deal. Word got around quickly. The next morning before dawn, one vehicle after another rolled into our yard, literally, because there was no more room in our driveway. Twelve men showed up to help track that bear. Some had even taken a vacation day upon hearing of the situation. Less than two hours later, the bear retrieval posse showed up with the bear in tow; Kenny had made a good shot. The bear hadn't gone far or suffered long. Rick still insists it was the easiest pack out of a bear he had ever done, noting that 12 sets of arms and legs made light work of it.

Hunting also bridges the gap between cultures. My brother Bobby, his wife, and their friends met members of an Amish community while hunting in Canada many years ago. The common bond of hunting brought the vastly differing groups together in friendship. They began coordinating their hunting trips to Canada for the same week each season. Over the years, instead of waiting to see each other during hunting season, the friendships grew into taking turns visiting each other's homes. One summer, the Pennsylvania group heads to Ohio to visit the Amish in their world. The next summer, their Amish friends hire a driver and come to my brother's house.

Even in Pennsylvania, which is known for its Amish settlements, it's not often you get invited to a pig roast where these less-modern-living people are the guests of honor. Heck, I had never even considered that the deeply religious agriculturalists hunted. Throughout Bobby's yard, women were wearing long conservative dresses with bonnets on their heads talking to women wearing shorts and T-shirts. Meanwhile, men with trousers, suspenders, beards and broad-brimmed hats were scattered about speaking with men wearing jeans and ball caps.

You can't help but be intrigued with such a vastly different lifestyle: a culture sandwiched between two worlds in many ways. It was a wonderful opportunity to talk with them as friends, to learn about their customs and way of life firsthand, instead of from a book. All thanks to hunting.

In Tanzania, hunting had also bridged the gap between vastly different cultures. The camaraderie that formed allowed us a peek into each other's lives.

Anytime I look up at the *dagga* boy's worn face and horns on the wall of our home, I remember the bond formed between people of two vastly different worlds and how blessed I was to become a part of their lives for even just a short while. I remember how they patiently answered my questions to satisfy my curiosity and help me understand their worldview. I relive the mishmash of emotions, the heartfelt appreciation, the jubilation of success, the deep respect for a living being, and the sadness and sense of loss that accompanies each sacrifice. I remember my body groaning from the punishment of the bucking Land Cruiser as we journeyed along roads pocked by elephant footprints. I feel the sharp pierce of my skin from the Tsetse fly's quest for blood. I remember hours in sweat-plastered clothing from the sun's brutal assault. I smile when remembering the pursuit of a tiny antelope that had suddenly changed into three huge *dagga* boys leaping to their feet. I see the scars left on the Cape buffalo's time-ravaged body, scars that told of his surviving an attack from his fiercest enemy. I remember exotic lands that touched my soul. The sights, the sounds, the feelings. It is visceral. Emotional. Alive.

The *dagga* boy did not die in vain. His rugged grandeur is celebrated and immortalized, preserved in all his glory. His hide and horns were not left to rot on the savanna floor, his essence lost. Gone forever. His story never told. As long as Rick and I live, the wondrous dik-dik turned *dagga* boy, will survive. He will be known.

15

KWENDA! KWENDA!

Geez, Sue looked frazzled. Typically, she sauntered into breakfast bright-eyed and bushy-tailed, perfectly put together, and raring to go. The dark circles under her eyes and a slightly disheveled appearance spoke volumes. *What in the world had happened during the night to put her in such a state?* we wondered. There of course had been the typical hair-raising concerts, including *Simba's* beastly serenades. That wasn't new. With our eyes glued to her, she melted into her chair and began sipping coffee. Still, she said nothing.

"Elephants," Rod explained with a smirk, shaking his head. "She barely slept a wink."

During his routine middle-of-the-night nature call, Rod slid his legs off the bed and bumped into a lump of flesh on the tent floor. Sue, dead silent and frozen in fear, sat scrunched in a ball with her arms wrapped protectively around her knees.

"The elephants are just outside," she whispered gravely.

During the night, the resident elephants had been feeding just yards from our tents. Periodic trumpets had been accompanied by short squeals and a steady stream of gurgling sounds, almost like giant stomachs rumbling from hunger. The strange vocalizations are an elephant's way of communicating and keeping track of each other.

We, too, had heard the distinctive blasts; but instead of fear, we had been delighted. Rick and I had seen many elephants during our daily excursions, but that was the first time the jumbos had added their serenades to the African Symphony. Unlike Sue, we were thrilled. Their vocals seemed a fitting addition to the primal choir. Elephants, after all, are synonymous with Africa. You simply can't think of one without the image of the other popping into your head.

Like the rest of the world, I was infatuated with the giants; excitement ran through my veins each time we came across them. Unfortunately, like most animals we saw, the feelings weren't mutual. They scooted. A huge part of my heart silently pleaded for Mike to drive faster. Catch up. Get closer. Follow them across the savanna. I wanted to watch them tear limbs from trees, caress their calves, and frolic in any remaining waterholes. Enthralled by the massive pachyderms, I was aching for more.

Instead, Mike slowed down and proceeded with the utmost caution. If elephants disappeared behind some brush, Mike would make wide arcs around the trees so as not to round the corner, surprising them. I sat on the edge of my seat draped in anticipation hoping we'd spy them again once we *f-i-n-a-l-l-y* rounded the tree. Most often, however, the humongous creatures disappeared like a fart in the wind.

Although I was deflated with disappointment, my crew was relieved. They knew better than to go barreling around the bend and chance running headlong into the massive beasts. Our Tanzanian counterparts treated the behemoths with kid gloves. The caution and respect given to the elephants forced me to recognize that, no matter what human characteristics we bestow upon them, they are wild animals and must be treated as such.

Sue knew this better than any of us. Her history with Mr. *Tembo* was far different than ours. Experience had taught her to equate elephants with sheer terror.

Elephants, or *tembos*, are beloved the world over for their charisma, intelligence, and tight family relationships. The herd animals follow a matriarchal structure composed primarily of female family members and their young offspring, typically in groups of 6 to 20 members. If a group gets too large, it may split into smaller groups, staying generally in the same area. Young males, upon reaching puberty at 13 or 14 years old, are booted from the herd and forced to go it on their own or join bachelor herds.

The matriarch is usually the oldest female. Responsible for the herd's welfare, she uses her vast experience and memory to lead the group to the best food and water sources, finds refuge from the elements, and protects her family from harm.

Just like humans, they demonstrate good manners, kindness, and care; they communicate with each other, both verbally and nonverbally; they form coalitions to solve problems; they get angry with members and then reconcile later; and they do what they can to protect and help the sick or injured members of their herd.

Thanks to the digital world, there are plenty of video clips affirming an elephant's incredible compassion, understanding, and cohesiveness, as well as selfless bravery. Baby elephants, in their clumsy vulnerable state, tend to find themselves in all kinds of compromising, sometimes life-threatening, positions. With watery eyes, I find myself cheering elephants on as they free a newborn from the jaws of a lion or pluck awkward calves from potential muddy graves. How can we not feel a deep emotional bond to such intelligent, caring, protective creatures who display almost humanistic behavior?

Truly, elephants are the gentle giants we think of with fondness, devotion, and adoration. Nevertheless, the very things we love about them--intelligence, strong family bonds, and protective nature--also make them a force to reckon with. If they detect risk to their herd, the gentle giants can turn into grey mountains of mayhem, changing from Dr. Bruce Banner into the Incredible Hulk, as many species do. These versions of the Incredible Hulk, however, are mammoth-sized. It doesn't matter whether the perceived peril is a pride of lions or a bunch of people. Alone, or as a group, they will not hesitate to protect their family.

In "Death in the Long Grass," Peter Capstick describes the public's perception of Jumbo as "big, gray, good-natured slobs who spend their time running in terror from mice, vacuuming up peanuts, and remembering things."[1] To rural Africans and anyone who spends even a short amount of time in wild elephant territory this perception is quickly shattered. He goes on to explain that "Nothing, but nothing, is as overwhelmingly attention-getting as an elephant that has just decided he doesn't like you; and nothing in the animal world is better equipped to do something about it." He adds "If you are not afraid of elephants, then you've either had no experience with them or you're not especially bright."

Their sheer size is the main reason any clever person should keep a respectful distance. Elephants are big. Really big. African elephants are the largest land mamals on earth. A normal bull will weigh between 5 to 7 tons and stand between 10 to 12 feet tall at the shoulder. You'd think any creature weighing 10,000 to 14,000 pounds would be slow and clumsy, but not so. With grace and agility, Mr. *Tembo* can run up to 25 miles per hour. If the sheer mountain of flesh isn't enough, both sexes are equipped with curved ivory tusks. These handy dandy instruments are primarily used for foraging and digging but work just as nicely as weapons, capable of goring or disemboweling foes when threatened or provoked.

Some elephants are born tuskless, ironically making them even more dangerous than their tusked sidekicks. Lacking the tools necessary to peel the bark from trees and dig holes for water, tuskless elephants typically are much more aggressive, bullying their way through life stealing food from others. Usually, these weaponless pachyderms are so hostile that the tusked victims of their thievery feel it isn't worth the trouble to contest.

Musth, an annual hormonal cycle that occurs in adult bull elephants, is another condition that can cause *typically* gentle giants to become extremely cranky, although cranky might not be the right word for describing an aggressive animal the size of a Peterbilt truck. During this period, lasting from a few days to a few months, their testosterone levels can increase up to 100 times more than normal, understandably causing physical and behavioral changes. The aggressive bulls often charge and attack other elephants, animal species, humans, and even trees.

Much like hormonal teenagers, musth seems to be more intense in younger males. As bull elephants age, they tend to mellow a bit. Therefore, their presence can help temper the aggressiveness of the younger testosterone-filled generation.

Elephants are myopically challenged but what they lack in sight, they make up for with the other senses. Their slinky-like noses contain millions of receptor cells providing a phenomenal sense of smell, enabling them to detect water and odors from several miles away. The trunk is also sensitive enough to detect distant thunder and the subtle vibrations of feet hitting the ground. In reality, the appendage is an upper lip and a nose with two nostrils running through its entirety. The end has two agile finger-like digits that can pick up one single blade of grass.

In addition to senses and dexterity, the trunk is loaded with thousands of muscles that are extremely powerful and highly maneuverable, enabling them to push down trees, and throw heavy objects. Acting as a snorkel in deep water, it can also suck up to 10 gallons of water a minute by bringing the water to its mouth to drink.

This versatile extremity is also a primary factor used for socialization to caress, soothe, calm, and reassure each other. Just like a human mother hugs her child, an elephant mother will wrap her trunk protectively and comfortingly around her young.

The elephant's massive ears are multipurpose instruments as well. Averaging 6 feet long by 5 feet wide and weighing up to 100 pounds each, the sail-like extremities trap sound like enormous funnels, allowing them to hear noises over two miles away. The giant wedges of skin, when in motion, serve to regulate the elephant's body temperature. Not only does the air movement cool the torso, but their blood is also cooled as it circulates through the veins of the earlobes. Just as important, the positioning of their ears is used as a communication device, indicating a whole host of emotions.

Of all of the elephant's attributes, it is their brawn that poses the most danger. Jumbo uses this quality in a manner of different ways. Some prefer grabbing their victim with their trunk and beating them against the nearest tree or hard object. Others favor stomping and kneading. Ultimately, the same basic result is achieved: the victim is smashed and pummeled beyond recognition. Fortunately for the target of their wrath, their plight is over pretty quickly.

Adding to the lethalness of the elephants' bulk is their incredibly unpredictable nature. What an elephant will do at any given moment is anyone's guess; an elephant may bolt at the first whiff of human scent on one occasion but carry through with a deadly charge five hours later. Each situation is different. It all depends on the circumstances, the habitat, and their frame of mind at the time.

Elephants are similar to people in that they each have their own personal space that makes them feel warm and fuzzy inside. We've all been a part of awkward conversations when a person invades our space. You start the conversation at one end of the room, slowly backing away, trying to maintain your little orbit until your butt is pressed up against the wall at the opposite end of the room. Invade a pachyderm's orbit and you might find yourself more than backed into a corner. Basically, the closer you get to one of these mountains of muscle, the higher chance you have of violating their sphere of comfort. Unless you are ready for hell in a handbasket, it's best to give *tembos* a wide berth.

Sue, unfortunately, didn't learn this from a book. She experienced a matri-arch's fury up close and personal, the incident embedded in her memory like it was yesterday.

During their first Tanzanian safari, Sue had stayed behind with the vehi-cle while Rod, the PH, and their game scout went in pursuit of an animal. With her feet propped up and the door cracked open, she sat reading as Mark, the driver, lounged beside her in the driver's seat. Without warning, they heard some trees gently rustling off to the left. Mark couldn't see from his seat, so he quietly slipped out of the vehicle to investigate. Just as he exited, a herd of 12-15 elephants strolled into view about 30 yards away.

One might ask how such a colossal entourage could suddenly appear with little warning. You'd think their heft would have the ground shud-dering and the brush crackling. Not so. For carrying around so much tonnage, elephants are amazingly quiet. A fibroelastic layer of tissue covers the bottom of their feet, basically creating pillow-like pads up to four feet in circumference. These oversized cushions not only act as built-in shock absorbers, but they also mold over objects effectively smothering anything beneath them, including sounds. Elephants are also designed to walk on their toes, further helping conceal their approach.

One would think that even with the titans quieter than expected, their sheer size and tendency to travel in groups would be a dead giveaway. Surely the giant herd animals would be easy to spot. Again, not so. Paradoxically, their huge proportions often serve as a type of camouflage. When passing through woodlands, it is impossible to see their entire frame. All that can be detected through the breaks in the canopy are glimpses of dirt-covered gray patches, making them very hard to distinguish.

With little warning, Sue and Mark found themselves much too close to an entire herd of the mammoth creatures. With the wind at their backs and the vehicle motionless, the elephants hadn't detected the human presence either.

The supersized family was strolling parallel to the vehicle with their trunks raised in the air like telescopes. The sight of so many elephants, so close, is enough to make anyone's hair stand on end--at least anyone with common sense. Instantly, Sue recognized the danger and, like a teenager sneaking in after midnight, *tried* to shut the door noiselessly. *Tried* being the operative word. The hushed click of the latch might as well have been a bull horn sounding off in the middle of a funeral procession. The matriarch heard the faint clink. Instantly, she whipped her body around to zero in on the threat.

Apparently, 30 yards on that given day was within the protective matriarch's bubble of safety. With her sphere of personal space violated, she was madder than a hornet. Declaring her fury, she stomped in place, trumpeted loudly, and flapped her ears aggressively. Sue could vividly see the tattered edges of the elephant's massive ears while hearing the *whoosh whoosh* created as air rushed over the sail-like extremities.

In just moments, the matriarch stormed directly at Sue. Mark stood motionless on the other side. Through clenched teeth, with his lips barely moving, he whispered, "Do not move. Do not make a sound or she will kill us." Having 20 years of experience under his belt, he knew elephants, as well as what they were capable of.

Sue didn't have to be told. She felt it in her gut. It took every ounce of restraint she could muster but she didn't so much as bat an eyelash. She remained statue still; frozen in fear. The matriarch covered the 30 yards in a flash, stopping just three feet short of the vehicle. With her entire mass blocking Sue's field of vision, she continued to trumpet her displeasure, flapping her ears wildly.

After a few blood-curdling moments, the protective pachyderm retraced her steps back into the herd, never taking her focus from the vehicle. Once with the herd, she violently kneaded the ground with her forelegs, still waving her ears aggressively.

Just moments later, she charged a second time. Hard. With much more force and hostility. Unable to contain herself, Sue swiftly slid into the driver's seat, putting just a few more inches between her and the angry matriarch. Almost inaudibly, Mark again repeated: "Do not move. Do not make a sound."

The second charge brought the elephant within inches of the vehicle. The elephant's bulk filled the window opening, blocking everything from view but a portion of her dirt-covered trunk and section of the wrinkled mud-plastered hide. More trumpeting. More ears flapping confrontationally. Finally, while never letting her focus falter, the protective leader retraced her steps backward into the enfold of her family a second time.

A few seconds passed before the angry giant charged a third time. Once more, her ears swung savagely, the *whoosh whoosh* sounds forever implanted in Sue's memory. The irate *tembo* stopped a third time just short of making contact, hesitated, and retraced her footsteps again.

The key to surviving an elephant charge is knowing how to read their body language, essentially to determine if they are bluffing or not. Since many elephants, especially females, don't like the sound of the human voice, yelling in a harsh, gravelly tone will sometimes scare them. Cows tend to bluff less often than bulls. In other words, they mean business. Their maternal instincts to protect the herd drives them to kill the threat. When other measures fail to stop an elephant charge, the rule of thumb is to stand your ground. Do not run. Try to out-bluff the animal.

Apparently, this matriarch hadn't read that playbook. Instead, she was thinking more in the line of baseball; *three strikes, you're out*. After the third retreat, her body language changed. The 8,000 pounds of maternal fury became deadly quiet, pinning her ears back, and tucking her head and trunk down. The show was over. No more warnings.

Mark knew it and Sue knew it. It was time to flee. As the matriarch initiated her fourth and final charge, Mark scrambled into the driver's seat shoving Sue out of the way and pushing the pedal to the floor. As the vehicle lurched forward, the matriarch stampeded behind them with her entire family in tow.

As noted, a speedy getaway is rarely possible in the bush. Sue stuck her head out the passenger window yelling "Faster! Faster!" The enraged elephants tried butting the rig with their heads, but the vehicle was able to stay just out of reach as it lurched across the pitted landscape.

Sue was doing her impression of an Indiana Jones movie hanging out the window screaming at the top of her lungs when she saw the two trackers sprinting towards the vehicle. They had been lounging under a shade tree 100 yards in front of them, the only tree amid sparseness. There was no cover. Nowhere for them to hide. Her pleas instantly changed from "Faster! Faster!!" to "Slow down! The Trackers! Slow down!"

Mark heard but didn't listen. There was no time. He knew the only chance of survival, for everyone, was the trackers jumping aboard with the vehicle in motion. Fortunately, the rig was still fighting for forward momentum, enabling the adrenaline-driven men to somehow clamber aboard. Sue's eyes were so focused on the elephants that only the sound of bodies banging against metal told her that they made it. Seconds later, both men began beating on the back of the cab, urgently shouting *"Kwenda! Kwenda!* Go! Go!"

Gradually, the Land Cruiser gained enough speed to put a lifesaving distance between them and the angry mob. Two hundred yards later, the entire herd buggered off into some brush, vanishing from sight. Just like that, tons and tons of raging elephant flesh was gone. The threat was over.

Once the ordeal ended, Sue had a complete meltdown. Still petrified with her nerves frazzled, she insisted Mark take her to an abandoned train station she had seen earlier in the day. No amount of persuasion could change her mind. He eventually did as she requested, left her there with the trackers, and returned to find the others.

Here is the thing. Sue is not a wimp. She is a confident, strong, assertive, take-charge individual who is comfortable carrying a gun and perfectly capable of taking care of herself. I, for one, want her on my side if I'm ever in a pinch. Mention the word elephant, however, and her body language completely changes. Each time she sees, hears, or talks about them, she relives the sheer terror of that day.

Rick and I knew the story. We knew *about* her fear. We'd also read many other such accounts. Therefore, in our brains, we *knew* their deadly potential. Still, the fear wasn't a ball in the pit of our stomachs like it was for Sue. Unless experiencing their ferocity firsthand, it's hard to imagine the Mr. Hyde part of an elephant's personality. Most of us are just too programmed to think of them as "big, gray, good-natured slobs."

Most of the time, that is exactly what elephants are. Gentle giants. Yet, on that day a perfect storm of circumstances led to a near-deadly encounter. If the wind had been different, the herd's keen sense of smell would have caught the human scent and avoided them. If the engine of the Land Cruiser had been running, the elephant's sensitive hearing would have picked up their presence long before they wandered into sight. Maybe the matriarch was just having a bad day and the human surprise was the straw that broke the camel's back. Who knows? With one slight alteration, they may have never known the elephants were there or they may have passed by peacefully.

As it was, circumstances did dictate a confrontation. Sue will never lose her dread of elephants. Still, she places no blame on them: "We were the intruders. The matriarch was just doing her job. Protecting her young and her herd. You can't fault a species for that."

Sue may not blame them but she sure as heck understands their potential. Surviving a full-blown elephant charge will give you a more realistic view of the massive pachyderms. Sure, their loving gentle nature takes precedence. Still, we must also recognize that once that switch is flipped, they can be savage and brutal. One itty bitty false move and Sue would now be fodder for worms instead of sitting across from us that morning at *Masimba* Camp, white-faced and unnerved. Sue was lucky. Not everyone is so fortunate.

Elephants are responsible for killing up to 500 humans a year in Africa. Many fatalities, of course, are never even reported. Either bodies are never found or there is no process to document such data. Hunters and wildlife professionals make up a minute portion of that tally. Most deaths occur to rural people while they are trying to protect their livelihoods or simply finding themselves in the wrong place at the wrong time when an elephant's protective instincts are unleashed.

Some human deaths can also be attributed to what many people call Nature Deficit Disorder: people living in cities and manicured suburbs out of touch with the reality of nature and its wild inhabitants. These animal-loving people quite simply enjoy a fairytale view of the natural world. They have no concept of what it is like to live among the creatures of Africa: a place where many species are mega-sized, destructive, and dangerous. Animals like elephants, lions, leopards, and hyenas.

In September of 2018, a German tourist at Mana Pools National Park in Zimbabwe was trampled to death after encountering a herd of elephants when she jumped out of her vehicle to take pictures. What aggravated the animal is unknown. The same article mentioned another man who attempted to drive an elephant herd into the open to take a photograph. This not-so-bright soul also lost his life.

Although people are cautioned to keep their distance from wild animals in national parks, some don't heed the warnings. Far too many people are programmed to view elephants *only* as gentle giants. Who in their right mind attempts to jockey a herd of dump-truck-sized pachyderms into position for the perfect picture?

The deaths of tourists, wildlife professionals, or hunters as a result of wildlife conflict typically make the headlines. The demise of local villagers, on the other hand, falls largely under the radar, unless specifically reading about human-wildlife conflict. Most of these victims are reduced to statistics, not individual names of people with mourning family and friends. Mothers. Fathers. Sons. Daughters. Siblings.

While these deaths may not make the newspapers, animal-loving people must recognize the consequences of human-wildlife conflict because, ultimately, it is bad for *both* species. If humans suffer, elephants suffer more. Those who wish to safeguard elephants cannot overlook this brutal reality.

Any elephant involved in a deadly attack, or even one demonstrating excessively aggressive behavior, is often put down for fear they will harm again. According to the World Wildlife Fund, over 200 people were killed by elephants in Kenya within the last 7 years, a country that banned all hunting years ago. In retaliation for the deaths, Kenyan wildlife authorities were forced to shoot between 50 to 150 elephants per year. That is a whopping 350 to 1,050 elephants in Kenya alone. This is, of course, only the government-sanctioned killings. Many more go unreported.

Elephants are happy to avoid human confrontation 99 percent of the time. Unfortunately, local people must live with the possibility of the other one percent. It is simply impossible for most Westerners to grasp what it is like to live amongst the iconic giants, who can, and will, pulverize you under the right circumstances.

The crux of the problem--for the people living with the *mostly* good-natured jumbos--is that they are eating machines. Elephants consume about 5 percent of their body weight, a stupendous 200 to 600 pounds of food, each day. That is a pile of vegetation. The megaherbivores spend 16 to 18 hours a day feeding on grasses, small plants, bushes, fruit, twigs, roots, and tree bark. The latter, aiding in digestion, is one of their favorite staples. The desire for this roughage leads to a lot of destruction as they break branches, strip bark off trees, or even topple entire specimens to get the food they need. They scatter and uproot almost as much as they eat. Their preferred dining areas often resemble twister-ravaged landscapes. As notoriously messy eaters, they are not the guests to invite to Christmas dinner.

Yet, these colossal uninvited guests often bring their huge appetites and destructive way of feeding to the fields of small rural farmers, causing destruction and devastation to many crop-dependent villagers. One elephant can quickly wipe out several acres of crops in one overnight raid. That modest plot of land is the entire livelihood for a small local farmer. Many of the rural people affected are already food-deprived and gravely poor. Obliterating their entire year's work leaves them in desperate situations. No crops to feed their family. No income to buy supplies. No extra money to educate their children. While people in the West regard *tembo* with affection and admiration, elephants inspire fear and anger for the local people who must share the land with them.

The land plundered by elephants, oftentimes, is habitat that was previously available to them. The exploding human population has forced local people to trespass further and further into the domain of the plant-eating pachyderms. Elephants are just doing what they have always done, consuming any food source available to them throughout their daily wanderings. Whichever side of the coin you look at, this competition and encroachment into one another's natural environment is causing significant human-elephant conflict.

Tourism in Tanzania is a growing industry. One of their main tourist attractions, the Serengeti National Park, draws over 400,000 tourists a year to see its spectacular fauna. Part of the draw, of course, is the beloved elephants. *Tembo* is therefore considered a key resource for the tourism industry, generating great incentives to preserve and protect elephants in the Serengeti.

Although this can be good for the beloved giant, it is causing escalated human-elephant conflict among residents living near the park. Incidents of crops being destroyed and human deaths resulting from the frictions have increased.

Some communities originally living in the park were forced to relocate back in 1951. At the same time, hunting and eating wild food were forbidden in the park, eliminating a key source of sustenance for local people. These same individuals often find it hard to find employment in the tourism industry. More educated townspeople are typically hired over non-English speaking villagers. Also, a large portion of ecotourism revenue goes to the government or foreign enterprises running the operations. Therefore, the local people receive very little benefit from preserving wild populations, although they are the ones experiencing the costs and side-effects of living with such dangerous destructive species.

In an attempt to distribute tourism revenue more evenly, Wildlife Management Areas (WMA) were introduced in Tanzania in 2006. This enabled member villages to lease out their communal lands to tourism operators. Although it provided income to the five villages containing the largest density of animals, the program was largely unsuccessful because the other 20 villages in the district were too remote or didn't have enough wildlife to appeal to tourism operators. Ironically, these same villages were most adversely affected by elephant raiding.

Efforts are being made to keep the pachyderms at bay. Some have laid wire fencing along boundaries which has had some positive effects. An initiative called 'Living with Elephants' was created in 2016 by a group of young villagers. The members post sentries along various locations along the perimeter of the village. When elephants approach, they form groups of about 20 people using firecrackers to drive them off. This village group was able to reduce crop damage in the past three years. Still, they fear that the elephants will soon adapt to the countermeasures they have created.

Most of these efforts to combat elephants are being done at the expense of the already impoverished rural people while profits are raked in elsewhere. As William Adams and Jon Hutton from Conservation and Society put it in 2007: "Powerful governments and international tourism enterprises collaborate to drive out powerless local residents.[3] Their actions and the unequal distribution of tourism profits, therefore, tend to reinforce human poverty at the local level while celebrating global principles of wildlife conservation."

The same type of scenario is playing out throughout much of Africa. Rural people are dealing with the problems of conservation but are not benefiting significantly from the added burden placed upon them. Instead, they are losing their lives and livelihoods.

There is hope. Many in-country organizations are working diligently to find ways for the two to live close to one another. Research has shown that fields located even a half mile from an elephant corridor have a 50 percent less chance of being raided. Other ideas include encouraging growing practices that produce better yield from less land; planting crops that can be harvested before the dry season when elephants are most likely to go in search of them; finding methods to make crops easier to defend; burning chili-laced dung or planting chili and tobacco-based crops to deter elephants (smoke irritates their sensitive smelling receptors and respiratory system); growing crops that the elephants simply don't like to eat; using bee-hive fences as a deterrent; educating local people on the use of such dissuasions; and restoring habitat corridors that allow seasonal movement of elephants and other wild species away from human populations. Nevertheless, promoting such expensive life-changing ideas in villages where elephants are feared or even hated can be extremely difficult.

Elephants are at the center of complex multi-sided issues. While populations in many areas are decreasing due to habitat encroachment, some national parks have experienced sharp increases. While this is great for the tourism industry, too many of these mega-sized plant-eaters, confined in too small of a space, are putting stress on ecosystems. In the past, the iconic giants had all of Africa to feast on. Now, elephant populations are confined to small areas, relatively speaking, that are often fenced and managed by humans.

Their territory has changed but their food requirements have not. As mentioned earlier, these messy eaters destroy lots of trees, either by stripping away their bark or toppling them. Put quite simply, when elephant populations go up, trees come crashing down. If not enough habitat is available to maintain the population, trees cannot grow back fast enough to replace what is lost. The loss of trees coincides with the loss of shade. This in turn affects grass and predator-prey relationships, as well as allowing rains to wash away valuable topsoil. These habitat changes affect the beneficial relationships between species. A destroyed ecosystem is not only a future death sentence for the elephants, but it also destroys the habitat of countless other species as well.

In the 2018 Africa Geographic article "Research: Does Botswana Have Too Many Elephants" written by Gail Thomson, a wildlife conflict specialist based in Botswana, researchers did an elaborate study on the sustainability of Botswana's elephant population.[4] Based on their data, the recognized number of elephants within the country is deemed to be 130,000 animals (although some conservationists estimate the population to be significantly higher).

The study concentrated on an enormous, unfenced area almost untouched by human management, unlike many locations in South Africa. According to the researchers, female herds and their young typically remain within three miles of a permanent water source. Bull elephants typically remain within nine miles. Consequently, the habitat close to water suffers the most impact from their supersized appetites. Habitat outside of this zone is only minimally impacted. These varying tracts of elephant usage allow for the growth of different types and lengths of grasses, plants, and trees. Some grazers prefer tall grasses while others prefer short. Still, others prefer dense shrubs. In the end, elephants create a diverse ecosystem, or different ecological niches, for a large variety of wild populations.

In conclusion, the study found that elephants perform a key role in maintaining a diverse and healthy ecosystem. There was one caveat; there must be large distances (at least 31 miles) between permanent water sources. Put simply, artificial waterholes should *not* be created. The study also found that large tracts of land must be barrier-free, allowing them to migrate naturally, thereby, limiting the damage to particular areas and allowing the habitat the opportunity to repair itself.

An adult elephant must drink an average of 40 to 60 gallons of water a day. That's enough to fill a normal-sized bathtub. Lack of water during long dry seasons forces elephant herds to travel further distances. Inevitably, calves unable to endure longer treks will not survive. This is one of nature's ways of limiting its population. Severe droughts will even act as built-in contraception, causing elephants to yield fewer calves.

According to the article, harsh lessons were learned from places such as Kruger National Park. In the past, many parks introduced artificial waterholes to help more elephants survive, catering to tourism. More water meant more elephants and places to see the majestic giants. While the practice was a boon for the tourism industry--and, temporarily, the elephants themselves--it upset nature's delicate balance, causing detrimental effects to other species.

The added water not only attracted water-dependent species such as elephants, zebras, and buffalos, it drew the predators who fed on them. Some animals, like roan, for instance, are more susceptible to lion predation. Their main places of refuge were where fewer lions existed. The artificial water points created higher lion densities in more areas, giving roan little chance to find sanctuary. Roan, therefore, suffered tragic losses, with very few found in Kruger National Park today.

This begs the question. Shouldn't conservation be about more than just one or two species, even if those species are less charismatic or iconic?

At *Masimba* Camp, I was appalled when Joel told me about the hundreds of hippos dying in Ruaha National Park due to drought. At the time, banning the use of artificial water seemed insane, as well as inhumane. How was it possible to stand by and watch so many animals die? In my pea brain, I was thinking *only* of the hippos. Never did it occur to me that something as basic as supplying water to dying beasts was detrimental to the ecosystem overall. Nature, for sure, is an intricate web. Ultimately, as horrific as it was, letting those roly-poly water-lovers die may have been the most humane thing to do for the good of wild inhabitants overall.

It is the same with elephants. It doesn't take a rocket scientist to understand that too many of an animal that requires up to 600 pounds of food a day could wreak havoc on an ecosystem. Large life-giving specimens of trees, some hundreds of years old, are falling to the mighty herbivores, causing less significant scrub trees to grow in their wake. Some conservationists fear irreversible damage is already occurring to natural resources in areas where too many elephants exist; and if something isn't done soon, there will be catastrophic consequences for elephants, as well as other species. It is devastating to think of letting elephants eat themselves, and other animals, into destruction, especially in areas that are supposed to be protecting them.

In the past, culling was used to stabilize elephant populations in many national parks. Although mass off-take may ultimately preserve wildlife, it is an extremely unpopular business the world over. Many countries caved to pressures from international interest groups and stopped the practice. However, some countries including South Africa, are considering using the practice again in areas that are being ravaged by over populations and increasing human-wildlife conflict.

Anti-culling groups push for birth control or relocating elephants to countries that have too few. Both techniques are extremely expensive and often don't do the job. Separating elephants from family groups causes significant stress to all elephants involved. Plus, many find their way back to their original habitat, making all the money and effort null and void.

When culling is necessary, entire family herds are killed. Research has found that elephants left behind are traumatized, making the elimination of the entire herd the most humane and least intrusive way to eliminate elephants without causing stress on the entire elephant population. It is worth noting that these carcasses are not left to rot on the savanna. One hundred percent of each animal--meat, hides, entrails, and bones--is utilized, thereby creating a micro-industry of its own.

Even so, wiping out entire families of majestic giants is an unpleasant business. It is also an extremely expensive process that cuts sharply into a park's resources, using assets that could be used elsewhere, such as in anti-poaching efforts. Until other tactics are found, however, it is simply the only viable short-term solution. Detestable or not, if the scientific data confirmed that the sacrifice of a few would save elephants in the long run, I would painfully support the heartbreaking practice.

Since well-managed hunting uses quotas that are specifically established to maintain or grow animal populations, it is not a replacement for culling. It does, however, provide value to elephants, aside from photo-tourism, along with combatting several other issues facing the giant pachyderms.

The *selective* harvest of adult-aged bulls removes individuals who are consuming vast amounts of valuable resources, especially since the large males require more food and damage larger, older trees compared to younger elephants. Taking bulls that are past breeding age has zero impact on the population, especially considering only a few of thousands are hunted and new calves replace them tenfold every year. Also, extremely old elephants often wear down their molars to the point they are unable to grind their food, causing them to weaken and die a slow miserable death of starvation. Hunting these elderly pachyderms may be a much more humane way to die.

Hunting elephants is also an act of supporting a community. In many rural areas of Africa, the meat from animals harvested by hunters is the only source of protein available to them, especially in predator-infested regions where raising livestock is difficult and they aren't allowed to hunt wild game themselves. Many villages are located hours away from any type of market to buy meat. Consequently, when approximately 12,000 pounds of flesh suddenly becomes available from the harvest of an elephant, it is a huge cause for celebration.

Also, as mentioned, elephants are exceedingly intelligent. According to Gail Thomson in the 2020 Conservation Namibia article "Key Questions for Human-Elephant Conflict Research," there are a lot of unanswered questions on whether hunting increases or decreases conflict.[5] It is known that the absence of older males leads to the younger ones becoming more aggressive. Also, some question whether witnessing a hunt makes an elephant more aggressive. On the flip side, others suggest hunting creates a "landscape of fear," thereby reducing conflict. Just like humans, animals learn where it is safe to go and where it is not. Hunting them may teach the clever pachyderms to avoid villages, the crops surrounding them, and people in general. This sure seems to be the case regarding other species hunted in the United States.

When weighing the effectiveness of each method of conflict mitigation, one must also consider the drawbacks of each. Non-lethal options are very costly, often requiring a vast amount of time and effort. Even if external funds help cover the initial costs of such tactics (burning chili bombs, installing bee-hive fencing, pumping water for elephants to drink, etc.), the ongoing maintenance and expense are often left to the individual farmers.

Hunting troublesome elephants, on the other hand, provides meat to the affected people while providing money to the villages, helping them pay for any damages sustained. That is why lethal control is often considered a much more attractive option by those who are risking their lives and suffering the direct consequences of living with such colossal creatures. Villagers are much more willing to deal with the inconvenience and perils of living with elephants if protecting them improves their quality of life. Plain and simple.

No matter what deterrents are used, human-elephant conflict will occur on occasion. This forces wildlife officials, as well as villagers, to take matters into their own hands at their own expense. Game rangers may use a bullet for such actions, but impoverished locals--unless they have a valid reason not to--may turn to primitive snares or poisons, ultimately causing more living things to suffer and die.

Elephant management is also extremely costly to the government, the national parks, and the wildlife services. Money from hunting helps fund law enforcement, conservation programs, and anti-poaching strategies in these agencies.

Namibia is a major success story in elephant conservation using big game hunting as a strategy. Their population of elephants has almost tripled since 1995, with a large percentage of that growth occurring outside of parks. Many other species--including lions, rhinos, cheetahs, giraffes, leopards, and even crocodiles--have grown as well.

Forging a strong bond between conservation and rural development and poverty relief is critical to their overall strategy. Community-Based Natural Resource Management Programmes (CBNRM) was formed. In all, 70 percent of Namibia is under one form or another of conservation management making it one of the world's largest contiguous areas of protected land.

These areas give the community the right to manage and use the wild populations for economic and development opportunities. Putting value on the animals enables them to earn significant income and has created a great incentive for people to look after and protect wildlife, including elephants.

A 2017 National Geographic article entitled "Should We Kill the Animals to Save Them" also explores Namibia's success in using hunting as a conservation model.[7] Author Michael Paterniti says:

> If it pays, it stays. It was a phrase I heard over and over again, in myriad discussions about African conservation, in part to describe how money has changed the mind-set of rural populations regarding the value of big game. Too often people have seen an elephant destroy their annual crop, and some have known the pain of a lurking lion taking a child for food. Here there's no mythologizing or fetishizing, no fund-raising around a fuzzy face: the leopard is a killer, the rhino is a ruiner. To protect themselves against the enemy, villagers often shoot and poison these intruders, without an iota of sentimentality. And yet, the argument goes, if those animals are worth money to a local community, that community will work hard to conserve and protect its assets.

After spending time in Namibia, the author of the article testified that he witnessed the success of this approach to conservation firsthand. Land that was threatened by cattle grazing instead became habitat that game returned to. Well-managed quotas enabled an increase in wild animal populations while also growing the number of individuals that could be harvested. Profits were shared individually as well as communally. Adult members were issued yearly checks to be used as income. The hunting concessions were also required to hire and train local people as well as contribute toward development projects such as schools and health clinics.

Paterniti found that hunting for conservation wasn't without drawbacks. Unlike Namibia, which turned wildlife management over to local communities, some governments assume ownership of the animals and hunting grounds. This model can lead to corruption, hunting quotas being based more on money than on healthy wildlife populations, and not enough of the income being reinvested in wild habitat. Even so, Paterniti states the link between enlightened hunters and the sustainability of animal populations and the preservation of wild places is "inextricable."

Botswana, on the other hand, is a perfect example of what happens when the legalized hunting of elephants is outlawed. Between 2007 and 2014, while the rest of the continent experienced at least a 30 percent drop in elephant populations, largely due to widespread poaching, Botswana supported a relatively stable population of more than 130,000 elephants and had done so for the previous 15 years. According to the IUCN, this was accomplished while using lucrative well-managed elephant hunting as part of their strategy. Botswana was touted as a conservation success story.

In 2014, everything changed when then-President Ian Khama caved to outside pressures, imposing a hunting ban on elephants. He also armed anti-poaching units in national parks with military-grade weapons and issued a radical shoot-to-kill policy. Most people expected these measures to safeguard elephants and deter poachers. Instead, researchers found a nearly 600 percent increase in poached elephants between 2014 and 2018 according to the 2019 New York Times article "Poachers are Invading Botswana, Last Refuge of African Elephants."[8]

In that same period, human-elephant conflict increased significantly. The rural communities were not equipped to handle the unimpeded roaming of 12,000-pound creatures and the destruction of life-sustaining crops. Rural villagers, therefore, were forced into a precarious position; either drive off the impending giants with whatever tools they had at hand or watch their food supply, and sometimes homes and water supplies, be destroyed.

In the 2019 Africa Geographic article "Botswana Has Found Her Voice on Elephants--but Will We Listen?" Gail Thomson, the wildlife conflict specialist mentioned earlier, states:

> Elephants have killed 36 people in Botswana in the last few years, with 14 deaths and many more serious injuries record-ed since February 2018. Many crop farmers have lost their

entire annual yield in just a few nights, which severely compromises their food security. Elephants effectively impose a curfew on any human movement after dark. Women who have spent the day working their fields, collecting water, and feeding their families can no longer walk over to their friends' houses at the end of the day for a relaxing chat. To do so when elephants are around is life-threatening.[9]

In the past when hunting was allowed and people were permitted to shoot rogue elephants, conflicts between humans and elephants were rare. The money earned helped the village mitigate any damages, the meat was utilized as protein, and the problem animal was alleviated. Once hunting was stopped, the intelligent giants had no reason to avoid villages as they had done in the past.

Mike Chase, the director of Elephants Without Borders, and therefore a staunch advocate for elephants, understands the plight of the local people. He tells National Geographic, "When you've tried all kinds of alternative s....and they're still dangerous, the animal has to be destroyed. At least the communities should be able to benefit by letting a hunter come in and pay to do it."

Before the hunting ban in Botswana, there was an incentive to protect elephants. Because of that, many rural people worked with authorities to curb poaching. Once the hunting ban was put in place, the local people saw no benefits. Instead, they experienced destruction, mayhem, and death--causing many people to look the other way regarding illegal activities, rather than helping authorities stop them as they did in the past. Neil Fitt, an independent conservation consultant in Botswana, recognized this fact in the New York Times article mentioned above regarding three people being killed by elephants in just one week: "I'm not saying that poaching is O.K., but whilst we have these problems, it is difficult to get the communities on board to assist in protecting wildlife. Addressing poverty and unemployment in the rural areas would go a long way in protecting our wildlife."

This ban on hunting, resulting from outside anti-hunting pressures, also led to a much greater threat. The rural people of Botswana became antagonistic against western interference. Where communities were once conservation-minded, they became almost anti-wildlife. Because of their loss of commitment to protecting elephants, poaching became rampant and others who would normally report it chose to turn a blind eye. In fact, in one two-month period alone in 2018, Botswana authorities found 90 poached elephant carcasses rotting with their skulls chopped off and their tusks removed.

When you look at this scenario, it is simply hard to dismiss the fact that the nearly 600 percent increase in poaching materialized *after* legalized hunting was eliminated, even while enforcing the violent poaching shoot-to-kill policy. Common sense speaks loud and clear; once the people living with the animals no longer benefited from their preservation and instead suffered death and destruction as a result of elevated conflict, there was little incentive for rural people to protect the giants.

Then, in 2019, due to the devastation and uninhibited destruction caused by the lumbering pachyderms, President Masisi, the newly elected president of Botswana, lifted the ban on hunting after "extensive consultations with all stakeholders." Also lifted was the "shoot-to-kill" poachers policy of his predecessor. President Masisi explains "sacrificing a few elephants will allow us to save many, many more, and protect the people of Botswana."[10]

In the Smithsonian 2019 article "Five Things to Know About Botswana's Decision to Lift Ban on Hunting Elephants," Erik Verreynne, a wildlife veterinarian and consultant based in Botswana, states that it is also important to understand that while huge elephant populations were great for Botswana's photo tourist industry, the rural villages who bear the highest costs of human-elephant conflict rarely benefited from the tourism.[11] The article goes on to say that a night in a luxury safari lodge costs $355 on average while a legal elephant hunt costs approximately $45,000, not counting the tens of thousands of associated expenses. In addition, this income requires much less infrastructure, leaving a much smaller imprint on the environment.

Botswana's decision has been praised by conservationists, hunting groups, and local communities; but not surprisingly, there was significant backlash from celebrities and anti-hunting groups. While many may be well-intentioned, they are trying to impose their values on a culture across the globe without understanding the reality of living with such creatures.

Although the U.S. Fish and Wildlife Service originally decided to lift the ban on importing legal elephant trophies in 2017, they have since caved to anti-hunting pressure. Unfortunately, few hunters want to pay the high costs of hunting without the ability to bring home the memory. Consequently, the reversal of Botswana's hunting ban may not result in the desired trophy hunters that they were hoping for--at least not from America. A ban on importing legally acquired hunting trophies is as detrimental to the hunting industry as the actual ban itself.

In full disclosure, if it was financially feasible, my husband would love the opportunity to hunt one of these dangerous game species. Hunting elephants is simply the ultimate quest for some hunters. They willingly place themselves in peril for a number of insane reasons that probably only a fraction of people can comprehend. Whether it be to test their skills, overcome their greatest challenge, or prove a victory over one's mortality. To these hunters, it is like a climber scaling Mount Everest or a runner finishing the Boston Marathon.

It is not only the danger of hunting elephants that puts my stomach in knots. It is the idea of Rick being responsible for the death of one of the amazing creatures. Still, with a heavy heart, I would support him even though my emotional attachment to elephants screams *No! No!*

That, however, is exactly the problem. What right do I have to pass judgment or make decisions on wildlife management while safely tucked away in my American home? All the good intentions in the world do little good if the local people are not on board. They are the ones living with dangerous destructive animals. Not us. It is their crops and livelihoods lost. Their communities that suffer in poverty. Their friends and family who are injured or killed. Ultimately, they are the people who will decide whether beasts live or die. That is the hard truth.

After witnessing Sue's deeply embedded fear at breakfast, the thoughts of elephants and their plight were whirling through my brain: human-elephant conflict; shrinking and fragmented habitat; overpopulations in some places; decreasing numbers in others; hunting or no hunting; and, of course, poaching. It made my head swim.

Just then, my body lurched in the vehicle as we crossed another patch of sunken elephant footprints baked into the cracked earth.

A smile slowly materialized on my face as realization dawned on me. Those teeth-chattering remnants of the mighty pachyderm may be inconvenient and even brutal at times, but the gaping tracks also meant that I was in Africa. Amid elephants. Lots of them. I'd happily accept the jarring from each and every elephant pothole if it meant the giants were part of the landscape. A safari without them would be utterly heartbreaking.

A bull elephant disappearing into the long grass.

As if knowing my thoughts, a lone bull elephant suddenly appeared on the savanna several hundred yards in front of us. When *Mr. Tembo* heard us, his casual stroll morphed into a determined stride, heading towards a cluster of mopane forest. My eyes lit up and I slid to the edge of my seat in excited anticipation. The bull wanted no part of us. Logic told me that his retreat was a good thing. After all, I had no desire to relive a version of Sue's terrifying ordeal with pissed-off pachyderms. Still, the passionate side of me desperately wanted to shout, *Kwenda! Kwenda! Go! Go!* My screams, however, would have been to get closer to the captivating behemoth--not further away. Reluctantly, I kept my mouth shut and watched longingly as the huge bull melted into a clump of acacia trees.

16
The Heart of the Conflict

"*Hapana. Hapana.* No! No! You wait. I'll get someone to go with you." Joel quickly exclaimed.

In surprise, I looked to see Joel's face switch from joyful storytelling to one of concern. One of his elephant anecdotes reminded me that I wanted pictures of the elephant footprints just outside of camp, literally only 30 feet away. While grabbing my camera, I casually mentioned my intentions, ultimately triggering a major undertaking.

Joel scurried away and came back with Musa and Maugo to act as my escorts. Again, the footprints were *only* 30 feet from the edge of camp. What I had figured to be a one-minute quest turned into a 30-minute production as my Swahili-speaking protectors, beaming with pride and excitement, led me to every single elephant pothole in the vicinity. Needless to say, I now have enough *tembo* footprints to wallpaper our master bedroom.

Why all the fanfare you might wonder? Truthfully, it took only a few days for me to become complacent. *Masimba* Camp and its competent staff had allowed me to drop my guard. A hungry lion in the mood for a rump roast no longer filled my brain. At least, not during the day. In camp, I felt fairly insulated from harm, embedded in a cloak of safety so to speak.

Another time during an afternoon break, while deep in my fairytale bubble, I announced I was going to read my book by the hippo pond. Sitting on the rock embankment above the lounging hippos seemed perfectly safe to me. Surely, the *kibokos* couldn't climb rock boulders if they got sick of my meddling. What I forgot to consider was that the cantankerous creatures weren't the only things to worry about.

Being near water, even the putrid haven of hippos, was one of the most dangerous places to be. While lions can go for several days without water, they must eat every day. With waterholes drawing in a whole host of thirsty critters, they are the perfect spot to ambush prey. Therefore, the only way I was getting anywhere near that hippo pond was with an armed escort. Since Lilian, along with her machine gun, volunteered to act as a chaperone, my plans to read took a hike; a conversation with Lilian was much more fun and educational than the pages of any book.

Lilian acting as my bodyguard at the hippo pool.

Another afternoon when returning to camp we rounded the bend to see three Tanzanians walking on the trail. Thinking they might be poachers, Raphael, Rick, and Lilian readied their rifles. When it became obvious that the men had no weapons and showed no malice, we slowly pulled up to them. After an exchange of Swahili, the three young men jumped into the cargo hold to ride back to camp.

They had been working for a different outfitter about five miles away in an area bordering Rungwa West and needed medication for a sick worker. When we found them it was midafternoon--the most blistering part of the day. In my naïve mind, I couldn't understand why they didn't make the trek in the early morning or late afternoon when it was a bit cooler. When mentioning this to Raphael, he replied in his calm matter-of-fact manner: "It is the safest time to travel. The lions are bedded down in the shade."

This simple statement hit me like a punch in the gut. Can you imagine having to consider such a thing when doing your daily chores?

Simba's favorite food may be Cape buffalo and zebra, but it's understandable why one might rather sink his teeth into something a little less formidable. A domesticated cow, tame goat, or even an unsuspecting villager makes a practically effortless meal. While lions typically don't target humans, that doesn't mean they don't make exceptions. When ravaged by hunger or pushed to desperation, and sometimes just because they can, they will turn to humans for food. People in the bush are, therefore, always at risk.

Tanzania has a history of killer lions. Between 1932 and 1947, as many as 1,500 people were killed by an aggressive pride of 15 lions near the town of Njombe, Tanzania. The pride was soon dubbed the "Man-eaters of Njombe." The attacks were triggered when the colonial government took drastic action to control a rinderpest epidemic that was killing livestock. All wild species, vulnerable to the disease and capable of spreading it to cattle, were summarily slaughtered. Buffalo, zebra, wildebeest and many kinds of antelopes were exterminated. With most of their prey gone, the lions were soon starving. Faced with extreme hunger, they discovered that humans offered an easy plentiful food source.

Osama, one of the Arabic words for lion, was another famous Tanzanian lion responsible for killing over 50 people in the village of Rufiji between 2002 and 2004. He was less than 4-years old when he was finally shot. Since he was so young, some scientists believed he learned to eat humans from his mother. Others claim his preference for tender cuisine was due to an abscess on one of his molars.

Of course, lions aren't the only predators to fear in Africa. Leopards are far less likely to attack humans, but they still kill dozens of people a year. Typically, the spotted felines are more opportunistic, only killing people under the right circumstances while hunting their natural prey. As with anything, there are exceptions. Google 'man-eating leopards' some time and you will be shocked at the results that pop up. I know I was.

Fortunately, leopards seem to prefer livestock over humans. As the most adaptable of the large cat species, they can live in practically any habitat, including urban areas, using dogs and cats as a primary food source. Leopards, therefore, occupy more places on the globe than any other large cat.

While their versatility and ability to exist in many environments is good, it can also be a Catch-22, specifically *because* they *can* live near humans. This often poses a significant risk to livestock. In societies geared around domestic animals, it is easy to understand why leopards in the vicinity aren't viewed with any kind of affection. Especially any old, weak, or starving felines who look at livestock as easy pickings.

How many people lose their lives each year to lions or leopards is anyone's guess. Like most statistics in Africa, getting an accurate count is like trying to squeeze water from a stone. Accordingly, statistics are all over the place. Let's just say, the consensus seems to be that lions kill approximately 70 people a year in Tanzania (the country with the most lions in the world) and 250 throughout Africa overall. The number of people killed by leopards is much sketchier and far lower. Since the root cause of attacks is human interference and encroachment into one another's habitat, many sources expect the tally to rise in the future as human-wildlife conflicts increase.

With detailed accounts of such grisly deaths passed down from generation to generation, it is no wonder rural people have a healthy dose of fear for the carnivores. The gruesome details are etched in their minds. To them, a mauling is not just a statistic or a number. Each victim has a name with family and friends who love them: a four-year-old tending a goat herd; a wife stepping outside after dark to relieve herself; a grandfather fallen asleep by the campfire, a farmer protecting his crops. Imagine the torment of losing a loved one in that way, either never knowing their fate or finding little left to bury.

The majority of Americans simply cannot grasp that kind of danger while doing the most normal daily tasks. For most of us, hell will freeze over before we get mauled by a cougar walking to the mailbox. Mothers don't get eaten by grizzlies while taking a bath. Fathers rarely get trampled by deer when defending their gardens. Children don't get attacked by wolves while playing in their backyards.

Westerners also have little to fear from property damage or loss of livelihoods as a result of wildlife. Moles digging tunnels through our lawns, bats taking up residence in our attic, squirrels nibbling on our wiring, or deer invading our garden may be inconvenient; but most of us will still have food on the table at the end of the day.

Even so, most Westerners will not let fur-covered visitors destroy, eat, or harm *whatever* they want just because someone in Tanzania loves squirrels, deer, and bears. Instead, they will build fences, insert mesh shields, install traps, buy animal-proof containers, or use other deterrents. These things, of course, take time and money. Both of which most Americans *do* have.

One must also recognize that we aren't talking about a problem that affects a small number of people. In Tanzania, for instance, about 90 percent of the population lives in rural areas. Of those people, about 90 percent depend on agriculture or livestock for employment, and more importantly, to provide food for the country's population.

Understanding the fear and dangers that rural villagers live with daily is vital to understanding their mentality. Each activity, including simple daily chores, must be carried out with forethought and prudence to avoid dangers that most of us simply can't imagine.

While writing this chapter, my mind jumped to the sight of three distorted carcasses. Lions. Once regal magnificent beings now slaughtered. Claw marks and shredded dirt marked the ground, telling of their desperate struggle to break free of the snares. I couldn't help visualizing the pain, confusion, and terror of their final moments. The more they resisted, the tighter the cables gouged their necks, ultimately choking the life out of them. My heart sank in despair and grief at the sight of the previously regal lions twisted awkwardly amid the loops of wire.

Just as Lilian and the others had explained to me, the deaths had nothing to do with poaching for money. All three lions, while deformed from the struggle, still had all of their "money" parts. Teeth. Skull. Paws. Claws. The lions were killed simply in retaliation or as a preventative measure against future predations.

While the mangled lions were a very real and vivid example of what I had learned from Lilian and *Masimba* Camp, I didn't witness the gruesome scene firsthand. The tragedy was featured on "The Heart of the Conflict" episode of Carter's W.A.R. Ivan Carter, the conservationist and wildlife investigator mentioned earlier, had spotted a kettle of vultures circling the sky. Upon investigating the telltale sign of death, he and his tracker Livvy found a dead lion, or the little that was left of it. When questioning the people of a nearby village, they learned of a missing donkey, an extremely expensive and important beast of burden in the African bush.

Carter's instincts told him the death of the lion and donkey were related so he went searching for the lost animal. Upon finding its remains, the signs in the dirt indicated that the domesticated equine had battled not just one, but four lions.

Soon, the stench of decay drew their attention. Moments later, they found the three mangled lions, all strangled in simple wire snares. Someone, presumably the donkey's owner, had discovered the lions eating its carcass. In retaliation, the lions were driven off allowing time to set the snares, knowing that they would return to feed.

Carter was outraged by the needless destruction of the predators who, as he put it, "...do not understand borders. They only understand the source of an easy meal."

The carnage, in his eyes, simply did not fit the crime. His anger sent him barreling towards the village anxious to confront the man responsible. Along the way, their vehicle was stopped by a herd of cattle blocking the road. In furious aggravation, he demanded they move.

The local cattle herder engaged him just as antagonistically, admitting that the donkey had belonged to his brother.

"You get your water from a tap," the villager shouted. "Where do you think we get our water?" he vigorously inquired.

Carter's body deflated in resignation as realization dawned on him.

"From a dam!" the man hurled back in frustration. "To haul it, we must use a scotch cart! What do you think pulls that cart?" With a sigh of exasperation, he again answered his own question, "a donkey."

As distressing as it was, Carter was forced to see the scenario from the eyes of the villager. The man, who was defending the actions of his brother, had 25 head of cattle, a few goats, and a couple of donkeys as his entire livelihood. The herder explained to him that without the lions, he would have many more heads of cattle.

As mentioned earlier, cattle in Africa are not only livestock, they are symbols of wealth, status, and quality of life. That donkey was a huge expense in their part of the world. Its loss may seem insignificant to us, but as a beast of burden, it was critical to their daily life. Plain and simple.

While watching the episode, I was in sync with Carter, rooting for the evil killer to be found, arrested, and put in jail with the key thrown away. Gradually, I was forced to see what Carter saw. They weren't poachers killing for money. No animal parts had been taken to be sold for profit. The deaths had absolutely nothing to do with the illegal wildlife trade. The destruction had been done in retaliation for the loss of the donkey and to prevent it from happening again.

With Carter's acceptance of the hopeless situation, their exchange transformed from hostile to civil. The herder switched to his other role in life, a loving father. Excitedly, he invited Carter and Livvy to meet his three sons. As the two men gently shook the hand of each shy, bashfully smiling child, the father proudly introduced the boys as Prominent, Prosper, and Provide.

It's funny how tiny things can affect you; my heart melted. In those names, the parents poured their hopes and dreams for the future of their children. A future in a hostile, often food-deprived, land where a few cattle make up their entire livelihoods, and a donkey is needed to get a family's daily supply of water.

Seeing the situation through the eyes of the villagers, my whole view changed. Instead of feeling *only* revulsion and outrage for the death of the lions, I felt compassion and understanding. While it is convenient to characterize the people responsible for such deeds as vile beings, it would be unfair, as well as a lie. The hard truth is, most are desperate people; they are providers making sure their children have food to eat, water to drink, and protection against the dangerous realities of village life.

We have all seen the peaceful Mom in our culture morph into a mama grizzly bear protecting her kids. Name-calling, a shove on the playground, or a child not getting the starting position on the football team can send reasonable parents into an outright tizzy. How can we expect mothers and fathers across the world to react differently? Against threats like these?

Seeing the love and pride on the face of that father as he introduced his sons Prominent, Prosper, and Provide reminded me that parents--no matter where they are in the world--want the same thing for their children: safety, security, love, nourishment, quality of life, and opportunity.

I'd like to say that the incident was unique, but that would be a lie. The morning I had first seen the elephant bones, Lilian had awakened me to these realities, teaching me that the illegal killing of animals was much more than simply killing for tusks, horns, and claws. Many rural Africans kill carnivores, quite simply, to make their lives safer and easier. Nothing more.

Knowing this, many in-country conservation organizations are working diligently to find non-lethal methods to mitigate human-wildlife conflict. Ruaha Carnivore Project (RCP) is one such group. Its founder and director, Dr. Amy Dickman, is a conservation biologist and National Geographic Explorer who has spent her entire life trying to protect wildlife, especially carnivores.

RCP recognizes the welfare of lions is inextricably linked to the welfare of the local people. They work with rural communities to reduce predator attacks on livestock while also helping pastoralists implement better non-lethal livestock protection methods.

Their research reveals that 65 percent of attacks occurred within poorly protected enclosures, or *bomas*, usually made of thorn bush. As a result, they developed stockades made of diamond-mesh fencing that proves to be 95 percent effective. The reinforced enclosures require locals to take responsibility for part of its cost, as well as its upkeep. The *boma* owners who devote their assets and time to such non-lethal techniques are given subsidized veterinary medicines for their livestock. Although this has been extremely successful in reducing conflict, each fortified enclosure costs around $500 for materials and labor costs.

Approximately one-third of livestock predation occurred during daily grazing, away from the protection of fortified paddocks. The farmers often move their cattle from area to area depending on the seasons. Livestock is often so spread out that herders can't keep track of them to prevent threats.

The Hwange Lion Research Project in Zimbabwe is experimenting with canvas enclosures that can be rolled up and moved along with the livestock. The highly mobile barriers offer a line of defense against the carnivores, plus they can be situated around fallow farm ground to fertilize the spent soil with dung, thereby providing another benefit. While still in the experimental stages, there is hope that this too will lower livestock predation.

Another fascinating and heart-rending method these organizations are experimenting with is the use of specialized guard dogs. These dogs, such as Anatolian Shepherds, which grow to be large and intimidating, live alongside the livestock, bond with them, and become very protective of them. Unlike herding dogs, they do not move the livestock when a threat is perceived, since fleeing animals often spur a predator's chase. Instead, the protective dogs stand their ground, barking loudly against any threat. This alerts the herder who can come help drive off any carnivores. Since most predators rely on surprise for a successful attack, once their cover is blown, most are likely to retreat. These dogs have proved very effective in successfully chasing off lions and other threats. Amazingly, no livestock attacks have occurred while being guarded by these four-legged guardian angels.

While this sounds promising, it isn't without problems. Only ten of the dogs have been imported into Tanzania so far. From these, some have died from snakebites and diseases. Another was killed by a lion while defending its charges. Just as significant is the financial cost. Each dog costs about $1,000 to purchase and support during its first year alone. That is a whopping pile of moola for rural Africans. Even if the canine is initially purchased by outside sources and gifted to herders, local families are still finding it difficult to feed such sizable guardians. The canines can weigh up to 150 pounds; that is a lot of hungry dog to feed, especially in communities where humans eat very little protein themselves and often deal with food scarcity in general.

Trials are underway to combat these issues by breeding the specialized canines with local dogs, hoping that the crossbreeds will retain their protective guarding instincts while also making them easier for economically challenged families to care for. Even if the right dog is developed, thousands upon thousands of these amazing watchdogs are needed throughout Africa. Even when, and if, the kinks are worked out, widespread use will not happen overnight. It will take time. It's an extraordinarily worthwhile venture, yet daunting just the same.

The RCP also employs local people as Lion Defenders and Conflict Officers. These villagers are trained to respond when livestock is attacked and to use their conflict mitigation skills to stop retaliatory killings. These committed individuals will even sleep outside the homes of those threatened to chase lions away to protect the people, their livestock, and ultimately the lions themselves. In addition, they help reinforce *bomas* using traditional means to provide temporary relief until the money can be saved to fortify the enclosure with wire. They are also trained to collect and record data digitally so that the RCP can gather baseline data to help develop appropriate conservation strategies. These local people are instrumental in collecting data and understanding the patterns of carnivore attacks and how to develop the best strategies to prevent them. Some of the Lion Defenders are members of warrior societies who used to gain wealth and prominence by killing lions. Now, they are showing others in the warrior community that they can gain income and status through conservation rather than the killing of lions.

Another successful program initiated by the RCP is Community Camera Trapping (CCT). Game cameras are set up around the participating villages and credit is given for each animal seen in the images. For instance, lions and leopards may be worth 15,000 points while a Cape buffalo is worth 4,000 points. Groups of four villages compete against each other to get the highest tally. Then every three months, monetary prizes are awarded to the communities that have spotted the most wildlife on camera. The money awarded to each village must be split between health, education, and medicines for the livestock. The villagers themselves decide on what the funds are spent on. To distribute the money, a big party accompanied by food is organized to celebrate and share information so that the community can see firsthand that preserving wildlife in an area reaps a higher reward, incentivizing them to preserve animals instead of killing them.

The RCP is not the only organization working to find strategies for humans and carnivores to coexist more peacefully. There are many throughout Africa. Botswana Predator Conservation, in my opinion, gets an award for thinking outside the box. They are currently studying the effects of painting eyes on the backsides of cows. As noted, predators will often abandon the hunt once they have been spotted by their prey. Consequently, the organization worked with local herders to test the idea, hoping to minimize killings.

Amazingly, during the four-year study, none of the 583 painted "eye-cows" were killed by predators, while 9 of the remaining 378 cattle became victims. Their concern is that the predators may eventually ignore the deterrent. As of 2020, this study was still in its initial stages with much more to be learned.

Overall, many strategies have proven successful in decreasing both carnivore attacks and carnivore killings in the core study areas, some by as much as 60 percent. Once they are deemed to have merit, they need to be maintained and expanded further into lion country.

Still, decreasing predation is not enough. On a 2020 "This Wild Life Conservation Podcast", Dr. Dickman makes the comparison that if your home is being burglarized and a burglar alarm helps cut thefts in half, it still doesn't make you fond of the burglars.[1] There has to be more. Local people must feel real tangible benefits from living with such creatures – safety, education, empowerment, health care, and improvement of the human condition. In other words, by placing ownership and a value on wildlife, there is an incentive to protect it.

During the podcast, Dr. Dickman explains that, while she is a non-hunting vegetarian who views hunting as horrific, her time in the field has convinced her that well-managed hunting provides benefits that currently have no replacements. Retaliatory and preventive killings are almost nonexistent in hunting concessions compared to non-hunting areas. But *the most* important aspect of legalized hunting is the benefit it provides to local people while also preserving huge chunks of land in its wild state. Land that is unsuitable for general tourism for the various reasons mentioned earlier.

Dickman's boots-on-the-ground experience has convinced her that stopping trophy hunting without *first* having a viable alternative will increase snaring, poisoning, and habitat conversion while depowering and harming the local communities that depend on it economically--all of which will negatively impact wildlife populations. She asks, "shouldn't conservation's goal be to grow species, not further reduce them?"

Human-wildlife conflict is a heart-wrenching reality for both two-legged and four-legged species. It is easy to pass judgment on a reality that we can't begin to grasp; our lives are not intertwined with the dangerous and destructive species. We adore them from thousands of miles away without understanding the truth of Africa's harsh existence.

Step into the shoes of a food-insecure local villager. Would you, lacking the basic necessities of life, find the money and time to build *bomas* for your livestock when a snare or poison would be much cheaper and easier? Imagine your child walking to school, knowing that *Simba* could be lurking in the shadows. Picture yourself hauling water or gathering firewood in predator-prone areas. Envision caring for and guarding the livestock that is the center of your economic well-being, as well as social status. Put yourself in the "Heart of the Conflict." Now ask yourself, what strategies would give your family food security, a better quality of life, hope for the future, and ultimately a reason to protect wild creatures instead of killing them? Common sense will tell you everything you need to know. Statistics are irrelevant when faced with these harsh realities.

17
THE CHERRY ON TOP

"*Twiga*," I announced excitedly, upon spotting two giraffes stretching their long necks to feed on the leaves of the acacia trees. For once, the long-legged browsers ignored us as we passed by, allowing me to gawk in wonder at their gracefulness. A mile later, Rick calmly muttered, "*swalapala*," gazing in the direction of a group of impala grazing in the distance. I glanced questioningly at Raphael.

He smiled and nodded "*ndiyo*". Yes.

A little later, our nemesis and their grazing partners kicked up their heels, heading for the horizon. By then, naming the zebra and hartebeest was easy: *punda milia* and *kongoni*. How could we forget those two after eating their dust so many times? *Kongoni*. I adored that name. It was fun and silly sounding, perfect for such a peculiar-looking antelope. Next, we passed a dried-up mud bog as warthogs hoisted their tails in the air, sprinting to their burrows. "*Ngiri,*" Rick announced. An hour later we entered into terrain with patches of wooded thickets. Mgogo silently pointed to a small group of sable browsing in the distance. Enthusiastically, I whispered, "*hala pala*."

Raphael grinned and replied in a hushed voice, "*pala hala*."

Darn! I always screwed that one up.

Class was temporarily over. Sable was one of the primary species on Rick's wish list and somehow the ones just spotted hadn't seen us yet. While Raphael lifted the binoculars to his eyes, I silently uttered, "*pala hala, pala hala, pala hala*" over and over in my head. For some reason, I always transposed those two words.

After a few minutes of studying the antelopes, Raphael lowered his glasses, shaking his head: "No mature bulls." With a tap on the window, Mike was off again.

While I loved traveling through the savanna and seeing all the wildlife, there was one problem; Rick and Raphael were like peas in a pod. Both were reserved, quiet by nature, and focused on the task at hand. Silence for them was easy. Me? Not so much. Oodles of questions rattled around in my brain as we shimmied through the African bush. While en route, everyone was confined to their little station, making talking with anyone other than those two anti-conversationalists impossible.

Fortunately, our frequent stops allowed for lots of *Lilian* time. At only 23 years old, her manner was far beyond her years; she was smart, level-headed, dedicated to her job, and generous with her knowledge and time. She was warm and friendly, essentially a much more social creature than our male counterparts. Therefore, unless questions needed to be answered en route, I saved most of my inquiries for her. Like water over a dam, questions spilled from my lips practically before the engine quit rumbling, unless we were stalking or tracking, of course.

While the guys did their thing at various pit stops, we did ours. Our *thing* revolved around friendship and learning; therefore, when Lilian's official duties as Tanzanian game scout weren't needed, she stepped into the role of *mwalimu* and *rafiki*. Teacher and friend.

Along with sharing her wealth of knowledge about Africa's plants and wildlife, Lilian taught us snippets of Swahili. *Asanta sana*, thank you very much, was of course the first thing we learned. From there we moved on to other things: *jambo,* hello; *hujambo,* how are you; *sijambo,* I am fine; *karibu,* you're welcome; and *maji baridi tafadhali*, cold water please. That was an essential one. We guzzled enough water during the day to sink a small ship.

Although *asante sana* was my all-time favorite, *kazi nzuri,* good job everyone, was a close second. That phrase just oozed out of my mouth like butter over a steaming hot ear of corn. It also reminded me of a superhero exclamation. Shazam! Although my view is most assuredly biased and romanticized, I felt like each of our Tanzanian hosts had their own unique superpower of sorts. Whether it be spotting a kudu's ear in the brush, determining which Cape buffalo was an aged male among the hundreds stampeding by, piloting a vehicle safely over pitted terrain, cooking bread over hot coals, or transforming strips of meat into jerky, their savvy and expertise in a foreign world deserved superhero status. *Kazi nzuri!* When I said those words to our crew, they meant much more than a simple "good job everyone."

Before long, it wasn't just Lilian teaching us Swahili. With an amused smile, Raphael would correct us when we botched a word or when I appealed to him with a big question mark in my eyes. Back at camp, all the English-speaking staff--Joel, Thomas, Michael, Andrew, and Hilary--joined in as well. My vocabulary grew to encompass another one of my favorite phrases; *lala salama,* sleep peacefully. Those two words sound just like a winsome lullaby, the perfect way to end each evening.

You can't come to Africa and learn bits of Swahili without learning the names of its wild creatures. Honestly, this was more fun than a barrel of monkeys or, in this case, a barrel of *tumbili.* It became a game of sorts. Any time Rick and I spotted an animal, we'd race to see who could name it in Swahili. With names like *fisi, digi digi, tohe, kongoni, popo, pongo, fungo, pofu, kiboko, twiga, korongo,* and *kaboko,* how could you not have a blast?

As mentioned earlier, foreign languages had never been my forte. I took Spanish in junior high school but barely scraped by with a passing grade. Normally a good student, I struggled endlessly to make sense of the foreign words spouting from the teacher's mouth. They all sounded pretty much like the teacher in the "Charlie Brown" cartoons, the endless "wah wah, wah wah, wah wah" boring the Peanuts gang to death. I dropped Spanish class like a hot potato the minute the term was over and never attempted a language again.

Tanzania changed that. My eagerness and fondness for learning Swahili caught me totally off guard. I loved the playful sound of the words and the way the syllables rolled off the tongue. The real selling point, however, was the reaction we received from the staff when we used those simple words rather than our language. That, more than anything, sealed the deal. We, of course, butchered some of the words, but that didn't matter. It only mattered that we tried.

Learning Swahili was just the beginning. Once Lilian, Raphael, and Mgogo knew we were hungry for more than just the pursuit of game, the bush became one giant classroom.

Lilian teaching us about the Mkwaju fruit.

Whenever the guys were busy, Lilian would search out nearby plants to give us mini-lessons and sometimes even a taste test. After sampling the so-called fruit of the *Mkwaju* tree, however, we learned to nibble instead of dive in wholeheartedly. The brown sausage-like pods were unlike any fruit we had ever seen or tasted. The hulls crack open when mature, revealing a fibrous sweet-sour fruit surrounding seeds that are also edible. Loaded with vitamins, the odd delicacy is used for cooking, flavoring drinks, household purposes, tea, and medicine. Interestingly, the seeds are one of the ingredients in Worcestershire sauce.

While the tree and all it bears may be extremely valuable, the taste of the fruit itself must be an acquired taste. While I don't remember the exact flavor, I do remember the strange pulp-like texture, as well as my lip-puckering response to its bitterness. If Lilian hadn't taken a bite herself,

I'd have thought she was pranking us. While stifling her laughter at our puckered faces, she assured us that vervet monkeys also love the delicacy. Well, the *tumbili* frolicking nearby had nothing to fear; there was not a ghost of a chance we'd steal their lunch.

Raphael's methods of teaching were much more subtle. He was always focused on the black dot on the horizon that may be a *pala hala* or a curled branch in a thicket that could be the corkscrewed horns of the grey ghost. Since I tried not to cloud his vision with questions, he shared his knowledge bit by bit as situations arose and features of the landscape presented themselves--just not always at the moment one might expect. This came into play during one of our normal excursions.

One of the many termite mounds.

Oodles of termite mounds dot the Tanzanian landscape. The earth structures pop out of the ground like pimples on a hormonal teenager's face, only the monstrosities can be 40 feet high by 60 feet wide. The ones we saw were typically about half that size. Still, that's some pretty ginormous mounds of dirt.

Some formations took the shape of mud-encased skyscrapers, while others appeared as intricate giant sandcastles. Most were more simplistic with mud heaped into rounded mounds or cone-shaped bulges.

No matter what they looked like, the towers of dirt *supposedly* housed huge colonies of termites, the notorious rice-size insects. Yet, each mound looked completely vacant. Zero activity. None. We never even caught a glimpse of the voracious wood munchers.

While passing another desolate-looking heap, curiosity got the better of me. I leaned over and whispered into Rick's ear, "How come we never see any termites?"

Rick, exceedingly helpful, shrugged his shoulders while murmuring "No clue."

Gee, what a blabbermouth. Anyway, I made a mental note to ask Lilian at our next stop.

My thoughts then jumped to the *twigas* we had just passed. The Maker's creative juices kicked into overdrive when designing these stunning ungulates. Along with their beautiful gold-mottled bodies, their long legs and soaring necks give them the height to nibble on treetops, the green leaves providing all the moisture they need. Giraffes can go days without a trip to a waterhole, giving them the freedom to roam into dryer terrain while much of the animal kingdom is held prisoner to the availability of daily water. Shockingly, giraffes can even go longer than camels without water. Who knew?

Twiga's quality that held me completely spellbound, however, was their gracefulness. The giraffe's stretched-out torso, coupled with its elegance, made their sprints across the savanna appear as if they were running in slow motion. Their endless legs reached forward in massive flowing strides, carrying their dappled bodies gracefully into oblivion. Simply mesmerizing.

The captivating scenes caused conflicting emotions. Part of me wanted them to stay put each time we saw them so that I could enjoy them as long as possible, while the other part of me anxiously waited for them to flee, allowing me to watch their unique grace and beauty in motion. Grasping that the dazzling performance could only be seen in the wild, I was humbled and grateful every time. The confines of a zoo simply would not allow for such exquisite freedom of movement.

Although there were plenty of giraffes striding across the lands of Rungwa West, overall giraffe populations have decreased 40 percent in the last 30 years. It's the same song and dance: habitat loss, human encroachment, and poaching for bushmeat and its hide. In a handful of countries, civil unrest is also a factor. Sadly, giraffes are already extinct in 7 of the 28 countries where they once roamed. The IUCN has therefore recently listed the giraffe's conservation status as Vulnerable to Extinction. While this listing may intend to save giraffes, it may set in motion policies that ultimately undermine conservation.

Africa, as you well know, is honking *HUGE*. On top of that, it is extremely diverse. Applying a one-size-fits-all strategy to a continent three times the size of America may not be the golden ticket. According to studies performed by the Giraffe Conservation Foundation, there are four distinct species of giraffe and five subspecies--not all of which are threatened.[1] For example, Namibia and South Africa--as a result of well-managed conservation efforts--have nearly doubled their giraffe populations in the last 30 years, using legalized hunting as a strategy. Interestingly, and possibly no coincidence, six of the seven countries where giraffes went extinct had no form of organized hunting. The fear is that a blanket policy will hamper the conservation efforts of countries with stable and growing giraffe populations.

This same scenario plays out with other species as well. According to a 2021 Zimbabwe State of the Nation video, it has 85,000 elephants. While that number initially makes an elephant-loving person want to do a backflip, unfortunately, their park systems only have space for about half that amount. Not only is the giant herbivore overpopulation having devastating effects on the habitat, but human-wildlife conflict is on the rise. Understandably, many people believe strategies should be based on each country's needs instead of lumping them all together.

While my thoughts were still absorbed in the graceful magnificence of *twiga* and the nightmare of determining sound conservation strategies, Raphael, out of the blue, interrupted my daydreaming, going into a fascinating explanation of termites. Rick and I glanced at each other in bewilderment. Over the bumping, grinding, and din of the motor, he had heard the question I whispered to Rick earlier. Again, I repeat a line Rick's grandma used to use, "*Raphael could hear an ant peeing on cotton.*"

That was quite a feat in itself, but why had he waited until the termite mound was ancient history? We still shrug our shoulders over that one. Apparently, he had been focused on more critical things at the time, like fresh *tandala* droppings splattered on the ground or footprints in the dirt. Or maybe he was just putting his thoughts together in English.

Raphael's feedback may have been postponed but we did learn where the termites were; remarkably, they were right in front of us. Well kind of. Up to 3 million of the gnawing insects live inside each one of the mud-baked structures. They are full of air shafts and elaborate tunnels, leading them directly to dead wood and plant roots for food. The hidden passages allow them to bring home the bacon, so to speak, without exposing themselves to danger. Under the cover of darkness, some of the workers venture out to feast on vegetation above-ground as well. From deep underground, the industrious builders gather mud, haul it to the surface, and use their saliva and feces to bond the dirt into cement-like fortresses. Now that is ingenuity.

Like bees and ants, termites have a strong social structure, emphasizing the power of the group over that of each individual. They, too, have a queen. While we may assume she rules the roost, in reality, she is no more than a slave, a captive ovary responsible for laying up to 30,000 eggs a day. The grueling effort to build and sustain each mound can last up to 15 years, essentially until the egg-producing servant dies of her labor. Literally.

Aside from the queen, the colony is divided into workers, soldiers, winged alates, also known as the reproductives or *kumbikumbi*. These specialized winged termites know which group the colony is lacking, fertilize the eggs accordingly, and tend to the eggs. Periodically they swarm from the mounds, ditch their wings, and form new colonies. We missed out on this phenomenon since the *kumbikumbi* don't take flight during the dry season. They wait until the rains when the ground is softer and easier to penetrate, enabling a mass exodus of fleeing insects. Leaving their mound in a swarm increases their chance of survival against the gauntlet of predators waiting outside.

Termites or *mchwa* are a valued food source for all kinds of predators, including humans. Since the flying termites are easily snagged by a host of predators, they suffer the most risk. The *kumikumbi*, packed with proteins and healthy fats, are considered delicacies by the local people. Supposedly, the scrumptious treats have a delicious nutty flavor, savored whether roasted, fried, or eaten raw. Even so, I'd prefer mine hidden in gobs of chocolate.

While the land-based termites aren't as valued as human food, plenty of insectivores feel differently. The aardvark has powerful claws, capable of breaching the mud-plated armor, while aardwolves wait to feast on the ones venturing out at night. Both of these termite-loving species can consume tens of thousands of insects in just one night. Their protein-rich bodies also make them a favorite among other insects, including ants.

Not only do termites offer nourishment to a host of insect-eaters, but they are also critical to the African habitat. Their elaborate tunnels and storage chambers used to transport, break down, and cache plant material for later consumption, as well as their digging ventilation systems for heating and cooling the colony, are extremely beneficial to the ecosystem. All the dirt movement changes the soil texture, creating porous topsoil which plays a key role in rainwater absorption. Along with retaining moisture, feces and food scraps from the creatures feeding on the mounds offer further nutrients to the soil. All of this allows for a dense collection of assorted vegetation. Healthy diverse plant life attracts a wide range of herbivores which, in turn, draws the meat-eating predators.

Wildlife, both predator and prey, also use the tall structures as observation posts. Even the smallest of species can scramble to the top, allowing them a great view of the grasslands. Once the architectural marvels are abandoned, they become useful for a whole other purpose. The caverns and intricate tunnel systems offer shelter and burrows for at least 18 different species, including warthogs, porcupines, spotted hyenas, mongooses, and snakes just to name a few.

All the life-giving aspects of the termite towers make the lands surrounding them some of the most biologically diverse in the entire habitat. The further you go from the amazing feats of nature, the more wild populations and reproductivity decline. Who could imagine such an inconspicuous insect could be so important?

By then, we had passed scads of the termite-filled sandcastles. It was their sheer size and unique formations that had piqued my interest, not their vital role in the ecosystem. We had thought of them as lifeless mounds of dirt, yet they were teeming with vitality. Thanks to Raphael, and his slightly deferred lesson, we came to view the dirt cathedrals with awe and gratitude.

Nevertheless, one troubling fact did come to light. Snakes. The slithering reptiles understandably are also drawn to the abandoned network of tunnels. Most notably, the snake of my nightmares. The long empty shafts are favorite hiding spots for black mambas. Essentially, don't go blindly fishing in a termite mound hoping to discover a coveted porcupine quill. Not unless you have a death wish. We were warned to keep a safe distance from termite-abandoned mounds. Fortunately, the gaping holes in the dirt made them easy to spot. No one had to tell me twice.

It will be no surprise that much of our schooling from Raphael had to do with snakes. After all, my fear of Africa revolved largely around the reptiles. I was obsessed with knowing anything I could about them.

Tanzanians often referred to black mambas, or *kabokos*, as *ropes* due to their long rope-like appearance. To me, that name seemed much too innocent sounding for such a lethal being. Raphael also informed us that the black-mouthed serpents tend to smell like rice. Basically, if you get a whiff of the fluffy white stuff, it's time to skedaddle.

During our long hours together, we even discussed what to do if bitten by Mr. Mamba and other snakes. If a *kaboko* sinks his fangs into you, there isn't much to discuss. Unless you have a vial of antivenom stashed inside your pocket, which is highly unlikely, you might as well start digging the hole. Fortunately, Raphael reminded us that while they are among the fastest snakes in the world, traveling up to 12.5 miles per hour, they are also very shy. The speed demons prefer to use their swiftness to escape threats, rather than attack. I latched on to that tidbit like it was a life raft on the doomed Titanic.

Our discussions didn't end there. Plenty of African snakes will kill you deader than a doorknob pretty directly if left untreated. As I touched on earlier, puff adders are responsible for more African snakebite fatalities than any other snake. Weirdly enough, this is also the snake that I feared the least. The puff adder's perfect camouflage, wide distribution, potent venom, tendency to bask on footpaths at night, and slothful nature creates a perfect storm of conditions for unwary villagers. Ironically, it was the very fact that they are short, fat, lazy, and nocturnal that made me less fearful of them. There was not a chance in hell that you'd find me traipsing around at night like so many of their victims were forced to do.

Fortunately, for villagers who do fall victim to a puff adder's bite, it is not an automatic death sentence. Their venom causes severe tissue damage, but with treatment and/or large doses of antivenom, their bites are highly survivable. The key words here are *with treatment*.

In the African bush, there is little and limited access to medical treatment. Appropriate health care facilities are few and far between. You can't just call an ambulance or race to the emergency room a few miles away. No life-flight helicopters are going to pluck snakebite victims from the savanna floor, buzz through the skies, and take them to the life-sustaining medical treatment needed. Without proper care, the puff adder's potent venom will cause the necrosis to spread throughout the body, causing a loss of limb or loss of life. An untreated healthy adult male may die in as little as 12 hours. By the time many Africans get the help they need, it is either too late to save their lives or an amputation must be performed to stop the continued loss of tissue.

Rick and I must be gluttons for punishment. We went so far as to consider the gruesome process, visualizing no anesthesia and using hunting knives instead of scalpels. In reality, however, Rick and I would probably not die or need amputation from such a bite. Unlike most rural Africans, we had the resources to purchase a global life-flight insurance policy. If tragedy struck, the cavalry would arrive on a white horse to save us (the white horse being an airplane of course).

That safety net, or insurance policy, barely cost us the price of a new pair of Nikes. Yet for many impoverished villagers, you might as well ask them to fly a spaceship to the moon. According to the 2020 National Geographic article "Snakebites Kill Tens of Thousands of Africans a Year," an estimated 30,000 people die each year from snakebites in sub-Saharan Africa.[2] Another 90,000 survive with amputated limbs and permanent disabilities. Those, of course, are just the ones reported. Doctors and snakebite experts feel the real toll may be double that.

Not only is there a huge global shortage in snake antivenom, but most of the ones required for African snakebites need refrigeration to stay stable and effective. With frequent power outages, even in cities, this is a nearly impossible task. In addition, many victims lack transportation to get to treatment facilities or don't get there in time. When and if they do arrive, the staff are often insufficiently trained or not equipped to treat snakebites. Even if the drug is on hand, it is too expensive for many victims. To draw attention to the snakebite crisis and attract funding for research and treatment, in 2017 the World Health Organization (WHO) took the unprecedented step to add snakebite envenoming to its list of neglected tropical diseases, even though, technically, it is not even a disease.

There are many factors leading to the shortage of antivenom but for simplicity's sake, it comes down to money. The antivenom is very difficult and expensive to produce and since the victims are mainly impoverished people lacking the funds to pay for the serum, there is little incentive for manufacturers to produce it in volume. On top of all of that, many researchers, politicians, and people, in general, are entirely oblivious that the issue even exists. Consequently, there is a lack of advocacy to resolve the problem. Now that the WHO has recognized snakebites as a priority, hopefully, efforts can be made to sift through the complicated components of the problem, thereby reducing the number of snakebite fatalities and injuries.

While the snakebite crisis and lack of antivenom are already disturbing, it is even worse when learning that a disproportionate number of snakebite victims, especially of puff adders, tend to be women and children. Their smaller body mass and lighter footsteps create less intense earthly vibrations warning snakes of their approach. With little time to react, the sluggish snakes are unable to move quickly enough to avoid itty-bitty, often barefoot, feet. For many people in rural Africa, footwear is a luxury, not a given. To make matters worse, the smaller the person, the more dangerous the venom is to their systems.

Joel's older brother came to mind. A black mamba had killed him when he was only 10 years old. His pint-sized body didn't stand a chance against such a lethal serpent, with no antivenom or medical care available. It is simply heartbreaking imagining the helplessness and anguish Joel's parents must have felt upon losing their firstborn. Being so young himself, Joel had few details to offer. I couldn't help wondering why the *supposedly* shy snake hadn't fled. Had his brother reached into a termite hole? How did he catch the snake unaware? Did the snake not feel his vibrations? Even though Joel's brother was a nameless faceless child to me, the thought of his final moments still haunts me.

Fortunately, our discussions with Raphael didn't include snakebite statistics. The staggering figures didn't come to light until researched further. For that, I am very grateful. Sometimes the less you know, the better.

My favorite bits of information from Raphael came when I didn't even know enough to *ask* a question. Suddenly, he would tap on the cab telling Mike to stop. Excitedly, Rick and I would scan the terrain searching for an animal. Instead, he'd rattle off some Swahili to Mgogo, causing him to lunge from the cargo hold on a quest of some sort.

On one occasion, Mgogo whipped out his machete as he hopped off. Whoa! Our eyes opened wide wondering what in tarnation he needed his 20-inch blade for. He then carefully grabbed a nearby spiked caveman-like limb from a supersonic-sized thorn bush. Barbs the size of pencil ends jutted from its inch-thick stems. After slicing off an eight-inch chunk of the weaponized tree, he handed it to us to inspect. Raphael explained that the tree is referred to as the Medicine tree. While it may look like something from a torture chamber, it does the opposite.

Some perceptive Africans learned this eons ago by watching injured lions heal themselves by chewing on the Medicine Tree's spike-covered limbs after suffering gashes in their hides from battles over territorial disputes or breeding rights. Mimicking the lions, humans found that boiling the bark into a tea offered pain relief while helping to prevent bacterial infections.

Raphael explaining the medicinal qualities of the Medicine tree.

Although we didn't always know what triggered Raphael to share tidbits of knowledge, we didn't have to wonder when it came to the Baobab tree. The beloved whimsical tree, also known as the "Tree of Life", is as much an icon of the African continent as the elephant. Anyone who has seen "The Lion King" or "Avatar" knows exactly what tree I'm talking about. The prehistoric species is easily recognizable from its root-like branches sprouting from an immense trunk. Its appearance gives rise to one of its nicknames, the upside-down tree. It looks like the tree was flipped on its crown, with its roots growing into the sky. The Baobab tree, for me, conjures images of Medusa, the snake-haired monster from Greek mythology.

No matter what label it goes by, the tree makes you feel like you are in the presence of divinity. It has an almost magical aura, partly due to its distinctive shape and partly due to its sheer size and prominence in the landscape. Reaching heights of up to 90 feet tall, the titan towers over the acacia scrublands below. Its thick trunk can reach a diameter of 50 feet wide, having a circumference of up to 154 feet. The inside of the monstrous trunk often becomes hollow, forming cave-like openings that wildlife, and even people, can live in. In tourist areas, small bars and gift shops are sometimes located inside these vast caverns. The ancient trees, amazingly, can live well over 1,500 years. Some, according to carbon dating, are even 3,000 to 5,000 years old. Such longevity in a habitat as hostile as Africa simply boggles the mind.

Rick and me standing at the base of a
Baobab tree or "Tree of Life".

Aside from the Baobab's enchanting beauty, its significance to the habitat is worth its weight in gold. Every single inch of the tree is incredibly valuable to both humans and wildlife. The tree's fibrous flesh is used by animals for food or by humans for making ropes, cloth, soap, rubber, and glue. Their leaves can be eaten by both two-legged and four-legged species or pressed into a powder form for use in flavoring and thickening in soups and stews. The oblong fruit is high in fiber, has six times the vitamin C of an orange, twice the calcium of milk, and six times the potassium of bananas, all while containing one of the highest amounts of antioxidants of any fruit in the world. Besides its nutritional benefits, it is quite tasty, and a favorite among locals and animals alike.

As the icing on the cake, the tree acts as one living, breathing pharmacy. The bark, leaves, and fruit--powered by their high antioxidant and vitamin content--offer multiple health and beauty benefits including supporting heart health; protecting against inflammation-related conditions such as diabetes, arthritis, and allergies; preventing cancer; boosting the immune system; aiding in digestion; promoting weight loss; supporting radiant skin; and too many more to mention. The women of Africa have been using the tree as a natural source of beauty and health for centuries.

The Baobab even sustains its own ecosystem providing food and shelter for a myriad of species from the tiniest insect to the mighty Mr. *Tembo*. Thousands of creatures find sanctuary as they scurry in and out of its many crevices: birds nest in its branches; baboons devour the fruit; bush babies and fruit bats drink the nectar and pollinate the flowers as well as find shelter in the hundreds of hiding places within the tree. The tree's numerous cave-like hollows also create perfect spots for larger critters as well, snakes included.

Of all the tree's merits, there is one in particular that blows my mind. The Baobab is composed of almost 80 percent water; essentially it's a humongous gnarled living sponge. During the rainy season, it soaks up gobs of water, storing it throughout its bulbous body. Later when the land is arid, these vats of moisture enable the tree to produce water-packed nutrition-filled fruits smack dab in the middle of the dry season. This extraordinary feature provides fluids and nutrients to multiple species exactly when it is needed most. A single tree can hold more than 30,000 gallons of water, essentially 171 gallons per cubic meter of the tree. No wonder it's referred to as the "Tree of Life."

The Baobab's worth doesn't stop there. With all its amazing health and beauty benefits, it may hold the key to social and economic improvements for Africa's rural people. Its fruit is the only one in the world that dries naturally on its branch; instead of dropping to the ground and rotting, it remains fixed to the limb. Baking in the sun for months turns its velvety coating into a coconut-like shell, while the nutritious pulp dries within, thereby needing no refrigeration (critical to land like Africa). It only has to be harvested, deseeded, and sieved to produce a ready-to-use "superfood."

The pure powder is packed with nutrition, antioxidants, and medicinal qualities.

The trees exist scattered amongst the driest, remotest, and poorest parts of rural Africa and are wild harvested; there is no such thing as a Baobab plantation. Approximately 10 million rural households can provide this fruit from the crops of already existing trees. In many areas, the fruit is so abundant that much of it goes to waste. National Geographic estimated that if there was a global demand for this African 'superfood,' it could be worth a billion dollars a year to the rural people. That is billion with a "B".

There is one major problem. Over 95 percent of people have never heard of this "superfood." I, too, was clueless about its existence. If its health benefits were known the world over, the Tree of Life could potentially be another piece of the puzzle in sustainably providing food security, economic opportunities, and a better quality of life for the local people, thereby protecting wildlife as well.

Posing in the Baobab tree.

Elephants may not know of the Baobab's superfood status, but they know of its existence; its fruit is one of their favorites. Interestingly, the two giants, both icons of the African continent, have a symbiotic relationship with each other. By eating the fruit, running it through their digestive system, and depositing the softened seeds in huge piles of dung--the ideal conditions for germination--elephants greatly help in spreading the Baobab tree far and wide.

Unfortunately, there is a downside to their relationship. In times of drought or elephant overpopulation, the pachyderms use the tree like their very own water tank. They rip off huge chunks of bark or tear off entire branches to access the water stored inside. The ancient trees are resilient, thereby, withstanding quite a bit of abuse from the destructive giants. Still, even their hardiness is limited. If elephant populations cause too much damage, injured trees will wither and die. Termites and other insects will quickly devour what is left. Within one year, an icon of Africa will be returned to the earth like it never existed, completely and utterly gone, a victim of habitat out of balance.

This phenomenon is especially prevalent in some of the national parks throughout Africa where elephant populations run unchecked. My heart sinks when thinking of losing the ancient symbols of life, such magnificent specimens that survived thousands of years, performing their own checks and balances, before we interfered.

Aside from sometimes getting water from the Baobab trees, *tembos* will use their tusks and feet to dig in dried-up riverbeds for water during the dry season. When finished drinking, they fill the holes back in so that other animals can't use them. Initially, I was shocked when Raphael mentioned this little fact. From my human perspective, it seemed pretty selfish. *Why not let the little guys have a swig?* I thought. My surprised expression must have warranted further explanation because Raphael added: "where there is water, there are carnivores."

Enough said.

Throughout our journeys, we not only learned about Tanzania, we learned how truly blessed we were to have Raphael as our Professional Hunter. As mentioned, Raphael was quiet, reserved, and unassuming; yet he also exuded skill, confidence, and command. As PH, he was in charge, but it was his leadership that created such cohesiveness among our little group. He led with subdued respectful grace, appreciating everyone's worth. With tons of bush experience, he could have rambled on about past exploits, but unless specifically asked about something, he never did. He also wasn't too proud to rely on Mgogo's expertise. Not only was Rungwa West essentially in Mgogo's backyard but he had worked the hunting concession for many years before Hilary took over. Raphael would, therefore, confer with Mgogo from time to time. Although I couldn't understand the Swahili, it was obvious that he wasn't too big for his britches to listen to advice from someone who knew the area like the back of his hand.

Unlike many of the staff, Raphael had only one wife and several children to provide for. During the off-season, he worked a small farm like much of the staff. The respect and admiration I have for this humble gentle skilled man simply cannot be put into words. Maybe everyone feels the same about their PH; but as far as Rick and I were concerned, we hit the jackpot when Raphael crawled aboard our Land Cruiser that first day.

Mgogo may not have spoken English but he, too, jumped on the *educate Rick and Sue* bandwagon. We'd be motoring along and suddenly he'd utter a few words to Raphael. Next thing you know, he'd jump from the cargo hold and saunter off after something of interest. One time he came back with a coconut-looking fruit from a *Mikoche* tree, a type of palm tree. Once again, his 20-inch machete or *panga* came out. After pounding it against a tree to break it open, he cut pieces of fibrous orange flesh for the whole crew. The inside of the fruit neither looked nor tasted anything like the white milky

Mgogo opening the coconut-like fruit of the Mikoche tree.

coconut heaven I think of when seeing a palm tree. Amazingly, there are over 200 varieties of the tropical tree that we equate with pina coladas.

After trying other such fruits on our excursions, Rick and I were pretty hesitant upon taking our first bite. Our apprehension paid off. The stringy cantaloupe-looking delicacy was just as mouth-puckering as the fruit the *tumbilis* love. Again, it must be an acquired taste. Either that or our new friends were simply enjoying our entertaining facial expressions. Raphael admitted that the local people enjoy *mikoche* fruit only to a certain degree; but *tembo,* on the other hand, absolutely loved the bitter-tasting nastiness. We were learning there wasn't much the gentle giants *didn't* love.

Mgogo not only joined in our education, but he was also warm and giving, always ready with a smile, and always a gentleman. He regularly presented me with small treasures he found during our treks: a tuft of lion hair, lucky beans scattered on the ground, and, my favorite, mega-sized porcupine quills. By now, you get the concept that almost *everything* in Africa is supersized.

Mgogo slicing the Mikoche tree fruit for us to sample.

For some reason that I can't exactly put my finger on, I had a soft spot for Mgogo. His skill and expertise in the bush were undeniable. It also didn't slip my attention that after exhausting hours on safari, his day didn't end. Instead of lounging, he was knee-deep in processing meat into jerky to take home to his family. During the offseason, he also farmed a little plot of land in his home village. All his efforts provided him the wealth to have two wives and four kids. That kind of dedication to family is endearing.

It was more than that though. Mgogo was almost always paired with me during our stalks through the bush so, basically, I considered him my protector of sorts. Although I like to think of myself as pretty self-sufficient, there just may be a little bit of damsel in distress hidden deep down in my bones. Mgogo, the strong silent type, was the perfect knight in shining armor.

Perhaps, it has nothing to do with that. Maybe, it was just the simple, but priceless African treasures he presented me. Even Rick, quite a thoughtful husband, never gifted me tufts of lion hair or giant porcupine quills. Whatever the reason for my attachment to him, one thing was very clear to me. I liked Mgogo, or as Joel would say, "*Oh, I liked him a lot.*"

No matter how well-protected and vigilant, unforeseen perilous situations can burst forth at any time. Even so, being surrounded by such competent skilled individuals as Raphael, Mgogo, Lilian, and Rick gave me peace of mind. Therefore, most of the time I felt pretty insulated from harm.

Everywhere, that is, but in the *long grass*. Until you are actually in the wilds of Africa, I don't think you can get the true gist of Peter Capstick's book "Death in the Long Grass." Those five words are *not* just a catchy title.

Me dwarfed by Africa's long grasses.

Grass is by far the most abundant plant in the savanna ecosystem. With nearly 75 species, it comes in a whole host of sizes, textures, colors, and heights. For simplicity's sake, let's just say that many grasses are supersized, like everything else in Africa, easily reaching 10 feet tall. The tips of some specimens brush the shoulders of adult giraffes and elephants.

Such habitat is, no doubt, seventh heaven for the many beasts who depend on it for food and shelter. For humans trekking through the lofty thickets, it is quite another story. Unless you are clinging to the neck of a giraffe, there is no way to see what is hidden within the towering grasses. Elephants. Lions. Snakes. Any creature--fanged, elephantine, or slithering--could be less than a stone's throw away and you would be clueless.

When slipping through the long grasses, we were normally tracking, not stalking. Consequently, our typical formation went out the window. Instead, Mgogo was front and center reading any signs. Right on his heels, with his rifle ready, was Raphael. Rick was next with his gun also in position. Basically, I planted myself in Rick's back pocket. In an insane situation, he was my tie to sanity. Abdalah and Lilian followed close behind. Her AK47 was no longer casually flung over her shoulder. It was cradled in her arms. Quite simply, slinking through lofty foliage was a nerve-wracking endeavor.

During these excursions, I felt relief the moment we exited the blinding maze of foliage into shorter grasses where our views were reinstated. Once in the open again, surrounded by so much experience and firepower, I blissfully entered back into my little bubble of safety.

Fortunately, for us, there was no "Death in the Long Grass" or even any close calls. Still, after experiencing just a taste of the dread it inspires, Capstick's title now hits me viscerally. In other words, I *get* it.

Luckily, those nail-biting episodes were countered by moments of lightness and levity. One minute I'd have butterflies in my stomach and 30 minutes later I'd be chuckling as all six of us looked like ostriches with our heads tucked in the ground, bent over searching for water in hollows in the ground.

During the dry season, discovering even small sources of the liquid gold was like hitting pay dirt. Where there is moisture, there are wild things. Consequently, almost every day entailed some sort of hunt for the precious commodity. Places that were once muddy bogs in the rainy season were the perfect places to explore first. The previously wet Meccas turned into dried-up dust bowls littered with pits, indentations, and caverns that could still hold life-saving puddles. Such areas also tended to have water that trickled up from the subsurface.

Breaks like these--searching for liquid gold, educational pit stops, and unsuccessful stalks--were as much a part of our safari as anything. They allowed precious time for social interactions and friendships to develop, ultimately opening the door to knowledge and awareness.

We had expected to see lots of wildlife on safari and, of course, for Rick to harvest some species; but neither of us had imagined such memorable and gratifying in-between times. To me, that aspect of our safari was the cherry on top of the hot fudge sundae. Although I've said it before, I must say it one more time; we felt truly blessed that these *particular* people were placed in our lives for even just a few short weeks. Weeks that changed us forever. Raphael, Lilian, Mgogo, and all of *Masimba* Camp will forever live in my heart. Our *rafikis* and *walimus*. Friends and teachers.

CRIES OF THE SAVANNA

S imba! We spotted our first lion. His tawny coat blended perfectly with the golden grasses that partially concealed him, lounging 40 yards off the trail. The dappled shade added to the camouflage effect. Looking like he had not a care in the world, his eyes followed our slow-moving vehicle. We expected him to leap up and run like most species we'd seen. Instead, the lion remained rooted to the spot. The rolling chunk of metal with its human cargo appeared to be little more than a small distraction from his afternoon siesta.

Raphael assured us this was typical behavior for the king of beasts. Apparently, lions in the wild tend to look at vehicles and the souls on board as one large entity, not as an object with a smorgasbord of dinner options plopped on top. This was good. Call me crazy, but I preferred not being viewed as an afternoon snack. Instead, we were regarded as a hulking creature too big for *Simba* to waste his energy on.

Suddenly, it dawned on me why photo safari vehicles, overflowing with tourists, could stream by lions in national parks without being molested. If we appeared too sizable to tangle with, the larger vehicles oozing with humanity must have seemed even more formidable.

Viewing us as a risky meal wasn't the only reason the lion seemed disinterested. It was midafternoon, and it was hot, scorching, searing, sweat-running-down-your-back, Africa hot. This is the time of day when lions pretty much put their stomachs on hold. This isn't just for comfort, it's a necessity. Lions have very few sweat glands. As a result, they most often rest in the shade, staying cool during the heat of the day, saving their heavy hunting for nightfall and early morning. This preference is not exclusive. If prey is available, they aren't about to look a gift horse in the mouth just because it's broad daylight.

The *Simba* in front of us was a young king. According to Raphael, he was probably about 3 years old and, most likely, had only recently been booted from his pride. The size and scope of his mane were a dead giveaway. The distinguishing feature begins growing at about a year old, then continues to grow throughout his life, often darkening with age. We may look at the lion's golden halo of hair as a regal adornment, but to the lion, it may mean the difference between life and death. The bigger the mane, the more intimidating he looks to enemies, while also protecting his neck and throat during territorial fights.

Male lions are considered mature at about 3 years old, which is about the same time, not coincidentally, that they are ousted from their maternal pride. It isn't until they turn four or five that they would even dream about challenging an adult male in an attempt to take over the kingdom. The lion we saw lounging in the shade, watching us in apparent boredom, had a while before he was ready for that bold move. Raphael figured he'd been on his own for just a short time.

Being a loner meant he had to hunt on his own without the help of teamwork. Solo lions are successful in their own right, but they must depend on ambushing prey and bursting forth in surprise attacks, instead of working strategically with a pride.

Young lions often form small bachelor groups or coalitions, frequently made up of related males recently ousted from their birth prides. Usually, the expelled nomads move at least 16 miles away from their natal group and wander 100 square miles of territory. Bachelors may have to spend years in this mid-phase before they are fierce enough to take over a pride. Prides, both males and females, are typically very hostile to outsiders who enter their domain. Once in a while, a lucky loner might chance upon a lioness in estrus away from her pride, thereby allowing him a little lovin'.

Lions are the most social of all wild felines and the only cat species to live together in a close-knit family group. The pride usually consists of a couple of adult males, related females, and their cubs; their natal bond does not tolerate outside females. While a pride typically consists of around 15 individuals, it can grow to as many as 30, basically an army of lethal fangs, power, and skill. Once a pride gets too large, the youngest generations of females may be booted out, and forced to find their own territory. On occasion, females will leave a pride entirely and become nomadic like their male counterparts.

Lionesses start reproducing at about 4 years old, giving birth to one to four cubs in a secluded den, thicket, or other secure location away from the pride. The newborns are born blind and helpless for the first few weeks of their lives. Consequently, for up to eight weeks, the cautious protective mothers will hunt solo, fending for themselves to keep their defenseless babies away from the pride.

You've heard the saying that it *takes a village* when it comes to raising young'uns. Well, lion prides are totally on board with that philosophy. Once cubs are integrated into the family group, caring for them is an all-out community effort. The cubs build strong bonds with most members of the pride, even suckling from any or all nursing females. Females work together to protect the cubs and teach them how to survive. Often two or more females give birth around the same time, allowing them to raise the cubs together, forming even tighter bonds.

Like the young of most beings, the cubs are extremely playful, practicing their hunting, social, and caregiving skills early on. Typical of human toddlers, most cubs aren't content to cause a ruckus simply with their peers. They attempt to draw adults into their games as well. Lionesses who have their own cubs are much more tolerant of the antics, including from the offspring of others. Females without their own youngsters are a little less forgiving. Sound familiar?

The entire pride works together to defend their territory and hunt prey. While both males and females are perfectly capable of assuming either duty, a division of labor tends to develop, allowing each individual to fall into their specific roles.

Any male lions leading a pride didn't just waltz into the position; they had to fight for it. Winning such an honor doesn't mean game over. To stay king, lions must continually defend their standing in the pride as well as against rivals who want to take over. According to National Geographic, those lucky enough to become rulers typically only last two to three years before being dethroned.

While adult males attached to a pride must constantly battle to keep their status, they usually get off easy when it comes to hunting. Growing to 7 feet long and weighing nearly 450 pounds, their powerful stockily built bodies are better suited for defending and patrolling their hard-won territory. Lionesses, on the other hand, are about a foot shorter, weighing closer to 280 pounds. Their slighter, more agile build makes them better suited for hunting. Consequently, the females tend to do most of the heavy lifting when it comes to bringing home the bacon.

As with the males, the females tend to assume precise roles in the pride, as well as in hunting. Some will stalk the quarry while others advance from the wings. Other lionesses will be stationed to attack the fleeing prey. While all this mayhem is going on, somebody's gotta keep an eye on the cubs. Consequently, there are some lionesses, and even males, who take on the role of babysitter.

A lion's arsenal of weapons includes muscular bodies capable of 36-mph bursts of speed, razor-sharp claws, powerful vice-like jaws, and canine teeth up to four-inch-long. On top of their brute strength and savagery, they have terrific night vision, six times better than humans, giving them a distinct advantage over species whose vision suffers in the dark. Their gel-like padded feet and hide color allow them to creep silently, almost invisibly through the savanna, earning them the nickname *silent snipers of the wild* by the National Geographic channel.

Even oozing with stealth and death-dealing weapons, the king's pursuit of prey is not a slam dunk. Thanks to the Creator's infinite wisdom to give each species a fighting chance, lions were given one pitfall. Compared to their body size, lions have relatively small hearts. This rather compact muscle limits their stamina, preventing them from long-distance chases. Much of the lion's prey, on the other hand, is equipped with speed and stamina. Since lions rarely pursue their quarry more than 100 yards, many targets are free to graze another day.

For this reason, lions try to be within 50 feet of their mark before bursting forth in pursuit. Getting within striking distance of vigilant flight animals, accustomed to having a bullseye on their backs, is not like taking candy from a baby. *Simba* must lie in ambush, stalk silently through the savanna, or use the cover of darkness to get within range. The instant the intended victim is close enough, they spring forward covering yards in a blink of an eye. Their jaws, which are five times stronger than humans, are the perfect weapon for strangulation, their preferred method of killing. The lion will use his powerful jaws to clamp onto the animal's neck, effectively shutting off its air supply until suffocation occurs. While this works great for smaller victims, lions must sometimes resort to more ghastly methods when it comes to larger wildlife.

Aside from lacking stamina, lions tend to suffer from tunnel vision. Once lions choose their target, they become so locked on their mark that other potential victims pass within easy reach, without *Simba* so much as batting an eye in their direction. While this attribute may save some quarry, it is easy to see how the lion's dead-on focus prevents them from darting back and forth after multiple fleeing animals, like balls in a pinball machine, quickly depleting their limited energy store.

Even for the most skillful lions, hunting is hard work. Therefore, compact species such as dik-diks, vervet monkeys, hares, and the likes are typically spared from the lion's menu. Quite simply, there is not enough meat on their bones to make the effort worth the payoff.

While many creatures depend on their minute size, speed, or endurance to survive in the world of the deadly carnivores, some rely on power and might; most notably elephants, hippos and rhinos. Lions typically avoid confrontations with the jumbo-sized pachyderms. Not only are such species a daunting chunk of flesh, but their brawn and tusks also make them extremely dangerous. Being trampled under the feet of an elephant or impaled by the incisors of a hippo can cause instant death or serious injury. A crippled lion is, most likely, a dead lion walking. Having said that, the infants of these massive beasts are fair game. Lions will seize any opportunity to take down younger, less threatening, members of the behemoths.

One lion is deadly. A pride is deadly times ten, twenty, or thirty. Since they aren't equipped for long-distance runs, lions work as a team, taking turns chasing their fleet-footed targets to tire them out. The lions' coordinated efforts not only allow them a much higher success rate for antelopes and zebras but enable them to tackle the more fearsome game as well.

For every victim that falls to the mighty lions, there are many more that escape. With an overall success rate of only 10 to 30 percent, life is not guaranteed, even for the king. Life is brutal for *all* wild creatures. Predator and prey alike.

Successful hunts aren't the only concern for a lion's survival. Other predators are a threat as well. Lions kill other carnivores, especially leopards, cheetahs, wild dogs, and hyenas at every opportunity. Conversely, those predators respond in kind. These slaughters have nothing to do with hunger. The sole purpose is to destroy their opponents, wiping out the competition.

While this may seem cold-blooded, it makes perfect sense in the animal kingdom. All of these predators exist in basically the same ecological niche, competing for the same food sources. Any predators eliminated increase the chances of their survival.

The lion's biggest adversaries are Spotted hyenas. These two are mortal enemies. The dog-like creatures may look nothing like the majestic lion, but they have many similarities, making them a huge threat. They eat the same prey, have strong social structures, and are skilled hunters that hunt as a team, while also being opportunists.

Most of us tend to think of lions as stately hunters who kill *all* their food. While it is true they are expert killers, it is also true that they'd much prefer to lay in the shade and let other critters take on the blood, sweat, and tears. In other words, lions are also thieves and opportunists, stealing much of their food from other predators.

Most of us view hyenas as the scavengers of Africa, assuming they survive by plundering the kills of others. This is far from the truth. They are skilled killers who hunt in groups. A pack of hyenas can easily bring down targets much larger than themselves.

Also, scavengers of all kinds know that a parade of circling vultures signals death. It doesn't matter which predator gets there first or which did the killing. *First come, first served* is not a mantra in the animal world. It only matters who is more powerful. Surprisingly, lions steal more booty from hyenas than the other way around. Some lions exist almost entirely on the victims of the less prestigious hunters.

Hyenas are extremely bold and will feed right alongside lions if the situation allows, often diving in to grab chunks of meat and retreating, always keeping just out of reach of the larger predators. If the hyenas' numbers are in their favor, however, they will challenge lions and even force them off of a kill.

While a confrontation between the two enemies, one on one, would be a fierce battle, the king would typically prevail. With that said, all bets are off if a lion finds itself outgunned. The same holds true for the hyenas. Essentially, it's all about numbers and circumstances. The bitter adversaries are always looking for a fight and willing to assault each other even when food isn't present.

This bitter rivalry is most detrimental to the younger generation of each. Slaughtering one another's offspring is child's play. Any predator snuffed out in the early stages of life is an adult that the other species won't have to compete with later on. Consequently, the pursuit to destroy one another's babies is an ongoing battle, raging throughout the wilds of Africa. Lions kill 70 percent of hyenas overall.

The competition between lions, cheetahs, and leopards is a little less contentious, primarily because lions tend to dominate these two felines. While lions will kill a full-grown leopard or cheetah if the chance arises, rarely can the smaller cats reciprocate unless a lion is wounded or sick. Lions aren't particular about who they steal from. They are just as happy to confiscate the kills of spotted felines as they are any predator and there is little the smaller cats can do about it.

Since leopards often have time to get their kill high into the treetops to avoid their bulkier relatives, they fare better. Cheetahs are much more vulnerable to losing their hard-earned booty. As the fastest land mamals in the world, they are built for speed, not climbing. Having dog-like non-retractable claws greatly limits their ability to scale a tree; thus, dragging their spoils into the treetops is not an option.

Once a lion pride has acquired its meal, there is a distinct hierarchy involved among the pride members. The cubs eat last and, therefore, suffer the most in times of scarcity, making them prone to dying of starvation or abandonment. Still, most cubs die as a result of other carnivores. Only about 20 percent of lion cubs will survive until the age of two.

Knowing that lions require a pile of food to sustain them didn't help as we slept, or tried to sleep, behind the thin canvas shield of our tent, listening to their vocal cries. There is nothing in the animal kingdom that will send shivers up your spine quite like the lion's blood-curdling low-pitched thundering roar as you lay like pigs in a blanket behind a veil of fabric. Learning that these prolonged calls could be heard up to five miles away allowed me to imagine that they were nowhere near our tent. *Simba* five miles away was hunky-dory. *Simba* outside our tent was not.

The lion's roars were different from the long rumbling sounds instilled in my memory. Typically, several longer thunderous vocal displays were followed by a series of increasingly shorter grunts. Either way, the lion's cries were easily distinguishable. Almost like clockwork, they shattered our sleep between 2 and 3 a.m., the bewitching hour so to speak.

Aside from the roars that most people are familiar with, they have a whole language: grunts, moans, growls, snarls, hisses, meows, purrs, hums, puffs, and woofs each with a variance in volume, intensity, tempo, and tone. Our time at *Masimba* Camp didn't offer us the pleasure of hearing *Simba's* entire vocal collection. Mainly, it was their low guttural grunts or *umphhs* that penetrated our slumber each night.

The lion's status as king of the kingdom is well justified. Lions are apex predators, as well as keystone species. Put in layman's terms, they occupy the top of the food chain and have a large effect on their habitat, even though their numbers are small relative to other types of animals. Lions have a unique function within an ecosystem, critical to keeping the ecological community in balance. Without *Simba*, habitats would differ dramatically or cease to exist altogether.

On top of their critical role in Africa's biological community, lions are charismatic species who have been revered throughout history for their power and fierceness, symbols of strength, courage, royalty, and stateliness. Still, their iconic nature has not prevented them from undergoing dramatic declines in both their range and numbers.

A century ago, over 200,000 lions roamed throughout Africa. Since then, lions have vanished from over 80 percent of their historic ranges while becoming extinct in 26 countries where they previously reigned.

Today fewer than 25,000 lions are remaining in the wild. Tanzania contains 40 percent of that number, along with a quarter of all their remaining territory. Ruaha National Park alone holds 10 percent of the global population. Tanzania is, therefore, *the* most important country in Africa for lions and lion conservation.

The lion's demise came to worldwide attention in 2015 with the death of Cecil, a magnificent 13-year-old lion who lived primarily within the boundaries of Hwange National Park in Zimbabwe. Many of you probably know the story, or at least a version of it. The incident was broadcast throughout the globe, sparking an international outcry. The National Geographic article "Cecil the Lion Died Amid Controversy--Here's What's

Happened Since," considered it to be possibly the biggest response to a wildlife story ever seen.[1]

Cecil wasn't just any wild lion. He was a study subject of WildCRU (Wildlife Conservation Research Unit). Being a wild lion, he did what wild lions do. He went hunting. On that pivotal day, Cecil crossed outside of the park's border and into the line of fire of a bowhunter legally hunting lion in the adjoining area.

Being that wild lions rarely reach 12 years of age, Cecil--at 13 years old--was well past his prime and nearing the end of his natural lifespan. According to hunting regulations, this made him a perfect candidate for harvest.

With the lion's collar hidden by its mane, the hunter had no idea he was shooting a studied animal. To make matters worse, his arrow wounded the lion instead of killing him instantly. This not only caused suffering for the lion, but it also made him extremely dangerous. Accordingly, the hunter did as ethical hunters do; he, along with his PH and trackers, pursued the injured beast for 18 hours, ultimately putting an end to its suffering and preventing it from harming others. If he hadn't, circumstances could have ended worse. The hunter did what was right, confirmed by the article above. Investigations found the hunter had hunted legally and ethically, without breaking any laws. As a result, he was never charged with a crime. None of that mattered. Few people waited for the facts.

Because Cecil had been given a name and was known to some visitors at Hwange National Park, his death made the headlines. Instantly, the news spread worldwide, making the hunter a target of international contempt among ordinary people, celebrities, and TV hosts. Before the facts were known and without justification, the hunter was raked over the coals and his wife and family were threatened. They were not alone. Trophy hunting, in general, was pummeled.

Trophy hunting, or selective hunting, was, and is not, the cause of plunging lion populations. Again, the truth was irrelevant. The furor over Cecil's death created a cash cow for many organizations. Fact or fiction, many charities were happy to exploit the incident, even though it generated sentiments that could ultimately hurt lion populations.

Panthera, a team of biologists, law enforcement experts, and wild cat advocates, put out a report entitled "Beyond Cecil: Africa's Lions in Crisis."[2] The report states, "Contrary to popular belief, trophy hunting is a small factor in the fate of the African lion--a relatively minor battle in the larger war on lions."

The report points to habitat loss, agricultural expansion, and human population growth as the biggest threats to lions. Cultivated land area in sub-Saharan Africa is expected to increase by 21 percent and livestock by 73 percent within the same period. Not only will the lion's prey have to compete for grazing lands, but the human expansion will also result in more interactions between lions and humans. This, of course, is rarely good. Any livestock deaths resulting from lions will provoke retaliatory and preemptive killings by herders and ranchers.

The report also acknowledges that bushmeat poaching is a severe threat to lions. Even lands in the largest protected areas are seeing vast regions emptied of large ungulates such as wildebeest, zebra, buffalo, and impala – all of which the lions depend on for food. According to Panthera, tens of thousands of wildebeest are killed each year in snares. The traps are also indiscriminate and lions are caught and killed. Wire nooses account for 52 percent of all lion casualties in Mozambique's Niassa National Reserve.

The IUCN supports Panthera's report. The premier conservation organization recognizes that trophy hunting did cause declines in poorly managed areas at times, but overall trophy hunting "has a net positive impact." They continue, "Regulatory measures which reduce the profitability of lion trophy hunting could have widespread negative impacts for wildlife-based land use, anti-poaching, and tolerance of lions outside protected areas."

Although hunting has proven to be a great tool for conservation, the industry is not without its thorns. Nothing is 100 percent sunshine and roses. Hunting for conservation requires that wildlife is managed using accurate scientific data and sustainable quotas. In some areas, not enough of the money goes to the local people. Also, some nations have had issues with corruption leading to unsustainable animal allocations or awarding hunting concessions based on factors other than qualifications and bid price. Thankfully, the scrutiny thrust upon governments in recent years has helped reduce these types of profiteering.

These issues in the "pay to play" system were noted in a study done by a group of international scientists led by Enrico di Minin.[3] Even with its hiccups, they found that hunting offers revenue to developing countries that would otherwise turn natural habitats into people-oriented land uses.

In addition, they concluded that if there was an outright ban on lion hunting, or even restrictions on trophy transport and lion products, most of the 8,000 lions on privately owned land in South Africa would cease to exist. Poachers would then fill the gap with lions from national parks and their numbers, too, would plummet.

Therefore, instead of throwing the baby out with the bathwater, they recommended changing policies to become more effective. Panthera agrees that progress is being made. Many countries, recognizing that poorly managed hunting was unsustainable, enacted reforms, including reducing their lion quotas.

While some nations need improvement, others have proven beyond a shadow of a doubt the effectiveness of good policies. Again, we go to Namibia as a shining example. As lion populations in other countries dwindled, Namibia used hunting tourism and ecotourism in conjunction with each other to increase its lion population by 700 percent.

Other data analysis conducted by researchers from the University of Pretoria indicated that if lion hunting were to end in Mozambique, Tanzania, and Zambia, almost 15 million acres of conservation areas would lose value, thus becoming vulnerable to other uses. That is an area seven times larger than Yellowstone National Park.

Even with all the statistical evidence, there are high-profile campaigns to ban trophy hunting, prohibit lion and elephant trophy imports, and list them on the Endangered Species Act. The research indicates that banning the import of legal trophies has the same effect as banning hunting altogether.

As the director and founder of the Ruaha Carnivore Project, Dr. Amy Dickman is a non-hunting, vegetarian, carnivore expert and Kaplan Senior Research Fellow at Oxford University who has committed her life to save wildlife. In the March 2021 edition of Science + Story, she offers this heartfelt plea:

I have spent more nights in my tent crying over lion deaths than I wish to count. Given my lifelong passion for this incredible wild cat, each death cuts me to the core, but some stand out more than others.

The lioness whose hind legs were cut off, and whose swollen teats suggested she had only recently given birth – I spent days agonizing about what was happening to those newborn cubs, almost certainly starving to death where she had carefully hidden them. Three other tiny lion cubs speared and piled up in the bush with a wooden stake through their fragile bodies. A young lion, perhaps only two or three years old, whose ravaged paw showed the agony of hours in a wire snare before it died from multiple spear wounds.

Bodies of three lion cubs speared in the bush.
©Ruaha Carnivore Project

A big lioness in the prime of life – one of our collared females – whose poisoning led to utter carnage, with the bodies of five other lions and over 70 critically endangered vultures scattered around her in an orgy of appalling, indiscriminate death. A heavily pregnant poisoned lioness, who we cut open in some vague hope that we might have reached her in time to save the cubs. But no – we instead found the still bodies of three perfect, full-term cubs, never able to play their role in the continuation of the species.

The bodies of lions, critically endangered vultures,
and other wildlife after a poisoning event.
©Ruaha Carnivore Project

And it goes far beyond lions. The horror of a leopard who died in agony, its right paw trapped in the unforgiving steel of a gin trap. The hyena we found decapitated in the bush, the beautiful tawny eagles sprawled lifeless on the ground after being poisoned. We see countless deaths, but they still emotionally impact me every time. None of those animals was named, or globally loved like 'Cecil' the lion--but their deaths count at least as much, if not more, because their very anonymity shows they lived in wild areas which receive little attention. They died because they had no perceived value to people in those areas, and the sadness I feel for every one of these deaths is awful.

I know, without a shadow of a doubt, that I am deeply, passionately and emotionally committed to the conservation of these incredible animals and the landscapes they live in. The same goes for all our team, who work tirelessly to protect them, and for every field conservation scientist I know. That is why it is always surprising when--for example in a recent Science+Story post--we are portrayed somewhat robotically, apparently surprised that 'the science' does not outweigh emotional or moral considerations in conservation debates, such as over trophy hunting. This fits within a wider narrative, which portrays those of us who warn about the risks of banning trophy hunting without viable alternatives as heartless and uncaring about wild animal killing. Literally nothing could be further from the truth.

There is good scientific evidence that banning trophy hunting, without better options ready to protect wildlife, habitat and livelihoods, risks amplifying major threats such as land conversion and poaching. But my colleagues and I who engage in these debates are very aware that 'science' is not enough to win hearts and minds. We have no problem with people getting emotional about wild animal killing: we want that passion, it would be an appalling world without it. Importantly, we feel it strongly ourselves--I am deeply fearful that hasty bans could lead to far more terrible wildlife deaths like those described above. We also have no problem with having celebrities involved in conservation: if well-informed, they can raise awareness of major threats and mobilize positive global action.

But the frustration comes when complex conservation topics are presented as simple soundbites and fragmented snapshots of reality, without discussing the wider context or the risks of extremely serious unintended consequences. We all know that simplistic narratives do very well on social media--it is easy to generate global outrage against an obese trophy hunter grinning over a dead lion, or a woman holding up a giraffe heart on Valentine's Day. These images are extremely powerful and, crucially, have a clear 'villain' that can be used for campaigning and fund-raising. But in truth, conservation is immensely more complicated than it first appears.

The Science+Story post suggests that we 'might be able to connect with the emotions, morality and aspirations of millions by telling the full story of how conservation fails and might succeed.' But this is the absolute core of the challenge. How do we as conservation scientists 'tell the full story' when it is complicated and messy? How can we reach people, and would they actually be prepared to listen to that full story, especially if it goes against their preconceptions? The fact that trophy hunting--even if it turns our stomachs--can help protect vast areas of habitat, guarding against land conversion, poaching and terrible conflict-related killings, simply doesn't have immediate power on social media. Facts and statistics, as we all know, usually don't change minds. Even when we post photos of the killings I describe--which are usually far more damaging for conservation than trophy hunting killings--there is a startling lack of public interest or concern, as if those deaths somehow don't count in the same way.

And this is for *lions,* one of the most loved species on the planet. The chance of generating public passion for entire healthy ecosystems or conserving the myriads of less publicly appealing species such as invertebrates or reptiles seems impossibly low. Most of the true conservation threats just don't lend themselves well to campaigning. For example, when conflict-related wildlife killings do hit the headlines, the backlash against local people risks actually intensifying conflict, not reducing it. The reality is that field conservation is complicated, with dizzying minefields of unintended consequences. But no-one wants to hear that--it is just not sexy, simple or compelling, unlike the simple (albeit usually false) narrative that trophy hunting is a major conservation threat and that banning it will automatically make things better. Oh, how I wish it were that simple.

In the field, we see the very real consequences of well-meaning but poorly considered actions. Trophy hunting blocks are increasingly lying vacant--this might be a success for some campaigners, but once you actually spend time in them, and see the degree of poaching, habitat conversion and wildlife killing in vacant blocks, you realize it is often far from a win for wildlife. Yet the pressure is only growing for bans, although I'm unaware of evidence for viable alternatives ready to avoid many more vacant blocks.

So, we know that the evidence presented is not winning the battle--that is painfully clear to us as conservation scientists, as well as to millions of affected rural people who get virtually no voice in these debates. So, what to do? I'm not sure, but I know what I would like to see as an important step in the right direction. Far from scientists having a 'disdain' for emotion, marketing campaigns and celebrities, I would love to see all those things used to safeguard wildlife habitat, and to deal with real conservation threats such as prey loss, poaching and conflict with vulnerable local people. I want us, at the very least, to agree that our aim should be to work with local people to reduce *overall* wildlife killings, rather than only caring about animals killed by trophy hunters. To do otherwise risks hugely increasing the silent loss of much more habitat and wildlife. Most people won't see those impacts--land will gradually be cleared, savannahs will fall silent, and we will respond to many more appalling deaths of nameless but vital wild animals.

So, this is an unashamedly emotional plea, including to celebrities--if you truly care about reducing wildlife killings, then please make space for hearing that 'full story' of messy, real conservation challenges. Listen to the perspectives of field conservation scientists and local communities, work with us as well, and together we can take action and reduce the despair we feel about the destruction of our natural world.[4]

For those who are looking for even more scientific evidence, you can read the 2019 *Science* article entitled "Trophy Hunting Bans Imperil Biodiversity" written by Dickman, Rosie Cooney, Paul J Johnson, Maxi Pia Louise, Dilys Roe, and 128 additional wildlife specialists.[5] It essentially says the same thing in a more matter-of-fact unemotional way. Each signatory, along with their qualifications, is listed at the end.

A heavily pregnant lioness killed due to conflict.
©Ruaha Carnivore Project

Cecil's death, the media firestorm, and worldwide outrage are proof that citizens of every country are impassioned about preserving the lion for future generations. To do this, however, the warriors of lion conservation must accept the real challenges facing the iconic species and embrace tactics, both hunting and non-hunting, that are proven to succeed, even if some of the methods go against every fiber of their being. If not, we are just putting another nail in their coffin.

An Africa without *Simba's* majestic, but menacing, allure would lose much of its mystique. The African Symphony, too, deprived of the lion's guttural cries and blood-curdling roars, would be amiss--void of a presence that makes your spine tingle, fills you with awe, and compels you to feel resolutely alive.

19
THE BIG PICTURE

Usianguke Mgogo! Don't fall! I cried out nervously. Twenty feet above me, our head tracker scooted across a barren branch, his legs encircling the limb to prevent him from sprawling to the ground. My anxious appeal, spoken in Swahili, caught Mgogo so off guard that it had the exact opposite effect; his stable grasp wavered just slightly as a grin spread across his face.

Mgogo had already scaled the pole-like trunk. No ladder. No shoes. No climbing gadgets. Just feet, legs, arms, and hands maneuvering skillfully up the limbless tree. It seemed like the perfect time to add "don't fall" to my vocabulary since Lilian, my impromptu language teacher, was safely planted on the ground beside me.

Raphael, holding a rope with a chunk of Rick's *dagga* boy attached to one end, waited below. Once Mgogo was in position, the empty end of the line was thrown up, allowing him to grab it and launch it down the other side. Using the setup as a pulley, the ground crew hoisted the piece of meat into the air until it rested against the limb where Mgogo sat. Through a series of loop de loops and various maneuvers, the hunk of flesh was soon anchored securely to the limb of the tree. Once tied in place, Mgogo attached green-leafed branches to it, totally hiding it from sight. The bare limb suddenly looked like it had sprouted a leafy shrub from its midst.

Now the all-consuming question. Why? Why on earth, after so much effort to attract an animal, did they hide the bait? That was the question burning in my brain.

Raphael didn't miss a beat. Recognizing my puzzled expression with a smirk, he offered, "Vultures."

Mgogo preparing to attach the bait to the tree.

Expanding on the one-word answer, Raphael went on to explain that the flying scavengers have keen eyesight, enabling them to spot carcasses from up to four miles away. If they saw the bait, it would be picked to the bone within minutes. Vultures are ravenous; they can eat up to two pounds of food in a single sitting. When a meal is sighted, the highly social birds circle the sky, signaling their kinfolk to join in the feast. It's, therefore, not uncommon to see one carcass feeding up to 100 birds; a swarm that can devour 100 pounds of flesh in less than 3 minutes.

Africa has 11 varieties of vultures, 8 of which live in Tanzania. The most prevalent species, by far, is the White-backed vulture common to the savanna and woodlands. Weighing up to 15 pounds, they can reach 40 inches long while having wingspans almost 6 feet wide.

The bait hidden behind green foliage.

Since the scavengers' sharp beaks are not designed to tear open the thick skin of large victims, they must wait their turn to feast on the leftovers of others, ultimately, reducing a carcass to a mere skeleton. While vultures are often regarded as repulsive, fierce and barbaric, they have a vital role in keeping wildlands free of decaying remains and disease. Their stomach acid is so corrosive that it allows them to digest meat at any stage of decay, as well as tolerate nasty diseases that might kill many animals. Their insatiable appetite is responsible for eliminating up to 70 percent of all decaying flesh within their ecosystem. They are, therefore, essential in protecting the health of all other species, including humans and their livestock.

Although vultures are critical to the African ecosystem, they are the fastest declining group of birds in the world. Recently, the IUCN lowered the White-backed vulture's conservation status to Critically Endangered.

Sadly, poaching of other game is the biggest reason for their drastic decline. The wide-open savannas which allow hordes of scavengers to locate a feast from miles away are also their downfall. Just as a carcass can be spotted from miles away, so can the soaring birds; a sight that signals death as clearly as a blinking neon light. This instantly alerts any nearby rangers, outfitters, and legal hunters of potential poaching activity. Poachers cannot have this. Consequently, many illegal killers poison the birds in mass numbers to lessen the chance of being discovered.

One large poison-filled carcass can kill all the vultures that feed upon it, basically massacring hundreds of birds at a time. An example of this played out in Botswana in 2019 when 500 of the threatened birds fed on the tainted meat of three poisoned elephants.

Sometimes, they aren't even the intended targets. As mentioned in Dickman's essay, the poisoning of six lions due to human-wildlife conflict also killed the 70 vultures that fed on the poisoned carcasses.

Aside from poisoning, vultures suffer from habitat loss and reduced prey. Many, too, are poached for the use of their body parts in tradition-al medicines. Finally, their extremely slow reproduction rate is partly to blame. Not only are the ghastly-looking birds monogamous, mating for life, but they also produce only one egg every one to two years. Who could have imagined a bird with such a distasteful reputation would have such a strong sense of loyalty?

Vulture

Until spending time in Africa, my view of vultures had been one of indifference, neither hating them nor loving them. The homely birds had simply been the bearers of the misfortune of others. I was utterly clueless about their value in keeping ecosystems disease-free and how their tattle-tale behavior put them in such peril.

Recognizing the assault upon the scavengers of Africa, as well as my own indifference, was troubling. How many people like me are only concerned about the cute, endearing, or majestic species and dismiss the ones that are aesthetically challenged? Each has a critical role in the overall scheme of things. Each has great value. Yet, there is no doubt that most of us tend to dismiss the creatures who are short in the looks department.

Suddenly, the muffled thud of Mgogo's feet hitting the ground snapped me out of my reverie. Although the vultures couldn't smell the rotting meat, most assuredly plenty of other critters could. That was the point; to pervade the area with the lovely scent of putrid flesh. As an extra enticement, Mgogo tied a juicy piece of entrails to the end of a rope and dragged it hundreds of yards through the surrounding bush forming a large perimeter around the bait tree.

No doubt, plenty of opportunists would pick up the foul-smelling stench. I was just hoping that Mgogo, towing the tempting morsels, didn't return with a lion on his tail. Not only did I want our tracker to come back in one piece, but lions weren't the intended targets. Our crew's goal was to attract leopards, specifically mature males, hoping that one would be unable to pass up a free meal.

Leopards, or *Chui*, are extremely agile climbers. Streamlined bodies, packed with powerful muscles, allow them to negotiate the canopy of trees with little effort. They prefer spending most of their time, including eating, in the security of treetops rather than exposing themselves to the dangers on the ground. Leopards, therefore, carry their victims high into the limbs to stash them out of reach of other predators, much like Mgogo had done, not coincidentally, with the chunk of buffalo meat.

Simba can climb admirably, but his skills are nothing compared to a leopard. Lions are stronger, but they are also heavier and less nimble so they prefer the ground. Besides, they don't have much need to climb trees. As kings of the animal world, they can pretty much eat wherever they choose. Still, lions aren't above a little pirating. A tempting, almost effortless, treat nestled a few feet above the ground can send them clambering to the heights.

Consequently, Raphael and Mgogo did not choose bait trees randomly. They selected specimens that had long trunks with no low branches, basically lessening the chances of *Simba*'s success while increasing the chance of *Chui's*. Any higher protruding limbs had to be strong enough to hold the weight of a leopard but *not* sturdy enough to maintain the bulk of a lion.

By now you have put two and two together; Rick was hunting leopard as well as plains game species. In the decades that Rick had dreamed about our once-in-a-lifetime adventure, he had plenty of time to pin down the aspects that were most important to him. He was firm that the experience should resemble an old-time African hunt as much as possible, essentially camping deep in the African bush where animals remained wild. Once those conditions were met, his top priority was a place where he could hunt the elusive spotted feline. Fundamentally, Rick's entire hunt revolved around this primary species.

The *license* one gets corresponds to the number of days on safari. Typically 7, 10, 14, 21, or 28-day licenses are available to hunters. Essentially, the longer the safari, the more game the client is entitled to hunt, both in terms of variety of species and overall quantity. If certain animals are abundant, more than one of that type may be available to hunt. For example, Rick could have legally harvested two zebras, two impala, and three Cape buffalos *if* he wished, paying the corresponding trophy fee for each.

Just because an animal is listed on quota, however, doesn't mean it is hunted. After Rick harvested one zebra, he had no desire to hunt a second one. There were also other game animals on the permit that Rick chose not to hunt for various reasons. In addition, there are no guarantees. It is hunting after all. A hunter may pursue a specific species the entire time but never have an opportunity for a harvestable animal.

A well-managed hunting system works like basic economics. Supply and demand. Each species is assigned a trophy fee that corresponds to its perceived value, ranging from a few hundred dollars to many thousands of dollars. The more limited and in demand a species is, the higher the value that is placed on it. The more abundant or less desirable the species is, the lower the trophy fee. For example, an elusive and coveted East African greater kudu will require a much higher trophy fee than the prolific impala, seen around nearly every bend in the road. In addition to the safari license fee, the trophy fees for each animal harvested are apportioned for the benefit of the Tanzania government, the local community, and the hunting outfitter.

Trophy fees and animals available for harvest are not randomly drawn from a hat. Each year the Tanzanian government performs a census to determine wild populations and distribution, as well as other factors. Based on the government's findings, they determine what can be sustainably harvested and assign quotas for each safari area accordingly.

Often when hunters are pursuing dangerous game, such as leopard, the outfitter hires an additional PH for added safety and success. Hunting carnivores is very labor intensive. Baits must be put in multiple trees which are checked and monitored daily. Once a desired feline is determined to be feeding on the bait, a blind large enough to conceal up to four people is built. All of this requires extra personnel, as well as large blocks of time dedicated to just this one species, making this the primary reason for the 21-day requirement in Tanzania and the corresponding jump in price.

Truth be told, if it would have been financially feasible for us, Rick's ultimate dream would have been to hunt a lion. With that said, the trophy fee for a leopard, along with all of the other associated expenses, was a big enough stretch for our budget. Fulfilling a dream requires walking a tightrope so to speak; balancing the weight of future responsibilities with that of seizing the here and now. Rick's hunting leopard, rather than lion, was our way of seizing the day while still keeping our financial equilibrium in check.

The quest for *Chui* was the primary reason we chose Tanzania over so many other wonderful destinations in Africa. Tanzania has plenty of leopards and provides an authentic, remote experience in the African bush that is second to none.

The first few days of our safari had been geared towards hunting plains game to supply the camp with meat and baiting material. Once that goal was accomplished, Raphael decided it was time to focus on *Chui*.

The common strategy for hunting leopard is to *attempt* to bait one of the elusive nocturnal cats out of the darkness and into the daylight with the promise of an easy meal. This is much easier said than done. Leopards are very intelligent and extremely wary while having acute senses that can detect danger from afar; aged leopards, even more so. Like all wildlife, leopards don't grow to a ripe old age by being stupid. The longer they live, the smarter they become, making them much more difficult and dangerous to pursue.

Just because bait is set doesn't mean it will be hit, and if it is, chances are the cats will wait until after dark. Therein lies the problem. In Tanzania, it is only legal to hunt *Chui* during daylight hours. Their nocturnal disposition, along with their acute senses, makes them one of Africa's most difficult animals to hunt.

Once a leopard is interested in a bait, a blind is built. The enclosure, often made entirely of native vegetation, must blend seamlessly with the surroundings, while also being large enough to conceal the hunter, game scout, and up to two PHs. After that, it's a waiting game. Hunting leopard requires sitting statue-like for hour, after hour, after hour. Sometimes day after day. Waiting. Waiting. Waiting.

Imagine sweat running down your back in the stifling heat of the cramped blind. Although it tickles, you can't even twitch. Your eyes burn as salty perspiration trickles into your eyes. Just pray you don't have a heat stroke. Next, the cramped position causes your butt and your back to start throbbing incessantly. Doggone it, just try to forget your aching muscles. Then, surprise, surprise, a Tsetse fly lands on your nose. Too bad. Suck it up. Suffer in agony as the angry little devil gorges on your blood. If you swat the nasty bugger, it's game over. Any leopard in the neighborhood will spot you dead to rights.

Now after sitting semi-paralyzed for countless hours over multiple days, *Chui* suddenly glides onto the bait branch seemingly from out of nowhere, just as dusk descends over the restless bush. Here's your chance. Your heart is pounding. Your body is trembling. Somehow you manage to force your eye to the scope and struggle to align the crosshairs on the one rosette you've picked as your target. Now he's clearly in your sights. His lithe silhouette is backlit against the colorful hues of sunset. Whoa! Wait! Utter disappointment washes over you. No gonads. There's no question--it's a female. Better luck next time.

This whole scenario sounds excruciating to me. If I had to sit mute and immobile for even one hour, I would go bonkers. Listen, I said I understood my husband, brothers, and many hunters; but that doesn't mean I don't think they are a bubble off plumb at times.

The torment hunters are willing to endure for the opportunity to hunt is utterly mind-boggling. No matter how ludicrous and wretched this all sounds, hunters pay big money in the hope that a mature male leopard will drop its guard just long enough for a few seconds of opportunity. As I said, part of the reason they are so appealing to hunt is that they *are* so challenging.

Why, you might ask, did I wait so long to tell you that Rick was also hunting leopard? As you may be aware, the hunting of leopards, lions, and elephants is a hot-button issue that incites passionate emotions. Often not good ones. Quite frankly, I'm scared to tell you more.

With the intense anti-hunting sentiment so prevalent in today's polarized world, we fear this book could cause serious backlash. Aside from the outrage over Cecil the lion, some radical people mount vicious social media campaigns against hunters, even when hunts are perfectly legal. Non-hunters, biologists, and wildlife officials aren't in the clear either. Not if they support well-managed ethical hunting. My social media accounts are already a target for threats and harassment.

Still, the verbal bashing I've received is nothing compared to the vile way I've seen others attacked. In an earlier chapter, I spoke of Claude Kleynhans, the PH and family man, who was gored to death by a Cape buffalo. Below an online article detailing his death were the following comments: "the hero bull delivered justice to the evil, cowardly human trash"; "I hope the hunter died in agony"; "a fitting miserable death for a trophy hunter"; "good riddance"; "trophy hunters are human garbage"; "I sure hope it was a slow painful and undignified death as befits the lowlife of humanity"; "I wish I could have seen the buffalo strike--beautiful shot, right in the femoral, would have bled for a while but the outcome was great."

While these most horrid remarks are probably the result of a very few extremists, it is still unsettling. You could see why I might be apprehensive about exposing our hunting safari. Hateful sentiments like this are all over the internet anytime the topic of harvesting wildlife, especially the most beloved species, is involved.

Even people who condone other types of hunting can have intense emotions against hunting lions, leopards, and elephants. People like me for instance. Before visiting Africa, I existed in a middle ground, essentially acknowledging a gray area. I accepted subsistence hunting and, as much as I hate to admit it, I felt some species had more value than others.

Still, I had no ill will towards the hunters themselves. Growing up immersed in a world of hunters--who I know to be upstanding citizens--enabled me to have a completely different perspective. Taking the emotion out of it, I was able to see the big picture--placing a monetary value on wildlife, especially dangerous destructive species, is critical to their survival.

Part of the problem is that many well-meaning people have fallen victim to the hype of the media and anti-hunting groups. Many groups are experts at spreading disinformation that is emotionally based and extremely biased while providing no facts to back up their claims.

Facts don't lie. *Well-managed* hunting's success in growing wild populations throughout the world is undisputed. Most of the arguments provided by anti-hunting organizations, accidentally or conveniently, fail to acknowledge the statistical data. As far as Africa is concerned, they also fail to address the *reality* of rural people living with dangerous destructive beasts. Rarely, if ever, do such articles mention habitat loss as the most significant threat to Africa's wildlife. Over and over, photo tourism is touted as the saving grace; but they fail to mention that most areas suitable for ecotourism have already been tapped. Seldom do they address the fact that rural villagers see very little, if any, of non-hunting tourism money. Anti-hunting groups berate putting a cash value on a species but neglect to disclose that in doing so, remote lackluster lands remain valuable in their wild state. They portray "trophy" hunters as foul human beings because they choose to keep the memory, but don't mention that all the meat is consumed, much less of the animal is wasted, and only a few old males at the end of their lifespans are sacrificed. They also fail to address who will cover the cost of anti-poaching programs, lost employment, revenue generated, and meat for local communities if legalized hunting is stopped.

These groups also like to equate trophy hunting with poaching. Yet, comparing the two, as Dr. Amy Dickman puts it, is like comparing shopping to shoplifting. The former is legal, regulated, and generates wider benefits. The latter is illegal, unregulated and plays a key role in wildlife decline.

Truly, I believe *most* people's motives are pure and motivated by love. Even so, that is not the case with every organization. *Some* of the largest, most well-known, and vocal anti-hunting or animal-rights organizations are motivated by greed. Preying on the emotions of Westerners is their money ticket. Any controversy or headline adds wads of money to their coffers. You would be appalled if you knew the small fraction of money, from some multi-million-dollar budgets, that actually goes to helping wildlife or preserving their habitat.

According to Dr. Brian Child, University of Florida associate professor of African studies who specializes in African conservation and resource economics: "in many instances, it is extremely hard to find out where the money went and what impact it had. We often just don't know. A lot of people raise a lot of money in the name of saving rhinos or lions or whatever without ever checking to see where the money goes. I rarely see it having much of an impact on the ground...." On the other hand, the benefits of hunting can be seen and documented.

Don't get me wrong, there are many wonderful lesser-known organizations backed by both hunters and non-hunters, working diligently to save wildlife. Donations to these groups improve the human condition of local Africans, offer education, introduce alternative income opportunities, find solutions to help people live safely with wild species, fund anti-poaching efforts, rescue animals, and preserve habitat. Instead of being broad-based, each tends to concentrate on specific problems and localized solutions, while having boots on the ground.

Still, it must be recognized that Africa's wildlife cannot be saved *simply* through charity. The continent of Africa is over three times the size of the United States. That is a monstrous amount of land to protect, with only small areas currently safeguarded by park systems. One also must remember that well-managed hunting is self-sustaining while donations are not.

It twists a knife in my heart when I see disinformation about hunting's role in conservation, along with vilifying *all* hunters as cowardly, violent, evil people who kill for entertainment. They are talking about the people I love: my husband, father, stepdaughter, brothers, nieces, nephews, and friends. People who, while imperfect, are still respectable human beings.

With that said, it would be remiss to say that all *so-called* hunters live by the standards set by the majority. It is doubtful that anyone becomes more infuriated with unprincipled killers than hunters themselves. Not only do they hate unfair pursuits, inhumane treatment, and disrespecting the creatures they love, but the rare unethical hunters sully the name of all hunters. Each bad apple gives anti-hunting groups the ability to put another nail in the coffin.

If all the emotional and greed-driven hype wasn't hurting wildlife populations, the slander could be overlooked. Hunters, hunting organizations, or anyone who supports them will survive the nasty words. Africa's wild species may not.

It is also interesting to note that few people, when casting judgments on hunting and hunters, recognize their culpability in killing animals. Death is a byproduct of our mere existence. The food we eat, the homes we live in, the fuel we use for comfort and transportation and the industries producing these necessities all exact a toll on the environment.

While I detest the thought of killing an animal myself, I am an omnivore. In my twenties, I attempted living as a vegetarian for three *long* months before caving in a weak moment to the lure of a *Sharpy* burger from the local Burger Hut, putting an abrupt end to a plant-based lifestyle.

My not wanting to kill an animal, while at the same time being a meat eater, is a bit hypocritical. Although I may help with the work involved in processing the kill, I let someone else pull the trigger, thereby maintaining my sensitivities. Simply put, I let others do the dirty work. Hunters, at least, take responsibility for the food on the table.

Growing up in cities and suburbs, many people are completely detached from where their food comes from. Our grocery stores are filled with sterile cellophane-wrapped packages of meats. We plop it in the basket, carry it home, unwrap it, and throw it on the grill. Voila, easy-peasy. Even so, make no mistake about it. Just days before, that package of protein was oinking, clucking, baaing, or mooing.

This point was made quite clear in the 2017 Washington Post article "A surprising number of American adults think chocolate milk comes from brown cows."[1] Aside from 7 percent of adults being unaware chocolate syrup is needed to make chocolate milk, a study of fourth, fifth, and sixth graders in urban California found that 4 out of 10 kids had no idea that hamburgers came from cows. Three out of 10 were also clueless that cheese is made from milk. More than half had no idea that pickles started as cucumbers or that onions and lettuce were plants. This gives an idea of the disconnect. While this detachment may seem harmless or even a bit funny, it is hard to make informed decisions without such basic knowledge.

Vegans and vegetarians, also, don't get off scot-free. Large-scale agriculture, with its row upon row of well-manicured weed and insect-free crops fill our lands with chemicals and fertilizers while chewing up untold amounts of real estate, land that previously was home to native plants and animals. Organic farmers may spare the chemicals, but they still need a large patch of dirt, void of natural vegetation and varmints. In addition, cultivating and harvesting crops with high-tech mega-sized machinery is brutal for any critter in its path, slicing and dicing those too slow to escape the churning blades.

Looking at the hundreds of thousands of acres of wheat and canola fields lining the roads near our home, you will see very little diversity. There are a few varieties of cultivated crops that inadvertently support mice, owls, coyotes, deer and a few other species--most of which the farmers and ranchers consider pests and, therefore, employ strategies to keep to a minimum.

Before these prairie lands were cultivated, the grasslands and diversity of vegetation supported bison, elk, deer, bear, prairie dogs, coyotes, foxes, tons of birds, and countless other species of all sizes, shapes, and forms. When looking at Idaho's rocky pastures, rugged canyons, desert expanses, white-water river corridors, and mountain woodlands--essentially lands not suitable for crops--there is still an overwhelming diversity of habitat, plant life, and wildlife.

Many people with plant-based lifestyles don't recognize their contribution to the loss of habitat and, therefore, the wild creatures that are displaced. Few also fail to recognize that deer and other "pests" were often killed directly to protect the food they eat. In "Mindful Carnivore: A Vegetarian's Hunt for Sustenance," Tovar Cerulli came to the same conclusion.[2] His statement, "we weren't eating animals, but our vegetables were" hit the nail on the head. Yet, quite a few vegetarians look down on or even vilify those who eat meat for doing the same thing that they do by proxy.

The argument from the plant-based industry is that crops are mainly used to feed livestock. But according to the United Nations FAO, grain makes up only 13 percent of global livestock feed. In all, 86 percent of their food is grass and leaves, crop residues, fodder crops, oil seed cakes, and other by-products--all inedible by humans.

All of this is just the tip of the iceberg. As Cerulli put it: "We maim and kill in a million other ways, our industrial, economic, and agricultural machinery incurring a massive debt in animal lives and, worse, in habitat. But I had always found such harm – regrettable and unintended – easier to accept than premeditated violence." His heartfelt thought-provoking journey from vegetarianism to veganism to omnivore and ultimately to hunter will give you a whole new perspective on the toll our survival takes on other beings.

Please don't get me wrong. I'm not suggesting that everyone start dressing like Davy Crockett or begin a starvation diet to save the planet. There is nothing wrong with eating domestic livestock, wild game, or embracing a vegetarian-type lifestyle. There is also nothing wrong with wearing a leather coat or a pair of leather sneakers. Every person must do what speaks to their heart and works for their body, while also doing their best to ensure the survival of wild populations for future generations.

My point in all of this is that there is a real cost to the environment and living things for basically *everything* we do. None of us are squeaky clean or blameless in our quest to survive. Like it or not, one way or another, we are all responsible for the killing or displacement of wildlife.

Mgogo came tramping towards us from the surrounding brush with the smelly entrails in tow, thankfully without sacrificing any skin to a hungry carnivore. Seeing he was safe triggered another concern I was having. So many of us take meat utterly for granted; yet, in many nations, it is a luxury. Despite Tanzania's large livestock population, rural people consume very little animal protein compared to other developed nations. Knowing this, it was impossible not to feel pangs of guilt when looking at the meat dangling from a bait tree rather than being made into jerky--protein that could feed Mgogo's family and other villagers.

Nevertheless, my misgivings had to be put aside to look at the bigger picture. After just a few days in *Masimba* Camp and seeing Africa's reality through newly awakened eyes, I accepted the sacrifice. Like so many aspects of hunting, I had to look past my emotions to see that the loss of the protein, as well as the leopard, was for the greater good of both species; humans and wildlife.

I'd like to say that only one piece of meat was used and that there was no more tree acrobatics; but, since you can't put all your eggs in one basket, the search for a couple more trees with the perfect leopard-sized branches began. Yet, instead of the baiting process making me anxious, I found myself looking forward to them. Not only was the task fascinating to watch, but it allowed plenty of time for visiting with Lilian and the others, while also continuing my Swahili lessons.

Mgogo using foliage to hide the bait from vultures.

Once all the baits were in place, dropping by to check for spoor became a part of our daily ritual. To keep human scent to a minimum, we typically parked a few hundred yards away while Mgogo snuck off to look for footprints, claw marks, tufts of hair, gnawing, or other signs that *Chui* had dropped by.

If any indication of a larger, presumably male, leopard was discovered, the plan was to build the grass cocoon, sit like statues, and let Tsetse flies gorge on human blood. Waiting. Waiting. Waiting. Hoping that just before dark an aged male would slink onto the branch, letting his guard down for just a few seconds. There was no guarantee that such a leopard would find one of the baits, or that he'd yield to temptation. And so, the wait for *Chui* began.

If Rick's hunt proved successful, part of me would cringe. The other part of me would remember the words of Dr. Amy Dickman: "It is a cause for celebration that so many people love lions, elephants, and other wild animals--but we should be extremely wary of basing decisions on emotion alone, in case we worsen their conservation outlook, and effectively love them to death."

I, for one, refuse to love wild creatures to their death.

Deeply Stirring to the Blood

The death of Cecil, and the corresponding worldwide outrage, occurred just three months before our Tanzania safari. Amid filling out forms, stocking medications, getting poked for immunizations, and finalizing travel arrangements, we watched as the media firestorm exploded across the globe. While Rick's primary goal was hunting leopard, Rod's was hunting lion. Understandably, the implications weighed heavily on our minds.

Our trip to Tanzania was Rod's second attempt to harvest a lion. He had pursued *Simba* several years before in Tanzania's Selous Game Reserve. After 21 days on safari and scads of hours spent huddled in a lion blind, he left without a lion, never having an opportunity for a mature male. While this may not have been the outcome Rod was looking for, his pursuit injected wads of money into the Tanzanian economy and was, therefore, a definite win for conservation and the local people.

Many anti-hunters like to think of "trophy hunters," or selective hunters, as super-rich, entitled, opulent, revolting people born with a silver spoon in their mouths. While there are exceptions, most hunters are simply not the foul, horrid people that the media portray them to be. At least not with the hunters I've met and certainly not with Rod and Sue.

Sue and her three siblings were raised in rural Washington state. Although their rustic home had running water in the kitchen sink, they had no indoor bathroom until she was 13 years old. Trips to the outhouse and bathing in a galvanized tub were run-of-the-mill aspects of Sue's daily life. She also spent time fishing and subsistence hunting with her Dad. Though her life was filled with love, it was a far cry from the life of a child raised with a silver spoon.

Only 30 miles away, as the crow flies, Rod grew up with 3 siblings on the outskirts of a small rural town. He hunted with his Dad until he was

17 years old when both parents were killed in a tragic accident. Needless to say, losing his mother and father simultaneously, while so young, was devastating. For the next few years, Rod floundered about rather aimlessly, trying college and a series of odd jobs.

Sue came into the scene after taking a waitressing job at a local burger joint that Rod frequented. Apparently, Rod was impressed with more than the burgers and fries; only 11 months later the two of them were married. Four years later, in the midst of raising children, they saw a business niche in the community and pursued it full-bore. Being a top-notch team, they grew their business to over 50 employees while simultaneously raising four responsible hard-working children.

Hunting is something Rod and Sue began doing together early in their marriage. In the beginning, their hunts consisted of local deer and elk. As their children left the nest and the business continued to flourish, they became more passionate about hunting and were able to incorporate guided hunts into their lives.

As avid hunters, wildlife conservation is of deep concern to them. Aside from supporting local organizations and veteran's groups, they contribute to various hunting organizations that focus on purchasing, improving, or protecting animal habitats.

That is where our lives intersect. We were introduced by friends at a Rocky Mountain Elk Foundation benefit. Although we live several hours from each other, we connected again and again at various conservation events. Our personalities clicked, our friendship grew, and the next thing you know, we were battling Tsetse-flies together on the top of a Land Cruiser in the wilds of Tanzania.

Why is any of this relevant? Even before the death of Cecil, big game hunters were vilified by many media outlets and animal-rights groups. Since Cecil's death, emotions have escalated, especially for anyone hunting lions. Hunters are often crucified on the sheer premise that they hunt. Nothing else about them is known. It doesn't matter that they are real people with life stories that may make you laugh, as well as make you cry. People who grew up in childhoods where hunting was the norm. People who give freely of themselves and their resources to help others, wildlife, and the environment. People with strong family and community bonds.

I hope that by telling just a bit of their story, people will view them with humanity, instead of painting them as disdainful beings simply because they choose to legally hunt a lion.

Since hunting a lion was Rod's primary objective, their quest began on day one. Hunting lions using bait is similar to hunting leopards, except that the rotting delicacies are hung on a stout branch about eight feet off the ground, still accessible to the more terrestrially minded lions. The key is to keep the bait out of the jaws of hyenas, but still entice the lions.

Their elevated blind, or *machan*, was six feet above the ground on top of a large flat rock. Made of branches and grass intertwined together, the enclosure was snug but still large enough to fit Rod, Sue, two PHs, and their game scout. As with leopard blinds, the shelters offered safety and concealment but not much in the way of comfort. Typically, they sat a few hours in the morning and again before dusk. Staying hidden in the cramped torture chamber during the heat of the day when lions are napping, instead of roaming, was pointless.

Their first day in the *machan*, both morning and afternoon, was a bust. As they approached the bait early on the second day, they spotted a male lion laying directly under the bait but, upon their approach, he slipped off into the bush. Quickly, they climbed the makeshift ladder into the blind. Barely had they situated themselves when the same lion waltzed right under the *machan*, only inches from their feet. The only thing separating the two species was a thin covering of parched grass.

Paralyzed in fear, Sue envisioned *Simba* standing on his hind legs to slice through the thatching. She communicated her terror by digging her fingernails into Rod's arm for support. His nonverbal answer came in the form of a slightly raised hand, gesturing: *Be still. Remain calm. It will be fine.* Staying composed in the tension-filled *machan,* as the lion investigated just inches below, was easier said than done.

Instinctively knowing that something was amiss, the curious lion examined the mass of dried grass above him, slowly circling the entire boulder. Inside, the hunting party huddled motionless. After minutes that seemed like hours, the lion slowly wandered into the bush.

According to their PH, Paul, the lion was probably about four or five years old; not yet old enough to hunt. Experienced hunters can read the tell-tale signs to closely estimate a lion's age: mane development, leg markings, nose pigmentation, tooth wear, and facial markings, all provide good indications of age. Other than the fingernail gashes in Rod's arm, everyone, including the lion survived the ordeal unscathed.

The morning of day three was again a bust, although evidence showed a young male had explored the bait during the night. During their late afternoon session, however, the same lion from the previous day came in, seemingly no longer having qualms about the *machan*. He leaped up to the dangling meat, ripped off a piece of flesh, and plopped on the ground to eat his prize. After finishing the yummy morsel, he repeated the process several more times. The safari party was trapped inside their stifling grass cell until *Simba* sauntered off on another escapade.

Day four started like all the others. Rod, Sue, and their entourage left *Masimba* Camp at dawn working their way towards the lion bait. Within ten minutes, they passed two young male lions, probably brothers, walking across the savanna away from them. Sue's stomach was still in a knot from the first sighting when Salum, their tracker, pointed in the distance and whispered, "*Simba*". Partially hidden in the distant tall grass was another male lion. Stalking to get a better look with binoculars, the PH confirmed it was a mature, harvestable male. The hunt was on.

Things can get pretty dicey at this point in the game. When hunting a lion, any normal person's heart will be beating like they just ran the 100-yard dash and their hands will be shaking like a desert dweller in the arctic--all of this while barely breathing. Then a lethal combination of speed and strength comes charging forward while the person's heart is still doing flip-flops. A deadly blur of fur in a frontal charge offers a relatively small target with little room for error. If the lion is close, but not hit just right, his adrenaline can tear a person into something that will give even hyenas the dry heaves. Anyone who doesn't hunt lion with a healthy dose of fear is suffering from soft spots in the head.

Needless to say, wounding a lion is bad news for everyone: the lion, the hunter, the PHs, and the trackers. You don't want a lion to suffer. You also don't want a lion in a pained aggravated state roaming freely where it can maul unsuspecting victims. Hunting lions is risky enough. Pursuing an injured one is treacherous. That's why two PHs are sometimes used for lion hunts. If an animal is wounded, it is the PH's responsibility to go after it. They may allow the client to assist, depending on the hunter's abilities and the circumstances, but ultimately it is the PH's duty to end the lion's ordeal.

It's impossible to track a wounded lion and be prepared to stop a charge at the same time. It takes one person to place their entire focus on tracking while the other (or others), depending on the situation, will cover the possibility of an ambush. Also, since lions sometimes travel in small bachelor groups, the lion may not be alone; his chums might be romping through the same dense thickets. There isn't much room for error. Just one good bite to the skull and a person's troubles are over. Lions typically give a small grunt before charging, thereby giving a hunter a split second to get their act together. Understandably, wounded lions are the cause of many human deaths and maulings to hunters.

Another thing to consider is that lions tend to do funny things to people's minds. Even the most stable competent hunters can turn into blundering idiots when aiming their rifles at one of these amazing creatures. There are stories of clients, upon hearing the blood-curdling roar, who never even get a shot off. Capstick spoke of a client who actually threw his gun down and ran like a lunatic directly towards the big cat. While it's a tough story to sell, it's easy to get the crux of his meaning.

While Rod and Sue were pursuing lion, we were off on our adventures. Upon returning to *Masimba* Camp for our afternoon break, we were slightly baffled. Although the staff appeared to cheerfully greet us as usual, most were wearing weird ensembles of clothing: funny hats, pillows stuffed under their shirts and in the seat of their pants, blankets tied around their waists, and even a supersized tie reaching Musa's knees. Initially, we thought that the entire staff had been sipping on some kind of African moonshine or that the sun's rays had finally fried their brains; but then Rod and Sue sauntered over with glowing smiles and wreaths of green leaves draped around their necks.

The crazy dress-up party was a celebration. Rod had not run like a maniac towards *Simba* as Capstick's client had done. He overcame the fear and adrenaline that often comes with facing one of the world's deadliest, most magnificent animals; his shot had been true and Rod had fulfilled his version of swimming the English Channel or sailing the world.

The lion celebration with Kaumba leading the chant.

Little in Africa get the local people as excited as the death of a lion. Though some are now seeking alternatives, men in certain East African warrior societies have historically, and still are expected to prove their manhood by killing a lion. A young man's ceremonial kill and his subsequent entrance into maturity are considered a cause for celebration. The same type of jubilation is triggered any time a lion is killed that has been preying on livestock. In today's world, killing a lion as a rite of passage is highly frowned upon by outsiders. Warrior cultures are being encouraged to find other ways to prove their manhood. Still, it is a deeply rooted tradition that lives on in certain corners of the bush. The staff's elaborate costumes and wild displays were all part of that heritage.

Although we missed the initial celebration, Sue filmed it for us. When they pulled into camp honking and yelling with both the Land Cruiser and Rod decorated in greenery, everyone knew what that meant. The staff soon appeared dressed in outlandish attire. With the wreath still draped around Rod's neck, they put him in a chair, hoisted it in the air, and carried him around while chanting in Swahili. Once back on the ground, the entire group circled him in tribal dancing. Kaumba belted out words in Swahili and everyone repeated back. A few basic lines were chanted over and over amid dancing, gyrating, clapping, and stomping. While we didn't understand the Swahili, we didn't need to. The gist of it was clear as a bell.

One might think that celebrating the death of a lion would be cause for angered repugnant thoughts, especially since I originally had been against it. Yet strangely I felt no outrage or repulsiveness. The moisture in my eyes were tears of sadness for a magnificent animal's sacrifice; tears of happiness for Rod's success; tears of wonder for the opportunity to step into a foreign culture, witnessing a primal ritual; and most of all, tears of gratitude for the whole African experience and newfound awareness.

Bearing witness to such a display, even digitally, awakened deep powerful emotions within me. Numerous times I have tried to put these feelings in words, but I keep coming back to a memorable, but somewhat corny, line from one of my all-time favorite movies, "The Last of the Mohicans". The European-born heroine describes her feelings of life in America's wilderness as "deeply stirring to the blood." Although the words aren't any less sappy today, they've remained etched in my mind all these years. "Deeply stirring to the blood" is how I felt. Corny or not.

A black cloud loomed overhead. The death of Cecil was still very fresh in the media. Even so, I knew in my heart that Rod's hunt had helped the conservation of lions overall. The Ruaha Carnivore Project puts it this way: "For long-term conservation, local people need to recognize real, tangible, and relevant benefits from the presence of wildlife." Rod's hunt and the sacrifice of one majestic lion did just that. His hunt made *Simba's* habitat valuable in its natural state, while also providing an incentive for rural people to *protect* lions, instead of killing them. Without the support of locals, the king of beasts may someday disappear from the wilds of Africa, preserved only behind the gates of sanctuaries and zoos. A fate I will fight with every fiber of my being.

21
GROUCHY LITTLE MONSTERS

Grrrrrrr, hiiiiiiisssss! Ear-piercing snarls slashed through the tent walls as I lay like a sacrificial lamb. Alone. Rick had stayed up talking with Rod, leaving me to brave the beastly symphony on my own. *Surely,* I thought, *I could handle a measly hour without my almighty protector by my side.* Besides, he was close. Surely he'd come to my rescue if I needed him.

After dodging our quota of bat feces for the evening, Sue and I had decided to call it a night, leaving the menfolk by the fire to combat the guano attack on their own.

While Rick's calm, competent presence *always* filled me with a sense of ease, it gave me even more peace of mind in Africa. You know, a place where death "takes a thousand forms" as Capstick put it. Without Rick in the tent, I was a bit more on edge.

Just moments before the terrifying screeches surfaced from the riverbed, I had been lying on my cot, exhausted but vigilant, listening to the familiar sounds of the night--bellows, chirps, cackles, *hee hees*, grunts, whistles, squeaks. Slightly comforting was the lack of *Simba's* easily recognizable *umphhs*. That part of the serenade typically didn't come until later.

Then, out of the blue, the harrowing high-pitched vocals of two cats--two large cats--shattered the relative peace. Instantly, I knew two leopards were engaged in a fierce battle. Surely it could be nothing else.

A similar ruckus had exploded just outside our bedroom window in Idaho a few years back. Thinking two mountain lions were fighting 10 feet from my bed, I peeked cautiously through the curtains to investigate. Instead, I saw Jinx, our panther-sized tomcat, savagely driving off a newcomer. If I hadn't seen the battle with my own eyes, I would have never believed that two domestic cats could create such bloodcurdling sounds. Once I grasped the situation, I pounded on the window, distracting Jinx, and allowing the small intruder to make a run for it.

Not only did the scuffle put a whole new meaning to the words *cat fight*, but it also answered why our humble abode wasn't plagued with stray or "dropped off" cats like so many country homes. Jinx was the answer to that mystery.

As loud and fierce as that battle was, it was nothing compared to the skirmish taking place outside our tent. I jumped up, and ran to the zippered screened door, screaming for Rick. No way was I stepping outside my canvas sanctuary.

Rick, however, didn't show. Instead, my urgent pleas brought Joel scrambling toward me from his sleeping area behind the dining hut. Through the screen, I watched our unarmed host advance hastily toward me. Seeing that he had nothing with which to protect himself, I frantically cried, "Joel, go back, Go back! Leopards are fighting!" My calls only slowed him a bit. Even more urgently, I again screamed "Joel! Stop! Go back! Go get help!"

As Rick's Grandma Alice used to say, he *listened like shit on a barn door*. In other words, he didn't listen one teensy-weensy bit. He continued his approach, bypassed our tent, and skulked carefully toward the sounds of vocal murder.

By that point, I was panic-stricken. I was sure that Joel, who I had completely fallen in love with, was going to be ripped to shreds right in front of my very eyes. Like a ping pong ball, I bounced between screen windows in the tent. One opening gave me a view of what was sure to be a leopard making mincemeat out of Joel. The other gave me a view of the patio as I continued to scream for Rick at the top of my lungs. I'd dart to one window, peek at Joel; then bolt back to the other screen to yell for Rick. Nothing. Back and forth again.

I was beside myself; terrified to step one foot from my little refuge but horrified at the possibility of watching our enchanting storyteller and comedian get torn to smithereens. Sweat, resulting from my maniacal tizzy, rolled off me like the water over Niagara Falls.

Finally, Joel's shoulders relaxed, and he turned and ambled toward my tent: "*Ahhh*. It's okay. It's okay. It's only honey badgers fighting."

Well, gee-whiz, that was just swell. The medium-sized member of the weasel family is known for its super-sized attitude. They are notorious for their strength, ferocity, toughness, and all-around meanness. Weighing up to 35 pounds with bodies up to 30 inches long, these pugnacious creatures have enough strength in their jaws to break the shell of a tortoise. Although they are mainly carnivorous, they can eat anything and everything, plant or animal, including bones, skin, hair, feathers, and flesh. Even deadly snakes, including black mambas, aren't immune to their skills, making up almost a quarter of their diet.

The only thing sweet about honey badgers is the fact that they love feeding on honey and honeybee larvae. Other than that, they are pure nastiness. Related to the skunk family, they are even equipped with a stink bomb to release when in distress, different but just as rotten as its smaller relative.

Although their long claws and powerful arms allow them to easily dig up the ground, tree trunks, or even termite mounds to build their burrows, they are just as happy to forego the trouble and steal the dens of others. The invasive and eager-to-fight species will even pick a fight with a porcupine. It says a lot about the ferocity of a bucket-sized mammal when their only real enemies in the animal kingdom are hyenas, lions, leopards, and pythons. Even then, they don't throw in the towel easily. It would be a brutal battle.

Honey badger

The thick-skinned omnivores, and I mean this literally, have a dense layer of rubbery epidermis that enables them to writhe around, breaking loose from predators. While honey badgers are somewhat resistant to snake venom, their dense skin also helps prevent fangs from penetrating in the first place. According to Raphael, the honey badger is only one of the two species (the other being the mongoose) that will kill a black mamba. If the badger gets bitten during this seemingly crazy endeavor, the venom causes him to act drunk for 20 minutes or so. After a possible hangover, he then goes about his business.

To sum it up, despite its small size, the honey badger has a reputation for being, pound-for-pound, Africa's most fearless creature. Even so, I was quite happy to know that honey badgers were brawling in the riverbed--not leopards. Badgers are a handful, but at least they were less likely to transform Joel into scraps from a woodchipper.

Joel informed me that the skirmish had been between two males fighting over a den on the riverbank; therefore, one of the grouchy little monsters would most likely become our new neighbor. In fact, it was likely that one of the quarrelsome critters had been there all along. We just hadn't seen him because honey badgers adapt easily to nocturnal behavior when humans are around.

During this whole nerve-racking ordeal, I saw neither hide nor hair of my knight in shining armor. At least, not the one I married. It still baffles me that no one but Joel heard my frantic screams. After all, I've never been accused of having a delicate voice. Yet, somehow, Rick and Rod--tranquilly smoking cigars, reliving the day's events, and dodging volleys of *popo* feces--were clueless. The garish cries of a crazed woman and two battling beasts had melted in with the rest of the sounds of the night. A typical evening under Africa's moonlit skies.

22

WELCOME TO CHUI CAMP

S lowly we rolled out of camp, heading for our next adventure. Joel was waving cheerfully, crying words of encouragement: "Ahhh. You'll like *Chui* Camp. It's a nice camp. You'll like it a lot."

Gee, he seemed pretty chipper to see us go. Maybe he also *liked it a lot* that, for at least a few nights, he'd have peaceful slumber, instead of being awakened by a lady's frantic screaming and grouchy little monsters battling over territory.

Normally, multiple people saw us off, but this day was different. Rod and Sue were staying at *Masimba* Camp and were already gone for the day. Joel was the total sum of our send-off party. A good portion of *Masimba* Camp's staff was squished into the Land Cruiser along with us. The poor ol' Toyota looked like a pin cushion on wheels with people, instead of needles, poking out of every nook and cranny.

With the remaining days of our safari ticking by, Hilary had decided it was time to concentrate wholeheartedly on Rick's leopard. The baits around *Masimba* Camp were only attracting females or young males. Consequently, it was time to pull out the big guns, so to speak. That *big gun* was *Chui* Camp, a smaller spike camp situated on a different section of the Mzombe River at the far tip of Hilary's hunting concession. *Chui* is the Swahili word for leopard. Hence, while *Masimba* Camp was prime lion habitat, the area near *Chui* Camp was prime habitat for its namesake.

The African leopard with its beautiful golden spotted coat is the most secretive and elusive of the big cat species. Primarily nocturnal, they typically spend their days lounging, hidden in the camouflage of trees or within the recesses of a cave. At night, they leave their concealment to hunt for prey, either on the ground or within the treetops themselves. There are exceptions to this, of course, especially in national parks, giving some lucky ecotourists the rare privilege of watching their magnificence in action. In hunting areas, leopards are rarely spotted during the day.

Since trees and caves are their strongholds, it is no surprise that they favor rocky landscapes with dense bush and riverine forests. In other words, *Chui* Camp habitat. It was the ace up Hilary's sleeve.

Not only is *Chui* secretive, generally evading other species, but they also have the same regard for their kin. Opposite to lions, these predators prefer to prowl their territories alone, avoiding their own kind as much as possible, making exceptions only for a few days each mating season. Each individual has a home range that overlaps with its neighbors. Like other species, territories are marked with urine, feces, and claw marks to warn trespassers away.

Leopards don't have a wide range of vocalizations like their cousin the lion, but they still communicate effectively with one another. They bark, saw, or make a hoarse, raspy cough sound when they have something to say. They also growl when angry, hiss when threatened, and, like domestic cats, purr when happy and relaxed.

While we didn't hear leopards nearly as often as other animals, we did periodically hear their strange barks and primal coughs, telling us they were near, not necessarily a comforting thought. Leopards have the most powerful bite of any of the big cats, making them killing machines. The honey badger holds the title of being Africa's most *fearless* creature pound-for-pound, but *Chui* holds the title of being the most *powerful* mammal pound-for-pound.

A female leopard usually weighs less than 130 pounds, while the male, much stockier with a larger head and claws, weighs closer to 165 pounds, growing up to 7.5 feet long. Leopards may have a slighter frame than lions, but are capable of speeds up to 36 mph, leaping 20 feet forward, and springing 10 feet in the air, making them just as deadly.

Like other cats, they are primarily ambush predators who depend largely on sneaking close to prey. Their spotted coat allows them to blend perfectly with the dappled shade and leaves of the trees. Once their prey is spotted, they crouch low, slink silently to within striking distance, typically 15 to 30 feet, and pounce before victims can react. Typically, the graceful, but ferocious, feline kills the prey with one swift bite to the throat or neck, often breaking the victim's neck instantly, crushing its spine, or severing an artery. Smaller prey, such as birds or mice, often receive one powerful fatal blow from a huge paw.

As the strongest climber of all the big cats, they can easily haul prey two times their size into the safety of the trees, sometimes carrying them 30 to 40 feet high. Perched aloft in the canopy, the leopard can eat in relative safety, well away from the reach of *Simba* and *Fisi*. The leopard has another huge advantage; getting the essential moisture they need from their prey, making drinking at waterholes unnecessary, although they do visit them when possible.

Hunting leopards is dramatically different from hunting most African species. With most game, hunting amounts to tracking and stalking to get close enough for a shot. The leopard's elusive nature and acute senses make it practically impossible to sneak up on them, effectively nullifying the spot and stalk technique.

Hunting leopards demands that you do the opposite. You have to make an immensely shy, mostly nocturnal animal disregard his normal habits and come to you instead. That means he must be lured into an open area of a tree that he would normally shun. This magical spot must also be located within 60 yards or so of a blind to allow for a single death-dealing shot, so that he doesn't escape, wounded and savage, into thick cover.

A wounded leopard in the bush is one of the most dangerous creatures in the world. They do not kill as many people as lions, but more professionals, hunters, and safari staff are injured by leopards than by any other wild game in Africa. An injured cat will slink off into the bush and snuggle up under cover until a person is within striking distance. Unlike a lion who will give a warning roar as he charges, *Chui* explodes from his hiding place in total silence, making mincemeat of whoever is in his path, slicing and dicing until his final moment. One of the hosts of the television show "Tracks Across Africa" put it this way: "Being mauled by a wounded leopard is like being thrown into a clothes dryer with an activated chainsaw."

To decrease the chances of getting anyone shredded, it may be tempting to let some time pass if *Chui* is wounded, hoping the cat will die on its own. Not only is it inhumane to let an injured cat suffer, but it also increases the chances that the cat will never be recovered. Bait trees also draw other predators. If hyenas are in the area, they can devour an injured leopard within minutes, leaving little, if anything, to retrieve.

Aside from selecting a bait tree less suitable for lions, its branches should be slanted in a way that will silhouette the leopard as dusk sets in. Every second of light is precious. The bait must also be securely fastened so he can't take it with him. Better still if it frustrates him enough to draw him in even earlier the next evening when there is enough light to shoot. This is all for naught, however, if the tree isn't situated in heavy cover. To entice a cat to approach during the daylight hours, he must be able to sneak in unseen.

Leopards don't like to be spotted by anything, two-legged or four-legged. Once a leopard is discovered by potential prey, cries of alarm sound off warning others of its deadly presence, thereby ruining his hunting. Therefore, you can have the best tree in the world with the juiciest piece of meat, but a cat will not cross open ground to get to it. He will, instead, wait until darkness. Providing a location offering concealment is innately the problem. Giving him cover to approach unseen also gives an injured leopard the cover to escape.

If the perfect tree is chosen, the blind is as close as it should be, and *Chui* is enticed into a daylight visit, the shot should be relatively easy. Still, hunters who can typically shoot the bullseye out of a 500-yard target are known to miss completely. Imagine sitting for hours in a cramped blind peering blearily through a tiny peephole at bait fastened to a tree. Waiting. Waiting. Waiting. The anticipation, adrenaline, fear, pressure, or even exhaustion can cause even the best of hunters to make mistakes.

There is another problem as well. Just like lions, leopards tend to do strange things to the most put-together people's demeanor. Rick's military and hunting experience keep him attuned to his surroundings, looking for the storm so to speak. His calm in the face of peril allows me to be-bop through life *without* carrying all that weight on my shoulders. This was a leopard hunt. His dream for so many years. There was no guarantee his calm, cool, collected manner would hold true.

Thoughts of the deadly spotted feline clouded my brain as Rick and I hastily packed our few belongings for our stay at *Chui* Camp. We had no idea how long we'd be there. Two days. Five days. Ten days. Presumably, we wouldn't return until Rick had harvested a leopard. If, and how long that might take, was anyone's guess. Rick was cramming clothes into his pack with much more gusto than the task warranted. I, on the other hand, was a bit torn. Part of me wasn't ready to leave the comfort and familiarity of *Masimba* Camp. Yet, my thirst for adventure and different scenery also tugged at me.

Loaded up and heading to Chui Camp.

By 9 a.m., we were loaded and ready to go, crammed like sardines in a can. *Chui* Camp was a smaller camp but it needed staff as well. I was only slightly exaggerating when I said that most of the staff was with us. Since hunting leopard was the most important aspect of Rick's hunt, Hilary was even part of our excursion. He squeezed up front with Mike and Lilian. Raphael, Rick and I had the bench seat, the best seat in the house, as usual. Mgogo, Abdalah, Kaumba, and Maugo were all in the cargo hold, along with packs and tons of camp supplies. The Land Cruiser was full to the gills.

Rungwa West Game Block was composed of approximately 540 square miles of a huge T-shaped mass of land. *Masimba* Camp was located on the extreme tip of one end and *Chui* Camp was located at the other, basically a four-hour jaunt across the savanna. Seeing new countryside for the first time is always exciting. Then throw in a herd of elephants, lots of giraffes, another hyena, kudu, steenbok, impala, warthogs, zebra, oribi, and two lions to get your motor really running.

Both lions we saw were male. One was a huge black-maned older male, and the other was younger and smaller. Just like the other lion we had seen, they were lounging comfortably, partially hidden, in the dappled shade under a small grove of trees plunked in the middle of a vast stretch of open savanna. Neither gave a whit about the Land Cruiser chock full of humans rumbling by. Neither did they care about the lunatic jockeying for the perfect camera shot, which I never did get. Meanwhile, their regal eyes just casually followed the roving sardine can as it motored through their little slice of the kingdom.

A few hours after seeing the lions, we experienced déjà vu. *Chui* Camp was essentially a smaller-scale version of *Masimba* Camp. It had a *mesi*, patio area, kitchen enclosure, skinning shed, and sleeping huts--all sitting along a different section of the Mzombe River, still bordering Ruaha National Park. Other than being nestled in the trees instead of along the riverbed, our sleeping quarters were practically identical, a secure zippered tent underneath a thatched shade shelter with a grass enclosure for a toilet, sink, and shower.

To keep us in the lap of luxury that we'd become accustomed to, Thomas, the tent attendant, and Andrew, the other PH, had come a couple of days earlier to set up camp and prepare. I'm not sure how many days or weeks the camp had sat vacant since its last guests, two-legged or four-legged, but it was immaculate and fully operational when we we arrived. Barely had we stowed our gear before a delicious hartebeest spaghetti lunch was served in the *mesi*.

As is often the case, full bellies seemed to be synonymous with disappearing acts. While I can't speak for the others, Rick, most assuredly, snuck off for a power nap. Within minutes, Andrew and I were the only two remaining. Like Raphael, Andrew had worked with Hilary for almost 19 years, starting as the camp's water boy, progressing to a tracker, and then earning his PH license.

Thomas and Kaumba preparing dinner at Chui Camp.

As he was a native Tanzanian with tons of bush experience, our initial chit-chat quickly turned into an afternoon lesson on how the country's land management program worked. From his pack, he pulled out maps showing me detailed views of Rungwa West, the Ruaha National Park boundaries, and the whole of Tanzania. He explained that land is broken down into different categories: Hunting Game Reserves (Game blocks), Game Control Areas, Open Areas, Wildlife Management Areas (WMA), and National Parks. Each one is slightly different, permitting different activities. National parks, for instance, only allow ecotourism, while some areas allow hunting, grazing, and farming. Still, others allow the harvesting of honey and timber as well. The WMA's are managed by the local people. Consequently, those areas vary depending on the management tools chosen for each community. These locally managed areas also have their own village game scouts in addition to the Tanzanian wildlife rangers such as Lilian.

Once I got the gist of all that, our chat turned less technical. Spellbound, I listened to story after story of his experiences in the bush, typically accompanied by some type of cautionary warning.

When the conversation turned to snakes, as it so often did, the subject of bushfires came up; intentionally setting fires to sections of the savanna is a common practice in Africa. Typically, people will fashion a circle around the potential burn area before using a torch to ignite the perimeter. Forming a ring allows the fire to eventually burn itself out. These fires are often fast spectacular blazes that not only destroy much of the habitat where snakes hide but also destroy some of the snakes without doing much damage to the larger trees and plant life, many of which have evolved to survive such wildfires.

Aside from making the savanna a safer place for humans, many wild species are equally fond of the burnt terrain. The fires remove dead plant matter, and the resulting ashes act as fertilizer, invariably launching new green growth. Many varieties of antelope prefer this younger, more tender vegetation over the taller dried grasses. It also enables the grazing animals a better view of predators while they feed. The fires are a win-win for most creatures. Snakes and predators, maybe not so much.

When researching this further, I found, like everything, there is a delicate balance that must be maintained. Both savanna and forest habitats are critical to support wildlife. Grass fires keep forests from encroaching into those critical open areas while replenishing themselves quickly. Forests, on the other hand, take much longer to recover, if ever, depending on the habitat and the circumstances. Therefore, if fire destroys too much forest, that is not a good thing. Human activity such as land clearing, encroachment, disruption of natural fire paths, fragmented patches, and climate change can, unfortunately, knock the equilibrium between forest and savanna out of whack.

Another crucial consideration for bushfires is the time of year. It is best to burn during or immediately following the rainy season. Blazes set at the end of the dry season can burn too hot, sometimes killing the roots of the grasses. This can not only lead to soil erosion but can also destroy important plants that wild populations rely on for food.

Spending a couple of hours with Andrew was fascinating. Aside from covering management areas, fires, and snakes, we touched on a dozen other things that reminded me to keep my butt anchored to the safety of *Chui*

Camp. No leisurely walks on my own. No way. No how. Not that the staff would have let me anyway.

By the time I was done picking Andrew's brain, the camp came alive with preparations. It was time for Rick to truly start his leopard hunt. Along with setting up camp, Andrew and Thomas had set up several bait trees, one of which showed signs of a promising male.

For several reasons, we decided it was impossible for me to go along. First of all, Rick didn't want to have to worry about my sorry butt if something went horribly wrong. Plus, the cramped blind would already be plum full, with Rick, Raphael, Mgogo, Andrew, and Lilian. Another derrière was something they could do without. Most notably, I was nowhere near insane enough to subject myself to that kind of tedious agony for hours at a time.

As I said, hunters are a different breed. The pain and torment they are willing to endure for their hunting pursuit boggle the mind. Not only was I smarter than my husband in this capacity, and not willing to expose myself to such abuse, but quite honestly I wasn't capable of it even if I wanted to. There was about a snowball's chance in hell that I would make it one hour in that torture chamber.

By now, you've got the gist of my personality. Do you think I could stay quiet for hours on end?

The ultimate deal breaker was the need to stay completely and utterly still. Never would I be able to go hours without flinching. Heck, even if the rest of my body agreed to cooperate, my bladder would have led a revolution.

Leopards not only have great senses, but they are also exceptionally clever. Recognizing that life rarely offers a free meal, they investigate thoroughly before giving in to the temptation. Even a wisp of something out of place will send them packing.

Part of me ached desperately to be in the leopard blind with Rick. After all, it would be the only real chance I'd have to see *Chui* in the wild. The odds of seeing the elusive, clever feline while perched on the back of a vehicle were slim to none. Avoiding the torture chamber *machan* was also surrendering my opportunity to watch the magnificent spotted feline in person.

Putting the finishing touches on the ground blind.

As the hunters gathered supplies and jumped aboard the Land Cruiser, electricity filled the air. Hunting leopard was a big deal. Everyone was excited. Especially Rick. He wasn't jumping up and down, doing cartwheels, or performing a happy dance. That's my style, not his. Nonetheless, his face said it all. Finally, after years of preparation, his leopard hunt was less than an hour away.

As the hunting ensemble rumbled away from camp heading toward the blind, four of us stood waving, shouting words of encouragement: *Good Luck. Be safe. Shoot straight. Come back with Chui.* Then suddenly they were gone.

As the dust cleared, I felt heavy-hearted. It was the first time I hadn't been with Rick on a hunt since we'd arrived in Africa. Although I knew I'd be no good in the blind, I also didn't want to miss even one second of this magical environment: a giraffe's graceful exit, a Baobab's towering magnificence, umbrella trees silhouetted against an orange sunset, or *Chui* slinking across a branch. Every animal, every tree, and every new adventure was priceless. Saying goodbye to the crew was also saying goodbye to unrealized experiences, as well as sharing firsthand in Rick's possible fulfillment of a dream.

The preparations had been made. The wheels set in motion. Expectations were high. Still, it also takes a smidgeon of luck. All I could do was wait and hope that Lady Luck, skill, and calm coincided.

After the hunters had disappeared, Kaumba ambled off to busy himself with dinner while Thomas hustled about in the dining hut. With Hilary and I the only two remaining on the patio, our small talk soon turned into a continuation of the lessons I'd started with Andrew.

As the owner of the outfitting business, Hilary was kind enough to explain the financial details around hunting management, including sharing the actual dollar amount. Each outfitting company must purchase a license to operate the hunting operation. For instance, the license fee paid to the government by his safari company was in the thousands of dollars. On top of that, another huge portion of money is paid for the sole use of *each* designated hunting block. Although I won't share it here, I'm not talking about some piddly amount, I'm talking about a jaw-dropping amount. Other outfitters, of course, pay similar fees for each of their hunting concessions.

Hilary Daffi, the owner of the outfitting business
in Chui Camp's patio area.

The above expenses don't count the individual trophy fees paid by each hunter, part of which goes to the government and part which is kept by the outfitter. On top of all those expenses, each outfitter for each hunting block is required to contribute a specified amount of money to projects for the betterment of local communities. For instance, providing funds to dig a well for a village, enhance their educational system, or initiate health programs.

Hilary reminded me of the hunting industry's other benefits that are just as important, if not more so: the trickle-down effect on the Tanzanian economy and the smaller environmental impact hunters make on the landscape along with much larger payoffs. He also repeated what Lilian had stressed earlier: the hunting concessions are situated to create buffer zones around national park systems. For poachers to gain access to the animals in Ruaha National Park, for example, they must first navigate through miles of wild rugged bush. That means no villages or communities to offer shelter and supplies. Plus, that ring of protection is loaded with game scouts, PHs, trackers, and camp staff.

The concept made total sense. Every day, with no expense to the government, two Land Cruisers packed with skilled gun-toting entourages of anti-poachers more or less patrolled every corner of Rungwa West Game Reserve's 540 square miles.

This, of course, may not stop all the poaching, but it offers one more line of defense against the illegal killers who don't give a hoot about quotas, or animals' pain and suffering, young or old, male or female; men whose quest for bushmeat, horns, ivory or animal skins drives them to use poison and snares causing torturous deaths along with significant collateral damage to non-targeted species.

Hilary also affirmed that even with all these benefits, the most important aspect of hunting is the protection it gives to the habitat that most tourists would shun. Making wild lands valuable for the wild populations that exist on them is imperative to stop human encroachment. Hilary has lived in Tanzania his whole life. He has seen the country's growth and has watched habitat disappear where hunting was minimized.

Unsurprisingly, since Rick was hunting leopard, our conversation drifted to leopards, more specifically the threats against them. Instead of using Hilary's words, I'd like to share with you a Public Guidance Position Statement entitled "The Leopard and Its Endangered Species Ranking" aimed at the United States Fish and Wildlife Service (FWS).[1]

The article, written by the True Green Alliance, a South African conservation group, captures the leopard's predicament.

In rural areas African villagers persecute leopards, killing them indiscriminately at every opportunity. These big cats are of no value to rural folk. On the contrary, they are a great liability because they become adept at killing domestic stock. Few rural Africans possess a firearm, so they kill leopards with poisons and cable snares, which cause horrible and inhumane deaths. Most rural people in Africa, however, have no other choice. Furthermore, when a man is fighting for his survival in a harsh environment, and looking after the well-being of his domestic stock, how the leopard dies is of no consequence to him.

Commercial farmers in Africa, on whose domestic stock leopards also prey, kill them with poisons, too, and/or they trap and/or shoot them. And because it is illegal to kill a leopard in most parts of Africa, the farmers avoid conflict with the authorities by simply applying the 'Triple-S Solution' to their perceived leopard problems: They 'Shoot, Shovel and Shut-up'. The vast majority of leopard deaths in Africa today are the result of these kinds of killings. By comparison, the numbers of leopards killed by hunters is minuscule.

What is abundantly clear is that declaring leopards to be a so-called endangered species, and registering them, as such, on the American Endangered Species Act listings, will have not one iota of effect on the behavior of indigenous rural villagers in Africa or well-to-do commercial farmers. They will still kill leopards, as they have always done, for the same reasons!

On the other hand, it has been the experience of professional hunters and wildlife managers that if they work with Africa's rural folk, and with Africa's commercial farmers, convincing them that it is in their own best interests not to kill leopards indiscriminately but to make them available as huntable tro-

phies to the professional hunting industry, they can benefit
greatly from their sale for a very high price. It takes a little
bit of extra effort on their part to protect their livestock from
predator attacks, but the dividends they can accrue from doing so, by them becoming part of the wildlife industry in this
manner, is well worth the effort. And pre-emptive killings,
which are the most damaging to local leopard populations,
STOP. This approach works best for Africa's leopards!

What *will* endanger the leopard is if the FWS declares it to be
an endangered species and denies American hunters the right
to take their African leopard trophies back home to America,
because THEN the species will become totally valueless to
Africa's people who will slaughter it at every opportunity.
This would be another great indictment on the wisdom, the
integrity and the science of the FWS, and on America itself.

Further, they contend that the FWS pays far greater heed to the
anti-hunting rhetoric than to genuine wildlife management. Many African
nations are getting restless with Western interference, stating that they do
not "accept the divine right of the FWS to enact domestic American laws
that will adversely affect another country's wildlife. We believe this is not
only an arrogant assumption it is also another indictment on the Service's
professional integrity."

Hilary may have used slightly different words on the patio that night at
Chui Camp, but the meaning was the same. Knowing the love and respect
that our Tanzanian hosts have for their wild creatures, I had no reason to
doubt him. Still, as an owner of an outfitting business, he did have skin in
the game. That is why it is even more impactful and relevant coming from
an African in-country conservation group.

Fortunately, many conservation organizations throughout Africa now
understand that the future of leopards, just like lions, lies in an integrated
approach to conservation that looks not only at the needs of the species
but also at the needs of the local people, land use, and the ecosystems as a
whole.

While leopards face the same issues as other predators, they have fared better than most. The leopard is probably the most widespread and successful big cat in the world thanks to its extreme adaptability, secretive nature, and indiscriminate diet. Leopards aren't picky eaters, helping them adapt easily to different environments and the delicacies offered at each. In Africa, carrion, fish, reptiles, birds, rodents, hares, warthogs, antelopes, cheetah cubs, baboons, domestic livestock, as well as dogs and cats are all yummy tidbits to the leopard. For these reasons and others, the leopard population in every major national park in Africa is safe and stable.

Nevertheless, it is no time to rest on our laurels. Due to habitat loss, their numbers are declining. It is estimated that leopards have disappeared from nearly 37-40 percent of their historical range in Africa. Yet, trying to learn the current population of sub-Saharan leopards is like trying to pull a genie out of a bottle. Even with Lilian's help, I was unable to find any kind of statistical data. Even so, it is abundantly clear that Tanzania is considered one of its remaining strongholds.

It is easy to see why establishing an accurate count of the elusive feline would be a daunting task. It's kind of like trying to count ghosts flitting about in a graveyard. It is their very secretive wispy character that gives the impression that they are so rare. While lions and cheetahs are easily spotted on the plains lounging around in grand fashion, leopards are tucked away in a cave or hidden in the camouflage of a tree's leaves. Just because you don't see them, however, doesn't mean they aren't there.

One thing for sure, the likelihood of my seeing a leopard while chatting with Hilary at *Chui* Camp was slim to none. No self-respecting leopard was going to come slinking into the camp in broad daylight with human activity around. While it made me sad that I was missing out on that opportunity to see a leopard in the wild, my time alone with Hilary was significant as well.

Hilary was the perfect host. He could laugh, joke, banter, harass, schmooze and tell stories with the best of them. As a young black Tanzanian, Hilary worked his way up the totem pole, spending many years as a camp helper, tracker and PH, ultimately owning his own outfitting business. Hilary was not only a huge success story, he was a wealth of information. Speaking with him one-on-one allowed me to part from the typical entertaining tales and jovial banter to delve much deeper into the hurdles facing rural Africa and its wild inhabitants.

Much of what I learned was deeply troubling. In some ways, I wish I had remained naive and completely oblivious. After all, ignorance is bliss. Nevertheless, to be a champion of wildlife, one must understand the reality of the situation, no matter how distressing, alarming, and unsurmountable the challenges seem.

Although my time with Hilary shed light on truly important things, it also made me ridiculously aware of how spoiled I'd become. While *Chui* Camp had most of the luxuries of *Masimba* Camp, it was indeed lacking a few of life's simple pleasures. The first became excruciatingly apparent as I tried to drink lukewarm diet cola, not a frosty one with the ice cubes I had been anticipating. *Masimba* Camp had an ice maker. *Chui* Camp did *not*. Water, albeit warm water, became my drink of choice.

Even more than the ice, I missed the four-legged parade at the waterhole. Even though the riverbed ran right past camp, there were no pools of water in view of the patio area. Hilary assured me that the animals were nearby. The waterholes were just a few hundred yards up the riverbed. Since it was too dangerous to go alone, he promised someone would escort me the next day.

Dinner was quiet compared to the liveliness of a table filled with spirited people, riveting stories, and plenty of laughter, but it certainly wasn't lacking in tastiness. Even with limited supplies at a more remote location, Thomas and Kaumba whipped up a to-die-for pumpkin soup, followed by eland steaks from the animal Rod had harvested the day before.

As dark began to set in, the foodstuff was stored away to deter any nocturnal visitors. Soon after, the generator sputtered and died, ending its ceaseless hum for the night. Just like *Masimba* Camp, only a few solar-powered lights remained to light the darkness. Within minutes, the camp was eerily quiet as each of us retired to our respective sleeping areas. Hilary's shelter was only 30 yards from ours; but as I entered our tent alone, it suddenly seemed like hundreds. Kaumba and Thomas slept in the kitchen hut area about 30 yards in the other direction. With the aroma of eland steaks still wafting through the air, I didn't envy their sleeping quarters one tiny bit.

After crawling into bed, I couldn't bring myself to turn off the light hovering overhead. With darkness in full bloom and camp silent, the African Symphony began its nightly serenade; screeches, cackles, grunts, squeaks, guttural cries. The ghostly, but seemingly distant, babble of hyenas was going strong. Missing was the gurgling sounds of nearby elephants and the bellowing of the hippos. Thankfully, *Simba*, too, was quiet. As much as I looked forward to the beastly compositions, the eerie vocals were much easier to enjoy when Rick was in the bed beside me.

Lying wide awake reading a book under the reassuring glow of the light, I waited for Rick's return. I knew it would be a while. The hunters would stay in the blind until dark. Then they had to radio the crew, wait for pick-up, and make the 45-minute jaunt back to camp.

After a time, I heard the distant rumble of the engine. No honking. No yelling and screaming. Only the sound of a motor grew louder as the seconds passed. The lack of noise told me everything I needed to know. No leopard. Success would have meant a celebration much like the lion celebration for Rod and Sue. We were sure to hear the triumph long before we caught sight of them. That night there was only silence.

Expecting Rick to be disappointed, I was surprised when he came into the tent excited and smiling. Although no huge males had come to the bait, two other leopards had. He watched a female drop onto the branch from out of nowhere to feed for a while. Then, a few minutes later, a young male chased her off, taking his turn. Not one, but two, leopards had come to the bait, offering him a peek at one of Africa's deadliest animals in their natural environment. Neither were mature males, but it didn't matter. Rick was thrilled just the same.

Surprisingly, he raved about Raphael, Andrew, and Mgogo *almost* more than the leopards. Even knowing the stillness that the blind would require hadn't prepared him for their level of immobility. If it hadn't been for the occasional blinking of an eye, he'd have sworn they were all dead, insisting they never moved a muscle the entire time. Meanwhile, his whole body ached from fighting the instincts to react to the Tsetse flies and sweat trickling down his face.

What a day it had been. Saying goodbye to *Masimba* Camp, a four-hour trek across a new landscape, lion sightings, elephants, giraffes and so much more. Most importantly, Rick had been on his first official leopard hunt and had been graced with the privilege of seeing two of the elusive felines.

Of course, we had no way of knowing what the next day would bring, but we were full of promise. Hilary's claim that the Mzombe riverbed woodland was a leopard Mecca seemed to be right on the money. It was sure to be a part of the African experience that we would never forget. Welcome to *Chui* Camp!

23
SAVAGE CRIES AND GHASTLY GIGGLES

WHOOooooooOOP! WHOOooooOOOOP! WHOOP! WHOOoooP!
Terror-stricken, I hid underneath the covers. Alone. Frozen in fear. The screened windows on my side of the tent were only a foot away, but there was no way I was peeking in that direction. If ravenous eyes were peering through, I didn't want to know. Instead, I stared straight up, seeing nothing but blackness.

After surviving the previous night in *Chui* Camp with no four-legged intruders, I idiotically turned off the solar light. In all the nights listening to the African Symphony, I had never heard so many hyenas, so close, belting out their savage cries. *WHOOooooPPP! WHoooPP! Heeheehee! WHOooPP! WHOoooPP!* Their insane giggles, along with roars and whoops and screams and growls, seemed closer than ever before, like they were prowling within *Chui* Camp itself.

Lying petrified on my cot, our staff's stories came flooding back to me, especially the tales of villagers falling asleep near campfires, and having their faces eaten off by hyenas. It was a ghastly thought but one that had some merit. While performing my pig-in-a-blanket impression, I tried to convince myself that the stories had been grossly exaggerated, simply attempting to enhance the thrill and danger of living in the bush.

With that said, our hosts weren't the only ones to tell of such savagery. Ernest Hemingway, in the *Green Hills of Africa*, wrote: "*Fisi*, the hyena, hermaphroditic self-eating devourer of the dead, trailer of calving cows, ham-stringer, potential biter-off of your face at night while you slept, sad yowler, camp-following, stinking, foul, with jaws that crack the bones that lion leaves, belly dragging....."[1] While it is apparent that Hemingway was no fan of hyenas, the words that thoroughly got my attention were *potential biter-off of your face at night while you slept.*

An equally vivid description by Robert C. Ruark in "Horn of the Hunter" attests to the same reality: "You will come upon natives with a portion of their faces chewed off, with horrid scars and welts healed over into grotesque masks. You ask them, how come? The answer is always *Simba*--lion. It is seldom true. The truthful answer is *Fisi* -- hyena."[2]

Hemingway, Ruark, and *Masimba* Camp's staff weren't the only ones to make such claims. Even when later researching hyenas on the internet, it was a fairly common theme. The descriptions, however, were far less explicit. Most material skillfully disguised it by saying "They are known to attack humans sleeping in the bush."

Some writers have even suggested that the hyena is a greater man-eater than the lion and leopard put together. Not a comforting thought. Fortunately, much of the human flesh that scholars are referring to was long dead before any hyenas scarfed it up. Let me remind you that the Maasai people of Kenya and Tanzania purposely leave the bodies of their dead to be eaten by hyenas. Hyenas are also very good diggers. Grave diggers to be exact. Any shallowly buried remains are simply inviting a feast. *Fisi,* understandably, became a walking symbol of the graveyard for many African cultures. It is no wonder there are countless myths and legends about the carnivores, including stories of witchcraft, grave robbing, and sexual deviance.

The hyenas' ghastly deeds are made even more ominous by their ungainly, sinister-looking appearance. Visions of the menacing creature filled my brain as another *WHOOP! WHOOoooOOOOP!* cut through the darkness. Their maniacal choruses were a part of every single night, but it was several days before we spotted one. Before that, they had been like ghosts in the darkness, always there but never seen. Only their voices told of their presence.

Fisi! Raphael whispered pointing across the savanna, just minutes into our morning trek. Following his finger, I spotted the peculiar-looking animal 100 yards away. Being only a few miles from camp, it was exciting to think that we might finally be putting a face to the primary voices we heard each night.

While the hyena didn't stick around long, I was still able to absorb its unpleasant, almost repugnant, features firsthand. He wasn't beautiful, graceful, and elegant like so many species. Neither was he cute and cuddly with an endearing personality to fall in love with.

Ruark describes him a bit more colorfully: "Of course, the hyena is a ridiculous beast. God's mind was absent the day he built *Fisi*. He gave him a dog's face and a lion's ears and the burly body of a bear. He permanently crippled his hindquarters, so that his running motion is a slope-spined, humping shuffle." He goes on to say "*Fisi* is such a terrible creature that he almost isn't true...an errant coward nearly always, and anything whole and brave can chase him."[3]

Spotted hyena

The unflattering portrayal of hyenas in books, along with their displeasing looks, psychotic banter, and penchant for eating the dead--whether fresh or withering in a grave--doesn't bode well for a beast's reputation. Essentially, *Fisi's* standing in the animal kingdom is in the gutter.

Even Walt Disney's *The Lion King* movies had them wallowing in the sewer. While most members of the realm were portrayed as regal, cute, beautiful, brave, and wise, the hyenas were thrown under the bus. Not only was their appearance distorted and freaky looking, but they were also depicted as gluttonous, brainless, and sinister. As Scar's evil sidekicks, their greedy behavior led to the collapse of the entire Pride Rock ecosystem.

As it turns out, however, *Fisi* has a huge public relations problem. Many of the traits associated with them are completely off base. Not just a little bit--I'm talking way out of the ballpark.

Their appearance leads to the first fallacy. Hyenas may have some dog-like features, but they are not related to man's best friend, or even wild dogs, in any way. Incredibly, it is almost the opposite. They are more closely related to cats and, therefore, fall under the scientific classification of cat-like carnivores.

The misconceptions don't end there. Although hyenas are personified as simpleminded, a study done by Duke University showed just the opposite. Their intelligence, along with their loving nature toward clan members, allows them to form intricate social bonds rivaling that of primates. In addition, the study found that captive hyenas were better at problem-solving and social cooperation than chimpanzees. Even more amazing, the hyenas solved the issues in total silence, using only non-verbal signals. Hyenas are, therefore, considered the most socially complex carnivores in the world, surpassing even the beloved lion.

The hyena Raphael spotted was alone, apparently a male. I say apparently because determining the sex of a spotted hyena can be a bit tricky. Not only do they not have horns to announce their maleness like so many species, but the most obvious method--looking for the male organ--is also null and void. Both sexes have penises or at least pseudo-penises. The female has dangling genitals that can be up to seven inches long, appearing to be the real thing. If that doesn't muddy the waters enough, then flip-flop almost everything you know about gender in the animal kingdom.

Female hyenas, almost 5 feet long and weighing up to 190 pounds, are typically 10 percent larger than males. They are also more muscular, more aggressive, and loaded with up to 3 times as much testosterone. Spotted hyenas are strictly matriarchal societies. Even the youngest females dominate ruthlessly over mature males.

In the hyena's female-dominated world, the males are literally at the bottom of the totem pole, thereby living a brutal existence. While still cubs, they are treated a little less severely. When they reach maturity at age two, any niceties come to an abrupt and bitter end. Young males are forced to leave their clan to search for an unrelated group, an extremely violent and vicious process. When, and if, a new clan's alpha female accepts him, he is faced with constant harassment and forced into struggling for food and sex his entire life. Mating is essentially the only reason males are tolerated.

The clan size depends largely on prey availability. Desert dwelling clans may have only 10 members while others can be huge, having up to 120 individuals. These supersized groups exist only in a few resource-rich national parks. The clans are tight-knit family groups led by an alpha female whose cubs inherit the rank immediately below her, similar to a monarchy. The rest of the clan is made of lower-ranking females, the young, and then the males. Like lions, mothers share the responsibility of nursing the cubs whether it is their offspring or not. Some members also act as babysitters, while others wrangle dinner.

While hyenas may not look the part, the females are doting mothers who invest much more time raising their offspring than most other carnivores. They wrestle and play with their cubs for hours at a time. Maternal clan members will even allow the young to drink milk until they are almost two years old, long after they begin eating solid foods.

With that said, a cub's entrance into the world is not so cushy. It is downright horrendous. The pseudo-penis making up the female hyena's reproductive system is also used for urination, copulation, and birth. Quite simply, that means newborns must enter the world through that tiny tube-like organ. Understandably, that makes the birthing process extremely difficult; many cubs die from suffocation before they even take their first breath. Incredibly, an estimated 60 percent of newborns are lost this way. The process is also hazardous for the mother; the lining of the birth canal is sometimes torn, killing her as well.

Litters typically consist of two to four cubs. If more than two survive the grisly birthing ordeal, they must overcome other hardships. Hyenas only have two nipples, forcing the offspring to fight for survival. The weakest ones, unable to obtain enough milk, die slow deaths of starvation.

The cubs who pull through grow into powerful hunters, a fact that blows the illusion of hyenas as lowly scavengers to smithereens. The hyenas' beautiful sandy-colored coats highlighted with dark spots blend easily with the landscape, offering the perfect camouflage. Yet, the killing machines genuinely take shape when studying their heads: wide-set eyes allow excellent night vision; large, rounded ears provide superb hearing; and powerful jaws, with 1,100 pounds of pressure per square inch, make crushing bones—even the bones of elephants—a piece of cake.

Their massive upper chests sloping to stubby hind legs may give them an awkward appearance but the design increases energy efficiency, allowing them to lope 37 mph flat out or 25 mph carrying a 40-pound antelope in their jaws. Unlike the lion, *Fisi* has strong lungs, a large heart, and wide nostrils allowing them to pursue prey for long distances, instead of counting on short bursts of speed.

Their indiscriminate palate is another great asset. They are ready, willing, and able to devour almost anything and everything in the animal kingdom: antelopes, buffalo, elephants, hippos, rhinos, birds, lizards, snakes, and even insects--including the flesh, hooves, horns, bones, hair, and feathers of each. In certain situations, they will even eat their own kind. Once bones are shattered and eaten, the hyena's highly acidic stomach breaks down the skeletal remains into small shards expelled effortlessly, creating easily recognizable strange white dung.

The hyenas' most lethal trait is their ability to work effectively as a team, just like their archenemy the lion. Clans work effectively to isolate a member of a herd and pursue it until death, allowing them to take down prey much larger than themselves. Though their reputation portrays them as scavengers, almost 95 percent of their food is from hunting. You may remember the hyena's kills are much more likely to be stolen by lions than the other way around. Hyenas are, therefore, *the* most successful hunters in all of Africa.

While clans have a sophisticated social structure, mealtime brings out the beast in them, causing feeding frenzies the minute the prey hits the ground. Amid fierce squabbling, ripping, clawing, and fighting, a group of hyenas can finish off an entire zebra--bones, hooves, hair, and all--in under half an hour. They, of course, also clash over kills with other powerful carnivores, including lions, wild dogs, and leopards. These hardy predators can live between 10 to 25 years in the wild, much longer than *Simba*.

Hyenas, like lions, are apex predators crucial to controlling prey populations. Also, as the best-known members of Africa's sanitary squad, they are vital to maintaining a healthy ecosystem, effectively eliminating every single morsel of decaying or disease-carrying flesh.

Hyenas are facing the same main threats as all African wildlife: loss of habitat, human encroachment, bushmeat poaching, yada, yada, yada. Like other large predators, their tendency to enjoy the easy pickings of domestic livestock also gets them into trouble. Retaliatory and preemptive killings are, therefore, an adult hyena's primary cause of death. Since trapping and poisoning are the most efficient killing techniques, other living things are harmed as well.

The hyena's bad reputation and PR problem certainly doesn't help their conservation status. Less attractive species lacking endearing qualities tend to be overlooked when it comes to wildlife preservation.

These negative perceptions are something I had to confront myself. Like most of society, it is easier to rally behind the furry inhabitants that speak to your heart: adorable lion cubs, gentle giants, elegant leopards, and roly-poly hippos. Thoughts of a rather displeasing-looking predator gorging on a beautiful zebra or antelope while it is still alive don't instill much affection.

While writing this chapter and facing my prejudices, I recognized an interesting fact. My low opinion of *Fisi* was largely based on their reputation as thieving scavengers, *supposedly* lazy animals stealing the booty of others to survive.

A lightbulb went off in my head: minus the thieving part, I was a scavenger myself, the very thing I detested most about hyenas before I learned that nearly all their food is a result of their skill and painstaking labor. The hamburger I eat is long-dead flesh from a cow; eggs are unborn chickens; and a halibut sandwich is a dead fish on a bun. All this stuff was dead as a doornail long before I ate it; I didn't have to kill anything myself. Heck, even my vegetables, grains, and fruits are typically the result of someone else's sweat.

Truly, few of us in today's society--other than farmers, ranchers, hunter-gatherers, and subsistence hunters--are eating *directly* from the results of own elbow grease. Of course, people, including me, work their butts off to earn the money needed to buy food for their tables. I'm not disrespecting that. Each person has his own skills or specialties to contribute to the world at large.

Still, the concept of our dependency on others for nourishment hit a nerve with me, especially since I was judging hyenas poorly on the same premise. A dead wrong assumption. It seems a predator with such great hunting prowess, who wastes diddly squat, should be placed on a pedestal rather than in the gutter.

While the public may never fall in love with the hyena or treasure its every breath like we do so many other species, hopefully, we can give them the respect and protection they need.

With all this said, I was petrified and alone, lying in the African bush listening to hyenas in a murderous-sounding collaboration, seemingly just outside our tent. True, I wasn't sleeping out in the open alongside the fire. Heck, I wasn't sleeping. Period. Still, at that moment, it mattered not that the hyenas' wicked reputation was unjustifiable and their role in the ecosystem was critical. Not when all that lay between me and the unsightly predators was mesh screens and a few millimeters of canvas.

WHOOooooPPP! Heeheehee! WHoooPP! Doing my best not to become an appetizer, I tried to determine *Fisis'* movements by focusing on their ghostly serenades, trying to decipher the meaning of each cry.

Hyenas have up to 14 distinctive calls that communicate specific information to the clan. As you might have guessed, one of the most notable vocalizations is the strange whooping call. Each individual has its unique whoop, an equivalent to us signing our names, making it easily identifiable to its clan. This loud vocalization is typically used to call for reinforcements, coordinate movement, and keep track of clan members, especially during a hunt.

As I lay paralyzed listening to the haunting dialogue, I was hoping they were just in a chatty mood and not getting themselves worked up for a hunt. At least, not of the two-legged variety.

Aside from whooping and lowing, there are shrieking squeals, grunts, rumbling, bass growls, chortles, chuckles, giggles, purrs, and howls. Heck, they can even mimic a lion's roar.

Probably the most notorious of all hyenas' calls are their *heeheehee*s, or high-pitched cackles resembling a human laughing hysterically. Hearing this maniacal giggle makes it easy to understand where the nickname *laughing* hyenas came from. Surprisingly, this iconic call is no laughing matter. At least not for the hyena.

The eerie chuckling is used when a hyena is deeply stressed, possibly being attacked, chased by another predator, or even assaulted by a higher-ranking member of their own kind. Low-ranking members lacking food also show their anxiety this way. The intensity and volume of the sounds are thought to correlate to the distress or excitement that a hyena is feeling.

Our tent at Chui Camp nestled among the trees.

Clang. Ting. Clunk. Suddenly new sounds surfaced from the other direction. Not primal sounds. As an amateur sleuth, I quickly realized that metal objects had banged together in the kitchen area. Either Thomas and Kaumba had caused the clamor or varmints were raiding the food. With my stomach in a knot, I waited for new clues, but none came. The clanking ended as abruptly as it started. In my role as a detective, I assumed that no noise was a good thing. If it had been a result of furry visitors, the ruckus would just be starting.

Still, affixed to my cot in heightened awareness, every sound seemed amplified. Hoping that Rick would return soon, I tried distracting myself by retracing the day's events.

Since no mature male leopards seemed to be hitting the bait they had sat on the previous night, they decided to try another blind a bit farther away, meaning they had to leave practically in the middle of the night to get there at least an hour before dawn. The African Symphony had been in full force when Rick left, but it hadn't mattered. Adrift in my morning haze, the primal music hadn't seemed any more threatening than normal. Waking up just briefly, I mumbled *good luck*, rolled over, and fell back into a deep slumber.

Hours later, they returned. No honking. No yelling. No celebration. Again, no leopard. Sitting in the leopard blind during the midday hours was pretty much fruitless.

The hunt hadn't been uneventful. While they hadn't seen hide nor hair of a spotted feline, on two separate occasions, one had skulked directly behind the *machan*. Two different cats. Yet, both had been too wary, and too clever, to take the bait.

According to Rick, it wasn't so much a sound that announced the leopard's presence. It was instinctual. Suddenly, Rick's hairs stood on end and his gut twisted in a knot. Then moments later, the intuitive awareness faded, telling him the deadly presence was gone.

Once they were back, Hilary sent the whole crew, including me, back out on safari to concentrate on harvesting an impala, another species on Rick's quota and plentiful in the area. The meat would be a welcome addition to *Chui* Camp since most of that had been left behind.

No one had to tell me twice. After missing out on the previous evening's adventures, I was raring to go. We had pursued two different groups of impalas. Each herd had a large mature shootable male, but Rick wasn't able to get a clear shot on either one before they vanished into the brush. Later, we crossed the path of a mature warthog boar whizzing across the savanna with his tail pinned in the air. Soon, he, too, was gone like the wind. We'd also crossed the paths of two separate *dagga* boys, each a lone bachelor. One's tracks were only four hours old, the other's two days old. Apparently, the tracks in the dirt were time-stamped. Trekking through the bush slinking behind Raphael and Mgogo kept me totally and utterly captivated.

Even as a non-hunter, I found that part of hunting exhilarating. If I denied it, I'd be lying through my teeth. Like it or not, it is thrilling to spot game, track its almost imperceptible spoor, and dart from cover to cover trying to get close enough for a shot, without being seen. Then if we made it that far, the shooting sticks had to be set in place and the shot set up. That means determining the precise distance and factoring in the wind to aim the appropriate inches high, low, left, or right. All of which I knew little about.

Then another waiting game, holding your breath until any non-targeted prey clears the line of fire. Sometimes animals are standing in front of the quarry. Other times, they are *behind* the intended target. Hunters can't take a chance that a shot will hit the wrong one or worse, strike multiple victims. There are also branches, trees, leaves, and rocks that must be worked around. Once everything falls into place, the target must offer the correct profile, allowing a good clean shot, hopefully killing him instantly.

Sometimes all of this happens in just a few seconds. Sometimes it takes many long minutes, hours, or even days for all the stars to align. The whole process of stalking and pursuing creatures on their turf, whether we succeeded or not, was challenging, fascinating, and slightly intoxicating. Recognizing my complicity helps me understand the *why* of hunting. Essentially, I piggy-backed on the adventure and excitement of the hunt, without needing its culmination. It's only that last step, pulling the trigger, that separates the two of us, as hypocritical as that is.

After a few hours, we rolled back into camp so the guys could squeeze in a siesta before the afternoon *Chui* hunt. No meat was brought home to add to the coffer but, still, I enjoyed every second.

As soon as nap time was over, the entire crew, minus me, headed off for the afternoon leopard hunt. Again, only Hilary, Thomas, Kaumba, and I remained at the camp. Anticipation was once more in the air as we shouted words of encouragement and waved our goodbyes.

Once they were off, Thomas accompanied me to the waterhole's viewing platform. It was certainly a weird experience having my movements so restricted. In America, we can stroll pretty much anywhere without the threat of a wild animal ruining a perfectly good day. That wasn't the case here. Even so, after a few days with no life-threatening incidents, I found it a little hard to stay cooped up. Luckily, the chat I had with Andrew the day before, with its ample warnings of dangers, came flooding back to me. This time an escort to the waterhole sounded like a great idea.

Thomas and I walked about 100 yards, just out of sight of camp, to a log platform nestled in a grove of trees above the riverbank. Very quietly, we snuck into position, already seeing plenty of activity. A troop of baboons and a flock of guinea fowl were skittering all over the opposite riverbank and between several waterholes. Some of the baboons were scrambling up trees or swaying on the edge of limbs. Others seemed to be keeping vigil over the waterhole. Younger ones frolicked as mamas rested with little ones clinging to their stomachs. I could have watched them for hours, but that didn't seem fair to Thomas who had more to do than babysit the likes of me.

Grrrrr. Zzzzzz Grrr. Zzzzzz. New sounds joined *Fisi's* sinister-sounding choir, startling me from my reflections of the day's events. Though my mind was reeling, my body remained paralyzed, hidden under the covers of my cot. Still not daring to glance out the screen, I focused my ears on a deep rumbling outside my tent. Gradually, awareness dawned on me. Human snoring. Coming from Hilary's tent 30 yards away. With that realization, I let out a huge sigh of relief. Seemingly, the hyena clan's proximity and intense dialogue were nothing to get in a tizzy about. If hyenas were about to storm the compound, surely Hilary wouldn't be contentedly sawing logs.

Although slightly relieved, I remained plastered to my bed on high alert listening to every spine-tingling sound of *Fisis'* uproar. Finally, after what seemed an eternity, I heard the din of a motor in the distance. The racket I didn't hear, however, was equally as telling. No horn blowing, yelling or screaming. *Chui* again had won the day.

While part of me was saddened by Rick's lack of success, the petrified part of me was thrilled that he had returned, even if that meant no leopard.

A few minutes later, Rick dragged himself inside. His demeanor was less chipper than the night before. Sitting immobile in the confines of a blind for hours on end was not as physically demanding as elk hunting; but mentally, it was grueling.

For a second time, a leopard had come to investigate but was too smart to approach the bait. Just like the morning hunt, they sensed more than heard a cat prowling behind the *machan*. Rick's gut had announced the cat's presence clear as a bell.

Shortly after they intuitively knew that *Chui* had left, darkness set in. Raphael radioed for the crew, but the transmitter was unable to make contact for some reason. Moseying through Africa on foot in the black of night when a leopard is nearby is not a bright idea. Raphael and Mgogo made the trek to reach the waiting crew while Andrew and Rick waited in the relative safety of the blind. You may remember, it's bad for business to send a client home in a pine box.

As Rick recounted his escapades, the fear that had gripped me for almost two hours largely faded. Suddenly, the hyenas' vocal crusade sounded more distant and less menacing than it had only moments ago when I was alone. Funny how that works. Ironically, *Fisi* on the prowl taught me that I, too, was capable of remaining motionless for hours. The key was to be solidified in fear.

The hyena's otherworldly chorus may instill dread but without it, the bush would not *feel* like Africa. Each evening's composition was a unique blend of primitive voices. A primal symphony that never repeated itself exactly. Every single time we crawled under the covers in our tent, we did so with the anticipation of what melodies would unfold. Often, the arrangement lacked the elephant's distinctive trumpet or their soft gurgling sounds. Other nights, although rare, it was the hippo's deep bellow that left a huge gap in the chorus. Even *Simba,* from time to time, refrained from adding his chilling vocals to the melody, but the hyenas *never* let us down. *Always,* their maniacal voices were present. Loud and clear, varying from rhythmical choruses to explosive crescendos. More than any other creature, it is their savage songs that remind us of the beauty, the horror, and the reality of life in the long grass.

Peter Capstick's vivid description of the hyena's chorus embodies the words that elude me:

> The sound of Africa is not the thundering rumble of a distant lion, nor is it the hollow trumpet of a bull elephant. If Africa has a voice, it is the hyenas. Deep in the blackness of night it gropes through the bush in rising and falling echoes that come from nowhere, yet everywhere, insane choruses of whoops, chortles, chuckles, giggles, shrieks, and howls that have a way of reaching out into the guts of a man as he sits by a lonely, dying fire and of raising the hackles of ancient, long-forgotten apprehension. From the first, faraway *wooooo-uppp* of the pack gathering to the sniggering chitter of

the kill, the hyena is telling you something you don't want to be reminded of: *you're just meat, after all, and your day will come.*[4]

There is no doubt that *Fisi* -- an unwieldy ridiculous-looking ghoul who is loathed, shunned, and laughed at by all--is as synonymous with Africa as the mighty lion or the beloved elephant. Their squeals, roars, growls, and insane mirthless hysteria is fused with what makes the continent so extremely special. Their eerie nocturnal serenades, even when they chilled me to the bone, became treasured memories. Savage cries and ghastly giggles that will *forever* remain entrenched deep in my soul. A vital, visceral part of a magical, exotic, harsh, troubled land.

24
WE ARE THE BAIT

"You've got to be kidding!" I exclaimed, eyes wide in disbelief. "They dropped you off in the middle of the jungle for two days and nights, all by yourself, with nothing but a knife, sleeping mat, and mealie meal?"

Lilian flashed a brilliant smile. "Well, they stopped by to check on me once a day."

With a look of incredulity plastered on my face and my jaw almost hanging to the floor, I must have looked like a character from a comedy show. The concept of sleeping alone in the wilds of Africa, basically unarmed, was beyond ludicrous to me. Heck, I'd barely survived the previous night's hyena extravaganza without having a heart attack, even *with* Hilary sleeping only 30 yards away.

Until Lilian's last revelation, we'd been sitting atop the Land Cruiser with our noses buried in our cell phones like two schoolgirls. There was no internet connection, but thanks to solar-power phone chargers, the digital record of our lives was still intact, enabling us to take a peek into each other's lives. Each photograph sparked a story, taking us to another time and place half a world away.

"Weren't you afraid?" I asked anxiously.

"Oh, yes. I was very afraid," she admitted. "At night, I huddled in my shelter and prayed."

The acknowledgment that she prayed didn't surprise me one iota. It made perfect sense, especially since her dad was a Lutheran minister. Besides, where better to ask the Creator for a little extra support than amid a "Solo Expedition Module" at the base of Mount Kilimanjaro?

While the solo outing she described struck me as an insane hellish suicide mission, she had no choice in the matter. Not if she wanted to earn her Technician Certificate in Wildlife Management. A mandatory part of her training was to spend time alone in Kilimanjaro National Park; build her own *bivouac*, a small *safe* waterproof nest made of natural vegetation; start a fire; cook her meals; erect a toilet; and forage for food. Of course, staying alive was also a prerequisite of the exercise.

Still reeling in amazement, I flung questions at her like a pitcher at a baseball game. "What about snakes?" I queried. She assured me that the training was done in an area with no venomous snakes. Frankly, I found *that* hard to believe.

Rather than obsessing over serpents, she had been focused on staying warm and dry. Lilian grew up in the scorching climate that covers most of Tanzania. The Kilimanjaro area was much rainier and colder than what she was used to. The waterproof *bivouac* she built was not only to provide safety against night visitors, it was critical to keep her from becoming a sopping-wet shivering piece of humanity.

Between foraging, building, and cooking, her days went by pretty quickly. The nights, on the other hand, dragged on endlessly as she huddled in her nest, shivering, scared, and praying for daylight.

The conversation, of course, moved to lions, leopards, and hyenas. I couldn't imagine being *so utterly alone*, with only grass walls as shelter, hearing *umphhs* or *whoooopppps* just outside. Yet, she had heard neither. Lions are now very rare in the park and, surprisingly, spotted hyenas and their ominous banter are completely absent. Surprisingly, most of the larger mammals we would expect to see--lions, rhinos, elephants, giraffes, buffalo, zebras, and antelopes--no longer exist in Mt. Kilimanjaro National Park in any significant number.

Some four-legged inhabitants still live on the fringes, but sightings are few and far between. Gone are the days of huge herds of these species grazing at the base of Africa's tallest mountain. Instead, its lowest section, referred to as the Cultivated Zone, is a ring of mainly coffee, avocado, and mango plantations. As the fertile belt at the mountain's base was overtaken by humans and wild habitats dwindled, wildlife numbers plummeted.

At 19,341 feet, Mount Kilimanjaro is the world's tallest freestanding mountain, as well as the tallest peak in Africa. For years, conquering this mountain was loosely on my bucket list, specifically because a normal person can do it without dangling on ropes from ice cliffs or scaling a ladder across glacial crevices. Read Jon Krakauer's book "Into Thin Air" detailing his account of a disastrous Mt. Everest climb and, if you have even an ounce of sense, that killer mountain will be crossed off your bucket list. Anyway, I figured with preparations, I could handle Mt. Kilimanjaro. *Just imagine the animals I would see in the process.* At least that was my thought process at the time.

It turns out the jaw-dropping wildlife pictures that I equated with Mt. Kilimanjaro National Park were taken in Amboseli National Park about 50 miles away, with the towering mountain presenting a breathtaking, but distant, backdrop.

Since Lilian's solo expedition took place in Kilimanjaro's Rainforest Zone she had little to fear from predators. But, she did hear a leopard's distinctive bark from her shelter and was fortunate enough to spot a Cape buffalo grazing in the distance.

Even with a lack of lions and hyenas, sleeping utterly alone in the cold, wet wilds of Africa had to be utterly terrifying. Not to mention miserable. Lilian was, no doubt, an impressive young lady. At 23 years old, she had already accomplished what I would never have the inner strength and bravery to do.

Her success is even more impressive when you learn that she didn't grow up in a rural village accustomed to such remoteness and the sounds of the night knocking at her door. She grew up in Moshi, known as the gateway to Kilimanjaro National Park, a city of approximately 200,000 people.

Lilian is the oldest of five siblings. While her dad was a Lutheran pastor, her mom worked from home taking care of their family while also growing coffee, bananas, and maize. Also, one cow made up part of their little homestead. Lilian's parents struggled to give each of their children a higher education as money on a pastor's salary was always tight. For her early education, essentially the equivalent of our elementary school, she went to the city of Arusha. After that, she advanced to what is called higher education, more or less an equivalent to our high school from what I gathered.

You may remember that Lilian took the position of Tanzanian game scout after the money needed for her ultimate goal of becoming a lecturer, or teacher, in wildlife studies at a university fell short.

Game scouts are the front line against poaching, so much of Lilian's time is spent in that endeavor. In addition, these scouts train and equip community members to protect and monitor animal populations; collect ecological data; generate and distribute environmental information to enhance awareness; promote community participation; work to minimize human-wildlife conflict; and, of course, accompany hunters to ensure regulations are followed and the harvesting of animals is documented. Typically, their duties focus on non-protected areas since the park systems have their own law enforcement officials.

Lilian had been a game scout going on two years before she received her first hunting assignment. Lo and behold, Rick was that hunter, enabling our fates to become intertwined.

Time whizzed by as Lilian shared pieces of her life with me. In what seemed like no time at all, hours ticked by as we huddled on the Land Cruiser's bench seat soaking up the precious shade as the rest of the crew sweated under the sweltering midday sun. Only a few yards away, their effort was transforming a barren tree into a torture chamber in the sky.

Our third day at *Chui* Camp had started almost nine hours earlier. By 6 a.m., we had already been motoring through the scrublands. Hilary thought it best to skip the morning leopard hunt and, instead, concentrate on something a little less elusive. Pure and simple, we needed meat. All eyes were peeled for any harvestable species on Rick's quota. Needless to say, I was thrilled to be on safari again.

While traveling through sparse woodlands with clumps of trees interspersed here and there, we passed giraffes, impalas, steenbok, and warthogs, but no shootable males worth pursuing.

Suddenly, we lurched to a stop without Mgogo or Raphael even signaling. While still looking around in confusion, we heard a tap on the cab window from inside. Lilian anxiously pointed to a tiny black blob hundreds of yards away in a patch of shade partially hidden by the shadows. The crew exploded into activity. They knew exactly what the mass of darkness belonged to: Cape buffalo, or more specifically, an old *dagga* boy. Since the herd animals rarely hang out on their own just for the fun of it, it was most assuredly an old bull who'd been booted from the herd. Although a *nyati* wasn't the animal we expected to replenish our meat stores with, Rick's quota did contain a third Cape buffalo.

With no discussion, we jumped into our serpentine formation and dashed to the first clump of trees. Then the next. And the next. You get the point. Somehow, with the wind working for us, we got within about 120 yards before the old boy sensed something was wrong and scrambled to his feet. Mgogo quickly arranged the shooting sticks, Rick placed the gun on the tripod, and I assumed my position. The massive horns, thick dull boss, and the buffalo being alone left little doubt that he was a harvestable male. Still, Rick waited for Raphael's word.

Seconds later, it was over. The *dagga* boy was a spectacular aged bull with massive horns. Although he was old, he had no lion scars to tell a bit of his story. His teeth were in better condition, more hair remained on his body, and his horns were not ragged and broken off at the tips. Even to me, it was apparent that he was a bit younger and had more recently been forced to go it on his own. Still, he was past his breeding age. He would no longer father future generations of the hardy beasts. Henceforward, his life would have been on a downward spiral.

That didn't matter. Tears still crept down my face. Rick's eyes, too, glistened with moisture. The typical emotions swirled through us. That is the thing. The harvesting of wildlife may be a worthy undertaking for the good of all, but that makes it no easier, no matter how many times it's done.

There was one aspect of the buffalo's death that no one was conflicted about. His death had been nearly instant, with minimal pain and suffering. Only adrenaline had carried him the ten feet to where he fell. There was also no wounded buffalo to pursue.

Mgogo looked down at the inert body of once powerful flesh and rattled off some Swahili, causing Raphael to smile. Raphael looked at Rick to translate Mgogo's words: "Rick American Army. One shot. Dead."

It sounds ridiculously stupid, but those simple words coming from our head tracker's mouth made me proud as a peacock, not only of my husband but of America's armed forces. Apparently, even in Tanzania, the skill of our military is held in high esteem.

After the moment of levity, we knelt and offered our thanks for the buffalo's sacrifice. Soon afterward, the crew jumped into action. Processing a carcass of approximately 1,500 pounds is no small endeavor. Fortunately, Maugo had also accompanied us from camp so we had one extra person to help with the massive undertaking. Even still, it is a wearisome task even for men who perform it consistently. Some of the meat would be used at camp, some made into jerky, and some used to make new leopard baits.

Once we were on the road again, we paralleled a tributary of the Mzombe River while scouting for a location to create a new leopard bait. A perfect tree offering plenty of cover, with huge leopard tracks just yards away, was spotted on an embankment above the riverbed.

So began the laborious task of hanging a bait. Although part of me felt bad watching the crew work their tails off, I loved the hour of friendly banter even though much of the Swahili still escaped my grasp. Besides, the whole process still fascinated me. By then, I felt little need to yell, "*Usianguke* Mgogo! Don't fall."

The last step, dragging entrails in a huge circle around the bait as enticement, was done a little differently. Instead of Mgogo making the jaunt by himself, Raphael accompanied him with his rifle. Not only were there fresh leopard tracks in the area, but there was also a waterhole only a few hundred yards away. That meant lions could also be nearby.

While the rest of us waited for the two of them to get back, Lilian and Abdalah strolled to the edge of the opening peering over the rocks towards the riverbed. A minute later, we saw Abdalah pointing and Lilian grabbing her rifle which had been hanging loosely in a sling across her shoulder. The rest of us rushed over to see what had attracted so much attention. We weren't disappointed. Only 30 yards down the embankment, partially hidden by rocks and scrub trees, was a young lioness. Presumably, one meant there could be others as well.

As our entire group kept an eye on her, Mike tried to warn Raphael by calling him on the radio. After all, the two men were dragging tasty entrails through the forested area. That's simply asking for trouble. Just like the previous night, the radio failed to transmit. Maugo began whistling loudly, hoping to draw their attention to warn them. The lioness continued skulking in the trees below us. She'd briefly disappear then show up again a few seconds later under a different tree. She heard the whistling and knew she had a human audience, but she didn't leave. Not when the smell of fresh meat lingered.

About 20 minutes later both men returned without incident. Whether the young lioness was alone or not was irrelevant. Once Raphael learned of her presence, his shoulders slumped slightly as he uttered a few words in Swahili. The crew jumped into action. Back up the tree they went, detaching the camouflaging greenery, untying and lowering the bait to the ground, and loading it back into the cargo hold. Within minutes, the previous hour's efforts were completely wiped out. Baffled, I looked at Raphael.

"*Chui* will not come with *Simba* here," he explained.

The bait had been placed high enough in the tree to deter the larger cats but that didn't mean they wouldn't make a gallant effort. Few lions would pass on such an easy meal, especially when it was their favorite cuisine. Besides, leopards would avoid the lion-infested area like the plague.

Hanging the bait before lions were discovered in the area.

We continued on our safari, basically weaving in and out of the sparse scrubland forest while remaining parallel to the riverbed. Less than an hour later, just as we were approaching the location of the next leopard bait, a mixture of impala, kudu, and roan was spotted grazing together several hundred yards away across a section of the river still containing several pockets of water. One of the impalas was a large mature male. While it was a perfect specimen to pursue, Raphael felt it was too near the leopard bait and our activity would scare away any of the elusive cats that may have been in the area.

Minutes later, none of that mattered. The trackers again found signs of a lion, another lioness to be exact. Even though the lure had been situated high on a limb, she had quite successfully made the little spot her personal diner. It appeared that she'd been coming and going for several days. Score two for *Simba*. Zero for *Chui*. We drove off without even adding fresh bait. Again, any leopard that fancied self-preservation was unlikely to approach once *Simba* had staked his or her claim.

Barely had we regrouped and taken off when the huge impala was spotted again. Now that the area was useless for hunting leopards, the firing of a rifle wouldn't matter. Into our serpentine formation we went, descending into the riverbed, leaping across pockets of water, and scrambling over boulders to reach the other side. From there, progress became slow, advancing from tree to tree. After we had pursued him for a couple of miles, the impala entered a thicker grove of trees. Although Rick was set up several times, a good shot never presented itself. Either non-targeted animals were in his line of fire or the impala was partially blocked by a branch, tree, or rock, effectively impeding his shot. Once the impala disappeared into thick cover, Raphael decided it wasn't worth the time and energy to pursue him further. The most scorching time of day was about to hit us head-on.

The game plan was to check one last leopard bait, return to *Chui* Camp for lunch, squeeze in an afternoon siesta, and hunt leopard in the late afternoon. With that said, *the best-laid plans of mice and men often go awry*. Raphael changed his mind within minutes of arriving at the next bait tree, the one they'd been sitting at for the past two hunts where they *felt* a cat skulking nearby.

While Mgogo, Maugo, and Abdalah refreshed the lure with some buffalo meat, Raphael investigated. Finding and following the leopard's spoor, he concluded that the leopard was much too cunning for a typical ground blind. That was a good thing. It was, indeed, an aged male; the hunters, therefore, had to *up* their game. Literally. The *machan* had to be *in* the trees. Not *under* the trees. The cat's keen senses were less likely to pick up the scent, sight, and sounds of the hunting party if they were nestled like chicks in a roost high above the ground.

Without skipping a beat, the crew flew into action. Raphael searched out the perfect tree while the crew's machetes hacked at branches. Within minutes, Mgogo was scooting up the pole-like trunk of a 30-foot-tall leafless acacia tree about 60 yards from the bait, the preferred maximum distance for harvesting a leopard.

The men building the "skyscraper" machan.

The tree's wide V-shaped canopy essentially became the bones of the skyscraper *machan* as Mgogo cleared any interior branches. The leafy vegetation gathered by the rest of the crew was hoisted up to him one by one. Equipped with only his supersized knife and manila rope, Mgogo tediously weaved each branch into the tree's framework, like the pieces of a jigsaw puzzle, until a sturdy platform was formed. The *machan*'s floor was no itty-bitty flimsy thing. It was large enough and strong enough to hold five people: Rick, Raphael, Andrew, Mgogo, and Lilian. Next, he built a bench seat for the five derrieres that would soon be lying in wait, hoping *Chui* would make an appearance.

While Mgogo was plugging away, the rest of the crew fashioned a 10-foot-long ladder to climb into the airborne structure, being that it was at least 18 feet off the ground. The Tanzanians might have been able to shimmy up a tree with guns in tow, but it was unlikely Rick could master such a feat. The ladder was also helpful in getting oodles of leafed branches up to Mgogo to complete the finishing touches of camouflage. After all, if the leopard saw them, it was game over. Covered with meticulously woven together greenery, the blind was entirely hidden.

Testing out the machan's ladder.

When the elevated *machan* was finished, its concealment was so complete that it was hard to spot from just a few yards away, even knowing it was there! Indeed, three weeks later when I was going through my African photos, I almost deleted pictures of it. Seeing an indistinct landscape with no wildlife, people, scenic beauty, or instructional value, I couldn't for the life of me figure out *why* I had taken the photos. Intrigued, I studied the pictures until the mystery unraveled. In that line of nondescript trees was the perfectly camouflaged *machan,* in fact, both *machans.* The original ground blind and the new monstrous nest were expertly hidden in the landscape.

Rick and I were little help in the amazing fabrication, although we did try. Briefly. Mostly, we were useless compared to our crew. Mike had strategically parked the vehicle under a shade tree so that we could sit atop and hide from the sun's brutal rays. Still, there was no breeze to turn our sweat into cooling relief. In addition, the buffalo in the cargo hold acted as one giant Tsetse fly attractant. Our netting and insect repellent did little to protect us from the angry little devils. Quite simply we were miserable.

Yet, we had little to complain about. While we hid in the shade, our crew toiled nonstop under the sun's blistering midday rays. It may have taken only four paragraphs to describe how the blind was built, but in reality, it took four sweat-drenched, Tsetse-fly-bitten hours. Plus, they had already processed and loaded a Cape buffalo, as well as built and replenished several bait trees.

Every once in a while, Rick and I would brave the sun's fierceness to watch in fascination as the branches, rope, and leaves transformed into a human birdhouse. Then we retreated to what little relief we had.

For me, there was one saving grace. Lilian. As a law enforcement officer, she was about as involved in the blind building as Rick and me, giving us plenty of time to visit. Time with Lilian was always a gift, one that I never took for granted. Although one of us was young and another slightly seasoned, we were able to share our worlds and unite in friendship. A friendship that started the moment she answered my first question with a smile. A friendship that grew as the days on safari grew.

By the time the shelter was complete, it was almost 4 p.m.--time for the afternoon leopard hunt. Since there was no time to take me back to *Chui* camp and get Andrew, another plan emerged. Raphael, Mgogo, Lilian, and Rick would stay to hunt and the rest of us would mosey several miles down the road to find a cozy spot to wait until sunset.

Twenty minutes later, Mike pulled into a small clearing with a lone shade tree, offering shelter from the sun. After the guys' jam-packed grueling day, I figured Mike, Maugo, and Abdalah would want nothing more than a little nap. I was wrong. Instead, they gathered firewood and dug a shallow fire pit between two fallen logs. Once the fire was crackling, they sliced off a hunk of buffalo meat, cut it into smaller strips, and draped it over sticks strategically placed across the logs flanking the fire. Within minutes, buffalo meat was roasting over open flames. Evidently, their empty bellies spoke much louder than the heat and their weary bones.

We were all starving. Since the plan had been to return to *Chui* Camp for lunch, no afternoon meals had been packed. The smell of sizzling meat made my mouth water in anticipation. Besides, what an opportunity: eating fresh Cape buffalo cooked over an open fire in the wilds of Tanzania. It was surreal. How could I be so lucky?

Maugo and Mike slicing up the buffalo meat.

Then, just a few minutes later, just one bite after tearing into the meat, the wind blew out of my sails. The no-frills *wildness* mixed with a little old-fashioned grit threw me for a loop. While I've eaten wild game my entire life, never have I eaten it straight off the hoof without spices, marinades, or being sautéed in gobs of butter. For those of you unfamiliar with wild meat, it has a distinctively different taste than beef.

While I'm clueless about how to translate this into words, it might help to remind you that wild species contain almost zero fat compared to fattened domestic livestock. That in itself makes a huge difference in taste. In addition, farm-raised animals are butchered when they are young and tender, whereas a lot of wild game is harvested when it is older, producing tougher meat.

Simply put, cooking wild meat calls for a lot more finesse than cooking domestic stock. Yet, with the right ingredients, skilled cooks can transform wild meat into delicious organic protein, much healthier than anything you'll find in a grocery store. Inferior cuts are often ground up into minced meat, concealing its gaminess within sauces, chilis, and stroganoffs. Cooked right, you will never know the difference. Heck, I'm even culinary challenged, and I can make delicious deer meat spaghetti sauce or scrumptious elk backstrap sautéed in butter and onions.

One bite of the buffalo was all it took for me to realize that hiding the gaminess was a little more challenging in the middle of a dusty clearing equipped with no more than Bowie-type knives and a pile of sticks. Our trio of impromptu cooks had done the best they could with the little they had to work with. Quickly, I learned that while my stomach was rumbling like a bowling alley on league night, I wasn't truly starving to death. If I had been, I would have appreciated the life-sustaining nutrition instead of wrinkling my nose.

Skewers of buffalo meat roasting over an open flame.

To lessen my guilt, I'm going to blame my reaction on Moses and Kaumba. After all, they had completely spoiled us. Each night they turned our wild protein, whatever species it was, into unbelievably delicious dishes. Even the soup, my favorite part of each meal, was a byproduct of each harvest. Although each broth-filled creation was made with vegetables--leek, pumpkin, green pea, zucchini, cauliflower, carrot, and even cucumber--the type of vegetable mattered little. The key was the bones and marrow used for making the soup's base. Never in my life, before or since, have I tasted any soup nearly as tasty.

Moses was even kind enough to invite us into his kitchen to share his soup secrets, but after one attempt at home, we threw our hands in the air. Our concoction didn't hold a candle to his. Maybe, Moses left out a few secret ingredients. One thing is for sure, while home in Idaho, there was no way to duplicate cooking over hot coals of an open fire in Tanzania with antelope-based bone marrow as the foundation.

Anyway, I took that first huge bite of pure, unaltered, straight-off-the-hoof, barbecued buffalo expecting the same flavorful yumminess that I enjoyed at dinner each night. Typically, my facial expressions read like the words in a book. Hopefully, for once, that wasn't true. After all their effort, I didn't want my squeamish reaction to insult the impromptu cooks. Once I choked down the first healthy-sized piece of meat, I altered my bites into delicate nibbles. With each piece, I did my best to brush off the bits of sand and dirt that had affixed themselves to the meat.

It also helps to remember that we'd been hauling that carcass around in the African sun since 8 a.m. There was nothing wrong with it. Meat is supposed to age for a time. Still, it was hard to forget the Tsetse-flies who had also enjoyed the feast. Psychologically, it messed with my head. I nibbled down just enough to quiet the rumbling of my stomach. Besides, it was important to save room for the evening's version of soup. Only when pigs fly would I pass on that treat.

After eating the buffalo, the guys sprawled out on the ground for a much-deserved nap while I stayed on the Land Cruiser's bench seat reading a book. Eventually, the sun drifted beyond the canopy of trees and the bright scorching sun faded into the hazy glow of dusk. With the loss of light, the quaint little clearing lost a little of its luster. It would soon be dark, time for the afternoon hunt to end. That also meant it was time for the critters of the night to begin their nightly shenanigans.

Chui. Simba. Fisi. Like honey flowing from a tipped jar, awareness slowly dawned on me. Less than a foot behind my rump were hundreds and hundreds of pounds of fresh buffalo meat. *Simba's* favorite. Heck, probably every carnivore's favorite. Like a giant invitation, the aroma of barbecued *nyati* drifted in the air. Finally, with mind-numbing recognition, I thought to myself., *My gosh, we **are** the bait!*

The hunters, equipped with all of the firepower, were attempting to lure *Chui* with a few pounds of protein while we sat within inches of an entire carcass. On top of that, we added further enticement by cooking it over open flames.

That realization put a new spin on things. Instead of burying my head in a book, my eyes began scanning the tree line surrounding us. It was eerie, but somehow enlivening, as well. Surprisingly, I didn't spiral into a state of terror like the previous night when the hyena clan had been causing such a ruckus. It certainly helped that three capable men with machete-sized knives were dozing nearby.

Soon, the haze of dusk turned into the pitch black of night. Stars began appearing. First slowly; then manifesting into a sky saturated with glowing embers. My eyes alternated between peering into the blackness for the glow of hungry eyes and gazing up at the stars. Sitting there near the dying embers of a fire in the wilds of Africa, spellbound by a foreign land, gratefulness washed over me.

A scratchy sound from a radio interrupted the peacefulness. Darkness had set in and the hunters were ready for pickup. There was no excitement in the voice. Just tiredness and hunger. *Chui* had again won the day. Though, in all honesty, that didn't surprise me. For once, Raphael had it all wrong. Why would a leopard go after a tidbit of meat when the whole kit and caboodle was a few miles away?

Off we went retracing our drive to pick up the hunters. An hour or so later, we rolled into camp to be greeted anxiously by Hilary, Andrew, and Kaumba. While the day's events were related to Hilary, the camp flew into a flurry of activity. The buffalo still had to be unloaded, further processed, and dinner prepared.

You didn't have to be a psychic to know that buffalo would be the protein on the dinner menu. What did knock my socks off was learning that the brown roast-like cut of meat resting on my plate was in fact the *dagga* boy's tongue. While gaping at the chunk of meat, my stomach transitioned from hunger pangs to flip-flops. Meanwhile, our hosts were beaming with pride. To put it bluntly, I was in a pickle. No way was I turning up my nose with all eyes glued on me.

Fortunately, the grilled organ didn't look nearly as icky as I had expected. It looked like a normal oblong slab of meat. Working up courage, I reminded myself of my hesitation when a slice of buffalo tail had been served in my soup. The bizarre-looking broth had been scrumptious. I daintily took a bite of the delicacy. Shockingly, its taste was not unpleasant; its weird spongy texture, however, was a deal breaker for me. The look on my face must have told the story because, amid chuckles, I was soon passed a good ole piece of grilled buffalo steak, minus sandy grit. Now *that* was yummy.

After dinner, we crawled into our cots recognizing that another day of our safari had slipped by. Rick had yet to fulfill his dream of harvesting *Chui* but, still, it was a day full of new adventures and further insights into a foreign land. Every moment of our journey was special, but there was something exceptional about our drive back to camp as the sun dipped towards the horizon that night.

Gazing into the blackness, I watched as each star, one by one, materialized to light up the night sky. Automatically, I'd searched for The Big Dipper as I've done hundreds of times in the past; but, on the other side of the globe, it was nowhere to be found. Instead, the Southern Cross and Orion the hunter were visible. That small recognition filled me with awe: hours earlier I had shared stories with Tanzanian friends; I had eaten Cape buffalo meat, straight off the hoof, roasted over open flames; and all this had been done while scanning the blackness for lions and hyenas. *Only* in Africa is any of that possible. Truly, I was fulfilling my dream, far beyond anything that I could have envisioned on my own. A dream that turned into a journey toward awareness, perspective, and insight. Ultimately, a journey that changed me.

25
A Dream Come True

The camp was quiet. Everyone not on the leopard hunt was tucked away in their little slice of *Chui* Camp, probably sound asleep. I for one had done little to warrant exhaustion. A grueling day on safari pursuing animals in the blistering heat had *not* been a part of my day. There had been no *Simba* sightings or treks through the bush. No studying the stars as the smell of roasted buffalo meat wafted through the air. No grand adventures, whatsoever, to wear me out.

The never-ending cries of *Fisi* and his pals, of course, still haunted the darkness, but I had learned a lesson from the other night's ghastly performance--every solar light in my tent remained on. The illuminating glow hovered above me like a guardian angel, making that evening's rendition of the primal chorus seem more distant and less threatening. Snuggled up reading a book, I listened for the tell-tale sounds of a Land Cruiser in the distance. Waiting.

Rick had left for the morning leopard hunt, seemingly, in the middle of the night. By midmorning, he returned with drooping eyes, slumped shoulders, and aching muscles. Luck was still not on his side; a large spotted feline had not shown up to make his day.

The minute lunch was over, he and most of the hunting crew disappeared into their hideaways for some shuteye. Lilian skipped the afternoon siesta to act as my chaperone to the waterhole for an afternoon of baboon-watching. Thanks to my bungled attempt at getting closer for a picture, they scattered into the brush amid a flurry of *ohhh ohh oh, ihhh ihh ih*, and *uhhh uhh uh* and a host of other grunts, screams, and cries of alarm. The primates are noisy little buggers.

By three in the afternoon, the hunting crew was again off to the skyscraper *machan*. While they battled the heat, cramped space, Tsetse flies, and immobility, I propped my feet up with a good book, visiting with Hilary and Thomas periodically, until it was lights out.

As the hyenas began their nightly clamor, my mind drifted back to the troop of baboons or *nyani*. More specifically, I was reflecting on the scarlet booties on some of the females; their behinds looked like they had been dunked in a bed of hot coals, giving the impression of utter rawness, making me cringe in empathy.

Having Lilian as a personal wildlife expert was pretty handy. She explained that the red puffy condition occurs in females for up to 10 to 20 days each month during ovulation. I'm not talking about just a smidgeon of swelling; I'm talking about some major inflammation. Their bottoms can supposedly swell to 4 to 6.5 inches larger than normal, reaching a peak when they are the most fertile, apparently as a way to say *come hither* to all the potential baby daddies. Eventually, their rumps do return to normal but, in my eyes, not for nearly long enough. Typical for many species, if I do say so myself, the males get off easy.

A baboon at Chui Camp's waterhole.

Baboons spend most of their time on the ground, mainly using trees for sleeping, eating, and scouting for trouble. That was fairly obvious as I watched the troop frolic at the waterhole with a few always camped in a tree appearing as lookouts. It was probably one of those primates that discovered my less than graceful picture-taking attempt, causing the troop to erupt into rowdy chatter while fleeing.

Twenty baboons in one troop seemed plenty big to me, especially when you hear the racket they make, but the group at *Chui* Camp would have been considered small. In habitats with plentiful vegetation, some groups can support up to 300 individuals.

Friendship in a troop of baboons can't be underestimated. The females spend their entire life, up to 30 years in the wild, basically within 100 meters of the same group of baboons. This group dynamic also means they spend their entire lives close to their rivals as well, putting a whole new spin on the saying "until death do us part."

For this reason, females take great care in choosing and maintaining friendships. Typically, they become closest to their maternal relatives, their mothers, aunts, and sisters. While the females stay with their families their entire lives, the males typically jump from troop to troop living with many different groups throughout their lifetime.

Baboons are governed by a complex hierarchy. Those higher on the totem pole can displace lower-ranking members from food and water sources and grooming sessions, and have more freedom, in general, to do as they please. Females typically inherit their mother's standing. Males, on the other hand, must earn their position, mainly by their size, age, and fighting ability.

As omnivores and opportunistic eaters, baboons eat a wide array of meats and plants including grasses, fruits, seeds, roots, bark, rodents, birds, young antelopes, sheep, and even monkeys. This indiscriminate diet also means they are happy to raid crops and steal any yummy morsels they can get a hold of. It is, therefore, no surprise that like the vervet monkeys, baboons can become quite a pest to humans. Unattended human food is fair game for any nearby opportunistic primates.

Just like at *Masimba* Camp, at *Chui* Camp food was never left unattended or unprotected, not only for the camp's protection but for the protection of the animals themselves. Once an individual learns of an easy food source, it often becomes nuisances, ultimately leading to its death. Our hosts took great care to keep that from happening.

Even worse than stealing a few scraps of food is the damage that the primates can do to crops. Depending on the species, baboons are about 20 to 34 inches tall, weighing an average of 33 to 82 pounds each. A troop of

100 to 200 *nyani* tearing through the neighborhood can do a lot of damage to crops that rural people depend on for their livelihoods.

To make matters worse, baboons have sharp canine teeth and powerful jaws that they are not afraid to use when their troop or food source is threatened. In most cases, the primates prefer to warn humans away rather than attack but, when push comes to shove, they will assault anyone failing to heed their warning.

The same theme dominating the rest of Africa is prevalent here as well. Any species that threatens the livelihoods of rural Africans is under threat of retaliatory and pre-emptive killings. The baboons' main cause of death is, therefore, human-wildlife conflict. Loss of habitat due to livestock farming and agriculture also plays a key role.

Fortunately, baboon populations are still holding strong. Truly, there are so darn many of them that it's hard to know exactly how many baboons are in the wild. Only the Guinea baboon, because they have lost nearly a quarter of their homeland over the past three decades, is classified as Near Threatened by the IUCN. One thing for sure, the olive baboons that frequented Rungwa West Game Block seemed to be in no peril. Plenty of their scarlet booties dotted the savanna.

As visions of scarlet butts danced through my head, a faint noise snapped me from my musings. Listening intently, I began hearing the muffled sound of an engine. Yet, there was more. It wasn't just the din of the motor. It was people sounds. As the noise grew closer, I suddenly recognized it. The horn was honking like a morse code, blaring on and off intermittently. Shouting could be heard. Clanging of metal against metal added to the melee. The uproar could mean only one thing.

Scrambling from my cot, I threw on my safari shirt, fastening just enough buttons to keep from embarrassing myself, before dashing out of the tent. Like ants coming out of the woodwork, Hilary, Thomas, Kaumba, and Maugo appeared from their little enclaves. In seconds we were clumped together laughing, crying, clapping, yelling, and waiting for the Land Cruiser and the cargo it held, knowing it would be more than just humans. *Chui* would be on board as well. Rick had fulfilled his childhood dream. Overwhelmed by a whole array of emotions, tears rolled down my cheeks.

Seconds later, the vehicle, covered in greenery and toilet paper, pulled to a stop in front of us. Everyone leaped down to a tangle of hugs, handshakes, slaps on the back, and chatter. Without saying a word, Rick and I grabbed each other in a long embrace, quietly weeping, savoring the exceptional moment.

Once we parted, the celebration continued. Rick, also draped in toilet paper like a half-wrapped mummy, was pushed into a chair and hoisted into the air as the camp erupted into a spirited celebration, with Kaumba leading the chant.

Celebrating Chui with Kaumba leading the chant.

Amid the rhythms, Rick was placed back on the ground in the middle of the circle of thrusting arms, gyrating hips, stomping feet, clapping hands, and whistling. Just like for Rod and Sue's lion, Kaumba belted out the words and everyone repeated them back. "Nani kaua, Rick nani kaua." *Who killed it? Rick killed it.* Next came "Kataa, kataa, kata Musa kata." *Shake your waist, shake your waist. Musa, shake your waist.*

Rick is not one for being the center of attention, especially when it comes to dancing, but, for once, he didn't mind. Though not nearly as rhythmic as our friends, he did a pretty good job. I, too, was alternating between shaking my booty, snapping pictures, and brushing tears from my eyes.

Just like the earlier celebration, I struggle for the words to convey the intense emotions I felt. Somehow, the dancing and chanting took me to another time and place. More ancient. More visceral. More authentic. I felt deeply privileged and extremely grateful to be embraced in an African tradition of primal joy, ingrained camaraderie, and deep-rooted purpose with people of a foreign culture who we now call friends. Quite literally, the leopard celebration was again "deeply stirring to the blood." Sappy or not, they are still the only words I can come up with to explain such intense emotions.

Rick in the middle of the leopard celebration circle.

Minutes later, the celebration died down and thoughts turned back to practical matters. With all the excitement, those of us at camp had yet to see the leopard. The entire group migrated to the Land Cruiser where we gazed upon the animal's elegant body curled respectfully in the cargo hold. Even in that position, I could see it dwarfed me in both weight and length. Reverently stroking the giant cat, I was filled with awe. The feline's fur was silky soft, like that of a housecat, but covered with large black spots resembling the shape of a rose. The distinctive marks contrasted sharply against its light-colored hide. Underneath the cat's magnificent coat, I could feel its muscles, attesting to its strength and power. Lying there, it looked peaceful, it's head mimicking that of a content oversized tomcat.

But upon studying its four, nearly two-inch long, canines and arsenal of razor-sharp claws, the lethal nature of the predator emerged, forcing me to see the deadliness that made his sacrifice so significant. With tear-clouded eyes, I paid homage to the exquisite creature, thanking him for his gift of life.

This leopard hunt had started like most of the others: the men hiding motionless for hours enduring relentless heat, incessant tedium, and voracious flies. The difference was the skyscraper *machan.*

Nested high in the tree, the hunting crew fixed their eyes on the bait waiting, hoping, and praying that their new perch would allow them to escape the shrewd cat's keen senses. As the moments ticked, the harsh shadows of full sunlight transformed into the haze of twilight. The day's hunt was nearly over.

Then, suddenly, there he was--the magical sight of *Chui* silhouetted against the sunset-lit tree. The leopard seemingly dropped onto the branch from out of nowhere, the bare limb unexpectedly holding a display of rippling muscles below a rosette-dappled hide. Everyone was caught unaware. Even the Tanzanians had not caught a whisper of his presence as he approached. Remaining noiseless, Rick slowly put his eye to his rifle scope and, as always, waited.

The instant Raphael gave the word, the leopard dropped from the tree, disappearing into a bed of tall grasses. There was no more to be done but to crawl down to see if Rick's shot had made direct contact or if he had, instead, created one of the most dangerous situations in Africa, sending a wounded leopard into the bush. Slowly and cautiously, the men covered the 60 yards. Although Rick felt confident about his shot, he was unwilling to relax until seeing the motionless cat.

His aim had been true. He had not buckled under the pressure. The beautiful mature male feline had died the second the bullet hit its mark. There was no pain or suffering or wounded leopard to pursue through the bush. No worries that a hyena would ravage the graceful, exquisite being, destroying its essence forever.

After a jaunt across the globe, a three-week stint on safari, a wad of money, and 23 motionless hours smooshed in a torture-chamber *machan*, Rick's childhood dream came true. Even so, all the sacrifices, aches, pains, sweat, and risks were worth it once that magical leopard appeared on the branch.

Here is the weird thing about hunting. The more grueling, miserable, and dangerous the hunt, the more treasured and memorable it becomes. This concept still baffles me.

Rick has dragged his worn limping body home on more than one occasion, almost becoming food for worms several times: nearly drowning when his friend's jet boat hit sweeper logs on Alaska's remote Kuskokwim river (hundreds of miles from help); surviving hypothermia from the same incident (rescued by native fishermen after five days surviving along the riverbanks); coming only yards from getting mauled by a furious momma brown bear who charged him in Alaska's Brooks Range (she finally backed down as Rick held his ground); hiking umpteen miles in ankle-twisting, energy-sapping tundra carrying 80-plus-pound packs; and having an Alaskan brown bear shove his nose in Rick's tent on Kodiak Island, watching the fabric's indentation move as the bear moved. Some of these hunts had been the most miserable, frustrating, and physically taxing as any he had ever experienced. Yet, even coming home empty-handed 75 percent of the time, his common statement was, "I can't wait to do it again."

While the leopard hunt was its own kind of agony, his Alaskan sheep hunts tested him to extremes. To this day, if you ask Rick which memory on our wall means the most to him, he will gaze up at that Dall sheep without a doubt, each time reliving the misery, danger, and aching muscles of each attempt until he was finally successful.

Hunters are literally gluttons for punishment. Quite honestly, most of us will never understand the drive to push ourselves to such extremes. While I love to join Rick, there is no way I could handle *that* amount of misery. Nor do I *want* to.

The next morning at 5 a.m., the entire camp was again alive, joyous, and posing for pictures with *Chui.* A second celebration of chanting, singing, and dancing was triggered, including a slick move on my part, causing my camera to somersault from my hand. As if in slow motion, I watched the indispensable piece of equipment spin through the air until it plunked, lens first, onto the rocky riverbed. Videoing a leopard celebration, while also *trying* to join in, was *not* a bright idea. The camera was technically usable *if* I wanted each photo to have a big blurry smudge smack dab in its center.

Thank goodness for cell phone cameras and solar-powered chargers. Me not having access to a camera when there is a sunset to capture or a warthog dashing across the savanna is equivalent to a hunter not having his rifle in elk season after hiking 10 miles when a monster bull grazes onto the skyline. It would have been devastating to be unable to capture the rest of our adventure. Granted, the pictures from my cell phone couldn't compare to the telephoto lens; but hey, beggars can't be choosers.

After the morning festivities, we were off again with our normal hunting crew while the others took care of breaking camp. We, too, had work to do. Our routes from the past several days were retraced, undoing all that had been done. All the baits had to be removed and left for the scavengers to eat. All the *machans* had to be destroyed, partly to leave the environment in its natural state and partly to keep poachers from using them.

During our rounds, the crew also discovered an older elevated *machan,* not of their handiwork. Hilary's people are the only ones who had the legal rights to hunt in the area, therefore, the blind had been built by trespassers during the off-season. It, too, was eliminated.

The hours of toil and sweat from building each network of grasses and limbs were undone in a matter of minutes. The dried remnants of each shelter were piled into little clearings where they were set ablaze. The flames crackled and spit, furiously consuming the withered vegetation. With the flames still leaping in the air, we pulled away, already intent on the next mission.

Tearing down the machan built by poachers.

Quite frankly, the last maneuver had thrown Rick and me for a loop, even after Andrew's previous explanation of fires. Watching our Tanzanian crew *purposely* start fires in a place so arid and blazing hot--and then driving away leaving them unattended--left us dumbfounded and, quite honestly, a little skittish. When Andrew had told me about the fires, I had assumed people would stand guard to oversee them like prescribed burns in America.

As we drove away with flames leaping into the air, I peered over my shoulder repeatedly. Surely, tiny embers would find their way to vast expanses of fuel, blowing up into infernos. Hours later, I still found myself searching the distant terrain for plumes of smoke. Despite that, I never saw any sign that the fires continued. That still amazes me.

Even with my concern that outrunning a bushfire may be in the cards, spirits were extra jovial. The successful leopard hunt, Rick's primary goal, had taken a lot of pressure off everyone. While traveling to destroy each bait site, we enjoyed sightings of kudu, impala, warthog, duiker, and a family of 12 elephants. We even spotted our first lizard resting on a big tree branch. The lizard was no itsy-bitsy Hawaiian gecko. It was a 6-foot-long monster!

When I excitedly asked Raphael what type of lizard it was, he calmly answered with a smirk, "A biiigggggg lizard."

Later, I learned it was some type of Monitor lizard, of which there are over 80 species, some getting up to 10 feet long. Still, Raphael's description seemed to sum it up best. It was a *biiigggggg* lizard.

Upon approaching the third bait site, we discovered a large troop of baboons hanging out by the waterhole. We were close enough to watch their antics, but far enough away that they didn't feel threatened. Front and center was a huge harvestable male. We watched him sit regally as baboons of all sizes and ages scooted nearby. A few played sentries in nearby trees; females had babies clinging to their stomachs; and others had young ones attached to their backs, piggyback style.

Watching Rick, it was easy to see the wheels turning in his head as he scrutinized the situation. Cringing inside, I remained neutral. Although I recognized that it was just as critical for baboons to have a monetary value, reason and emotion don't always coincide. After a few minutes of deep contemplation, Rick shook his head and in resignation said, "I can't do it. Not when he is just sitting there calmly with his whole family surrounding him." There is *shooting* and then there is *hunting*. There is a difference.

Every ethical hunter lives by a code of ethics. That involves the rules of fair chase that I talked about early in the book: the ethical, sportsmanlike, and lawful pursuit of free-ranging wild game in a manner that does not give the hunter an improper or unfair advantage. While technically the baboon fit that definition since he was free to flee in the wide-open country, the situation did not *feel* right for Rick.

Ultimately, hunting is an individual choice for every hunter, as long as it is legal and ethical. With that said, ethics can be highly subjective. What is ethical for one person may not be for another. Every situation is different. Every species is different. In the end, once the trigger is pulled, the hunter must be able to sleep at night. As far as the baboon goes, Rick not only had trouble with the species' humanistic features, but the situation had muddled the rules of fair chase. It didn't seem right or fair. In another situation, in another time, he might make a different decision.

Giraffes, too, are another animal that Rick struggles with in respect to his personal choice of hunting them or not. The Creator pulled out all the stops when designing the distinctive species of the African continent. Yet, even with so many incredible species, there is just something extra special about the giraffe. Not only for me but Rick as well. We were both mesmerized each time we were blessed with their presence.

Since it is illegal to hunt giraffe in Tanzania, it was a non-issue. The exquisite, long-legged creature is one of the country's national symbols and therefore, according to Lilian, hunting one is punishable by life in prison. Even if it had been legal, Rick was unsure whether he would feel comfortable harvesting the species.

That being said, it is just as important that a monetary value be placed on the giraffe as it is on any animal. Like all species, habitat is their biggest threat. They are also slaughtered for bushmeat, pelts, bones, hair, and tails. In addition, they can acquire diseases such as anthrax and rinderpest because of sharing habitat with domestic ungulates who carry the disease.

Thankfully, the long-legged ruminants do have one distinct advantage over many wild species. Since they pose minimal threats to the life or livelihoods of humans, human-wildlife conflict is of little concern. Also, their food source, primarily the canopy of trees, seldom competes with domestic livestock.

The rules of fair chase and personal choice apply to fenced hunting areas as well. When wild species are kept confined in small areas that offer no real challenge to the hunter, most *hunters* do not consider that *ethical hunting* and, therefore, are opposed to it. Nevertheless, it is important to distinguish the size of an area that is fenced. There are many vast game ranches in South Africa, Namibia, Zimbabwe, and other countries that are thousands, if not hundreds of thousands of acres. Large acreage like this, especially with varied terrain, allows the free movement of wild species, offering what most would consider an ethical hunt.

As noted earlier, large, fenced ranches managed specifically to safeguard and increase game populations have been instrumental in precipitating the drastic comeback of many wild species. Managing wild species suited to the terrain was found to be far easier and more lucrative than raising domestic livestock or growing dismal crops, both ill-suited for Africa's hostile climate and its predators.

Since wildlife ranches are operated with the underlying intent of making their land profitable, some people begrudge them. Yet, the system works. It not only increases the owners' bottom line, thereby offering an incentive to continue their efforts, but it also safeguards large and growing populations of wild species. If the ability to harvest the mature males on these ranches was terminated, preserving species would no longer be viable and the land would return to other uses.

Hunters, like all humans, do make mistakes. At a charitable auction, Rick won a bid for an affordable stag hunt in New Zealand. Although he knew it was in a fenced area, he hadn't taken the time to research it before bidding. The fenced area turned out to be much smaller than he anticipated, offering little challenge for the hunt. Rick came home disheartened. While he would someday love to hunt stag again, he would do so in a wide-open free-range area.

Once the last bait was lowered to the ground for the wild critters to feast on, we said goodbye to the family of baboons and headed back to *Chui* Camp one last time. By noon, we were packed and en route to *Masimba* Camp.

Four hours later, we arrived to see Joel and the others excitedly running to greet us, just like they did each time we returned from safari. It was a joyous occasion, especially once word spread of Rick's success with *Chui* and another Cape buffalo.

Our evening meal reverted to a packed table, spirited banter, hilarious stories, camaraderie, and friendship. We missed the lively dinners, along with our entertaining host and the rest of the staff. We were also happy to hear the bellowing of hippos from the hippo pool and to return to our tent sitting along the riverbed with our aquatic neighbors just yards away. We missed our *Masimba* Camp Shangri La. It was *home*.

Having said that, *Chui* Camp would also hold a special place in my heart. It was full of new adventures, different sights, and special moments with our hosts and friends. Most of all, *Chui* Camp is where skill, opportunity, and Lady Luck coincided. A place where Rick and I had been welcomed into an ancient, visceral celebration of primal joy for the harvest of a dangerous predator notoriously feared by rural people. A place where friend-ships and deeply rooted traditions coincided, allowing us the privilege of participating in a ritual "deeply stirring to the blood." A place where Rick's childhood dream came true.

But, far more important than one person's successful quest was that the leopard's sacrifice would allow many more of the magnificent felines to live.

26
THE GOOFBALL AWARD

Yet again, I found myself scooting from tree to tree in our typical semi-crouched formation. Another eland bull had been spotted in the distance. While the jumbo-sized antelope wasn't a primary species on Rick's wish list, it was an impressive, but kind of strange-looking beast. The large ungulates had been taunting us for days, with mature bulls popping up anytime we crossed large patches of open savannas.

With another potential target located, our hunkered-down sprints had already gained us about a mile; but, still, he was too distant for a clean shot. The bull was absorbed in his pre-twilight meal with a mixed herd of eland doing the same, making the task of evading his detection more difficult. Instead of one set of eyes and ears, there were multiple. Again, Raphael, with the train-like cluster of humans hot on his heels, darted forward to the last tree offering any kind of cover between us and the attentive herd. The bull, immersed in a cocoon of watchful eyes, was no easy target.

The common eland, or *pofu*, is the world's largest antelope, being slightly larger than its northwestern relatives. The common eland is taxonomically divided into three sub-species: the East African eland (also known as the Patterson's eland), the Livingstone's eland, and the Cape eland. The Central African giant eland, commonly known as the Lord Derby eland, and its highly localized cousin, the West African giant eland, are both longer in the headgear department but are slightly smaller in body mass. The three common sub-species, as their name suggests, are prevalent throughout most of the southern half of the continent. The eland is considered one of the most adaptable of all ruminants because it can survive in a variety of different habitats. In general, they prefer the drier savanna and grassland areas.

While elands are very common, they seem to be lesser known. I was clueless that the hump-backed ox-like herbivore even existed until traveling the grasslands of Tanzania. This, presumably, may be because they lack the graceful aesthetics and iconic nature attributed to many of Africa's grazers.

Eland

Surpassing almost all other antelopes in size, it will not surprise you that elands are big. Really big. The males can be up to 11 feet long, stand 6 feet high at the shoulders, and weigh up to 2,000 pounds. Females, only reaching about 1,300 pounds, are not exactly delicate little creatures. Eland calves are born tawny-colored but, over time, evolve into a bluish gray. Also, when young, the eland has slight white vertical stripes on their sides that fade considerably as they mature. Both genders of eland have tightly spiraled horns, dwarfing in comparison to many of the longer-horned species. The male horns tend to be shorter but thicker than their female counterparts.

The *pofu* (don't you just love that name?) is quite an odd-looking duck if you ask me. As stated, they lack the graceful elegance of most varieties of antelopes. Their ox-like impression stems from the hump on top of their front shoulders, combined with their very bulky torsos. Aside from the bulge on their backs, the bulls have a rather large *dewlap*, or fat and skin, hanging down from their necks. To add to these rather peculiar traits, the bulls have a large clump of bushy hair, called a *ruff*, on their foreheads, which increases in length and density with age. In all honesty, the wad of tresses, affixed to such a stout ungainly looking animal, does little to help their rather bizarre appearance.

Because of the eland's size and brawn, speed isn't an asset that will win them a Kentucky Derby. Able to run only 25 mph for very short distances, they are the slowest of all antelopes. But what they lack in speed, they make up for in endurance. Their powerfully built physique allows them to maintain a 14-mph trot indefinitely. Their size also doesn't hinder their athletic abilities; jumping a 4-foot fence from a standstill is a piece of cake. When frightened, 8-foot leaps are just as feasible.

Eland might not have the speed of their fleet-footed relatives, but they don't have to--their might is a pretty good equalizer. Rarely do they flee from four-legged predators. When attacked or threatened, the females will typically stand their ground protecting their young, either alone or in a united front. Groups will often create an impenetrable circle by bunching all their heads together, forming a lethal ring of kicking back legs. Male elands also rarely flee but, instead, go on the offensive. In a mixed group, large males will sometimes take front positions to help protect the calves and pregnant females.

Outfitted with almost a ton of flesh and thick spiral horns, even lions tend to think twice about including them in their dinner plans. The same can't be said for their calves, the young, and the sickly. *Simba* and his pride happily pick off any weak links.

Fortunately for the eland, their defensive strategy changes regarding humans. Experience has taught them that flight, even at only 25 mph, is a better alternative. Our witnessing their hindquarters fading into the savanna on several occasions proved that point fairly well.

The social organization of the eland is somewhat different from that of other antelopes. Typically, the herd lives in groups of up to 60 individuals, significantly larger than other types of antelopes. In the wet season or resource-rich areas like the Serengeti of Tanzania, eland herds can grow much larger. The herds we saw, however, typically numbered closer to 20.

While elands only exist in about 50 percent of their historic range, their population overall remains strong. The IUCN, therefore, lists their current status as Least Concern. Fortunately, many countries enjoy popu- lations that are considered stable and some countries are even showing increases in numbers, mainly Namibia, Botswana, Zimbabwe, South Africa, Malawi, Zambia and Tanzania. About half of their total population lives in protected areas, while another 30 percent live on private lands largely due to their value as trophy animals.

It should be noted that eland populations decreased dramatically in the 1970s due to civil wars and their aftermath in countries such as Uganda, Rwanda, Angola, and Mozambique. This is not a unique concept. Where there is conflict and war, wild species suffer catastrophic consequences, right along with human populations. Four-legged inhabitants are slaughtered to feed armies or desperate citizens. They are also poached to raise revenue for funding wartime operations. Hostilities often force existing park systems to crumble just when wildlife protection is needed most. Regrettably, but understandably, outside conservation efforts rarely exist under such hostile conditions.

Assuming that animals existing in Africa's national park systems will always be protected is wrong. If hostilities arise in their locations, for whatever reason, they too are at risk. According to a study by researchers from Yale and Princeton Universities, more than 70 percent of Africa's national parks have been affected by war in recent decades. The 2018 Nature article "Warfare and Wildlife Declines in Africa's Protected Areas", states: "Conflict frequency was the single most important predictor of wildlife population trends among the variables that we analyzed" in their 65-year database.[1]

With 54 continental African countries, each with its system of government, issues regarding conflict and governing properties are utterly complex and discombobulating. While I can't begin to explore this in its entirety, according to the African Renewal article "African Democracy Coming of Age", development experts sum up "the solution to Africa's socio-economic and political problems in two words: good governance."[2]

Fortunately, many countries and organizations are working hand in hand to achieve gains in these areas. According to the article, Africa is showing steady progress overall, despite hiccups, with data showing that good governance is trending in the right direction.

While I'll never truly grasp the intricate convoluted issues facing the African nations, it is absolutely clear to me that peace and wildlife conservation are inextricably linked, just as the lives of rural African people and the creatures they live amongst are linked.

While it is encouraging that the populations of elands in many countries are holding firm or even slightly growing, overall, their population is still gradually decreasing. It's the same song and dance time and time again. Aside from habitat loss, elands suffer a much greater risk from bush-meat poachers compared with many of the slighter species. Its massive size provides a large useful hide, as well as an abundance of meat. To make matters worse, their protein is superior in taste.

Rick and I can vouch for that. An eland was harvested by Rod early in our safari, making it the protein on our plates, cooked in various ways, for several days. Indeed, *pofu* was Rick's favorite of all the wild game we ate while at *Masimba* Camp.

Lump those three qualities together--tastiness, lots of meat, and large hide--and it's easy to see why the unique-looking antelope is a prime target for illegal bushmeat slaughter.

In addition to legalized hunting, some countries have even begun domesticating the eland as a way to place a monetary value on the animal. The wild species are better adapted to the African environment than cattle and, evidently, are easily domesticated. In addition to their highly prized protein, they offer a large amount of nutritious 'long life' antibacterial milk, far superior to a cow's. Currently, the eland is being farmed in South Africa, Zimbabwe, Kenya, Russia and Ukraine.

The eland may have been domesticated in a few countries, but it was obvious that no such thing was occurring in Tanzania, at least not in Rungwa West. We'd pursued *pofu* at least three times already. On one occasion, we'd stalked a bull eland two miles before determining he was too young. Another time, we followed a small herd for over a mile until we were able to get within 300 yards of a shootable bull. Although the shot was doable, it wasn't feasible with several other eland grazing in front of him providing a living shield. As soon as one animal moseyed on, another one parked right behind his torso. A bullet would have taken out both. So, we waited. Then we waited some more. Suddenly, the herd picked up their heads and trotted off into the sunset. Maybe, they winded us or maybe something else told them to skedaddle. Either way, it was late afternoon and too late to continue a stalk, so the hunt was over.

There was also a third eland pursuit in the mix somewhere, but that adventure is nothing but a highly telling note, *"went after pofu again"*, scribbled in my journal. The entry did very little to jog my memory. It would seem that the pursuit was either too uneventful to commit to memory or it whipped my butt, making me capable of only jotting down four words.

Anyway, we were hoping the fourth *pofu* attempt would end with better results. While we could easily see the mixed herd, the lack of cover offered quite a challenge. There was still approximately 400 yards of wide-open savanna between the attentive herd and our human brigade. A 400-yard shot, typically, is not difficult for Rick.

Nevertheless, the chance of wounding game increases with distance, no matter how skilled or prepared a person is. The memory of the elk Rick wounded in Idaho, which he was unable to track and finish, still twists a knot in his gut. I would guess that 100 percent of hunters have taken that gut-wrenching regrettable shot at least once in their lifetime; but if they are *true* hunters, great pains are taken to avoid such mistakes in the future.

It is also a case of economics. In Africa, may I remind you that a wounded animal is considered a soon-to-be-dead animal, therefore costing the hunter the trophy fee, as well as the opportunity to harvest that species listed on their license.

A few moments later, the quandary over a 400-yard shot didn't matter anyway. From a distance, the bull's large body gave the impression that he was older than he was. With further inspection, Raphael decided the eland's less dense horns told a different story, indicating the stout bull was closer to seven or eight years old. Considering common elands can live to 15 years in the wild, he was still in his prime and spreading some pretty incredible genes throughout the ranks.

After the eland stalk, we headed back to *Masimba* Camp. Another day on safari under our belts. While the eland pursuit had been a bust, we spotted hyena, giraffes, a jackal, waterbucks, impalas, hartebeest, roan, oribis, three families of elephants and a pair of lions. A 4-year-old male and a young lioness were resting under a tree with a zebra herd grazing nearby. Thankfully, the resting felines were more interested in shade than zebra steak.

Believe it or not, we also spotted more *dagga* boys, two old bachelor bulls, beside a thicket of scrublands a few hundred yards from the road. As the Cape buffalo jumped up, barreling into a thicket of dense bush, Rick excitedly asked Raphael, "Are they harvestable?"

With a look of incredulity and worry plastered on his face, Raphael asked, "For you?"

Rick had already used his quota of three buffalo. Rod and Sue, however, had been striking out when it came to *nyati,* even though it topped their wishlist. So, when Rick answered, "No. For Rod and Sue," relief washed over Raphael's face.

It was irrelevant anyway. Our American counterparts were off on their own safari in another sector of Rungwa West. The bulls we saw did them zero good. As luck would have it, we continued to see harvestable *dagga* boys again and again, so many that the staff gave Rick the nickname, *the buffalo whisperer.* Though every sighting was exciting for us, our good fortune was a little disheartening for Rod and Sue.

On their first trip to Tanzania, they hiked over 90 miles in the ten days before Sue harvested her bull. She was so spent from exhaustion, stress, and fear from so many extended and tense pursuits that she burst into tears upon success.

On this trip, unlike us, buffalo seemed to elude them no matter what they did or where they went. Their last nine days at *Masimba* Camp were dedicated almost exclusively to the pursuit of the old boys. Multiple times they chased herds through sections of long grass, producing some pretty hair-raising stories. They could hear the huge beasts grunting and snorting just yards away, catching glimpses of their shadowy blackness from time to time, but never getting a clear view. Another time, much like our earlier experience, they lost one when it crossed into the national park. While they had many close encounters, not once in the three weeks of our safari did they have an opportunity for a harvestable bull, a testament to the fact that hunting is not just about skill and perseverance, it is also about luck and being in the right place at the right time. Again, that is why it is called *hunting*, not killing.

The morning after our fourth unsuccessful *pofu* stalk, we were again bouncing along, at a snail's pace, through a section of road that looked as if a herd of elephants had done a jig amid the rainy season, drying it into a sun-baked obstacle course. Footprints cemented into the ground were prevalent everywhere, but some sections of roadway were worse than others. At the lightning speed of five mph, we were making our way through an open expanse of short-grassed savanna littered with a few sporadic trees when, lo and behold, a gray dot--all by its lonesome--was spied in the distance.

That *anything* could be spotted amid the rocking and rolling of the vehicle was a miraculous feat in itself. Through the binoculars, the gray dot transformed into an eland bull. While he wasn't as big-bodied as the previous bull, his thickset horns and his being alone indicated he was much older. The hunt was on.

Hiding behind shrubs attempting to get closer to the eland.

Jumping into our crouched formation, we scrambled from scrub tree to scrub tree. There was little vegetation to conceal our approach, forcing us to belly crawl 70 yards to reach the last tree offering any kind of concealment. Since I was the fourth in the line, the sparse vegetation was smashed to smithereens, offering me an easier go of it, as well as ensuring slithering serpents were long gone. Other than an occasional poke up my nose by a wayward blade of grass, worming my way forward proved to be not as horrendous as I had anticipated.

Once we reached the lone tree, the unsuspecting bull was still 220 yards away. As a loner, he didn't have the added protection of dozens of eyes and ears on high alert. Slowly, we wriggled from our 12 inches of cover into a shooting position. A few seconds later, Raphael whispered, "Shoot."

The bull dropped to the ground. Everyone sprinted to the fallen eland. Upon arrival, I froze in horror as the bull lifted his head slightly, turned towards me, and peered into my eyes. With our focus locked on each other, another shot exploded in my ear. As the *pofu's* huge dark eyes closed, my body melted to the ground in anguish. Of all my hunts with Rick, never had I approached a creature that wasn't already lifeless.

Earlier on, I tried to explain how some deaths affect me more emotionally than others; and, sometimes, there is no rhyme or reason for it. Well, on that occasion, there was no mystery why the eland hit me so dramatically. Looking into his beautiful eyes, even for just a few seconds, tormented me in a way that I had never experienced before. It crushed me. Tears didn't just gather in the corner of my eyes or trickle down my cheeks, they flowed like water from a faucet. Even putting this in words, tears roll down my cheeks, partly because it reminds me of other deaths. I remember my dad's larger-than-life presence and the gaping hole in my life after his passing. I remember my brother Mike--his "shitty" grin, sarcastic humor, selflessness, courage, and zest for life until the bitter end. Not a day goes by that my heart doesn't ache for them, and others, wishing they were in my life again. Death sucks. Period. Whether it be human or fur-covered, no matter how it occurs.

While I still get teary-eyed remembering the eland's sacrifice, it does bring me some comfort knowing that the last thing he saw were eyes filled with love, respect, and thankfulness. That had to be better than any of the fates that awaited him, possibly being eaten while life slowly drained from his body.

Processing the eland for transport back to *Masimba* Camp was no easy task. The bull weighed approximately 1,600 pounds, close to the weight of each Cape buffalo, making it too large to load in one piece. The eland had to be cut in half and some of its entrails and stomach contents left behind. Only the choice organs were scooped up, placed in a metal pan, and taken to camp. What remained would become a feast for the scavengers.

Once the eland was processed into two chunks, it took every trick in the book, plus all seven of us lifting to get it into the cargo hold. Several people lifted from the vehicle. Several positioned themselves on each side of a log placed underneath to help lift the weight. I, too, pocketed my camera/phone to help. After a lot of grunts on our part, the first half was heaved into the cargo hold with a plunk.

Suddenly, it occurred to me that I should be documenting the process. Pulling out my camera, I backed up, not knowing the guys had laid one of the lifting branches behind me. Just as I gained momentum, my feet hit the obstacle, pitching me into a backward swan dive. One that landed me smack dab on top of the monstrous heap of eland guts! Let me assure you, the viscera of a 1,600-pound antelope holds a lot of gooey nastiness, plus a whole lot of partially digested muck.

Me after falling in the eland guts.

For a few seconds, everyone just gazed at me in shock, trying to determine if it was okay to laugh at the klutzy American. When I burst into hysterical laughter, that opened the dam. Everyone joined in. My wonderful husband just shook his head with a huge smirk on his face; he was used to my lack of grace.

Anyway, other than my pride, I wasn't hurt in the slightest. A pile of soppy intestines, slimy organs, and digested greenery made for a pretty cushy landing zone.

While the fall itself was irrelevant, the smell was not: I stunk big time. Thankfully, I had a tank top crammed into my pack, enabling me to remove at least the first layer of stench. Still, the foul-smelling slime had oozed through my safari shirt onto my bra. While I wasn't entirely obnoxious, I still smelled like something the cat dragged in.

My klutziness wasn't all for naught. It earned me a highly valued prize, the "Goofball Award," presented to me by the one and only Lilian Mremi, Tanzanian game scout extraordinaire. The award was a rather scrumptious lollipop she found stashed in the bottom of her pack. Honestly, I was quite thrilled with the unique trophy. I just wish I hadn't eaten the treasured memory.

Me with the lollipop or "goofball" award.

After the rest of the eland was loaded, we all piled aboard for the sluggish trek across the pocked landscape. We hadn't rocked and rolled even 50 feet before White-backed vultures began dropping upon the gut pile amid a frenzy of goose-like hisses and cackles. With few trees dotting that section of grasslands, it initially appeared as if they had come from nowhere. When we turned our eyes to the distant skyline, however, we saw the birds approaching from miles away in every direction. Rick and I watched the swirling spectacle in awe. It felt like we were in a version of the Alfred Hitchcock horror movie "The Birds."

Greedily, they dove upon what was left of the eland. By the time we were 200 yards away, the ground was alive with squabbling, grappling, scuffling and gorging vultures. Oodles of them. We've seen plenty of vultures circling kills in the states, but nothing compared to this. Spellbound, we watched the ghastly, but gripping, display play out in front of us. Within 10 minutes, Raphael assured us the entrails would be completely and utterly gone.

Reading or hearing about it is one thing. Seeing the display unfold in front of your face is another altogether. Quite simply, it is a sensational phenomenon to witness. Most of Rick's quarry had been loaded whole or harvested in scrublands, hiding the entrails from immediate view. The eland was our first experience with the vultures storming upon remains.

It also reminded me of the poachers. We saw, firsthand, why the illegal killers despise the winged advertisements of death, and why they are poisoning them in droves. Once the original birds had taken flight, every bird from miles around had been alerted, pinpointing death like a beacon of light in the darkness. Any government patrols within miles would have spotted the birds, drawing them to investigate.

If we had placed toxin in that carcass, 50 to 100 vultures would now be dead, with very little effort. What a wretched reality. No wonder the IUCN put them on the Critically Endangered List. Yet, the fact that we did see hordes of the winged scavengers filled me with hope for their future.

When we pulled away from the whirlwind, it was only 9 a.m. The five-hour trek back to *Masimba* Camp delivered a fresh whiff of my foulness with each gust of air. As the stench swirled around me, so did my thoughts. Life is fickle. One minute I had been tormented, with tears flowing, looking into the eyes of the eland. Thirty minutes later, I was laughing hysterically after flopping onto a cushion of entrails. After another 15 minutes, I was entranced by a scrum of vultures in a voracious feeding frenzy. A testament to the web of life.

Pondering the eland itself, it was hard to believe that until just a few weeks earlier I didn't even know the magnificent animal existed. Yet now the *pofu* is forever planted in my memory. Although the look in his eyes still haunts me, his death was not in vain. We preserved his grandeur. Our family and friends now know his magnificence as well. People who, like me, never even knew there was such a creature. His eyes no longer have the sparkle of life, but I am still taken back to that morning in Africa; crawling on my belly across the crusty, pitted grasslands; the devastation when he looked into my eyes; the absurdity of falling into a bed of intestines; the wonder of a sky crowded with winged scavengers descending to recycle the *pofu's* remains and the laughter and camaraderie with friends. And yes, I remember the Goofball Award. Another day in Africa etched in my memory forever.

27
PALA HALA

The vehicle stopped as Raphael pointed through the haze to a thicket of sun-scorched trees. Blending seamlessly with the dried-up ravine were four lions, 3 younger males and one female. Like toddlers quarreling over a toy, the snarling quartet slashed and lunged at each other while swatting a doomed Guinea fowl back and forth. From our vantage point, the squabble appeared more playful than fierce.

The young lions took a short break to study the strange-looking metal elephant that had stopped 25 yards from their tussle. Fortunately, they showed no desire to move the skirmish in our direction. Once their curiosity was satisfied, they resumed their scuffle over the morning's appetizer.

Not long after the dueling felines, we passed a momma hartebeest nursing her offspring just off the side of the pathway. The maternal *kongoni* was so preoccupied with the baby greedily ramming her in the tummy that she hardly noticed us rolling by. The calf, too, was oblivious, its tail wagging a mile a minute during the hungry assault.

The delight of such moments made the days tick by much too quickly, bringing us to the end of our safari. Our focus, therefore, centered on harvesting a kudu and a sable, the two primary species remaining on Rick's bucket list. As Murphy's Law would have it, specifically searching for one particular type of wildlife often presents you with a whole host of other opportunities. We were seeing plenty of shootable males. Just not *the* ones we were looking for. Typically, we just enjoyed the sightings and moseyed on. With that said, once in a while an animal presented itself that tempted Rick's resolve to pursue *only* those two species. On that particular day, the temptation came in the form of a roan.

The roan, or *korongo,* is a close relative of the sable and, like its cousin, is one of Africa's most attractive antelopes. It is also one of the largest, exceeded in size only by the eland. Males typically stand about 5 feet high at the shoulders, weighing close to 620 pounds. Females are only slightly smaller. The *korongo* is a member of what is often referred to as the *horse* antelopes. It won't surprise you that they have horse-like builds, long sturdy limbs, and thick necks with an upstanding mane.

Roan

The similarities in appearance end there. The roan's head is shorter with a striking black-and-white face. White patches highlight its eyes and nose, giving it an almost clown-like appearance. His unique face is framed by long elf-like ears tipped with tassels of black hair. As their name suggests, their coat is a tawny reddish-brown, or roan colored. While both genders sport sickle-shaped horns, the male's horns reach approximately 26" on average, being slightly thicker and longer than their counterparts. Even with a clown-like face and elf-like ears, roan are strikingly beautiful.

Once a roan grows to maturity, its survival is made easier by a rather aggressive and courageous temperament, making it a formidable foe. When threatened, they will confront predators rather than flee. In some parts of Africa, they have even earned the nickname "Lion Killer" due to their tendency to gore any attacking lions with their curved horns and sideways stabbing technique. They are ill-tempered with competing bulls as well. When two adult males meet up, it is common to fight for dominance, often using an interesting method of getting down on their knees to battle with clashing horns.

Recently, while watching a YouTube video, I witnessed a roan's tenacity. Two lionesses had a bull on the ground, raking his hindquarters. Suddenly, the roan began striking the felines with its horns, driving off the attackers with his pointed weapons. Each time the cats lunged, the roan spun his body, facing them head-on, forcing them to retreat temporarily. The bull stood, appearing as if he had rebuffed the deadly encounter. Nevertheless, after several steps, his damaged legs gave out and he crumbled to the ground. The lions were watching and waiting. Seeing weakness, they moved in for another attack. The roan kneeled onto his front legs slashing at the predators with his horns, driving off several more assaults. But, its courageous fight could not overcome the initial injury.

Bearing witness, even on video, to the struggle was heart-rending, even *knowing* that the roan's death meant life for the lions.

The roan's will to survive may save them from some predators, but carnivores aren't their only threat. According to the IUCN, the roan's conservation status is currently listed as Least Concern with an approximate population of 50,000 to 60,000 made up of various taxonomic sub-species. Even so, it is now one of the most threatened antelopes in many parts of Africa despite its rapid breeding rate. Roan are particularly vulnerable to habitat degradation due to their picky grazing and their calves' dependence on the same optimal conditions. A pregnant female gives birth in a secluded place, leaving the calf hidden for most of the day for the first few weeks of its life.

This makes the roan a telling indicator of an ecosystem's health. The loss of *korongo* from large areas of their original range serves as a tragic reminder of diminished ecological qualities in those areas. As noted earlier, South Africa's Kruger National Park is one such place that suffered disastrous consequences in recent years by trying to provide artificial water sources throughout the park.

Along with moisture came many more predators, but, just as deadly, were the water-dependent grazers that were drawn to the new water sources. Species like zebra and Cape buffalo tend to act as mowing machines, leaving a swath of sheared grasses in their wake. The resulting loss of taller grasses, the roan's essential diet, destroyed not only their food supply but the cover they needed to conceal their calves. Roan populations in Kruger National Park plummeted to below 40 animals.

While the installation of the additional water was done with the best of intentions, it upset the ecosystem's natural set of checks and balances. Most conservationists now support managing habitats for preserving *all* species, not just the favored few. The manufactured waterholes have since been closed, hoping to regrow the populations that were detrimentally affected.

Aside from the water debacle and habitat loss, roan face the typical threats of bushmeat poaching and agricultural expansion. Although roan are considered Least Concern, most now survive only in protected areas, thankfully, one of which was Rungwa West Game Reserve. Our treks through higher-grassed terrain blessed us with many sightings of the fussy eaters.

While we'd stalked *korongo* several times, weaving eerily through the blinding walls of long grasses, they had outmaneuvered us each time. The herd Raphael had just spotted in the distance offered another opportunity. If the roan was a mature, harvestable male, it also offered a huge dilemma.

Earlier in the safari, we had budgeted for roan and pursued them when the opportunity arose. Nevertheless, the trophy fees associated with the eland and the additional Cape buffalos blew Rick's hunting budget out of the water. Since kudu and sable topped Rick's wish list, we left money in the budget for those two only. *If* he successfully harvested a roan, he would have to forego either the kudu or the sable.

Sure enough, lowering his binoculars, Raphael confirmed the roan was an aged bull. Kudu and sable were less prevalent than other wildlife, so there was no assurance Rick would have the chance to pursue either one. If we had a crystal ball, the decision would have been easy, but since we had no gadget to foretell the future, the choice became: pursue the roan in front of us or wait, hoping an aged sable or kudu crossed our paths.

Making that kind of decision after traveling so far for such an experience was no small thing. With a conflicted heart, Rick chose to forego the chance for a roan; it was time to head to sable habitat. Unlike the roan, sable tend to avoid wide-open savannas, preferring light woodlands instead, especially the miombo woodlands, a mixture of bush and grasslands.

The sable, or *pala hala*, is a close relative of the roan but slightly smaller, averaging closer to 500 pounds. They also have a horse-like sturdy build with a short neck, longish face, and dark mane. While there are several subspecies in small numbers, the most prevalent is the common sable. The older males are characterized by glossy black coats with white underparts and white facial markings similar to the roan, but less clownish looking.

Sable

Calves are born reddish-brown with virtually no markings. As they age, the white markings appear while the rest of their coat turns darker. The older the animal, the more striking the contrast, ultimately creating the black coats they are known for. While in many ways the *pala hala* looks similar to the roan, its ears are brick red at the back, significantly shorter, and lacking the tassel and elf-like quality. Both sexes also have horns that are ridged, curving drastically backward, creating almost a complete semi-circle. Essentially, they look like a roan's sickle-shaped horns on major steroids. With smooth and sharp pointed tips, a male's horns can grow over 40 inches in length, creating very useful weapons. The female's horns are shorter and slimmer.

While sable and roan habitat differ, they both hide their calves in tall grasses, drop to their knees to fight, and shun shorter grasses, preferring to eat taller vegetation. With that said, sables are even pickier. Sometimes, it comes down to nibbling on just select parts of plants. Sable also rely heavily on water and rarely stray far from moisture. They also leave the herd to give birth.

With a current population of approximately 75,000 animals, the IUCN lists the sable's status as Least Concern. Nevertheless, like all of Africa's wildlife, they face threats of habitat loss and poaching. The sable in Kruger National Park also suffered from the installation of artificial-water sources, leading them to plummet to about 300 individuals. The invading water-loving species not only cropped the grasses to short undesirable lengths but also changed the grasses' composition in the process, eliminating some critical nutrients previously on the sable's menu.

The story of sable in the country of South Africa is a contradictory one. The number of sable roaming in the national parks is currently minimal. However, because of their value as game animals, South Africa's game-ranching industry has kept their overall numbers up.

The sable's exquisite beauty--majestic curled horns, painted face, and sharply contrasting hide--make it easy to see why it is one of the most iconic species in all of Africa and why it is coveted by selective hunters.

Once Rick decided to pass on the roan, sable became our focus. We spent two more days bumping along from one sable hot spot to the next, searching for the elusive *pala hala*. Finally, three days later, a herd of bachelor bulls was spotted in the distance.

As is often the case, the herd of sables was grazing alongside a herd of hartebeest. The additional sets of eyes, ears, and noses were a win-win for both groups of prey animals but were a major impediment for any predators.

Fortunately, being in sable country meant we were in a light woodland area with a mixture of bush and taller grasses. After hiding the vehicle and staying downwind, we darted from cover to cover, until getting within 150 yards. Standing amid the herd was a harvestable bull, offering a perfect profile view.

Rick set his rifle on the shooting sticks. It was a dream shot, with one exception. Another sable grazed directly behind him. If the bullet passed through the bull, it would also hit the other. He waited. The younger bull took a step forward. Raphael whispered, "Get ready."

Then just as the young sable cleared the targeted animal, another one strolled in front of him. Again, with bated breath, we waited. Waited. And waited some more. Finally, the younger bull ambled forward. The second it cleared the mark, Raphael whispered, "Shoot."

As Rick pulled the trigger, animals exploded into action. Most of the sable and hartebeest charged to the left, but the targeted bull bolted to the right. We burst forth from our hiding spot, lagging only feet behind Mgogo as he dashed into the woodlands. Forty yards away, partially concealed in a thicket of trees, lay the powerful strong-willed sable. The hunt was over.

The *pala hala* was magnificent. His beautiful horns curled almost as far back as his shoulder blades. The white of his belly and painted face contrasted sharply against his deep ebony coat, a sure sign of a mature bull. Again, we felt sadness for the loss of such a regal creature while also being excited that Rick had accomplished his goal of harvesting such an exquisite species. We felt the guilt of taking a life, the wonder of experiencing its beauty, and gratitude for his sacrifice. There was even disappointment and regret that the pursuit was over, knowing that Rick may never again have the opportunity to hunt such an animal. Swimming in emotion, we progressed to hugging, handshaking, and congratulations from the rest of the crew. While embracing Lilian, I tearfully muttered, "Finally, *hala pala.*"

She smirked and corrected me one more time. "Sue, *pala hala.*" Hopefully, the majestic animal forgave me jumbling his name yet again.

One of Africa's most iconic antelopes made the ultimate sacrifice so that others could live. It was time that I gave the sable, *pala hala,* the respect he deserved, never screwing up his Swahili name again.

Like the eland and buffalo, his magnificence and beauty did not die when his body hit the earth. It was preserved. Each time we look at him, we remember the hartebeest grazing nearby, the tension waiting for the other sables to clear, the camaraderie of hunting with our Tanzanian crew, and the sable's strength and determination, fighting for survival even after a bullet pierced his heart. His soul may no longer be present, but his aesthetic splendor is preserved so that our grandchildren, friends and family can know the beauty, elegance, and grandeur of *pala hala.*

28
KWAHERI RAFIKI ZANGU

Finally, I spotted another smudge in the powdery dirt. For almost two hours, we'd weaved through sparse woodlands intermixed with patches of grasslands. Making eye contact, Rick and I silently acknowledged that we had both seen the telltale sign. Slightly different than our typical human train, Mgogo and Raphael were both up front with their eyes glued to the ground seeing details that escaped our eyes. Typical of our many stalks, minutes would pass leaving us feeling as if we were on a wild goose chase. Then, miraculously, a partial print or scuff would triumphantly materialize.

While spying the dead giveaway of an animal's trail was always oddly satisfying, as well as exciting, it meant even more on that particular day: the hoofprints belonged to two large male kudus. After days, another opportunity had come for Rick to pursue the *tandala*, the magnificent spiral-horned antelope that topped his priority list.

Time was running out. In less than 24 hours, we'd be on the bush plane back to Arusha, our first stop before the final legs of our journey taking us to the States. Sadly, that also meant saying *kwaheri*, or goodbye, to our friends from the opposite side of the world and an adventure unlike any we had ever seen or would likely ever see again. With that realization, Rick and I crawled aboard the Land Cruiser for our last safari with a heavy heart. Twenty-one days had passed in a blink of an eye.

With kudu as our main focus, we headed straight to their preferred territory. An hour later, we were rewarded by spotting two of the magnificent species on the edge of a clearing, both with horns spiraling to the heavens. For a few precious seconds, we stared in wonder before their elegant bodies were but ghosts in the wind, but fortunately, a glance was all Raphael had needed to know both were harvestable males. The hunt was on.

The kudus had hightailed it into the forested scrublands and were a might faster than our snake-like entourage. Even after three weeks on safari, Raphael and Mgogo's tracking skills thoroughly captivated me. It simply never got old. Stealthily, we'd zig to the left thirty yards, stop to study a twig or piece of grass, then zag to the right for forty yards. Another stop to read some minute sign in the dirt, forcing us to head through a stretch of tall grass. Minutes later, we'd be slinking through another grove of scrub trees. Not only did I relish the slow meticulous games of Follow-the-Leader, I felt a touch of pride each time I spotted a revealing detail for myself.

After two hours, we came to a large expanse of open savanna. As Raphael peered across the grasses, we could see the wheels turning in his head. He knew how badly Rick wanted an East African greater kudu. He also knew we had other plans for our final day.

After a few moments, he matter-of-factly informed us that if we stayed on the kudus' trail, we should be able to catch up to them in six to eight hours.

On any other day, we would have jumped at the chance. However, we had made different plans for our final day of safari. *Chui* Rock, the monstrous cathedral of stone jutting from the flatlands mentioned in an earlier chapter, had practically screamed *climb me* each time we passed under its shadow. Fulfilling that beckoning was a special treat we had saved as a kind of farewell tribute.

There was not enough time to pursue the kudu *and* scale *Chui* Rock. My heart sank: we had to scrap the climbing adventure that tugged at *my* heart or scrap the pursuit of the kudu which tugged at Rick's. It was decision time.

Rick looked at me momentarily, then informed Raphael that the kudu would have to wait. Just like that, the hunt was over. The spiral-horned wonders had again won the day. Even so, the mesmerizing pursuit and watching the expertise of our crew was the perfect ending for our last on-the-ground trek through the savanna.

A couple of hours later, we were standing at the base of the colossal mountain of stone. With Raphael and Mgogo leading, we were soon scrambling over the huge boulders forming the outside perimeter and lower level of the stone tower. Easy peasy. Next, we wormed our way through a network of stone tunnels formed over eons by boulders splintering from the main outcropping. No problem. Then, as I enthusiastically cleared the last stone passage, my heart skipped a beat. Before me stood a rather steep 100-foot stone face to reach the top.

Crawling up the steep section of Chui Rock.

While I love rock scrambling, scaling a sheer wall of rock was something quite different. Put me in an airplane, no problem. Stand me near the side of a cliff, fear grips my entire body. Anyway, with fright knotting my insides and Rick on my heels, I crawled on all fours, never looking down, until reaching the almost table-like crest. Lilian, too, was a little unsettled. In her three weeks of patrol, it was the first time she didn't carry her government-required machine gun. Have no fear; the weapon made the scramble to the peak in Raphael's arms.

Once we reached the summit, I forgot all about the butterflies in my stomach. *Chui* Rock towers above the savanna offering a 360-degree view of the Rungwa West Game Reserve. The crown of the stone mountain was about the size of a football field, basically flat, but interspersed with crevices, dips, and bumps that form caves, the perfect hiding spots for its namesake. Many of the chambers were large enough for the elusive spotted cats to slink into but too small for *Simba*. Bones, even giraffe bones, were scattered about the rock advertising the leopard's past meals. Porcupines also seemed to like the view; although instead of bones, they left behind their 8-to-12-inch quills.

It's hard for the passionate hunter in a man to climb such heights without using it as a lookout. Rick and Raphael had their binoculars glued to their eyes scouting in every direction. The rest of us roamed about exploring and taking pictures. Mgogo even tempted fate by investigating a few of the crevices and cave-like openings; but thankfully, we never saw hide nor hair of any elusive cats.

Abdalah, Mgogo, and Lilian having some fun while Rick and Raphael glassed the savanna below.

After winning the "goofball award" earlier in the week, I decided I might as well keep the theme going. No way could I pass up the opportunity to perform my best *King of the World* impression from the movie *The Titanic*. Fortunately, Lilian was a bit of a goofball herself. Both of us stood on the highest point, flinging our arms out wide.

Lilian and me doing our "King of the World" impression.

Abdalah, Lilian, Me, Mgogo, and Raphael

Taking a long winding loop back to *Masimba* Camp, we kept our eyes peeled for kudu just in case the grey ghost offered Rick one last opportunity. Waterbuck, zebra, hartebeest, duiker, impala, giraffes, warthogs, and monkeys graced us with parting sightings, but the *tandala* eluded us. Our last elephant-pothole-dodging miles across the savanna were bittersweet.

Much too soon, we arrived at *Masimba* Camp, a much-altered *Masimba* Camp. Hilary and Andrew had returned to Arusha after our leopard hunt to attend to business. Their huts had sat empty the last few days, but when we pulled in that last afternoon, the *hemas* weren't just vacant, they were gone. Toilets, sinks, water tanks, and tents rolled into neat bundles were bunched together, all waiting to be loaded on trucks and taken to Mgogo's village for storage. The thatched walls had been torn down and stacked in the riverbed. All that remained of the huts was the framework of logs that had supported the grass panels.

Tearing down Masimba Camp at the end of the hunting season.

The transition was no surprise to us. We insisted they break down as much of the camp as possible rather than waiting until we left. The staff had already been there for months and were eager to get home to their own lives and families: Joel had his grandchildren pulling his heartstrings;

Mgogo had two wives, four kids, and crops to attend to; each person had his version of family waiting eagerly for him to return.

Yet, *knowing* that the camp would be partly dismantled didn't prepare me for actually seeing its mutated form. The transformation was a very visible reminder that our time was nearing its end.

The next morning, as soon as we pulled away, the camp would explode into a flurry of activity finishing what had been started. The remaining shelters would be stripped, and the grasses added to the heaps already dotting the riverbed. The solar panels, generator, electrical supplies, radios, tents, cooking equipment, tables, chairs, shelving, etc. would be dismantled and loaded on the trucks and Land Cruisers. The convoy, spilling over with cargo and Tanzanians, would then begin the journey to various villages, returning the staff to their homes and loved ones.

While the destruction of camp was a major undertaking, Joel insisted that it was a piece of cake compared to building camp. When returning after the rainy season, the well-manicured cozy little encampment would be a large expanse of overgrown vegetation and partially hidden walkways. All the supplies and equipment would be hauled back; new grasses would be cut, dried, and woven into panels for the huts, fencing, and work areas; tents would be erected; toilets, sinks, water tanks, and bath fixtures reinstalled; electricity, radios, generators, and solar panels reconnected; and food and other supplies brought in to provide for the workers and the next season's clients. While all of this was occurring, others would set upon clearing and improving the roads.

Knowing that the camp's destruction would keep poachers from moving in, hopefully sparing the lives of many animals in the game reserve and bordering park system, made it a little easier to wrap my head around it. Poachers, after all, don't respect boundaries, quotas, gender, or age. That I understood completely.

Seeing my melancholy, Joel also reminded me that its rebirth would provide many desperately needed jobs year after year as long as *Masimba* Camp endured, and hunters continued to come.

Even understanding all this, my heart ached. I loved our little slice of paradise and felt a deep connection to it, as well as the people we shared it with. While it would be rebuilt, it would never be exactly the same again. There would be different hunting clients and possibly different staff members. Each new hunting season would bring a whole new dynamic with it. One that didn't include us.

Knowing that *Masimba* Camp would soon return to the creatures of the wild, however, did make me happy. The coming rains would allow the rising waters to swallow the thatching piled in the riverbeds as crocodiles and hippos took their place. The resident elephants, lions, leopards and other wild creatures would soon be wandering through the shaded oasis, with no human interference. The honey badger could go back to operating in daylight, no longer needing to wait until nightfall to go about his business.

After adjusting to the altered Shangri-La, Joel ushered us to the skinning shed which had exploded into a hotbed of activity. Harvested game doesn't just magically transform into tangible memories. It takes the time, effort, and skill of multiple layers of people to capture an animal's true aesthetic quality, preserve its glory, and allow its splendor to endure long after death.

From the moment each harvested animal took its last breath, great care had been given to transport and respectfully process its body, keeping its beauty intact. After the meat is processed for use, the next phase begins. Any flesh remaining on the hide had to be meticulously removed without damaging the skin. It was then stored in a bed of salt to dry and preserve it. The skulls, too, had to be cared for. The brain matter was tediously removed from the cavity before being placed into a vat of boiling water to remove any remaining tissue. After each element was prepared, it was stored on scaffolding or behind the walls of the skinning shed to protect it from scavengers. Although these first steps in processing are critical, both for meat quality and aesthetics, it is probably the least recognized.

Unlike in Idaho, all of the African skins, skulls, and horns had to be wrapped and prepared for shipping. Like a three-dimensional jigsaw puzzle, the hodgepodge of curled horns had to be loaded onto one of the safari vehicles for transport. With no room in the bush plane, the precious cargo would have to make the two-day overland trek to Arusha. By the time the priceless memories reached the next phase of their journey, we would already be sleeping in our beds on the other side of the globe.

Once they arrived in Arusha, the skins and horns had to be taken to a dipping facility where they were dunked in an anti-bacterial solution to make them safe for export. After drying for several days, they'd be repacked, crated, and taken to a shipping company for transport to America.

Upon arrival in the United States, U.S. Customs and the U.S. Fish and Wildlife Service had to perform their inspections and clearances. Once deemed legal, the cargo was shipped to the prearranged taxidermy studio. Since few taxidermists do their own tanning, the skins were sent to be processed into leather, and the horns were stored for later use. After that was completed, the tanned skins were returned to the taxidermist, allowing the real magic to begin.

Taxidermy truly *is* an art form. Wildlife artists, having a deep knowledge of their subjects, essentially mold a piece of lifeless hide expertly over a piece of styrofoam, recreating the magnificence, elegance, and beauty of the original being.

That said, all taxidermists are not created equal. Just like all artists, some are more talented or creative than others or excel in different art forms. An individual in Montana, for instance, may recreate the essence of an elk, a species he is familiar with, beautifully, yet, he may be less adept at capturing the spirit and elegance of a kudu, a creature he is less familiar with. For this reason, some hunters choose to have their taxidermy work done in Africa. There are also those who *believe* they are artists but would be better off choosing another line of work.

The time, effort, and stress that goes into choosing the perfect taxidermist can be a little crazy. For months, Rick scoped out the workmanship of taxidermists with expertise in African species before choosing the one he felt most comfortable with. One might joke that some hunters, including my husband, take more care choosing their taxidermists than they do their spouses.

When hunting locally, most hunters deliver the hides and other components directly to their taxidermist, lessening the chances of things going south. With that said, retrieving animal skins, etc., shipped from Africa is a tangled web of government agencies, processing facilities, and shipping depots--essentially nightmares waiting to happen. With so many entities handling the prized memories, a lot can go wrong. For sure, it is a nerve-wracking time for hunters. Rick did not breathe a sigh of relief until his taxidermist had the shipment in hand.

As it turned out, Rick had a good reason to worry. Several of his hides were destroyed in the dipping process, literally falling apart in the taxidermist's hands. His leopard skin, Rick's most prized memory, suffered greatly. Thankfully, the taxidermist, with finesse and patience, was able to salvage it by using a different pose and making it smaller.

Getting African game from the savanna to an American living room is a prolonged elaborate process, one that makes my head spin. Depending on the circumstances, the undertaking can drag on for over a year or two. Although Rick handled all of this himself, companies can be hired to oversee the entire process. Since nothing is free, it gobbles up another wad of money, adding to the chunks already dished out for each step, much of which stays in Africa where it is needed most.

After watching the flurry of activity at the skinning shed, Joel transformed the dining hut into a mini marketplace filled with Maasai souvenirs, relics, and keepsakes. The changing world has forced the nomadic tribal pastoralists to adjust their lifestyles. Tribal leaders are trying to find ways to preserve their traditions while balancing the need for education in modern society. While this has caused many members to move away from their nomadic lifestyles and find work in the cities, others have learned to survive by participating in Tanzania's economy by turning to farming and running tourist businesses. They sell their traditional medicines, meat, produce, jewelry, and other souvenirs to tourists. Tourists just like Rod, Sue, Rick, and me.

Every available surface of the eating area was covered with an assortment of unique tribal pieces, providing us with our very own private shopping spree. We bought Maasai swords, painted gourds, and an array of miscellaneous trinkets for ourselves and our families. Nevertheless, our prized purchase was a beaded talking stick bought in tribute to Joel.

You might remember that his dad carried one such stick with him everywhere, cradling his *little buddy* under his arm. In the retelling of stories, Joel had done the same. We knew that each time we saw the special piece of memorabilia, the memories would come flooding back, transporting us back to the *mesi* where Joel held us spellbound with one intriguing story after another.

A few hours after our shopping spree, we headed to dinner, much more subdued than normal, our cheeriness and excitement missing. Thoughts of leaving clouded our brains. Then just a few minutes after we'd taken our last bites of sable, the muffled sounds of tribal chanting could be heard. Soon the singing grew louder as every person at camp joined in the procession, half-dancing, half-walking into the dining hut.

In the midst of this, Moses placed a small cake in front of me, inscribed with *"Kwaheri! Rod and Sue. Rick and Sue. Karibuni tena!"* Goodbye. Come again soon. As you might imagine, that sent my already emotional state over the edge. Tears flooded my eyes. Even now, I can't put into words what that little celebratory treat meant to me. When in my life would I ever again have Tanzanian friends bake a cake over hot coals in a makeshift oven in the middle of the African bush? Few parting gifts, past or future, will ever mean as much.

Me dancing along with the staff during the

cake presentation celebration.

We were clients from a vastly different world, but they had adopted us into their world as friends, ones that I wasn't ready to let go of. Wanting to offer something, anything, to show our appreciation, my waitressing instincts kicked in. Jumping up, I grabbed a knife and cut the special treat into 21 bite-size pieces. Sue, too, instantly joined in. Together, with nothing else to offer, we dispensed the small tokens of our friendship to each member of *Masimba* Camp.

After the festivities died down, most of the staff left to get ready for the next day's departure. Rod, Sue, Rick, and I decided we couldn't end our time at *Masimba* Camp without one last cocktail on the patio. After a few minutes of reminiscing, our nostalgic sorrowful mood was rudely interrupted by those who gave a crap. Literally. Plop. Plop. The resident bats began their nightly assault, swooping in and out of the branches above our head, gobbling up insects while we ducked below, keeping a protective hand over our drinks.

Popo's parting gift caused us to erupt in laughter. As much as we wanted to prolong our last night, thoughts of guano-enriched hair and excrement-laced clothing put a damper on things. Somehow, the bombardment felt right. Africa's supersized flying mammals had shattered our glum mood while saying *kwaheri* in their own unorthodox, rather slimy, way.

Although exhausted from a day crammed with adventures and intense emotions, I couldn't turn off my thoughts. As the cries of the savanna began filling the night air, I wondered if I would ever again hear the hippo's distant bellow, the hyena's eerie cackle, the elephant's gurgling, the monkey's chattering, and the lion's spine-tingling *umphh*. Primal sounds that somehow chilled me to the bone, while also making me feel more alive than I had ever felt. The beastly symphonies, possible only in the African bush, stirred me to the core, becoming forever anchored in my heart.

The next morning brought a lot of teary goodbyes. First, we had to say goodbye to the staff who weren't taking us to the airstrip. That included Joel, Thomas, Michael, Moses, Kaumba, Maugo, Emilian, and others.

An hour later, amid hugs, tears, and laughter, we said our final farewells to Lilian, Raphael, Mgogo, Abdalah, Mike, as well as Rod and Sue's crew, Paul, Nikko, Salum, Ima, and Zefania. Sullen and hesitant, I climbed the steps of the bush plane. A plane that would take us back to our reality, away from so many people that will forever hold a special place in my heart. Saying goodbye is never easy, but saying goodbye to people you may never see again is heart-rending.

Instead of loading up and hurrying back to camp, our Tanzanian friends fanned out, waiting to wave a final goodbye as the pilot went through his checklist. A few moments later, with tears streaming down my face, I watched as the waving arms and smiling faces became smaller and smaller, ultimately disappearing completely, as we taxied down the makeshift runway.

Peering out the window, I wistfully soaked up every detail of Rungwa West, knowing that I may never see it again. As we gained altitude, the umbrella acacia trees, woodlands, and vast stretches of savanna transitioned into a faraway blur of brownish nondescript terrain. The drab, lifeless-appearing landscape had not been the Africa I had envisioned since childhood. It hadn't even been a footnote on my bucket list. Yet, paradoxically, I was already mourning its loss. Africa--with all its immenseness, magnificence, magic, wonder, brutality, and harshness--has a way of grabbing you. And never letting go. *Kwaheri rafiki zangu*. Goodbye, my friends. Hopefully, one day we *will* meet again.

Masimba Camp staff waving goodbye as the plane begins taxiing.

29
Wildlife Saviors and Greedy Villains

Africa has become very personal for me. It is no longer just an intriguing distant land. It is umbrella acacia trees silhouetted against the sunset, the medusa-like Baobab jutting its twisted limbs into the African skies, and scant pools of water waiting for the rains to begin. When I picture the continent's wild species, I see giraffes gliding gracefully across the parched landscape, warthogs darting for their burrows with tails hoisted in the air, and *dagga* boys scarred by *Simba's* quest to survive.

Most importantly, the people are no longer anonymous. I see Raphael's kindness in explaining the spike-covered medicine tree, Lilian's smirk as she presented me the "goofball" award, Mgogo's gifting me tufts of lion hair, and Joel holding us spellbound with story after story. Each person at *Masimba* Camp remains a fixture in my mind that I will forever hold dear. Yet, too often, these amazing people--and their day-to-day struggles--are overlooked in the world's view.

To say I understand their daily lives after just a few weeks in a bush encampment is ludicrous as well as arrogant. No way can I pretend to *know* their reality. Their hard work and oversight kept us in the lap of luxury, relatively speaking, largely shielded from harm. Having a bathroom inches from our tent was not just a convenience, it was a safety net. If nature called, we did not need to exit our cocoon and chance a run-in with things that go bump in the night. Most villagers don't have that luxury.

Food also wasn't an issue. Wild game and stashes of vegetables purchased in Arusha kept us well fed. There was no livestock to protect from hungry carnivores hankering for easy pickings. No crops were planted to tempt mountainous unpredictable herbivores. Therefore, scaring off *Jumbo* with beehive fencing or sentries armed with pots and pans wasn't necessary.

Anytime I wanted a little hippo therapy, an armed escort took me to the pools of stagnant water because even that nasty bit of liquid was a lure to predators. Many villagers *must* go to such perilous places every day with no such protection.

Now that the people of Africa are no longer nameless and faceless, the small-time farmer losing his entire crop to an elephant may very well be Mgogo. A game scout injured while in pursuit of poachers could be Lilian.

I found myself juxtaposing their children with my grandbabies, Harper and Trigger. The thoughts of our munchkins exposed to opportunistic predators and territorial hippos on their way to school or to access water made my blood run cold. It could have been one of them who had accidentally invaded Willy the hippo's domain, causing his two tons of fury to launch at them instead of that warthog. Imagine having to teach your children that the safest time of day to travel was in the heat of the afternoon because *Simba* would most likely be napping.

With my eyes opened to the perils that the rural, often food-insecure, people of Africa must face daily, it became utterly clear why, from their viewpoint, life would just be much easier and safer without having to deal with the dangerous destructive creatures we adore from afar. Agriculture could expand into previously wild territories, livestock herds could be increased with few predators to threaten them, and daily living would not pose the risk of getting steamrolled by a hippo or mauled by a carnivore.

Once this reality is understood, it is easy to see why rural Africans must have a say in the management of wildlife resources. Besides, isn't that only fair? Africa's unforgiving lands are home to them as well and have been for thousands of years. Yet, too often, their needs are disregarded and injustice is thrust upon them by the global community.

Conservation in Africa has a dark history. In her book *Nature Crime, How We're Getting Conservation Wrong,* Rosaleen Duffy contends "The war to save the planet is commonly presented as a just war, motivated by the highest morals and waged by dedicated conservationists."[1] But when examined more carefully, it is clear that the crusade to protect wildlife is often used to justify harsh and threatening policies against the world's most marginalized and vulnerable people. In other words, the need to save wild species takes priority over the rights of the people who live with them.

Africa has been sustaining indigenous people for eons, but the creation of national parks and protected areas suddenly made the continent's vast resources unavailable to them. Not only were many people forcibly removed from their homes, but their everyday practices and methods of survival were also redefined as criminal behavior. Suddenly, hunting and fishing were construed as poaching, grazing livestock and foraging for food as trespassing, cutting timber as theft, and setting fires as arson. With these activities outlawed, the rightful stewards of the land were characterized as criminals and small-minded, selfish villains, while those in the conservation movement were characterized as heroes.

During colonial rule, most trapping was deemed cruel and unethical. As a result, it was often outlawed, essentially criminalizing subsistence hunting practices even outside of protected areas. Hunting by Europeans was defined as legal and acceptable on the premise that a quick kill was much more humane. How we draw the line between hunting and poaching is still based on these past ideas and fraught with ethical and practical difficulties. According to Duffy, "White men have been portrayed as sport hunters and committed conservationists who were keen on defending wildlife, black men as greedy and cruel poachers, blamed for destroying wildlife."

Don't think that I didn't discover my hypocrisy in that last tidbit of information. Throughout this book, I have repeatedly referred to primitive traps and snares as inhumane, causing indiscriminate slow, painful deaths. While those methods still turn my stomach, I can't help but see the other side of the equation. After all, primitive snares were an accepted norm used throughout history as a part of human survival.

As you know by now, I have become passionate about well-managed hunting's role in saving wildlife. With that said, my observations weren't made to portray native Africans with any negative undertones. They were made with my understanding of "trophy" hunting's value in protecting habitat and wild populations in *today's* world. It is simply much more profitable and better for local communities to allow foreign hunters to pay large fees to harvest animals, rather than return to past practices. A statement made by a rural villager in Tom Opre's documentary *Killing the Shepherd* really drove that point home for me: "What's wrong with them taking the skins and leaving the meat for us?"[2]

With that said, if an African nation decides to end all foreign hunting and allow their people to return to legal sustainable harvesting or eliminate hunting entirely, that should be respected as well. As long as it is *their* decision.

It is also worth noting that the anti-hunting world often uses colonialism as an argument to attack trophy hunting. We must acknowledge that the current conservation model has deep colonial underpinnings, including land set aside for both photo-tourism and trophy hunting. But that makes it even more important to respect the decision-making and rights of African countries and their communities. Powerful countries trying to force their wishes and values on less powerful nations is modern-day colonialism.

While Duffy's book touched on trophy hunting, that was just the tip of the iceberg. She explores conservation in-depth and how many of us, totally unknowingly, have a hand in making things worse.

Tourists, with no concept they are doing anything wrong, illegally export endangered species as souvenirs, especially trinkets made from turtle shells, seashells, and some hardwoods. The use of young animals for photographs at tourist destinations also encourages the illegal wildlife trade, while being devastating to the creatures involved. Many times, these adorable photo opportunities are the result of baby animals trapped in the wild, with their mothers sometimes killed. The furry attractions are often drugged, with their sharp teeth and claws removed, to make them more docile for the constant handling of tourists. Other times they are captive-bred in horrible situations.

Aside from all these ways we can unknowingly harm wild species, there is the world's love affair with precious gems, mobile phones, game stations, and numerous electronic devices. Colorful jewels and coltan, a key raw mineral needed for mobile technologies, are mined in some of the world's poorest countries and areas rich in wildlife but torn by conflict.

While gold, coal, diamonds, sapphires, and coltan are highly coveted assets, that also makes them a curse. The high value of these industries draws crime syndicates, illegal mining, and conflict. The intricacies of this boggle the mind and go far beyond what I can detail here, but let's just say that regulations on such businesses are hard to enforce and easy to get around, often causing horrific human rights abuses, wildlife trafficking, and destruction of animal habitat.

For example, coltan is a prime target for illegal activity because of its high value in the international market. Since most of the world's supply of coltan comes from the Democratic Republic of Congo, the clearing of forests for mining operations is responsible for the major destruction of gorilla habitat within their country, resulting in drastic decreases in eastern lowland gorillas. Madagascar is another example. Illegal sapphire mining on reserves is destroying habitat and threatening the 38 endangered lemur species.

While "blood diamonds" mined in African war zones, often by forced labor, no longer make the headlines, there is still a vibrant illegal market in conflict diamonds, causing enslavement, torture, rape, and murder. The international certifications put in place to reduce the number of illegal diamonds are riddled with loopholes that allow conflict diamonds, far too easily, to get mixed in with "clean diamonds."

If we blame the local people of Africa for the problems facing gorillas, lemurs, elephants and rhinos, we are pointing the finger at the wrong people. The threats are not caused by the local communities. They aren't wearing jewels, decorating with ivory figurines, or buying rhino horn to "cure" ailments. The demand for these things comes from the wealthier communities of the world, and the high value associated with them draws organized crime and other unsavory characters into the mix.

Many people tend to believe that when wildlife is in trouble, nonprofit conservation organizations can save the day, but these groups must compete in a global market for our attention, and more crucially for our money. Therefore, it is difficult for them to find solutions if it means blaming their supporters for their role in creating conservation problems. Doing so risks losing donors and supporters who may not be willing to accept their own choices as part of the problem.

Truthfully, reading Duffy's book blew my socks off. It opened my eyes to many things--especially our part in making things worse for conservation, even unknowingly. One thing is for sure; when one looks closely at African conservation, the illegal wildlife trade, and poaching, the roles of wildlife warriors and greedy villains become quite blurred.

Nevertheless, Africa *needs* us to explore its nations, learn about its cultures, book safari adventures, purchase its souvenirs and trinkets, wear its diamonds and sapphires, and pay to hunt its game species. But, we need to do these things with awareness, ensuring items are harvested or produced legally. For instance, demand "gorilla-friendly' mobile phones, conflict-free diamonds, and sapphires that are produced under the highest ethical and environmental standards. The money we spend should empower the people of Africa, elevate their human condition, and give them hope for the future, not drive them into poverty, food insecurity, or worse--create victims of human rights abuses. We can do this by supporting conservation organizations, tourist enterprises, and mining industries that work with local people to create income opportunities and fair wages, especially when their livelihoods have been detrimentally affected by conservation efforts.

While there is no one simple answer, Western views of conservation must change to treat Africans as equals, respect their opinions, and value their lives as much as animals. Wildlife management--whether non-hunting or hunting--must use strategies that are advantageous to both rural Africans and wildlife alike because, ultimately, the fate of both species is inextricably linked. If rural people are suffering as a result of well-intended activism and legislation, atrocities in the bush will continue to happen--whether it be poaching for food, poisoning carnivores to protect livestock, killing elephants for their tusks, defacing the land for minerals and gems, or altering habitat for human-related uses. The fate of Africa's wild species lies in the physical health and economic well-being of the African people. After all, they are the boots-on-the-ground stewards of these incredible creatures. Not us.

30
PROMISES KEPT

I n 2019, the newest version of *The Lion King*, made its debut across the world. As someone who has experienced all three versions of the wildly popular movie--cartoon, Broadway, and photorealistic--I find it impossible for anyone with a love of Africa to listen to its soundtrack without swimming in a sea of emotions. "Spirit," Beyonce's song from the latest movie version, is publicized by the artist as a 'love letter to Africa.' It truly is a moving tribute to the magical lands of Africa that touches the soul. Well, to borrow that line, this book is *my* version of a "love letter to Africa." My story, however, is based on *reality*, the hard truth and complexities associated with the magical, wondrous continent.

While entertaining and incredibly moving, movies like "The Lion King" create a false narrative that draws people into a romanticized view of nature and the animals' existence in the wild. Some people even live with the fantasy that nature is some kind of paradise where creatures live happy lives, a place where premature miserable deaths are the exception to the rule.

With so much misleading information circulating on social media, it is understandable where these unrealistic views come from. Endearing wild creatures are shown contradicting their instincts, or so it appears. Recently, I saw a picture of an elephant cradling a lion cub in its trunk, *supposedly* carrying the baby to water. Two bitter enemies joining forces. Wouldn't that be wonderful? You bet the picture tugged at my heart, at least the idealistic part of me that would love to believe nature was a fur-covered utopia. Then, reality hit. Upon researching, I found it was, indeed, photoshopped.

On Instagram, there was a video of a leopard playing with a baby antelope. The endearing scene of predator and prey frolicking together was enough to make any animal-loving person's heart melt, evident by the comments. Most didn't question how the story ended; their remarks left one to believe they had no idea what was about to happen. As you might assume, the calf was eaten only seconds after the video cut off. Believe me, I asked.

With such charming lovable depictions of wildlife on the internet, it's no wonder that many people living in cities, largely isolated from the natural world, have such vast misconceptions of nature, or nature deficit disorder, as some like to call it.

There may be exceptions, but the reality is wild animals are at risk of dying, continuously, from the very moment they enter the world. The vast majority of babies never even make it to maturity. Some of their lives are so brief that their entire experience entails pain. Heck, many hyena pups don't even survive their mother's elongated birth canal to see the light of day.

The risks continue for any animal lucky enough to survive the brutal trials of youth. Some suffer physical injuries, illness, malnutrition, thirst, or extreme weather conditions, often causing drawn-out agonizing deaths. Many species, including many of our favorites, engage in cannibalism, infanticide, or fights to the death with siblings or rivals. Victims of predators, especially larger ones, also rarely experience a quick torment-free execution. Their end of life is often a grisly prolonged affair. Wildlife can even suffer psychological stress when an overpopulation of a species knocks an ecosystem out of whack, destroying resources that other animals need to survive. Nature is an indiscriminate ruthless killer that spares no pain. That, unfortunately, is the hard truth.

Many people are either oblivious to these facts or conveniently choose to ignore them. That is fine and dandy; everyone has a right to believe what they want to believe. It only becomes a problem when one's unrealistic views are used to scorn others or shape policies.

By glossing over the truth, many anti-hunters vilify hunting by claiming it causes pain and suffering to the animals. The million-dollar question is: As opposed to what? Being eaten alive? Dying a slow torturous death of starvation, thirst, disease, or injury? For those who have witnessed both--death in the wild and death by ethical hunters--there is no comparison. Hunting is probably *the* most humane way for an animal to die.

That is not to say that an animal's death is any less significant or sad. The *pofu* who locked eyes with mine for that brief moment still haunts me, even knowing his death in the wild would have been much more brutal. Also, in my heart, I know that the eland did not die in vain. His sacrifice paved a way for many others to live.

Anyone lacking an understanding of nature's cruelty, choosing to ignore it, or clinging to the idea of a utopian existence, free of pain and suffering, is living in a fairytale world. Much like *The Lion King* movies, its characters may have human-like qualities, but in real life Simba, Nala, Rafiki, Pumba, Mufasa, and Zazu would not be working together to overthrow Scar, the evil villain, thereby bringing peace and plenty to the realm. The kings would be eating their faithful subjects.

If we truly want to save the kingdom, we must dispel the idyllic view of nature and recognize the harsh reality of life in the wild--especially in Africa--where the sheer size and ferocity of many species causes havoc, destruction, and even death to the people living amongst them.

The "Disneyization" of wildlife, as it is often referred to, ultimately, sabotages conservation efforts. In Glen Martin's book *Game Changer: Animal Rights and the Fate of Africa's Wildlife*, he talked with Laurence Frank, a research associate of the Museum of Vertebrate Zoology at the University of California and one of East Africa's foremost predator researchers.[1] According to Frank, the greatest problem is the "growing disconnect between the ideal and the real--the sense that 'loving animals' is the same as saving wildlife. As animal rights advocates gain influence in East Africa...it becomes harder to implement effective conservation programs, because some of those programs may involve killing animals." The key to saving Africa's charismatic wildlife, Frank believes, is the rejection of the Disney ideal.

His conviction is supported throughout Martin's book which, while evaluating the rising influence of the animal rights movement, finds that the policies championed by animal welfare groups could paradoxically lead to the elimination of the very species--including elephants and lions--that are most cherished. His scientific debate, told without sentiment or prejudice, vividly shows how "The world's last great populations of wildlife have become hostages in a fight between those who love animals and those who would save them."

The bias against hunters and hunting, in general, has been building for years, but until Tanzania, I had no idea of the true scope of it or how it was affecting conservation and the local people of Africa.

Masimba Camp changed all that. Africa--its exotic animals, humble people, and unforgiving lands--captured my soul and lit a fire in my gut. The issue has become personal for me--not to defend the hunters in my life--but because I fear for Africa, a wild magical place that has seeped into my blood.

"Spirit," Beyonce's song from *The Lion King*, starts with the Swahili phrase meaning "Long live the King." This, too, is what I want with every ounce of my being. The thoughts of an Africa without the beastly choruses of *Simba, tembo, Fisi, Chui, kiboko,* or any creature, for that matter, is soul-crushing. This book is my attempt to comply with another line in her song: "Stand up and fight."

Previously, when encountering anti-hunting sentiment, it was just easier to keep my mouth shut, but that tactic does nothing to help the animals and people of Africa. People will never understand hunting's value to conservation and human lives if we choose to avoid confrontation by burying our heads in the sand.

Just as importantly, before leaving *Masimba* Camp, I promised Lilian that I would do what I could to help people understand. This book is my attempt to fulfill that promise.

While social media has its pitfalls, it also makes the world a much smaller place. Sometimes, just moments after a few keystrokes, I will hear the phone's ping notifying me that I have a message from the other side of the globe. Not only did this allow Lilian and I to keep our friendship alive but it gave me access to her knowledge, experience, and memory--all of which were invaluable in writing this book. Her young mind is like a steel trap. Anytime a detail escaped me, or I needed clarification on something, she was there to fill in the blanks. She also reviewed each chapter to ensure the information was conveyed correctly.

Lilian continues to be a game scout for the Tanzanian government and remains a wealth of information about Tanzania's wildlife and its management. Much of her time is still spent occupied with anti-poaching and research work. Recently, she noted "Anti-hunters are still challenging us, but we are trying our level best to explain to them with evidence. Maybe one day they will understand and allow us to do our work in peace."

Though Lilian's work life remains much the same, her personal life has changed drastically. She is now the mother of a healthy, active, fast-learning three-year-old son. Since much of her time is spent at work facilities or in the field, both of which lack schools and hospitals, raising a child is difficult. Consequently, Loseriani, a name that means "blessing" in Maasai, currently lives with his grandparents in the city of Moshi where he attends a preschool. Though Lilian finds it difficult to separate from him, she has no choice because of her difficult work environment. One day she hopes to be able to join her son in the city to raise him herself. She also hasn't abandoned her hopes of becoming a wildlife studies teacher.

The internet's sorcery also allows me to stay in contact with Hilary. His life has also changed significantly. The anti-hunting sentiment, banning elephant imports from Tanzania and the restrictions on lion imports, have caused significant drops in hunting clients, especially since Hilary's hunting concession is prized lion and leopard territory. Not all hunters planning to hunt only plains game are willing to spend the extra time and expense to travel to such a remote location when there are less expensive, more accessible hunting areas. When marketing his hunting concessions on his own became difficult and expensive, he joined forces with a United States partner and dropped several of his hunting blocks. Thankfully, *Masimba* Camp remains.

The changes allowed him to return to working as a PH, which he thoroughly enjoys. He also diversified by opening two small hotels near Arusha that cater to eco-tourists. Hilary explained that there is no longer a good profit in the hunting industry. Even though it is legal to hunt lions, most hunters are not interested if they can't import the memory back to their own country. According to him, they now "...seldom hunt lions, employ 50 percent fewer people than before, have fewer camps, fewer areas, and less of everything by and large." In addition, he indicated that many of the hunting blocks now sit vacant, something that was never seen ten years ago.

When researching, I found that there are, indeed, 76 hunting concessions no longer being used as of September 2021. As Dr. Dickman indicated in her essay, vacant hunting blocks leave habitat prone to poaching and habitat conversion, ultimately killing far more animals, while doing nothing to improve the welfare of the local people.

This is further supported by Ivan Carter, the conservationist and founder of the Ivan Carter Wildlife Conservation Alliance (ICWCA), on 2021 Blood Origins Podcast.[2] He states that Cecil the lion, and the resulting restriction on lion trophies, created such a loss of income from American hunters that Tanzanian outfitters started handing back their concessions. When that happened, the local communities wanted the land back to be utilized in other ways. The result was the resettlement of 15 million acres of wildlands. So, Carter emphasizes, "The uncomfortable truth is that the bans on lion hunting has killed, or is in the process of killing, 15 million acres of lion habitat and with it, the lions as well."

When double-checking these figures with Mike Angelides, the secretary of the Tanzanian Hunting Operators Association (TAHOA), I found that Carter was being conservative with his number. Each hunting block encompasses approximately 1000 square kilometers; with 76 vacant concessions, that leaves closer to 18 million unprotected acres. Angelides, however, couldn't be sure exactly how much of that was "resettled".

Our little Shangri-La amid Rungwa West Game Reserve has also changed significantly since we were there. Last fall, Lilian had the opportunity to return to *Masimba* Camp to oversee two hunters. Upon receiving the news, I was practically crawling up the walls wishing that I could go with her to visit everyone. For two weeks I waited anxiously for her to report back to me with all the scoop.

Her news, however, made me quite sad. Out of 20 people, only Mgogo, Musa, Kaumba, Moses, Emilian, and Hilary remained. In addition to those losses, *Chui* Camp, our second little piece of paradise, no longer existed because of a lack of water. Fortunately, a new satellite camp was built in a different location, thereby still allowing the employment of 20 people.

Mgogo, Musa, and Kaumba are reportedly doing well, still working in Rungwa West and maintaining small farms in the offseason. They were happy to see Lilian again and to learn that we are still in contact with one another.

Communicating with Joel and Raphael, who are largely off the grid, is difficult and very limited. For a while, we even lost touch altogether. Thanks to Lilian's network of friends and Joel's son, Joel and I reconnected this spring through WhatsApp. I can't tell you the joy it brought me to hear his cheery voice again. Fortunately, before heading into the bush for the 2021 hunting season, he had gone to visit his son and grandchildren, giving him access to the internet.

Although I'm not clear about the circumstances, Joel no longer works for Hilary; he works for a different outfitter instead. The lack of hunters resulting from the Covid-19 pandemic made 2020 a very difficult year. He is praying that 2021, with the return of hunters, will be much better.

Joel informed me that although Raphael and Andrew no longer work for Hilary, they still contract out as PHs with other outfitters whenever they can. All of them still farm during the offseason as well, mainly growing maize. In the few minutes that Joel became very solemn, he admitted that he is very worried and prays to God regularly about anti-hunting sentiment and what it means for his future and the future of Africa.

After a bit of seriousness, he was back to his cheerful self. While his dad has passed, his mother is still doing very well and now lives with him: "Ohhh, she is sooo old. I'm telling you. She's 110 years old but, ohhh, she can still see. You get in front of her and she knows who you are!" So, as evident by these bits of information, he still has a way with words.

Since time doesn't stand still, the twins--whose antics Joel entertained us with many evenings--are now in school. Since they live nearby with his daughter and her husband, he still sees them often. His son also added two more kids to the mix since our time in Tanzania. As you might imagine, discussions regarding his grandkids typically ended with a joyous: "Ohhh, I like them. I like them a lot."

Hopefully, by exposing you to these wonderful people and the challenges they face, you will keep them in mind when considering the conservation issues of Africa. Not only do they matter, but their lives are also inextricably linked to the welfare of wild species.

In July 2020, Resource Africa published an "OPEN LETTER" to the world entitled: "Celebrity campaigns undermine successful conservation and human rights."[3] It was signed by over 50 community leaders, representing millions of people from the southern African nations. Since the words of the African people are more valuable than anything I can put on paper, I offer the following excerpts:

As representatives of millions of rural Africans, the majority of whom live below the poverty line, we are urgently appealing to you, as celebrities with status, to stop undermining our globally recognized conservation efforts and our basic human right to sustainably use the natural resources on which our communities' livelihoods depend.

In recent months you have lent your names to campaigns to stop hunting in Africa. We acknowledge that you are doing so with the best of intentions and we welcome your interest in our wildlife. But you have expressed these views without full appreciation of the implications for our people or wildlife, and without consulting us, who live with and manage African wildlife and who will ultimately determine its future...

Successful conservation must start with those of us who live alongside dangerous large animals, whose value is deeply ingrained in our cultures. During colonial times, European colonists removed our rights to manage and benefit from these animals, and in many instances forcefully evicted us from our lands, often to make way for protected areas. This led to dramatic loss of wildlife and habitat—a disaster for conservation, our traditions and our livelihoods. Post-independent governments restored our rights, integrating wildlife into rural economies through inclusive conservation approaches. This provided socio-economic incentives to live with and sustainably manage our wildlife.

Although you may view elephants, lions and other wildlife through a romantic, idealized lens, our daily reality of living with these magnificent and valued, yet dangerous animals, requires more pragmatism. We worry that our children may be killed on their way to school, or that our ability to provide for our families will be destroyed within a few hours by elephants in our fields or large predators among our livestock...

Despite this, elephants, lions and other species live amongst us, not only in protected areas, and are multiplying because we want them to. The harsh reality is that if incentives for us to conserve and share our land with wildlife are removed, their future in Africa will be as bleak as that of wolves, brown bears and other large carnivores that were once plentiful in the UK, Europe and the U.S. You have every right to consider regulated, sustainable hunting abhorrent and we appreciate that for those not familiar with the realities of rural Africa, it may seem a counter-intuitive conservation strategy. But if your objective is conservation--not solely recognizing individual animal rights--we call upon you, before passing judgement, to understand the context of coexisting with dangerous wildlife: consider our perspectives, evidence base, success stories from a conservation method that recognizes the basic human right of our people to manage and benefit from the sustainable use of our natural resources. If we cannot feed our families through humane and sustainable use of wildlife, we will have no option but to adopt land uses that will invariably destroy our beautiful natural landscapes and exterminate our treasured wild animals – an all too familiar situation throughout the world.

It will be no news to you that many of our countries are not wealthy or endowed with rich resources. One of those which we do have, wildlife, is demonstrably managed responsibly and sustainably. We are tired of people from elsewhere, far removed from our realities, talking on our behalf and undermining our success. We are an integral part of the solution to illegal wildlife trade, poaching and unsustainable use of biodiversity. It is disappointing that while animal rights campaigns to stop hunting have raised enormous sums of money, we have yet to see evidence of those funds conserving African wildlife or benefiting any of our communities in their role as custodians of that wildlife. What and who do these campaigns benefit? Their impact will be to remove our incentives to manage and live side by side with wildlife. Imposing worldviews and value systems from faraway places, amplified through your powerful, influential voices, results in disastrous policies that undermine our rights and conservation success.

We recognize and respect the rights of Western celebrities and animal protectionist campaigners to discuss how best to manage African wildlife. However, these discussions must be informed by our voices as custodians of this wildlife. At the minimum this should acknowledge both our conservation successes and our communities' right to earn a livelihood through the culturally appropriate and sustainable management of our resources for the benefit of our people and wildlife. Anything less is to put the rights of animals before the rights of Africans.

We write this letter as the world is demanding the acknowledgment and righting of past and present wrongs in the form of historical erasure, plunder of resources, labor exploitation, structural inequalities and imposition of unjust Western values and belief systems based on privilege. We want you to hear our voices; our conservation successes and lived realities are not 'myths.'

Reading this letter, which can be found in its entirety on the internet with all its signatories, gives a clear indication of why African nations may feel resentment, exasperation, and anger toward the Western world.

A picture speaks a thousand words. At Marina Lamprecht's seminar last year, she displayed a slide with a group of African tribal leaders sitting in a circle on the ground. The caption read: "A meeting was held in Africa...to discuss the management of whitetail deer in the U.S."

Africa is a complex, unforgiving continent. It is also magical, wondrous, and intriguing--a land with sights that will take your breath away, exceptional people who will touch your heart, and wild species that will fill you with awe.

Like the pieces of a puzzle, so many things fit together to make our African safari so much more than just an adventure or hunting expedition. It was a journey of awareness. The people whose lives were meshed with ours were no coincidence. Experiencing their unique personalities, expertise, and friendships while immersed in a bush encampment enabled me to see Africa as it genuinely is instead of through rose-colored glasses. It allowed me to indulge my love of wildlife while also recognizing the need for sacrifice.

The thought of losing the untamed land and its spectacular creatures crushes my soul. The words of Dr. Amy Dickman bear repeating: "It is a cause for celebration that so many people love lions, elephants, and other wild animals--but we should be extremely wary of basing decisions on emotion alone, in case we worsen their conservation outlook, and effectively love them to death."

I urge you, travel to Africa! Immerse yourself in a life-changing journey and experience the magical, inspiring, wondrous yet harsh and dangerous land. Meet its fascinating people and witness the grace and beauty of its majestic species. It doesn't have to cost an arm and a leg. Not even for a hunter. Plains game can be hunted for the price of a Hawaiian vacation. If you aren't a hunter, go on a photo safari to one of Africa's magnificent parks and see wildlife swarming by the roadside largely unafraid, an experience that eluded me. If traveling to Africa isn't something you wish to do, help by sharing what you have learned with others and support organizations that advocate for the sustainable use of resources while empowering the African people. For recommendations, see my resources page.

If you are up for more of an adventure, search for an experience that will place you in the bush where you can build friendships with local people, a place where your sleep will be invaded by wild creatures conducting their nightly shenanigans. Listen transfixed to *kiboko's* throaty bellow, *tembo's* gurgling or distant trumpet, and *tumbili's* chatter. Lie chilled to the bone as *Simba's* guttural cries haunt the night. Let *Fisi's* ghastly laughter and *Whoop Whoooooop Whoops* send shivers down your spine. Allow Africa's moonlit skies and its primal symphony to stir you to the very core of your being. Imagine something creating such a hold on you that you cannot picture a life in which you won't return.

I am not the same, having heard the cries of the savanna. Not only their savage songs but their cries for the world to awaken. To understand the hard truth needed to ensure their cries *forever* remain a part of wild Africa and not just ghostly echoes from a distant past.

The **AUDIOBOOK** version of *Cries of the Savanna* is now available, narrated by **yours truly,** with guest narration by **Lilian** (Chapter 30). Also, the ACTUAL sounds of lions, leopards, hippos, elephants, leopards, baboons, and more will transport listeners to the wilds of Tanzania with primal dialogues that can't be captured in words. The audiobook is available on my website **www.suetidwell.com** and at most audiobook distributors.

Signed books are available at **www.suetidwell.com**

As you may have guessed, Rick and I did return to Africa. The land has a way of grabbing your heart, crying out for you to return...again...and again. **Join my email** list for new adventures and book updates....and, as a **BONUS**, receive the exclusive excerpt, "The Rhino Runners of Waterberg Plateau."

Buy audio or signed books
www.suetidwell.com

Email Sign Up

A Note From Sue

Thank you for reading Cries of the Savanna!

*If you enjoyed reading the book or were touched by the people and wildlife of Africa, I would love you to share what you learned, refer the book to others, and/or **leave a review** on Amazon, Goodreads, social media, or your own blog. In the book world, reviews and referrals are like rhino horn -- **more valuable than gold.***

Thank you....AND Happy Adventures!

ACKNOWLEDGMENTS

Asante sana to Lilian Mremi, Raphael Erro, Matoleo Mgogo, Joel Hhoki, Hilary Daffi, Abdalah, Mike, Michael, Anton, Andrew, Moses, Kaumba, Emilian, Thomas, Musa, Maugo, Paul, Mriru, Salum, Zefania, and Imma. I am forever grateful for your friendship, knowledge, guidance, protection, and care – all of which made our Tanzanian safari so much more than just an adventure.

To my editor and project manager Jocelyn Engel, thank you for believing my words were worth sharing with the world and for having the skill, insight, and resolve to guide this book – and the author – through the wilderness of publishing.

Thank you, Sharon M. Brown, your honesty allowed me to see my words from a different perspective. Your open-mindedness and support gave me hope and confidence.

To author Dwight Van Brunt, thank you for enthusiastically supporting this undertaking and reading each word when the book was still in its infancy.

Thanks to Rod and Sue, our friends and Tanzanian travel companions, for allowing me to share part of your story as well.

Thanks to the many beta readers -- both friends and strangers; your gift of time and knowledge provided intelligent feedback, helping to make this book the best it could be while also offering uplifting commentary.

To my family and friends scattered from coast to coast, thank you for believing in my ability to tell a story and for your love and support throughout my entire life. You know who you are!

Thanks to my Idaho family for accepting an East Coast girl and exposing me to ranch life, as well as a whole different set of adventures and experiences.

To my Mom and Dad, I thank you for giving my siblings and me the best of childhoods, one filled with love, laughter, adventure -- and yes, hunting -- exposing me to a world of outdoors, camaraderie, tenacity, and sustainability.

Thanks to my husband, for loving me through the good and bad; for exposing me to adventures I never dreamed of; for supporting me through endless hours camped at the keyboard; and for understanding the faraway trances of a mind embedded in the wilds of Africa. You are my rock.

To each reader, thank you for taking precious hours from your life to journey with me to Africa, to see the wonder and magic of a harsh continent, and to learn about the complexities of wildlife conservation.

Most of all, thanks to all creatures whose sacrifice means that others shall live.

SWAHILI WORDS

asante sana- thank you
bivouac – small safe waterproof shelter
chakula – food
chui – leopard
Chui Camp – Leopard Camp
chura - frog
dagga – mud
dagga boy – old Cape buffalo bull
digi-digi – dik-dik
fisi – hyena
fungo – civet cat
hapana - no
hema – tent
hujambo – how are you?
inyati – another name for Cape buffalo
jambo - hello
jangili – poachers
kaboka – black mamba
kanga - colorful patterned fabric
karibu – you're welcome
karibuni tena – come again soon
kataa – shake your waist
kazi nzuri – good job everyone
kiboko – hippo
koboko – black mamba
kongoni – hartebeest
korongo - roan

kraals – corrals
kwaheri – goodbye
kwaheri rafiki zangu – goodbye my friends
kwenda – go
kumbikumbi – winged alate, termites
lala salama – sleep peacefully
Maasaii- an ethnic group inhabiting Kenya, Tanzania, and Uganda
maji baridi tafadhali – cold water please
machan – elevated platform
Masimba Camp – Lion Camp
mamba - crocodile
mbogo – another name for Cape buffalo
mchwa - termites
mesi – dining hut
mikoche fruit – a type of fruit
mkwaju tree – a type of tree
mwalimu – teacher
nani kaua – who killed it?
narri – another name for Cape buffalo
ndiyo - yes
ndorabo – Tsetse fly
ngiri- warthog
nyati – Cape buffalo
pala hala – sable
panga - machete
panya – mouse
pofu - eland
popo – bat
pongo - bushbuck
punda milia – zebra
rafikas - friends
rafiki - friend
simba – lion
sijambo – I am fine
swalapala - impala
tandala – kudu
tembo – elephant

tohe - reedbuck
tumbili – vervet monkey
twiga - giraffe
ugali - mielie-meal
ujangili – poaching
usianguke – don't fall

RESOURCES

Here is a recommendation list compiled with the help of the experts mentioned in this book. It is just meant to offer you a starting point. There are hundreds of worthy organizations based in Africa. The key is to choose programs -- *endorsed by local communities and governments* -- that support human empowerment, wildlife protection and land conservation through the sustainable and measurable use of resources.

Blood Origins, www.bloodorigins.org
Botswana Carnivore Forum,
www.botswanacarnivoreforum.wordpress.com
Conservation Force, www.conservationforce.org
Ecoexist, www.ecoexistproject.org
Elephants for Africa, www.elephantsforafrica.org
Empowers Africa, www.empowersafrica.org
Giraffe Conservation Foundation, www.giraffeconservation.org
Ivan Carter Wildlife Conservation Alliance, www.ivancarterwca.org
Lion Landscapes, www.lionlandscapes.org
Lwiro Primate Rehabilitation Centre, www.lwiroprimates.org
Panthera, www.panthera.org
Namibian Association of CBNM Support Organization,
www.nacso.org.na/people
Resource Africa, www.resourceafrica.net
Save the Elephants, www.savetheelephants.org
Saving the Wild, www.savingthewild.com
Shepherds of Wildlife, www.shepherdsofwildlife.org
Space for Giants, www.spaceforgiants.org
Sustainable Use Coalition Southern Africa, www.suco-sa.org.za

The Rhino Momma Project, www.rhinomomma.com
True Green Alliance, www.mahohboh.org
Zambeze Delta Conservation, www.ivancarterwca.org

Notes

Chapter 2 – *Masimba* Camp
1. Peter Hathaway Capstick, *Death in the Long Grass* (New York, St. Martin's Press, 1977), p.267

Chapter 4 – Horns Curling to the Heavens
1. Team Africa Geographic, "Understanding Rinderpest", *Africa Geographic*, July 21, 2020

Chapter 5 – The Dark Side
1. Frode Smelby, Rune Henriksen, Christian Nellemann, "Combatting Poaching and Illegal Logging in Tanzania: Voices of the Rangers-Hands-on Experiences from the Field", *GRID-Arendal*, November 15, 2016
2. Jani Hall, "What is bushmeat?", *National Geographic*, June 19, 2019, https://www.nationalgeographic.com/animals/article/bushmeat-explained
3. Leah Asmelash, Saeed Ahmed, "African Elephant Poaching has Declined, but Study Warns They Are Still Vulnerable", *CNN*, June 6, 2019
4. Jani Hall, "Poaching animals, explained", *National Geographic*, February 12, 2019, https://www.nationalgeographic.com/animals/article/poaching-animals
5. Jason G. Goldman, "Where humans suffer, so do elephants", *National Geographic*, May 28, 2019, www.nationalgeographic.com/animals/article/poverty-and-elephant-poaching-in-africa
6. Annie Roth, "Poachers Kill More Rhinos as Coronavirus Halts Tourism in Africa", *New York Times*, April 8, 2020, www.nytimes.com/2020/04/08/science/coronavirus-poaching-rhinos

Chapter 6 – The Widowmaker
1. Robert C. Ruark, *Horn of the Hunter* (Long Beach, CA: Safari Press Inc.; New edition, 1993), p. 285,287,288

Chapter 9 – Eyes Wide Open
1. Priya Miller, "The Economic Significance of Hunting Tourism in Tanzania", www.socobilldurham.sites.stanford.edu/sites/g/files/sbiybj10241/f/miller_priya_tanzania_final_paper.pdf, 2017
2. Peter Lindsey, "Trophy Hunting in Sub Saharan Africa: Economic Scale and Conservation Significance", *Best Practices in Sustainable Hunting*, 2008, pp 41-47
3. "Sustainability and the Funding of the Timbavati Private Nature Reserve", *Africa Sustainable Conservation News*, February 28, 2020

Chapter 10 – Perception Vs. Reality
1. Rocky Mountain Elk Foundation, "North American Wildlife Conservation Model – Tenet #2", June 28, 2017, https://www.rmef.org/elk-network/tenet2/
2. Craig White, "What's all the Howling About?", Idaho Fish and Game, www.idfg.idaho.gov/old-web/docs/wolves/articleHowling.pdf, Winter 2010
3. "Our Conservation Success Story", PHASA, March 13, 2020
4. Bob Koigi, "NAMIBIA: THE CONSERVATION CAPITAL OF AFRICA", *Fair Planet*, March12, 2021
5. Dr. Joseph O. Ogutu, "Dramatic Declines in Kenya's Wildlife Demand an Urgent Response", *Earth and Environment*, July 31, 2018

Chapter 11 – Honey Put Your Shoes On
1. "The Dark Side of Hippos", *Real Wild*, YouTube, Why Hippos Are One of The Most Dangerous Animals, April 25, 2020
2. Simon Pooley, "When and Where do Nile Crocodiles Attack?", *The Conversation*, July 15, 2019

Chapter 15 – Kwenda! Kwenda!
1. Peter Hathaway Capstick, *Death in the Long Grass* (New York, St. Martin's Press, 1977), p.66
2. Yukino Iwai, "Human-Elephant Conflict in the Serengeti: The Side-Effects of Wildlife Tourism", globaljournal.org, October 30, 2018
3. William Adams, Jon Hutton, "People, Parks and Poverty: Political Ecology and Biodiversity Conservation", *Conservation & Society*, 2007
4. Gail Thomson, "Research: Does Botswana Have Too Many Elephants", *Africa Geographic*, March 12, 2018
5. Gail Thomson, "Key Questions for Human-Elephant Conflict Research," *Conservation Namibia*, December 14, 2020
6. Albertina Nakale Pohamba Shifeta, "Namibia's Elephant Population Grows to Over 22,000", *New Era Live*, September 9, 2018

7. Michael Paterniti, "Should We Kill the Animals to Save Them", *National Geographic*, October 2017
8. Rachel Nuwer, "Poachers are Invading Botswana, Last Refuge of African Elephants", *New York Times*, July 1, 2019
9. Gail Thomson, "Botswana Has Found Her Voice on Elephants—but Will We Listen?", *Africa Geographic*, February 27, 2019
10. Mokgweetsi Masisi, "Hunting Elephants Will Help Them Survive", *Wall Street Journal*, June 19, 2019
11. Erik Verreynne, "Five Things to Know About Botswana's Decision to Lift Ban on Hunting Elephants", *Smithsonian*, May 24, 2019

Chapter 16 – The Heart of the Conflict
1. Dr. Amy Dickman, "Lions, Trophy Hunting and the Ruaha Carnivore Project", *This Wild Life Podcast*, Episode 16, September 1, 2020

Chapter 17 – The Cherry on Top
1. "Africa's Giraffe, A Conservation Guide", Giraffe Conservation Foundation, www.giraffeconservation.org/wp-content/uploads/2016/02/GCF-Giraffe-booklet-2019-LR-spreads-c-GCF.pdf, 2019
2. Thomas Nicolon, "Snakebites Kill Tens of Thousands of Africans a Year", *National Geographic*, December, 2020

Chapter 18 – Cries of the Savanna
1. Jani Hall, "Cecil the Lion Died Amid Controversy -- Here's What's Happened Since", *National Geographic*, October 15, 2018
2. Panthera, Wildlife Conservation Research Unit, "Beyond Cecil: Africa's Lions in Crisis", www.wildaid.org/wp-content/uploads/2017/09/Beyond-Cecil-English.pdf, 2017
3. Ivo Vegter, "Hunting Bans Would Condemn a Lot of Game", *Daily Maverick*, September 25, 2018
4. Amy Dickman, "Science + Celebrity for Conservation – A call for partnership based on knowledge, not opposition driven by emotion", *Science + Story*, April 15, 2021
5. Amy Dickman and others, "Trophy Hunting Bans Imperil Biodiversity", *Science*, August 30, 2019

Chapter 19 – The Big Picture
1. Caitlyn Dewey, "A surprising number of American adults think chocolate milk comes from brown cows", *Chicago Tribune*, June 16, 2017
2. Tovar Cerulli, *Mindful Carnivore: A Vegetarian's Hunt for Sustenance* (New York, Pegasus Books), p. 52

Chapter 22 - Welcome to Chui Camp
1. Ron Thomson, "The Leopard and Its Endangered Species Ranking", *The True Green Alliance*, www.mahohboh.org/the-leopard-its-endangered-species-ranking/, January 18, 2018

Chapter 23 - Savage Cries and Ghastly Giggles
1. Ernest Hemingway, *Green Hills of Africa*, (New York, NY: Touchstone Simon & Schuster Inc.; First Touchstone Edition 1996), p. 38
2. Robert C. Ruark, *Horn of the Hunter* (Long Beach, CA: Safari Press Inc.; New edition, 1993), p.114
3. Robert C. Ruark, *Horn of the Hunter* (Long Beach, CA: Safari Press Inc.; New edition, 1993), p.116
4. Peter Hathaway Capstick, *Death in the Long Grass* (New York, St. Martin's Press, 1977), p.273

Chapter 26 – The Goofball Award
1. Joshua H. Daskin, Robert M. Pringle, "Warfare and Wildlife Declines in Africa's Protected Areas", *Nature*, January 10, 2018
2. Kingsley Ighobor, "African Democracy Coming of Age", *African Renewal*, 2016

Chapter 29 – Wildlife Saviors Vs. Greedy Villains
1. Rosaleen Duffy, *Nature Crime: How We're Getting Conservation Wrong* (New Haven and London: Yale University Press; 2010), p.82
2. Tom Opre, "Killing the Shepherd", shepherdsofwildlife.org, 2020

Chapter 30 – Promises Kept
1. Glen Martin, *Game Changer: Animal Rights and the Fate of Africa's Wildlife* (Berkeley and Los Angeles, CA: University of California Press; 2012), p.63
2. Ivan Carter, "On Moving Elephants", *Blood Origins Podcast*, Episode 112, September 9, 2021
3. "OPEN LETTER, Celebrity campaigns undermine successful conservation and human rights", Resource Africa, https://resourceafrica.net/open-letter-celebrity-campaigns-undermine-successful-conservation-and-human-rights/, July 14, 2020

About the Author

Sue Tidwell's love of travel and adventure took her to the wilds of Tanzania where she was infected with an extreme case of African fever, a condition that grips a person's heart like a vice and never lets go. In her multi-award-winning debut title *Cries of the Savanna*, Tidwell is determined to light that fire in the heart of her readers as well. Tidwell lives in rural Idaho with her husband, Rick, who tolerates her endless obsession with the faraway land. When not pining for Africa, Sue can be found atop a paddleboard or engaged in her latest outdoor excursion.

Made in the USA
Middletown, DE
30 July 2023

35957779R00257